ASEAN's Diplomatic and Security Culture

purpose

Member states of ASEAN – the Association of South-East Asian Nations – have developed a distinctive approach to political and security co-operation, which builds on the principles of sovereign equality, non-intervention and non-interference, quiet diplomacy, mutual respect, and the principle of not involving ASEAN in mediating bilateral disputes among the membership.

This book examines the origins of ASEAN's diplomatic and security culture and analyses how over time its key principles have been practised and contested as ASEAN states have responded to regional conflicts as well as challenges posed by the major regional powers, ASEAN's enlargement, and the Asian financial crisis. The book goes on to assess whether ASEAN's diplomatic and security culture is likely to remain salient as the political, economic and security context in which regional leaderships operate is undergoing further change.

Jürgen Haacke is Lecturer in International Relations at the London School of Economics and Political Science.

ASEAN's Diplomatic and Security Culture

Origins, development and prospects

Jürgen Haacke

Routledge
Taylor & Francis Group

LONDON AND NEW YORK

First published in hardback 2003
First published in paperback 2005
by Routledge
2 Park Square, Milton Park, Abingdon, Oxon OX14 4RN

Simultaneously published in the USA and Canada
by Routledge
270 Madison Ave, New York, NY 10016

Routledge is an imprint of the Taylor & Francis Group

Transferred to Digital Printing 2006

© 2003, 2005 Jürgen Haacke

Typeset in Times by
Taylor & Francis Books Ltd

British Library Cataloguing in Publication Data
A catalogue record for this book is available from the British Library

Library of Congress Cataloging in Publication Data
A catalog record for this book has been requested

ISBN 0–7007–1652–1 (hbk)
ISBN 0–415–37417–0 (Taylor & Francis Asia Pacific paperback edition)

For Mingqing

Contents

Preface and acknowledgements   ix
List of abbreviations   xii

Introduction   1

1 Early origins of the 'ASEAN way': the struggle for respect
  and sovereignty   16

2 Post-war origins of the 'ASEAN way': from estrangement
  and conflict to regional reconciliation and accommodation   32

3 ZOPFAN and the ASEAN Regional Forum: the extramural
  dimension of ASEAN's struggle for security and recognition   52

4 The Cambodian conflict and the 'ASEAN way': the struggle
  for a pristine interpretation of principles   81

5 China's relations with ASEAN: challenging or reinforcing
  the 'ASEAN way'?   112

6 The US challenge to the 'ASEAN way'   139

7 The concept of flexible engagement and the practice of
  enhanced interaction: intramural challenges to the
  'ASEAN way'   165

8 ASEAN's diplomatic and security culture after the Hanoi
  Summit: has 'old' thinking been dominating 'new' practices?   191

Conclusion: on the prospects for ASEAN's diplomatic and
security culture 214

Notes 234
Bibliography 251
Index 281

Preface and acknowledgements

This book began to take shape in the mid-1990s when I was struck by the ferocity of exchanges carried in the international press and scholarly journals on the so-called 'ASEAN way'. In the event, debates on the 'ASEAN way' would intensify further after the onset of the Asian financial crisis, and they continue to this day.

Contrary to many others, I have never been persuaded that it is best to dismiss the 'ASEAN way' as an analytical category, or its relevance as a diplomatic and security practice. Equally, however, I have felt that there are good reasons to treat with caution overly effusive claims by those celebrating its success in contributing to regional stability or its role in constructing collective identities in Southeast Asia.

My interest in the 'ASEAN way' has focused above all on exploring its meaningfulness and relevance as a normative framework for political and security co-operation as seen by regional decision-makers. It is this interest that has also led me to explore the circumstances and motivations underlying the endorsements of or challenges to ASEAN's diplomatic and security culture, and to examine to what extent collective understandings of its core norms and associated practices have developed over time.

The book is derived from a doctoral thesis examined in the Department of International Relations at the London School of Economics in October 2000. In writing and completing the original dissertation and then refining the argument for publication, I have benefited from the advice, comments and assistance of a significant number of people and organisations. First and foremost, I would again like to thank Professor Michael Yahuda, as my principal supervisor, who has proved a continuous source of intellectual stimulation and challenge, and without whose unfaltering encouragement and gentle guidance this project would not have been brought to fruition. Equally, I am very grateful indeed to Dr Peter Wilson for co-supervising the thesis and providing all-round support at all times. I am also grateful to Professor Michael Leifer and Professor Richard Higgott, the internal and external examiner, respectively, not only for having passed the thesis, but also for providing valuable suggestions on how further to improve it. I would, in particular, like to acknowledge the intellectual debt

I owe to the late Michael Leifer, whose scholarship on Southeast Asia I have found nothing short of truly inspirational.

In writing this book, I have, moreover, benefited from the opportunities and support offered to me by several institutions and their staff. I found the London School of Economics a wonderful place in which to conduct research and to grow intellectually. Numerous members of staff, in addition to my supervisors, made it a greatly enjoyable experience, not least Professor Christopher Hill, Professor William Wallace, Dr Hayo Krombach and Michael Banks, all of whom provided general guidance. I am also indebted to Dr Kay Möller of Stiftung Wissenschaft und Politik, who, in the summer of 1996, supervised some of my early work on China's stance on multilateral institutions in the Asia-Pacific. I am, moreover, grateful for having been given the opportunity to conduct research on ASEAN at the Institute of Southeast Asian Studies in Singapore in 1998. The excellent library facilities there proved very helpful indeed, and I have fond memories of conversations with staff. I also owe a particular debt of gratitude to the Shanghai Institute of International Studies, especially its former President Professor Chen Peiyao and its Academic Director Zhao Gancheng. Both gave very generously of their time in July 1998 and provided a helping hand in organising many of my interviews with representatives of a number of research institutions in Shanghai and Beijing. Last but not least in this context, I more than happily acknowledge the tremendous encouragement and support that I have received from Professor Jeremy Jennings, currently Head of the Department of Political Science and International Studies at the University of Birmingham, which I joined in the autumn of 1999. Without this encouragement and support, the book would have taken much longer to complete.

Research for this book could not, of course, have been undertaken without financial support. I gratefully acknowledge having been in receipt of a research studentship from the Economic and Social Research Council. I also gratefully acknowledge the additional research studentships awarded by the London School of Economics. A travel grant from the University of London Central Research Fund enabled me to conduct fieldwork in Singapore, Malaysia, Thailand, the Philippines, Indonesia and China. Funds granted by the Department of Political Science and International Studies as well as by the School of Social Sciences at the University of Birmingham allowed me to do further fieldwork in Vietnam and Laos.

I have also benefited from the kindness and helpfulness of numerous individuals. A large number of scholars, journalists and officials shared with me their insights into various aspects of the international politics of Southeast Asia. For this I am very grateful. I am also very grateful to Dr Dino Patti Djalal and his family for their warm hospitality extended to me in July 1998 while I was in Jakarta, and the generous time and organisational assistance then also given to me by Dr Kusnanto Anggoro. Similarly, my thanks go to Drs Stefan Fittkau and Kim Ong-Giger whose respective hospitality I enjoyed at various points in time between May and August 1998 when conducting fieldwork in Singapore.

In addition to my supervisors and examiners, several colleagues and friends have commented on various chapter drafts on the road to completion of this book. For their critical observations on all or some of the chapters I would, in particular, like to thank Comfort Ero, Hayo Krombach and Julie Gilson. I did not take on board all suggestions, but I found them very useful in clarifying my argument. I am, moreover, grateful to Peter Sowden for his suggestions, support and patience throughout. It goes without saying that I alone remain responsible for any errors of fact and misinterpretation from which the analysis may still suffer.

Chapter 7 is derived from an earlier article and is published here with the permission of the journal in which it originally appeared, *The Pacific Review*. I am indebted to Alan Chong, Sorpong Peou and John Funston for comments on this material.

I would finally like to acknowledge the assistance and encouragement that I have received from friends and family. It was not easy to complete the manuscript knowing that Edmund and Ailin were becoming increasingly frustrated at the routine postponement of agreed reading and playtime. Mingqing, while selflessly having supported this project throughout the last few years, is nevertheless probably more than anyone else pleased finally to see it off my desk.

Birmingham, July 2001

List of abbreviations

ABRI	*Angkatan Berendjata Republik Indonesia*; Indonesian Armed Forces
AFP	Agence France Press
AFTA	ASEAN Free Trade Area
AMDA	Anglo-Malayan/Malaysian Defence Arrangement
AMPERA	*Amanat Penderitaan Rakyat*; the Message of the People's Suffering
ANS	*Armée Nationale Sihanoukiste*
APA	ASEAN People's Assembly
APEC	Asia-Pacific Economic Co-operation (Forum)
APRI	Asia-Pacific Regional Initiative
ARF	ASEAN Regional Forum
ASA	Association of Southeast Asia
ASC	ASEAN Standing Committee
ASEAN	Association of Southeast Asian Nations
ASEAN–ISIS	ASEAN Institutes for Strategic and International Studies
ASEAN PMC	ASEAN Post-Ministerial Conferences
ASEM	Asia–Europe Meeting
ASO	Annual Security Outlook
ASP	ASEAN Surveillance Process
CCP	Chinese Communist Party
CGDK	Coalition Government of Democratic Kampuchea
CSCAP	Council for Security Co-operation in the Asia-Pacific
CSCE	Conference on Security and Co-operation in Europe
DEPHANKAM	*Departermen Pertahanan-Kaemanan*; Department of Defence and Security
DEPLU	*Departermen Luar Negari*; Department of Foreign Affairs
DK	Democratic Kampuchea
DPRK	Democratic People's Republic of Korea
DRV	Democratic Republic of Vietnam
EAEG	East Asian Economic Grouping
EEP	experts/eminent persons
EEZ	Exclusive Economic Zone

EIU	Economist Intelligence Unit
EU	European Union
FALINTIL	*Forças Armadas de Libertaçao de Timor Leste Independente*; Armed Forces of National Liberation of East Timor
FDI	foreign direct investment
FPDA	Five Powers Defence Arrangements
FPPC	Five Principles of Peaceful Co-existence
FRETILIN	*Frente Revolucionara do Timor Leste Independente*; Revolutionary Front for an Independent East Timor
FUNCINPEC	*Front uni national pour un Cambodge indépendent, neutre, pacifique et coopératif;*; United National Front for an Independent, Neutral, Peaceful and Co-operative Cambodia
GATT	General Agreement on Tariffs and Trade
GDR	German Democratic Republic (former East Germany)
HPA	Hanoi Plan of Action
ICK	International Conference on Kampuchea
IMET	International Military Education and Training (Programme)
IMF	International Monetary Fund
INTERFET	International Force in East Timor
ISA	Internal Security Act
ISDS	Institute for Strategic and Development Studies
ISG–CBM	Inter-sessional Support Group on Confidence-building Measures
ISIS	Institutes for Strategic and International Studies
JIM	Jakarta Informal Meeting
JIM-1	First Jakarta Informal Meeting
JIM-2	Second Jakarta Informal Meeting
KOGAM	*Komanda Ganyang Malaysia*; Crush Malaysia Command
KPNLF	Khmer People's National Liberation Front
LPRP	Lao People's Revolutionary Party
MCA	Malayan/Malaysian Chinese Association
MCP	Malayan Communist Party
MFN	Most-Favoured Nation (Status)
MILF	Moro Islamic Liberation Front
MNLF	Moro National Liberation Front
MOU	memorandum of understanding
MPR	*Majelis Permusyawaratan Rakyat*; People's Consultative Assembly
NAFTA	North American Free Trade Area
NATO	North Atlantic Treaty Organisation
NEP	National Economic Policy
NGO	non-governmental organisation

NLD	National League for Democracy
OIC	Organisation of Islamic Countries
PACOM	(US) Pacific Command
PAP	People's Action Party
PAV	People's Army of Vietnam
PKI	*Partai Komunis Indonesia*; Indonesian Communist Party
PLA	People's Liberation Army
PLAN	People's Liberation Army Navy
PMC	Post-Ministerial Conferences
PRC	People's Republic of China
PRK	People's Republic of Kampuchea
PULO	*Pertubuhan Pembebasan Patani Bersatu*; Pattani United Liberation Organisation
RVN	Republic of Vietnam
SEAARC	Southeast Asian Association for Regional Co-operation
SEACP	Southeast Asia Co-operation Project
SEAFET	Southeast Asian Friendship and Economic Treaty
SEANWFZ	Southeast Asia Nuclear Weapons Free Zone
SEATO	Southeast Asia Treaty Organisation
SLOC	sea lines of communication
SLORC	State Law and Order Restoration Council
SNC	Supreme National Council of Cambodia
SOC	State of Cambodia
SOM	Senior Officials Meeting
SPDC	State Peace and Development Council
SRV	Socialist Republic of Vietnam
TAC	Treaty of Amity and Co-operation in Southeast Asia
TNI	*Tentara Nasional Indonesia*, Indonesian National Army
UMNO	United Malays National Organisation
UN	United Nations
UNAMET	United Nations Assistance Mission to East Timor
UNCLOS	United Nations Convention on the Law of the Sea
UNGA	United Nations General Assembly
UNTAC	United Nations Transitional Authority in Cambodia
UNTAET	United Nations Transitional Administration in East Timor
US	United States
USSR	Union of Soviet Socialist Republics
UWSA	United Wa State Army
VCP	Vietnamese Communist Party
VFA	Visiting Forces Agreement
WGZOPFAN	Working Group on the Zone of Peace, Freedom and Neutrality
WTO	World Trade Organisation
ZOPFAN	Zone of Peace, Freedom and Neutrality

Introduction

Standards

Norms play an important part in mediating the fears and the identity claims of social actors insofar as shared understandings about expected behaviour and the perceived legitimacy of these provide for a stable context of social interaction. Over time, however, norms may become the subject of controversy and contestation. In some cases, this will lead to ambiguity in the practice of a particular norm. The previously shared understanding may also be in part superseded by a new dominant interpretation of the norm. Equally, a contested norm may give way to a new one. In other cases contested norms might be reaffirmed because the initial challenge to their continued validity is repulsed. In most cases more than one challenge is needed before longstanding collective understandings of norms are replaced by new collective understandings.

This book explores the origins and development of a set of norms and related practices – conceptualised as a diplomatic and security culture – that has guided the interaction of state/government leaders and senior officials representing the member states of the Association of Southeast Asian Nations (ASEAN). Its central task is to examine the extent to which the search for security and the struggle for recognition by ASEAN leaders and officials in the context of their identity-formation processes have led to new collective understandings and interpretations of a shared normative terrain. At the core of this normative terrain stand six norms:

- sovereign equality _a source of help in a difficult situation_
- the non-recourse to the use of force and the peaceful settlement of conflict
- non-interference and non-intervention
- the non-involvement of ASEAN to address unresolved bilateral conflict between members
- quiet diplomacy
- and mutual respect and tolerance

Importantly, this book is not only a study of norms. It is equally a work of foreign policy analysis and a study of the international politics of

Southeast and East Asia. The reason for this is that an exploration of the development of the normative terrain underlying intra-ASEAN diplomacy and co-operation cannot be meaningfully separated from an analysis of the reasons why ASEAN leaders espouse, defend or challenge the particular interpretations and practices associated with ASEAN's diplomatic and security culture.

The concept of diplomatic and security culture

The concept of diplomatic and security culture is not one often employed in International Relations. It brings together the two distinct concepts of diplomatic culture and security culture. The meaning of neither of these has been fixed.[1] Hedley Bull, broadly speaking, conceived of a diplomatic culture as a common stock of ideas and values possessed by state representatives.[2] According to James Der Derian,

> [a] diplomatic culture begins as a neutral link between alien quarters, but ... it becomes a cluttered, yet protected enclave, a discursive space where representatives of sovereign states can avoid the national tolls of the embryonic international society while attempting to mediate its systemic alienation.
>
> (Der Derian 1987: 42–3)

A security culture, on the other hand, may be understood as a shared body of ideas, norms and practices that serves to enhance the security of social actors, not least states. Notably, security has increasingly been thought about with respect to a variety of referents, sources of threats and approaches to security.[3] Beyond broadening and deepening the concept, the literature on security in International Relations has also moved towards a sociological understanding of security. This understanding focuses on the importance of 'ontological security', which stands for a sense of the individual as being in cognitive control of their interaction context (Giddens 1984). This notion of security is closely allied to the concept of 'trust'.[4] Broadly building on these conceptualisations, a diplomatic and security culture can thus be understood as a normative terrain on which leaders and diplomats have met and meet, and which serves the mediation of both their estrangement and insecurity.

A diplomatic and security culture should also be thought of as something particular. While some norms may have been endorsed universally, not all norms and associated diplomatic practices relating to the formulation and implementation of foreign and security policy should be assumed to be equally meaningful to even the majority of relevant actors. For example, there are clear and universally accepted rules about the privileges and immunities of diplomatic personnel (as stipulated in the Vienna Convention on Diplomatic Relations), but this does not mean that there is a universally accepted understanding of basic norms of international society such as sovereignty or non-interference. There is clearly also a wide range of views on the legitimacy of a reliance on public, quiet, informal or formal diplomacy, just as there is a wide body of opinion on the merits of strong or weak forms of institutionalisation. The reasons for this discrepancy in outlook are many, not least the fact that all foreign policy makers, by definition, operate in different lifeworlds.[5] Particular geo-strategic circumstances, perceived vulnerabilities, historical memories of interaction with outsiders and political aspirations, among many other factors, may influence what relevance and validity individual actors ascribe to the legitimacy of even basic international norms supposedly shared by all. Common understandings on these matters may of course still often be attained with some other actors, perhaps on the basis of similar experiences or political outlook, but such shared understandings tend to be partial in scope, limited in number and impermanent.

Thus, even though a diplomatic and security culture should be considered to be something particular, this does not mean that some of its core elements could not overlap with other regulatory and constitutive frameworks. In other words, particular diplomatic and security cultures may comprise a number of norms and practices that also form part of another diplomatic and security culture or are considered part of universally recognised norms such as sovereignty and non-intervention or the non-use of force. It is possible to distinguish between diplomatic and security cultures by virtue of the different meaning certain concepts and norms have for social actors, reflecting particular understandings and concerns that are the product of their particular histories and circumstances and socio-cultural settings. Just how many social actors subscribe fully or partially to a diplomatic and security culture is thus always an empirical question. That said, particular diplomatic and security cultures have often been associated, implicitly or explicitly, with particular regions.[6] A diplomatic and security culture may also be associated with a particular international organisation. The next section seeks to ascertain whether the principles, norms and practices under the label of the 'ASEAN way' are usefully conceived as a diplomatic and security culture of the leaders of ASEAN member states.

The 'ASEAN way' as a diplomatic and security culture?

The so-called 'ASEAN way' has not been explicitly conceptualised as a diplomatic and security culture (indeed there is no official definition of the term). However, that this is possible and would be useful emerges from the way in which the literature has already conceptualised the 'ASEAN way'. At least three distinct conceptualisations have emerged. The first focuses on the 'ASEAN way' as an intramural approach to dispute management and confidence building (Caballero-Anthony 1998; Kamarulzaman 1996; Hoang 1996). Hoang (1996: 63–71) lists five 'techniques' of ASEAN's informal dispute management. These are adherence to the ground rules enshrined in ASEAN's various declarations and communiqués stressing the virtue of self-restraint; adoption of the practices of *musyawarah* and *mufakat* (consultation and consensus); using third-party mediation to settle disputes; and agreeing to disagree while shelving the settlement of conflicts.

The second conceptualisation has centred on the 'ASEAN way' as a distinct decision-making procedure. Here, the 'ASEAN way' is primarily associated with processes of consensus finding (*musjawarah*) and consultation (*mufakat*) that are seen to originate from the practice of Indonesian village democracy. Pushpa Thambipillai once described the process of ASEAN decision-making as follows:

> Through informal channels ('feelers') the likely position of a particular ASEAN country on an issue will be known in advance. If the reaction seems unfavourable and with little chance of modification, then, that particular issue or a particular position will not be pursued or would be presented in a slightly modified version. Sometimes it will be pursued more obliquely if it is important to a particular country. This is to pre-empt the emergence of confrontational issues at regional meetings, where failure to reach a common agreement could be interpreted negatively and cast doubt on the workings of the organization. In short, only issues with some degree of acceptability will be presented at the regional level.
>
> (Thambipillai 1985: 14)

Third, and more recently, the 'ASEAN way' has been conceived of as a 'process of identity building which relies upon conventional modern principles of interstate relations as well as traditional and culture-specific modes of socialisation and decision-making' prevalent in Southeast Asia (Acharya 2001: 28).

Taken together, the above conceptualisations of the 'ASEAN way' suggest that this normative framework is of significance in mediating disputes, guiding interaction and underpinning a process of identity construction.

Interestingly, Acharya's conceptualisation of the 'ASEAN way' is actually more restrictive than the above quote suggests because he distinguishes between 'ASEAN norms' and the 'ASEAN way'. For him the former include principles like the non-use of force and the pacific settlement of disputes, regional autonomy and collective self-reliance, non-interference and the rejection of an ASEAN military pact in favour of bilateral defence co-operation (Acharya 2001: 47–62). He links the latter to particular social practices and culturally specific norms ('socio-cultural norms') that in an earlier work he claimed amounted to an 'organizing framework of multilateralism' and a specific process of multilateral institution building (Acharya 1997: 320, 324). The most important 'socio-cultural norms', Acharya suggests, are a preference for informality and a related aversion to the institutionalisation of co-operation, as well as consensus-building which builds on consultation on the basis of equality and tolerance (Acharya 2001: 68). In contradistinction to the brand of regionalism associated with the European Union (EU), the 'ASEAN way' is thus seen to imply the avoidance of both institutional over-centralisation and voluntary relinquishment of sovereign decision-making. Chin Kin Wah has reinforced this point by stressing the basic character of ASEAN as a 'cooperative, consultative but not supra-national organization' (Chin Kin Wah 1995: 436). As regards tolerance, Acharya has added that the process of ASEAN multilateral interaction involves 'non-confrontational bargaining styles which are often contrasted with the adversarial posturing and legalistic decision-making procedures in Western multilateral negotiations' (Acharya 1997: 329).

Noting not least Acharya's own apparent inconsistent usage of the 'ASEAN way', it is necessary to query the persuasiveness of associating the latter only with what he referred to as socio-cultural norms and practices, rather than also with what he termed 'ASEAN norms'.[7] Acharya's reasons for making this analytical distinction may build on the point that some of the latter norms are 'legal-rational' norms or basic norms or principles of international society. The implicit underpinning argument would seem to be that to speak of an 'ASEAN way' in relation to principles or basic norms of international society makes little sense, as the leaders and officials of most, if not all, countries subscribe to them. In other words, the logic driving this argument is that, as a culture is deemed particular in relation to other cultures, universally endorsed principles are best not to be considered elements of a particular culture.

Arguably, this does not necessarily follow. While it may be true that decision-makers around the world tend to endorse principles of the UN such as the non-use of force, non-intervention and non-interference, the relevance and significance of these principles to individual state leaders is likely to depend on the context of interaction in which leaders operate. The legal principles thus have varied political meaning. Interestingly, Acharya himself emphasises this point by noting four key different expectations held by ASEAN decision-makers with reference to the principle of non-interference. In accordance with these, decision-makers should be

(1) refraining from criticising the actions of a member government towards its own people, including violation of human rights, and from making the domestic political system of states and the political styles of governments a basis for deciding their membership in ASEAN; (2) criticising the actions of states which were deemed to have breached the non-interference principle; (3) denying recognition, sanctuary, or other forms of support to any rebel group seeking to destabilise or overthrow the government of a neighbouring state; (4) providing political support and material assistance to member states in their campaign against subversive and destabilising activities.

(Acharya 2001: 58)

None of these would, for instance, be likely to apply in the context of the European Union, either because there are no such shared understandings or because the stipulated context is simply not relevant. In contrast to Acharya, this study posits an intrinsic interrelationship between basic international norms (or legal-political norms) and 'socio-cultural' norms guiding the interaction between ASEAN leaders. Michael Antolik has developed this point to some extent by associating with the 'ASEAN way' a 'diplomacy of accommodation' that emphasises restraint, respect and responsibility (Antolik 1990: 8–9, ch. 9). For Antolik, the norm of non-interference is at the core of the principle of restraint.[8] This principle is thus seen to induce ASEAN elites to conform to a behavioural pattern of 'no public challenges, comments, or criticisms of other regimes' legitimacy, domestic systems, conduct, policies, or style' (Antolik 1990: 156). The principle of respect, as Antolik understands it, aims to ensure that ASEAN states do not fail to consult on issues important or of interest to other members. By the principle of responsibility Antolik means that ASEAN countries make a conscious effort to consider the interests and sensitivities of their neighbours, even when making decisions that could be described as affecting 'internal affairs' (Antolik 1990: 156).

Significantly, an intrinsic interconnectedness of the two identified normative strands mediating ASEAN member states' intramural diplomacy and foreign policy co-operation is also posited in the explication of the 'ASEAN way' offered by the former Secretary-General of ASEAN, H.E. Dato' Ajit Singh. Singh argued that

> [The 'ASEAN way'] ... is that undefinable expression that readily comes to mind when we want to explain how and why we do the [sic] things the way we do. Although the expression seems instinctive and intuitive, yet it is based on some very firm principles and practices. We respect each other's sovereignty and independence and do not interfere in each other's internal affairs. Bilateral issues are avoided. We treat each other as equals. Decisions are taken only when all are comfortable with them. Close consultations precede these decisions. Consensus is the rule. The question of face is very important and every effort is made to ensure that no party feels hurt in an argument or a discussion. This does not mean that we do not have disagreements. We often do, but we do not, as a rule, air them in public. It also means that knowing each other as well as we do, we can disagree strongly and yet, at the end of the day, play golf together, eat Durians or do the Karaoke. And Asean is none the worse for it.
>
> (A. Singh 1996)

Taking account of the above, three points emerge. First, the 'ASEAN way' can indeed be thought of as a diplomatic and security culture, a 'terrain' that has served both the mediation of estrangement that tends to accompany identity-formation processes. As such, it helps to build trust in the interaction context among ASEAN leaders and to promote interstate and regional stability. Second, ASEAN's diplomatic and security culture comprises six core norms: sovereign equality, non-recourse to the use of force and the peaceful settlement of conflict, non-interference and non-intervention, non-involvement of ASEAN to address unresolved bilateral conflict between members, quiet diplomacy, and mutual respect and toler-ance.[9] For the purposes of this study, the norm of mutual respect is linked to expectations that leaders may well agree to disagree without, however, being disagreeable, and that they should demonstrate awareness of – if not sensi-tivity to – the position, personal standing, and domestic and international achievements of one another. Third, other norms and practices associated with the 'ASEAN way' either derive from or are linked to one or more of these core elements. For instance, consultation, consensus and consent may be norms long established in the political processes of the region, but the search for them may also be considered an expression of the norms of sovereign equality and respect. The preference for informal institutions is similarly linked to the particularly strong regard for the norm of sovereignty. The norm of non-confrontational behaviour, which is linked to the norm of allowing others to 'save face', is an expression of the norm of respect, but in practice it is also tied to the norm of quiet diplomacy. The significance of the principle of respect and related norms as an element of ASEAN's diplo-matic and security culture must not be underestimated. As Singapore's senior official Kishore Mahbubani put it, ' "[f]ace" is important, and conflict can break out when it is lost' (Mahbubani 1995: 117).[10]

Reasons for writing this book on ASEAN's diplomatic and security culture

There are several reasons for writing this book. First, the question of whether and how ASEAN's diplomatic and security culture will change is arguably a core, possibly even the most important, question confronting the international politics of Southeast Asia today. It is, for example, widely held that if ASEAN's diplomatic and security culture does not develop along the lines that its critics demand, ASEAN will become increasingly insignificant.

While for a long time controversial as an approach to security, since the Asian financial and economic crisis ASEAN's diplomatic and security culture has advanced as the main target for criticism in relation to ASEAN, especially from outside the region. The general argument is that the 'ASEAN way' is no longer suited to the demands of the contemporary interdependent world, which is why it is widely perceived to have prevented ASEAN from acting appropriately in meeting a set of diverse challenges. More specifically, a torrent of criticism has been directed at the norms of sovereignty and non-interference, quiet diplomacy and respect. ASEAN's non-interference norm has come in for particularly strong criticism, as this norm is regarded as incompatible with a world of porous borders in which the insistence on the unqualified validity and priority of sovereign statehood over other norms is deemed anachronistic or politically suspect. The norm of non-interference is charged as being responsible, among other things, for ASEAN countries' failure to design an appropriate response to the economic crisis in Thailand in 1997, the smog-haze that emanated from Indonesia and the various dom estic crises in ASEAN states that have had repercussions for neighbouring countries.

For critics the choice is straightforward: 'Either interference becomes legitimate, or the association will become increasingly meaningless' (Möller 1998b: 1,104). Jeannie Henderson has taken the criticism one step further, arguing that the 'ASEAN way' 'lies at the core of a contradiction between ASEAN's claim to be a manager of regional affairs and its capacity to produce solutions to regional problems' (Henderson 1999: 12). These arguments complement the broader point that ASEAN's past achievements have been overrated (Narine 1997; Leifer 1999a). Notably, at the annual ministerial meeting in July 2000 even Singapore's Foreign Minister Jayakumar (2000) provocatively suggested that ASEAN might become a potential 'sunset organisation'. Ironically, until the outbreak of the Asian financial crisis in 1997 the Association was widely regarded as the most successful and effective regional organisation in the developing world. Also, ASEAN leaders (Jayakumar 1997b) and officials for years claimed that it was members' adherence to the 'ASEAN way' that helped them overcome or deal peacefully with their historical memories of bitter disputes and unresolved territorial conflicts.

Significantly, the question of how ASEAN's diplomatic and security culture will evolve will also have repercussions for intra-regional relations in Southeast Asia. Indeed, the question is no longer simply whether ASEAN's diplomatic and security culture stands in the way of preventing neighbours from appropriately dealing with 'domestic' issues of ASEAN states that have regional implications. Perhaps even more important is the question of whether ASEAN's entire normative terrain is crumbling as a consequence of divergent foreign policy interests, the assumption of new identities and attendant intramural disagreements, not least over the 'ASEAN way'. This process has now evidently also affected what is arguably ASEAN's single most important norm: the norm of the non-use of force and the peaceful resolution of conflict. In February 2001 a simmering dispute between Thailand and Myanmar erupted into a brief but relatively serious border skirmish in which the Royal Thai Army reportedly killed dozens of members of Myanmar's armed forces (*tatmadaw*). This was the single most deadly application of the use of force by one ASEAN member against another since 1967. It came a mere three years after the second Chuan Leekpai government had formulated a strong challenge to the consensus on the 'ASEAN way' in the form of 'flexible engagement'.

The magnitude of this development becomes clear when we recall that a wide agreement had emerged amongst policy-makers and analysts that the Association had left behind the times when the region was still seen to resemble the Balkans. Several scholars (Acharya 1991, 1996b, 1998 and 2001; Dosch 1995; Simon 1988 and 1998) have debated for more than a decade the question of whether the Association could be conceived of as a (partial) pluralistic security community or whether it was better described as a (limited) security regime, as argued, for example, by Huxley (1993).[11] The former, associated with Karl Deutsch *et al.* (1957), suggested that ASEAN leaderships, although not all liberal in outlook, had managed to develop 'dependable expectations of peaceful change, (Deutsch *et al.* 1957: 5) or, put differently, no longer expected to use force in their relations with one another.[12]

Origins of the 'ASEAN way'

It is also crucial to understand that ASEAN's diplomatic and security culture is still an immensely understudied phenomenon, notwithstanding the recent work on the Association or even on the 'ASEAN way'. The study of the origins of ASEAN's diplomatic has clearly been neglected in favour of studies on the genesis of ASEAN as an international organisation. Even those who in this context emphasise that the norms of the founding document (Bangkok Declaration) are essentially legal-political norms of international society have not been inclined to take the issue much further (Irvine 1982). A major exception is Acharya (2001: ch. 2), who consciously traces the evolution of 'ASEAN norms and the emergence of the 'ASEAN way' to events in the international politics of Southeast Asia. He relates the origins of ASEAN norms to the 1955 Bandung Conference, the experience of *konfrontasi*, major power rivalry and ASEAN's post-formation period. (He also introduces the socio-cultural norms of the 'ASEAN way' as part of a 'common cultural heritage'.) However, even his very useful account leaves unanswered some questions regarding how we might think about the origins of ASEAN's diplomatic and security culture.

For instance, did the 'ASEAN way' only come about after all its constituent legal-political and socio-cultural norms were implicitly or explicitly successively agreed, or was there a particular point in time when ASEAN's diplomatic and security culture was established, perhaps followed by a process of its further refinement? To what extent does it matter that ASEAN's organisational record for the first few years was blighted, for instance due to serious intramural friction between Manila and Kuala Lumpur (over Sabah, expressed not least in the Corregidor Affair, which involved an apparent attempt by Philippines-sponsored rebels to penetrate Sabah). Arguably, such points matter a great deal and, depending on what one understands by origins, it is possible to trace them back to different time periods, either before or after the formation of the Association.[13]

Development of the 'ASEAN way'

Another insufficiently studied theme concerns the development of ASEAN's diplomatic and security culture. Up to the third enlargement of the Association in July 1997, when Laos and Myanmar became members, or even until the full outbreak of the Asian financial and economic crisis, this issue was hardly addressed. It was generally assumed that by enumerating the individual norms making up the 'ASEAN way' a better understanding of the concept would be achieved. Very little attention was paid to whether members differed in their views about the relevance or validity of the principles that their leaders embraced in their respective diplomatic discourse, or whether new norms governing intramural conduct emerged. Only since 1998, in view of the proposal for 'flexible engagement' put forward by Dr Surin Pitsuwan, then Thailand's Foreign Minister, have more systematic inquiries into the evolution (of certain elements) of ASEAN's diplomatic and security culture begun to appear (for example, Funston 1998a, 1999). That this has happened should not surprise us. As Der Derian remarked, the '[e]xistence of diplomatic culture only becomes self-evident, and subject to inquiry, when the values and ideas of one society are estranged from another' (Der Derian 1996: 92).

That said, the proposal to allow for a more flexible interpretation of the norm of non-interference in intramural relations did not, in itself, represent an immediate change or even the demise of the 'ASEAN way' – as other ASEAN governments spurned the idea because of perceived problematic implications. The proposal did, however, amount to a challenge to the common understanding of the contours and substance of the terrain that ASEAN had endorsed to mediate insecurity and estrangement within its region. More recently, notwithstanding the consensus on 'flexible engagement', ASEAN has agreed on several innovations in the area of how ASEAN states should engage with each other, not least in the field of preventive diplomacy. Clarification is thus needed on whether a shift in the longstanding understandings of particular elements of the 'ASEAN way' has indeed occurred and what, if any, new norms have emerged (see Chapter 7).[14]

The major powers and the 'ASEAN way'

Finally, there are virtually no systematic attempts to analyse how ASEAN leaders have sought to make regional powers endorse the terrain of the 'ASEAN way'. Attention has instead focused largely on the extent to which other regional organisations have adopted processes of intergovernmental co-operation similar to aspects of ASEAN's diplomatic and security culture. Equally, there are basically no systematic works investigating the extent to which the major powers have supported or instigated challenges to the prevalent understandings of the 'ASEAN way'. This book contends that the question of the development and relevance of ASEAN's diplomatic and security culture cannot be explored in isolation from the broader evolution of norms in international society in general and from ASEAN's relations with the major regional powers in particular.

Theoretical assumptions

This book is situated in the constructivist camp of International Relations theory, broadly defined.[15] As regards its main theoretical assumptions and concepts, it draws on the insights of a number of different but not necessarily incommensurable works. First, the book follows scholars like E.H. Carr (1946: 149) and Manning (1962: chs 2, 3), in that states should only be regarded as 'notional entities' rather than corporate persons with a single will and possessing qualities or attributes that apply to human personality. In other words, reference to the behaviour of a state is shorthand for saying that individuals act in specific roles as agents for the state. Indeed, the recent sociological turn in International Relations stresses that the dynamic governing the behaviour of states cannot be divorced from the perceptions of state leaders as individuals and as representatives of the particular social-political setting in which they operate.

Second, the book assumes that state leaders and foreign and defence officials in particular are concerned with a search for security. The book employs a broad notion of the concept of security. It builds above all on Alagappa (1998; see also Paribatra and Samudavanjia 1986), who has emphasised how security threats, as perceived from the perspective of state leaders, extend from fears about the territorial integrity and political autonomy of their countries to concerns about their own political survival and well-being. This means that Alagappa invites scholars to widen the range of what might be conceived as possible security threats to incumbent regimes to include developments in state-civil society relations as well as in the national, regional and global economy.[16] Threats to political survival may also take the form of ideas which are perceived to compete or stand at odds with those underpinning the respective political system or particular policies. The book also takes seriously the idea that ontological insecurity experienced by particular leaders can readily translate into perceptions of threat in relation to, say, interstate or regime security.

Third, the book draws on the work of Axel Honneth, whose writings have focused on the importance of mutual recognition between subjects to the success of inter-subjective identity-formation processes. According to Honneth (1995a), recognition available to subjects in adulthood – cognitive respect and social esteem – is not necessarily guaranteed. For instance, subjects may be excluded as agents capable of acting on the basis of reasons in discursive decision-making processes on matters that concern them. Equally, subjects may find their identity claims in relation to status and achievement are ignored or repudiated. Following Honneth, such experiences can lead subjects to struggle for what they would regard as more legitimate forms of interaction, better representation in institutions and fairer social arrangements.[17] Such a struggle, especially if it is collectively undertaken, may be the start of a process of norm-rationalisation (Habermas 1984). Equally, subjects may challenge or defy those who seek to deny them respect or standing. In this sense, the ensuing conflict has what Honneth (1995a) calls a 'moral grammar'. Violence to identity-claims may set off social struggles that actually run counter to the perceived material interests (economic advantage, for instance) of those concerned (also see Moore 1967, 1978). Interests, then, are endogenous, not exogenous, to the process of social interaction.

Significantly, the struggle for recognition is an enduring process. As Axel Honneth argues, 'the experience of a particular form of recognition ... [is] bound up with the disclosing of new possibilities with regard to identity, which necessarily result in a struggle for the social recognition of those new forms of identity' (Honneth 1995a: 162). The abiding feature of new claims to recognition, Honneth argues, can be understood with reference to a psycho-analytic concept of human identity. In Honneth's words, 'the individual claim to recognition is anchored in every subject as an enduring motive which is continually capable of being activated' (Honneth 1995b: xxiv).

By implication, state/government leaders are also involved in constant processes of identity-formation. They no doubt wish to be respected as persons *and* as representatives of their political systems, as well as for any political, economic or social achievements they might have mustered.[18] State leaders have also acquired particular identity-claims in the process of their own socialisation, including possibly a sense of entitlement that is widely shared in society on the basis of common interpretations of history or specific contexts like successful struggles for independence. Importantly, in their role state/government leaders they are, moreover, constantly involved in a two-way identity-formation process, *vis-à-vis* their respective domestic society and *vis-à-vis* other actors on the international scene.

With this broad understanding of the struggle for security and recognition in mind, it is possible to understand the emergence of a diplomatic and security culture as the outcome of a process of mutual recognition, possibly through a process of reconciliation or accommodation. Whether a specific diplomatic and security culture emerges in this way is an empirical question. Moreover, as with all norms, a diplomatic and security culture will also fulfil three functions, as identified by Friedrich Kratochwil. It will:

- serve as a guiding device for dealing such situations in social life, whether co-operative or conflictual;
- create webs of meaning and structure expectations, providing for an intersubjective 'communications systems' which becomes the basis for criticising or justifying courses of action pursued by social agents;

• guide decision-making processes insofar as rules and norms influence choices through the reasoning processes of social actors.

(Kratochwil 1989: 10–12, 69–70)

To the extent that social actors adhere to the norms of a diplomatic and security culture, they will reinforce the latter's perceived validity. This will further reinforce expectations about the interaction context and is likely to have security-building effects, in the sense of a trust-building exercise. Importantly, social actors find that norms 'instruct [them] what interests *of others* [they] have to take into account while making [their] choices' (Kratochwil 1989: 95). Of course, actors may still monitor strategically their own and others' behaviour (McSweeney 1999: 140). Diplomatic and security cultures can be extended to include new actors. Theoretically, this is possible because, as Kratochwil suggests, 'it is precisely the internalization of the norms' *generalized* validity claim which bridges the gap among actors who know very little, or virtually nothing, about each other' (Kratochwil 1989: 48).[19] However, it may be that in practice the norms in question are contested by another actor, in which case the diplomatic and security culture cannot be extended in its particular form.

Finally, although it is thus possible to say that a diplomatic and security culture can mediate estrangement and help build trust and security, an existing diplomatic and security culture should not be expected to do so always. Indeed, elements of a diplomatic and security culture may themselves become contested in such a sustained way that a failure to agree on new interpretations of principles or the introduction of new norms may lead to its demise. At the same time, one needs to recognise that a diplomatic and security culture is only one part of the wider setting – both enabling and constraining – under which foreign policy decisions are formulated and implemented. Examples of other relevant considerations are developments 'at home', material needs or changes in the broader international sphere, not least in the balance of power.

Themes of the book

The book has three principal themes. The first concerns a continuous struggle for security, as well as recognition by government/state leaders and their senior officials (as with all human actors). The adoption of this theme is linked to the argument (Habermas 1992: 101) that normative orders are always orders of *interpersonal* relationships.

In line with the theoretical assumptions, the major second theme of this book is that of challenge and defiance in the international politics of Southeast Asia. The book examines both indirect and direct challenges to ASEAN's diplomatic and security culture in the Cold War and the post-Cold War era. Significantly, on the basis of the conceptualisation developed above, the book explores not only the challenges that individual leaders may have mounted to the 'socio-cultural' norms constituent of the 'ASEAN way' (see Nischalke 2000) but also, and perhaps more pertinently, those directed at the legal-political principles.

The third theme is that of the development of ASEAN's diplomatic and security culture, understood as shifts in the interpretations of its core and associated norms, as well as the emergence of substitute norms and practices collectively deemed legitimate by leaders of the member states. Notably, the book does not treat legitimate norms and practices as simple reflections of any underlying distribution of power.

Organisation of the book

The book is divided into eight chapters. Chapters 1 and 2 deal with the origins of ASEAN's diplomatic and security culture. They explore the early roots of the 'ASEAN way' in the form of the social, political and economic struggles of elites in Southeast Asia during the period of colonialism, and examine how and at what point after independence respect for the 'ASEAN way' was secured. Chapter 3 focuses on how ASEAN leaders, since the early 1970s, have sought to win a commitment from non-ASEAN states *vis-à-vis* the Association in relation to legal-political norms that were seen as the substantive basis of the Association's diplomatic and security culture. At first the focus will be on the Zone of Peace, Freedom and Neutrality (ZOPFAN) framework and then it will shift to the ASEAN Regional Forum (ARF). Chapter 4 discusses the extent to which proposals for a political solution to the Cambodia conflict clashed with an 'absolute' understanding of the validity of the norms of non-intervention and the non-use of force and should therefore be regarded as Cold War challenges to the 'ASEAN way'.

Chapter 5 examines the challenges posed to the 'ASEAN way' by the People's Republic of China. In particular, the chapter explores China's record of adherence to the norms of the non-use of force and the principle of restraint, with particular reference to its actions in the South China Sea dispute. It also looks at whether China has challenged or reinforced the norms or practices of the 'ASEAN way' in the aftermath of the Asian financial crisis. The post-Cold War challenge posed to ASEAN's diplomatic and security culture by the United States is analysed in Chapter 6. The key question here is to what extent the United States has sought to alter the approach that ASEAN members have adopted towards each other or towards those states that are signatories to the Treaty of Amity and Co-operation. Equally, it asks to what extent Washington challenges ASEAN's effort to extend its diplomatic and security culture to the interaction of regional states in the context of the ARF.

Chapter 7 examines the challenges to the 'ASEAN way' posed by Thailand's spurned proposal for 'flexible engagement' and the pursuit of 'enhanced interaction' by some ASEAN members in intramural relations.

The objectives of this chapter are to understand the nature of and the reasons for Thailand's formal challenge to the 'ASEAN way' and to investigate fellow members' response up to the Sixth ASEAN Summit in Hanoi in late 1998. The question of how, if at all, ASEAN's diplomatic and security culture has developed since the 1998 Hanoi Summit is further explored in Chapter 8. The chapter seeks to evaluate whether the creation of the ASEAN Surveillance Process, the initiation of the annual 'Retreat', the participation by some members in the International Force in East Timor (INTERFET) and the establishment of a Troika mechanism signal partial reinterpretations of the 'ASEAN way'. The concluding chapter of the book reflects on the prospects of ASEAN's diplomatic and security culture. It sketches three possible developments for the 'ASEAN way' – evolution, stasis or demise in the medium term – and seeks to assess which of these is the most likely. As will become apparent, not only the past and present, but also the future of ASEAN's diplomatic and security culture is likely to be intimately linked to whether internal and external security concerns and continuing estrangement among regional leaderships necessitate a normative framework in which the latter are mediated.

1 Early origins of the 'ASEAN way'

The struggle for respect and sovereignty

The present chapter is the first of two that address the genesis of ASEAN's diplomatic and security culture. This is an area of inquiry on which relatively little light has been cast compared to the efforts expended regarding the formation of the Association of Southeast Asian Nations itself.[1] Dating the origins of the 'ASEAN way' is an endeavour fraught with difficulty, primarily because of the different understandings one might espouse in relation to the term. If one focuses on when the norms of the 'ASEAN way' enjoyed respect by decision-makers of the founding states of ASEAN in their intramural relations, one immediately reaches the conclusion that the origins of ASEAN's diplomatic and security culture did not coincide with the formation of ASEAN. The 1968 Corregidor Affair, prompted by press reports in the Philippines that Manila had been training a secret army on the island of Corregidor in preparation for an armed incursion into Sabah, is a case in point. It suggested that member states were not necessarily inclined to rule out the use of armed force to press their own territorial claims. Conclusions about dating the origins of the 'ASEAN way' would differ if attention focused on the events or circumstances in which norms like sovereign equality, the non-use of force, non-interference and quiet diplomacy began to enjoy meaning with relevant decision-makers. This was clearly the case before the establishment of ASEAN. Indeed, a normative framework not too dissimilar to the basic tenets of the 'ASEAN way' was meant to underpin previous attempts at regional co-operation in the form of the Association of Southeast Asia (ASA) (Lyon 1969: 154–6). In some sense, therefore, the origins of the 'ASEAN way' could be seen to date back to before the establishment of the Association of Southeast Asian Nations. If one accepts this argument, however, the question then becomes how far back in time the origins lie.

In this context, it is useful to recall that while at the core of ASEAN's diplomatic and security stand modern legal-political concepts such as sovereign equality, non-interference and the non-use of force, these are relatively new to Southeast Asia. Indeed, indigenous conceptions of state, sovereignty, statecraft and interstate order were still common currency in Southeast Asia in the early twentieth century. The origins of the 'ASEAN way' might therefore also be understood as a process of abandonment of the latter understandings and related practices. Notably, extending our under-standing of the origins of the 'ASEAN way' to developments before members' independence seems useful for another important reason. The point here is that the political struggle accompanying the embracing of the concept of sovereignty, and in particular the nationalist struggle, directly involved those political leaders who would govern member countries at the time of the founding of the Association. To the extent that the embracing of the modern conception of sovereignty and nationalism in Southeast Asia preceded their active political careers, these arguably functioned as historical memories of the founding fathers of ASEAN.

As both notions of the origins of the 'ASEAN way' seem persuasive, this book will discuss both the early and the post-war origins of the 'ASEAN way' in this and Chapter 2, respectively. This chapter is divided into two sections. The first section provides an overview of traditional conceptions of interstate relations in Southeast Asia and the nature of the colonial chal-lenge to these. The second section focuses on the struggle for respect and sovereignty in what would later become the five founding states of ASEAN. In this context, a brief account will be given of how both a struggle for recognition underpinned by a moral grammar and security concerns guided the early nationalism of Malaya, Singapore, the Dutch East Indies, the Philippines and Siam/Thailand. Chapter 2 will then concentrate on the later origins of the 'ASEAN way' as a framework for the mediation of estrange-ment and insecurity.

Traditional interstate relations in Southeast Asia and international society

The state in much of traditional Southeast Asia has generally been considered a microcosmic reproduction of the universe in accordance with Hindu–Buddhist cosmological principles (Tambiah 1987; Heine-Geldern 1973). This had several implications for how traditional rulers thought about sovereignty and the character of interstate relations. Sovereignty was conceived of as the divinely sanctioned right to rule the universe, manifested in the qualities of the ruler or god-king. Striving to become supreme universal monarchs (*chakravartin*), rulers tended to seek the expansion of their circle of influence (*mandala*). This entailed a signifi-cant fluidity of state frontiers (McCloud 1986: 99). As Benedict Anderson put it: 'The traditional state is defined by its center, not by its perimeter' (B. Anderson 1990: 42).

Similarly to the conception of territorially limited states, the notion of sovereign equality was also alien to traditional rulers (Hooker 1988a: 335–6). Indeed, from the standpoint of the ruler aspiring to be a universal monarch, this was impossible. In the words of Suwannathat-Pian, it was 'imperative for a king to avoid at any cost committing an act that could be construed as recognizing the superiority of another' (Suwannathat-Pian 1988: 44). Notably, suzerain relations implied a *moral* relationship of superiority and inferiority between political units that translated into the suzerain's obligation to extend protection to the vassal state. Historically, in continental and insular Southeast Asia, tributary relations involved the symbolic offering of the *bunga mas* (ornamental plants with leaves and flowers of gold and silver) to the suzerain (Tate 1971: ch. 2; Hall 1981: 544–5). Examples of such relationships include those of Siam and what were later to become the Unfederated Malay states of Kelantan, Trengganu, Perlis and Kedah, or Siam's relations with rulers in Laos and Cambodia. In maritime Southeast Asia, suzerain relations may, for instance, be traced to as far back as the Kingdom of Majapahit.

Notwithstanding its inherent objective of bringing about peace and order, reliance on the conception of hierarchical relations between political units tended to produce seemingly unceasing rivalries and made war an important instrument of statecraft. Indeed, 'war ... was the arbiter of virtually all interstate disputes and the most common form of interstate action' (McCloud 1986: 98). Theoretically, the resort to warfare indicated weakness on the part of the aspiring universal monarch, as submission to his supreme power was held ideally to proceed voluntarily. In practice, however, war was the chief means of enforcing the authority of the god-king. Violence not only served to expand control over resources and populations, which augmented the royal power, but was also meted out as punishment when petty rulers failed to recognise the moral and virtuous superiority of their respective overlord.

Significantly, the moral authority of traditional rulers was contested not only from without, but equally from within the polity. To prevail, leaders required a strong support base. As Suwannathat-Pian argued, '[k]ingship in traditional South-East Asia was principally based on the real power and ability [charismatic leadership] of individual rulers, their command of wealth both in terms of materials and social rewards, and the support of their clan and followers' (Suwannathat-Pian 1988: 40). In other words, the moral authority of aspiring god-kings rested in no small measure on the support of individuals or groups wielding influence at the domestic level, usually the princes and other members of the ruling elite. When internal struggles turned virulent, this usually had repercussions for relevant suzerain relations, as lesser states would often seize an opportunity arising from problems of administrative control to wrestle free from their moral bonds.

The colonial challenge

The traditional understanding of sovereignty and practice of interstate relations did not immediately lose relevance when Southeast Asia was subjected to colonialism. Ironically, Europeans, some of whom found the character of overlord ties in much of nineteenth-century Southeast Asia morally objectionable, tended to end up assuming the role of a new 'overlord'.[2] The legit-imisation of relations of inequality between Western states and Eastern societies rested not least on the invocation of the 'standard of civilisation' (Gong 1984a). The standard, backed by superior force, became a tool by which the colonial powers secured economic advantages, in particular. As McCloud argued, '[t]he Dutch rejected the concept of state sovereignty in favor of the primacy of conquest and refused to acknowledge legitimate economic interests or needs in their drive for monopoly control' (McCloud 1986: 131).[3] To the extent that treaties between Asian and European coun-tries contained provisions emphasising equality, for instance the Treaty of Friendship and Commerce negotiated between the British East India Company representative and Siam in 1826, such symmetry was actually considered objectionable in Britain because it failed to satisfy certain key economic interests. In the case of the Treaty, these focused on the abolition of royal monopolies and the trading privileges enjoyed by Chinese merchants, as well as extra-territorial jurisdiction (Gong 1984a: 205). When attempts to redress this 'imbalance' failed, the resort to gunboat diplomacy ensued. The resultant 1855 Bowring Treaty resembled 'unequal treaties' already signed by China and Japan, stipulating the surrender of Siam's judi-cial and fiscal autonomy.[4] Notwithstanding the many reforms initiated, Western powers subsequently remained reluctant to relinquish the extra-territorial rights secured.[5]

The conventional argument has been that European powers 'socialised' the states of Southeast Asia into accepting European norms, not least by educating their colonial subjects. This is true to the extent that European powers insisted on and introduced administrative and legal structures that paved the way for the transition in political organisation from traditional polities (kingdoms) to a modern sovereign state. In many ways the reforms entailed a depersonalisation and secularisation of political legitimacy, as Western notions about functional bureaucracies and administrative effi-ciency replaced indigenous social practices. However, the embracing of a modern conception of sovereignty and other basic norms of an expanding international society in lieu of traditional conceptions of state and interstate relations by Southeast Asian ruling elites is arguably as much a consequence of interlocking struggles for recognition as a product of imposed socialisa-tion. The distinction is important insofar as it may help to account for the strong commitment to core norms of the 'ASEAN way' by ASEAN deci-sion-makers with long historical memories.[6]

Indeed, over time the experience of colonialism generated multiple strug-gles for recognition among both local aristocracies and the wider masses across Southeast Asia. This is not to say that many members of ruling elites were not able to benefit at all from colonialism. Those ceding land were usually materially compensated, with some receiving pensions for life. Others may have successfully played their part in colonial administrations. Nevertheless, over time, resentment *vis-à-vis* the colonial representatives would set in, leading to localised or national anti-colonial struggle. Analytically, those struggling for recognition pursued social, cultural, economic and/or political objectives. Some of these struggles also had racial overtones. Grievances arose, for instance, on religious grounds as a reaction to attempts at Christianisation, i.e. anti-*kafir* movements. In other cases it was fuelled by the erosion of authority of indigenous elites stemming from, among other things, new ways of organising the economy and the centralisation of colonial administration that were associated with the assumption of monopoly control over commercial trade in various product ranges. Not surprisingly, the effective denial of political equality and power in arrangements of governance set up by foreign administrators was seen as something that could be overcome only once political independence was achieved.

Anti-colonialism in Southeast Asia was also nourished by various intellectual influences from other parts of the world, and diverse historical events reinforced existing grievances. For instance, ideas about Islamic reformism or the 1902 conclusion of the Anglo-Japanese Alliance – the first international treaty on defence which an East Asian country concluded on the basis of state equality – accelerated in different ways the struggle for recognition by Southeast Asian elites. As did, if not more so, the collapse of the Qing dynasty and the establishment of the Republic of China, as well as Woodrow Wilson's espousal of the principle of self-determination in the Fourteen Points (W. Wilson 1918). Significantly, while these developments were occurring international society continued to be a closed shop for Southeast Asia's social and political elites, so that their nationalism also fed on the perception that the standard of civilisation applied to their societies was in fact a 'double standard'.[7] Arguably, this made the perceived status of inferiority all the more morally degrading, further propelling anti-colonialism. The question is how this stage in the development of the 'ASEAN way', which in essence involved a struggle for admission into international society, evolved in the five founding states of the Association? The following section attempts to recount a few relevant developments in the social and political history of the states concerned until independence was attained in order to substantiate the argument that the early genesis of the 'ASEAN way' is intimately tied to concrete struggles for respect and rights. Interestingly, the section points to a tension – which in a different form continues to exist in the present – between the struggle for recognition by elites and that of wider social forces.[8] This would have important consequences for intra-regional relations in the post-war/post-independence period.

The grammar of the anti-colonial and nationalist struggles[9]

Siam was the only kingdom in Southeast Asia at least nominally able to retain its independence, although in the Treaty of Friendship and Commerce of 1855 (Bowring Treaty) King Mongkut (Rama IV) granted extra-territorial rights to British subjects and conceded jurisdiction in legal cases concerning British subjects to London's Consul in Bangkok. Influenced by the forcible imposition of the 1842 treaty by Britain on China, King Mongkut had clearly sought to escape the humiliation of military defeat (Gong 1984a: 208). Siam subsequently sought to rely on Britain to balance the security threats arising from the territorial ambitions of France, which challenged Thailand's claim to suzerainty in both Laos and Cambodia, as well as her own territorial integrity. As Fairchild Busch noted, King Mongkut described the choice for Siam as either 'to swim upriver and make friends with the crocodile [France] or to swim out to sea and hang on the whale [Great Britain]' (cited in Gong 1984a: 208). In the event, Siam's quest for security through de facto alignment with London failed to halt French designs on territory claimed by the former (Hirschfeld 1968).[10]

As suggested above, the institution of extra-territoriality (implying the acceptance by Siam of foreign consular jurisdiction) and Bangkok's loss of fiscal autonomy (in relation to duties and tariffs) were at the heart of Siam's subsequent struggle for recognition.[11] Essentially, this struggle took the form of what today might be termed a drive towards 'modernisation', directed foremost at revamping Siam's legal regime and its form of political organisation. In the words of Gerrit Gong, Siam 'worked ... hard to fulfil the standard of "civilization"' (Gong 1984a: 219), the ultimate goal of which was to be recognised as an equal member of international society. Although initiated under Mongkut, this task fell to King Chulalongkorn (Rama V), who vigorously transformed Siam in accordance with many of the premises underpinning the constitutional and administrative example set by the Western powers. King Chulalongkorn realised that the European concept of law 'was an emanation of the state' and that this concept demanded 'that for a Siamese law or legal system to be acceptable to European powers, it must emanate from a state constructed on the same principles' (Hooker 1988b: 549). Siam's modernisation efforts were thus extended to the construction of a state founded on secularism and administered by an appointed bureaucracy, in which the authority of law flowed from the state and no longer from personal or religious rule (Hooker 1988a: 440).

The length to which officials would go over the years to win the respect of the Western powers in working towards the repeal of extra-territoriality was considerable, especially in the first two decades of the last century. The modernisation process included, for instance, a wide array of reforms ranging from the abolition of the practice of prostration in the royal presence, to the abolition of slavery, polygamy and public gambling houses. Craig Reynolds evocatively summed up the underlying motivation: 'Parity with the West was a preoccupation of the Thai elite at this time, and parity applied to dress and deportment as well as to sovereignty' (Reynolds 1991: 8). Siam also entered World War I on the side of the allies to demonstrate its commitment to humanity and to earning its proper place in the society of states (Gong 1984a: 233). While the war effort allowed Siam to be represented as an equal at the Paris Peace Conference and, subsequently, as a charter member of the League of Nations, the colonial powers refused simultaneously to rescind extra-territoriality. Indeed, as noted, it was not before 1937–9 that the remnants of extra-territoriality were revoked in response to the passing of Siam's 'modern' constitution and the promulgation of a civil and commercial code (Hooker 1988b: 574).

Meanwhile, two contending positions had crystallised within the 'People's Party' following the 1932 overthrow of Siam's absolute monarchy. One, led by Pridi Phanomyong, a French-trained lawyer, was associated with radical economic reform plans, the implementation of which were designed to secure Siam's emergence from her feudalistic, absolute monarchical past and to entrench the political survival of the new political system of constitutional government (Suwannathat-Pian 1995: ch. 3). The other, which united more conservative elements of the party and would prevail politically, had formed around Phibul Songkram, a French-trained military officer. This group shared the goal of ensuring Siam's break with backwardness and of winning international respect. However, it hoped to achieve this objective through economic self-sufficiency and nation-building. As it turned out, the latter involved a process of cleansing cultural practices that might cause embarrassment because they might be rejected by the *farang* (Westerner). At the same time, those aspects of Thai culture deemed genuine, unique and worthy in the eyes of the official were to be preserved. Indeed, Siam's leadership sought only to mould the outward Siamese identity on the basis of the modern state, while trying to conserve its inner strength against the threat of the *farang*. In other words, to learn English and Western technology was to preserve the essential core of Siamese identity, which was part and parcel of the spirit of Buddhism. In June 1939 Thailand replaced Siam as the country's official name, in accordance with the notion of *Muang Thai*, meaning 'the land of the free'. Moreover, to Phibul, who led Thailand's military dictatorship during the war, major power status (*maha prathet*) was the only choice for a country that wanted to overcome slave status (Suwannathat-Pian 1995: 106).

This led him to embark on an irredentist strategy that entailed concluding an alliance with Japan in December 1941 and declaring war on Britain and France in January 1942. Having already regained from France the territories of Battambang and Siemrap in Cambodia and the Laotian territory to the west of the river Mekong in 1941, two years later Phibul also recovered the four Malay States (Kedah, Perlis, Kelantan and Trengganu) which Thailand had ceded to Britain in 1909. Bangkok then also acquired the two Shan states of Kengtung and Mongpan.

In the face of the outcome of the Pacific War Pridi Phanomyong took over from Phibul the reins of power in August 1945, arguing that the declaration of war was null and void and vowing to return the territories, to pay damages and to revert to the name of Siam. However, Pridi's political comeback as prime minister lasted only from April to August 1946, and by April 1948 a coup had reinstalled Phibul as Thailand's head of government. His renewed rule paved the way for the assertion of a pro-US, staunchly anti-communist political identity to ensure the preservation of the country's independence, the recognition of its status as a state of sovereign equality, and the retention of Thai pride in its institutions and culture.

Malaya: contending struggles for recognition and ethnic security

The introduction of a new type of government and law in the whole of the Malay Peninsula by 1919 did not immediately arouse nationalist sentiment against Britain in colonial Malaya, although sultans and chiefs were by then effectively deprived of their executive powers. While one might expect the Malay aristocracy to have resented this and to have initiated a united struggle against the changes brought about by Britain, the colonial arrangements allowed for a semblance of power that proved acceptable to them, at least for a time. Also, the majority of Malay nobles were initially satisfied with the administrative positions they were able to secure in the civil service after receiving their English education in the elite Malay College, which was modelled on the British public school system.

The early Malay struggle for recognition is thus better associated with religious reformists, who – drawing on the Egyptian modernist movement – invoked a purified Islam. The chief target of their criticism was traditional Muslim officialdom, which was held responsible for Malay economic and educational backwardness. According to the modernists, traditional Islamic practices had been adulterated by impurities of custom and belief derived from *adat* (customary law) and from other religious sources. Significantly, it was not this backwardness *per se* that bothered the modernists, but the experience that such backwardness made Malays disrespected by the other ethnic groupings in Malaya. The Straits Chinese, for instance, gibed at

> their [the Malays'] slavish adherence to outmoded custom, the dissolute-ness of their traditional leaders (interested only in opium, women, and gambling), their lack of industry and ambition, their hostility toward anyone who showed exceptional talents, and their inability to practice mutual help.
>
> (quoted in Roff 1994: 54)

Taking offence, Malay religious reformers started to associate the colonial administration, rather than any lack of education, with their humiliation and complained bitterly that '[t]he knowledge that is given to peoples under foreign influence has no purpose other than to impoverish their intellects and teach them to lick the soles of their masters' boots' (quoted in Soernano 1960: 8–9). In the event, religious reformism failed to advance the nationalist struggle.

Malay nationalism was instead galvanised by the demands for equal rights and privileges put forward by Chinese and Indian immigrants, who had been imported by the British to help exploit natural resources in colonial Malaya. The nationalist attitudes of Malaya's immigrant population, and in particular their increasing aspirations for a dominant economic and political role, led many Malays to appreciate the attendant danger to Malay identity and to form the first Malay political party, the Kesatuan Melayu Singapura, in 1926. While more revolutionary-inclined elements – who had formed the Union of Malay Youths (Kesatuan Melayu Muda) under the influence of the communist revolts in Indonesia and Sukarno's mass movement and demanded independence and unity with Indonesia – ultimately failed in their political objectives, the traditional elite's struggle for recognition did not.

The reasons why Malaya's traditional elite, especially in the Federated Malay States,[12] ultimately embarked on the nationalist cause built on the increasingly pervasive feeling of a loss of authority and social prestige. As Khasnor Johan put it, '[t]he sense of deprivation of the ruling classes in the administrative and political spheres was undoubtedly magnified through their awareness of the better fortunes of their counterparts in the unfederated states' (Khasnor 1984: 13). However, the Malay nobility's resentment against colonialism fed primarily on the reality that the British ultimately presided over access to both jobs and status. The accelerated admittance and recruitment of the younger Malay nobility into Malaya's bureaucracy (the Malay Administrative Service) did for some time allay the struggle for recognition of those concerned. Despite the fact that they were partially accommodated by and on reasonably good terms with the colonial power, their struggle for position, status and riches nevertheless continued until the educated Malay nobility also won entry into the more prestigious Malayan Civil Service. There they became 'official spokesmen of unofficial Malay opinion' (Puthucheary 1987: 98), before the Pacific War.

Even more importantly, a wave of nationalistic sentiment gripped the traditional Malay elite after World War II as British plans for a Malayan Union were released (Hall 1981: 874–6). Two aspects in particular of this proposal caused considerable outrage among Malays. First, there was the abrasive manner in which a proposal had been introduced the substance of which, *inter alia*, called for the residual sovereignty of the sultans to be relinquished and the structure of government to be unified under direct colonial rule. If implemented, this plan would have emasculated the remaining influence of the traditional nobility. Second, there was the concomitant objective of establishing a system of equal rights for all people domiciled in the peninsula (excluding Singapore) by introducing Malayan Union citizenship.

The detractors of the Malayan Union scheme drew on organisational structures – overwhelmingly the network of Malay Associations, which had come into being only several years previously – to deal with this supreme threat to its identity and position, and formed the United Malays National Organisation (UMNO). According to Roff,

> Chauvinist or ethnicist rather than politically nationalist, the Malay Associations professed complete loyalty to the traditional Malay establishments ... and an almost equal enthusiasm for British colonial rule, as the bulwark for the time being of Malay interests against the rapacious demands of Malayan-domiciled aliens.
>
> Roff (1994: 256)

Under the leadership of Dato Onn, UMNO's first chairman, the challenge to the Malayan Union proposal proved successful, as evidenced by the eventual British acceptance of the UMNO Federation Plan in February 1948. Significantly, just as the Malays largely united in the struggle to maintain their privileged position in Malaya *vis-à-vis* the immigrant ethnic groups, so the latter continued to struggle for a more just and equal society. In the words of Wang Gungwu, the proposal for Malayan Union succeeded 'in releasing the energies of all three communities and inducing them all to consider their potential rights in a new Malaya' (Wang 1962/1992: 190). Ethnic Chinese, in particular, joined the communist uprising in June 1948, exacerbating racial tensions, although many Chinese and Indian merchants and professionals distanced themselves from the communist insurrection. To address the interracial friction and to build a united front against the communist challenge, Dato Onn proposed a reconsideration of the citizenship provisions of the Federation Constitution. He also proposed that UMNO should stand for United *Malaya* National Organisation and admit non-Malays to emphasise that UMNO should be pursuing the struggle for independence, which he considered the real objective of the 1949 UMNO Constitution (Ishak bin Tadin 1960: 73–9).

Resistance to these proposals made Dato Onn leave UMNO to form the Independence of Malaya Party, but his advice was in a sense heeded by the new leadership, under Tunku Abdul Rahman, as testified by the establishment of a multi-ethnic Alliance government. This government's consensualist nationalist goal was to gain independence at some unspecified point in the future, whereas Tunku Abdul Rahman himself relatively swiftly pressed for independence after his accession to power. Significantly, his drive for 'all-out independence' was also determined by personal experiences of disrespect in his dealings with Britain. This included not least the 'shabby treatment' that he received following the resounding electoral victory in 1955 by the Alliance – whose members comprised UMNO, the Malayan Chinese Association and the Malayan Indian Congress – which led to him becoming Chief Minister of the Federal Executive Council.[13] Whether the Tunku was more easily irritable because of his royal descent need not detain us here.[14] The Tunku succeeded in his quest for rapid independence, which he secured in the London constitutional talks. Importantly, especially given the failure of talks with Malayan Communist Party (MCP) leader Chin Peng in 1955, the Tunku had become a staunch anti-communist. This made him anchor independent Malaya's security in a defence agreement with the Western powers.

Singapore

The multi-racial leadership of independent Singapore, which had become a separate colony in 1946, consisted of convinced anti-colonialists[15], including Lee Kuan Yew, Goh Keng Swee and S. Rajaratnam. This anti-colonialism was the product of experiences with both British and Japanese rule. Indeed, any expectations that some might initially have harboured at the outset of the Pacific War in relation to Japan granting other Asian countries equal status in the establishment of a Co-Prosperity Sphere were dashed soon after the fall of Singapore in 1942. Indeed, Tokyo ended up by torturing or murdering both Chinese and Indians in 'Syonan' (Singapore), a factor which provoked the formation of the Malayan People's Anti-Japanese Army, the military arm of the Communist Party of Malaya.

When repossessing Malaya and Singapore, the British found they had effectively lost their mandate to govern, not least because of their failure to protect Singapore against the Japanese. Significantly, the anti-colonialism of the day, especially of Chinese-educated Chinese in Singapore, fed over-whelmingly on an abiding bitterness that was engendered by the flagrant discrimination the British continued to practise to their detriment. The Chinese resented the alleged and real threats to and attacks on Chinese iden-tity and the dearth of funding made available to Chinese institutions, especially because Malay and English-language institutions received substantial financial support. Indeed, Chinese-educated Chinese encoun-tered a three-fold deprivation, concerning citizenship, political rights and jobs. For instance, the Chinese-educated could not practise law or medicine or qualify for a white-collar position in the colonial bureaucracy. Anti-colonialism, as a response to violations of claims to identity and justice, not surprisingly found expression, *inter alia*, in the invocation of Chinese culture. In the late 1940s and early 1950s, however, following Mao Zedong's victory in China's civil war, the defence of Chinese culture became increas-ingly linked to the advocacy of Chinese communism. Young Chinese living in Singapore faced with the prospect of military service while remaining relegated to what was perceived as second-class-citizen status, sought to kindle Mao's revolution in Singapore. As Dennis Bloodworth stresses, '[t]he young Chinese would stake everything on winning recognition, for without it they had no future' (Bloodworth 1986: 61).

What Wang (1962/1992: 208) termed the English-educated elite of 'Malaysian' intellectuals was not attracted to the theme of Chinese culture and chauvinism, but nevertheless soon sought to exploit politically the frus-tration and outrage vented by the Chinese-educated in the direction of the colonial power. A key role fell to Lee Kuan Yew, who established connections with various unions to build mass support for a political party, the People's Action Party (PAP), registered in 1954. He succeeded not least because the Communist Party of Malaya was interested in supporting a political party that might serve as a Trojan Horse in the party's attempt at wresting power from the colonial regime.

The PAP vowed to remove the 'arbitrary powers' conferred on the colonial government by the Emergency Regulations. Meanwhile, its moderate camp hoped that British colonialists would not surrender Singapore to the leftists within the PAP, but to them. At the same time, both factions within the PAP and Singapore's wider political opposition sought to expose and exploit the depravity of the colonial administration, to diminish the latter's public repute and to promote the line of independence for Malaya and Singapore. Initially, both PAP moderates and leftist members (such as Chin Siong or Samad Ismail) supported the goal of a merger, if for different reasons. Lee Kuan Yew correctly believed that the United Kingdom would be reluctant to lose control over internal security and its military bases, at a time well before the withdrawal from east of Suez. In his view, this would help avoid a potentially revolutionary situation in Singapore that the radical faction could exploit. Ultimately the English-educated elite won the struggle for political influence and paved the way for Singapore's merger with Malaya. This was made possible by a political crackdown on leftist elements by the then Chief Minister Lim Yew Hock, the ingenious tactics adopted by the moderates and a series of errors of judgement by the radicals.

Dutch East Indies/Indonesia

The rise of Indonesian anti-colonialism and nationalism developed in response to fundamental changes in the basic structure of Javanese socio-economic organisation that had accompanied Dutch rule (McCloud 1986: 130–3). These changes were considered unjust by large segments of the indigenous population. Against the background of disappointed expectations of large sections of the peasantry, growing strains first surfaced in relations between peasant masses and members of the Javanese aristocracy (*priyayi*), many of whom had been co-opted by the Dutch colonial power.[16] In addition, economic and social discontent surfaced among the Indonesian middle class as the monopoly practices of foreigners and Chinese penetration of traditional domains of indigenous manufacture deprived them of economic influence and income. Educated middle-class aspirants were forced to seek personal fulfilment outside traditional fields of work. However, the remaining status-conferring jobs were effectively limited to positions in the Dutch colonial administration. And as was the situation in Malaya, access to salaried officialdom in the colonial bureaucracy was restricted, especially because of the Dutch language proficiency requirement. Until 1928 apparently only 279 Indonesians had entered Dutch-language schools (Legge 1972: 27). However, even those with Western training struggled for recognition because 'the large majority of Western-educated Indonesians were either given posts which they felt to be inferior to their educational training or were unable to get governmental or any other employment where their training was utilized' (McTurnan Kahin 1970: 49). Middle-class discontent led directly to the founding of the famous Sarekat Dagang Islam (Islamic Trading Society).

Popular outrage did not merely arise over discrimination in relation to employment opportunities. Indeed, the nationalist struggle gathered further momentum in reaction to various other forms of social and ethnic discrimination, often accentuated by a blatant attitude of superiority held by the Dutch, irrespective of the fact that they often had an inferior educational background. For example, the judicial administration and penal legislation allowed for the 'preventive detention' of Indonesians but not Europeans. Most Dutch and Eurasians were exempted from paying tuition, whereas Indonesians were not (McTurnan Kahin 1970: 52–5). Unsurprisingly, therefore, more and more Indonesians believed that personal ambition could be fulfilled only after the colonial order was overturned and that this would necessitate the invocation of Enlightenment claims against its European advocates. One of Indonesia's pre-eminent nationalists was of course Sukarno, leader of Indonesia's nationalist movement since 1926.

As Legge argued, 'Sukarno['s sense] … of insult and humiliation was deeply felt, and the determination to assert his own pride and to recover self-respect for himself and his people became the driving force of his actions' (Legge 1972: 34). In practice, this meant that in spite of Sukarno's familiarity with Jeffersonian democracy, Kant, Rousseau, Hegel and Marx, he did not first and foremost conceptualise freedom in terms of individual liberty but of national emancipation (Legge 1972: 53). The nationalist endeavour was intimately tied to a moral discourse about the reorganisation of the economy and politics of the Dutch East Indies. For tactical purposes, he also pointed to the supposedly shared nationalist foundation of religion (Islam) and communism, arguing for their mutual reconcilability. As an aside, we may note that the moral fibre of Sukarno's rhetoric did strike a chord with many 'ordinary' Indonesians because of his many allusions to the Javanese traditional worldview, particularly his references to the *ratu adil*, the Just Ruler in Javanese mythology (Legge 1972: 5–7).[17] Sukarno also developed the concept and ideology of 'Marhaenism'. This concept represented an attempt to define an ideology of Indonesian socialism with reference to indigenous agrarian experience. Marhaenism was essentially the ideology promoting the interests of the little man, of 'the destitute people of Indonesia' (Leifer 1996a: 168–9). Invoking such terms in his political struggle, Sukarno addressed and exploited politically not so much the cultural or ideological substance as the moral grammar of struggle. Sukarno's constant juggling of religion, communism and nationalism would not be without political consequence for the development of Indonesian domestic politics, however.

In the meantime, Sukarno had also sought to invoke a moral grammar in the conduct of Indonesia's foreign policy, not least to wrest recognition of Indonesian independence from the Dutch (Leifer 1983: 19–23). Although independence was originally proclaimed on 17 August 1945, the actual transfer of sovereignty occurred only in December 1949, following the nationalist leadership's combined resort to violent struggle (*perjuangan*) and diplomacy (*diplomasi*). In the event, this experience became deeply rooted in Indonesian political identity. Independence was perceived as the reward for the sacrifices made, but also as a belated confirmation of the justness of the nationalist cause.

> Early statements had been to the effect that the world would be obliged to recognize the justice of Indonesia's cause because of its moral strength. In the event, independence was achieved after a bitter and costly struggle in which the critical role of external powers was governed ... by self-interest and not by deference to the ideal of self-determination. This experience strengthened ... an attachment to the concept of an independent foreign policy.
>
> (Leifer 1983: 26)

Philippines: the interplay of moral outrage, economic interests and security

Early Filipino nationalism matured in the socio-economic context of opposition against Spanish friars who controlled access to education, taxation and governed the municipalities. Apart from the issue of being subjected to colonial rule, Filipinos felt that the Spanish treated them as inferior people. As José Rizal, one of the leaders of the Propaganda Movement, argued in an atmosphere influenced by social Darwinism, '[t]hey made the race itself an object of insult. They professed themselves unable to see in it any admirable quality, any human trait' (quoted in Kratoska and Batson 1992: 258).[18] Considerable ill feeling towards the friars was further accentuated by moral outrage over the ways in which the former had attained their dominant position. According to George Taylor 'Filipinos felt that the friars had come by their land holdings through fraud and deceit' (G. Taylor 1964: 45).

It was the *ilustrados*, the enlightened, who demanded the recognition of the Philippines as a province of Spain with representation in the *Cortes* (Spanish parliament), as well as racial equality, political rights comparable to those in Spain, equality before the law, and professional advancement. However, the grievances experienced also led to the rise of a secret revolutionary society, the Katipunan, led first by Andres Bonifacio, and subsequently by Emilio Aguinaldo, the country's first President. In the event, although the Katipunan received initial support from the United States in the latter's conflict with Spain, Aguinaldo depended on *ilustrado* backing, which whittled away the more the gulf between the two socially diverse elites opened up. Interestingly, the two discourses that underpinned these two movements – the elitist discourse of legal autonomy and the religious-moral discourse of *kalayaan*, both of which can be captured analytically as a struggle for freedom and recognition – were soon merged by the *ilustrados*. This convergence was sought for strategic reasons, given the sustained moral appeal of the normative claims contained in the discourse of *kalayaan* and the violence and political demands that, for a long time, it continued to generate on the basis of references to national rebirth and redemption. It was necessary for the educated nationalist elite to co-opt this discourse because the concept of *kalayaan*, drawn from the Sacred Passion of the Lord Jesus Christ, stood for a condition of brotherhood, equality, contentment and material abundance, which called into question the traditional Philippine understanding of the patron–client relationship.[19] This also appeared to have implications for the question of land tenure. In the event, however, both the *ilustrados* and the *cacique* class (the powerful land-owning bosses) emasculated this form of politics from below.

Significantly, however, US appreciation of the remaining moral texture of the nationalist agenda led to the preparedness to allow Filipinos to assume various positions of some authority at local and regional levels. This led to what R.S. Milne (1963: 87) termed a 'reconciliation of nationalism and colonialism'. Subsequent promises of independence helped Washington to further outflank respective demands for a long time so that, effectively, the Philippine nationalist experience became one of constitutional nationalism. Notably, it was the landed aristocracy that benefited from this turn of events as delayed independence implied the safeguarding of its interests.

Following the end of Japanese occupation of the Philippines, members of the ruling elite were again acting in the context of grievances that arose in Manila's relations with Washington. In part this happened because General MacArthur imprisoned some of those accused of collaboration with the intermittent Japanese puppet regime in somewhat arbitrary fashion, and in circumstances that amounted to a loss of their dignity (Aguinaldo 1957: 231–3). Notably, many of those concerned later regained positions within the post-war administrations. Other aspects concerned perceived US interference in financial and budgetary supervision of the process of independence, the question of war reparations and various symbols of colonialism. The Philippine Trade Act ('Bell Act') of 30 April 1946 evoked particular resentment because, among other things, it appeared to be designed to prevent the creation of indigenous (national) industries and because it required the Philippines to amend its Constitution to allow for the exploitation of natural resources by foreigners. Indeed, the 'parity clause' granted the same rights to Americans as Filipinos in developing the Philippines' national resources and public utilities. Philippine grievances were later addressed in the 1954

Laurel–Langley agreement (Fifield 1968: 63–7; Hall 1981: 900–1). In spite of the rhetoric, however, the Philippine experience of nationalism was not underpinned by a struggle for recognition as intense as that felt in Indonesia. The rhetoric of 'Filipino First' was simply meant to obscure the fact that some within the broader elite were pursuing particularistic interests, such as sugar interests, or that financial rehabilitation was to serve the purpose of pork-barrel politics. At the same time, the end of the Pacific War saw increasing attention focus on internal security, particularly with regard to the perceived political objectives of the National Peasants' Union, the repression of which resulted in rebellion (Kerkvliet 1977: ch. 4; Lachica 1971). At independence, the Philippines' identity in foreign affairs was decisively shaped by the ruling class in a direction that remained pro-American, favouring domestic constitutional arrangements similar to those in the United States, and a strong US commitment to the defence of the Philippines.

Conclusion

This chapter has argued that the early origins of ASEAN's diplomatic and security culture are located in the drawn-out struggle for independent statehood and sovereign equality in international society. More particularly, it has demonstrated how a strong commitment to the norms of sovereignty and independence developed out of a moral struggle against the denial of rights, discrimination and perceived disrespect. It found that much of the moral outrage feeding the nationalist discourse and political struggle arose from poor prospects for upward mobility of the social and intellectual elite. Ultimately, this struggle for recognition led to the displacement of colonial regimes and entry into the society of states. The onset of the Pacific War, and in particular Southeast Asia's incorporation into the Greater East Asia Co-Prosperity Sphere, reinforced this dynamic. As Peter Lyon (1969: 21) argues, 'World War II was the forcing-house rather than the seed-bed of modern South-east Asian nationalism' (Lyon 1969: 21). The subsequent return of colonial regimes in the immediate post-war years to Indonesia and the Philippines ultimately proved irreconcilable, albeit in different degrees, with the by then well-advanced struggle for national freedom and respect. This struggle was paralleled by a search for security by elites in their stratified societies, which in turn was expressed in the containment of others' struggle for recognition. Certainly at this stage, therefore, Southeast Asian elites accorded greater significance to the integration of their countries into the society of states than to initiating major domestic political changes that might have enhanced political liberties. Of the nationalist leaders from the founding ASEAN states, Indonesia's Sukarno arguably proved the most charismatic. Notably, his intensely felt sense of injustice not only found expression in Jakarta's struggle against the Dutch, but was also to play a crucial part in the post-war origins of ASEAN's diplomatic and security culture.

2 Post-war origins of the 'ASEAN way'

From estrangement and conflict to regional reconciliation and accommodation

As one would expect, the attainment of sovereign statehood by Southeast Asian countries gave rise to new claims for recognition by its political leaders in relation to themselves as persons and to the countries they had had the privilege of taking into international society.[1] This applied, in particular, to the case of Indonesia. Jakarta insisted on sovereign equality and far greater regional autonomy than the United States, as the region's hegemonic power, or other major powers were prepared to concede. Indonesia's leadership objected intensely to perceived attempts to undercut what Sukarno, in particular, regarded to be the Republic's entitlement, not least in the wake of its bloody independence struggle. At the same time, Indonesia worried deeply about its vulnerabilities, which were the product of its distended geographical character and its lack of development. Similarly to Indonesia, other countries which would be future members of the Association found that the post-war context was not one of their own choosing. However, in contrast to Jakarta, leaderships in Bangkok, Kuala Lumpur and Manila, all of whom harboured significant fears about subversion from within, aligned their political fortunes with the United States as the region's hegemonic power or maintained defence relationships with the former colonial power. Noting briefly some aspects concerning the construction of national identities in Thailand, the Philipppines and Indonesia in the immediate post-war period, this chapter goes on to explore how intra-regional conflict over identity and territorial claims not only wrecked prospects for early interstate co-operation, but also engendered significant estrangement and insecurity. The chapter then analyses the steps and building blocks that, over time, provided for mutual reconciliation or at least accommodation among ASEAN states.

The pursuit of security and recognition

After independence the social and political elite in the Philippines fostered an ever more staunch anti-communist identity owing to its perceived vulner-abilities and security concerns. In March 1947 the Philippine government concluded a Military Bases Agreement that accorded the United States the right to retain the use of more than ten facilities. A mutual defence pact was subsequently signed with the United States in 1951. Grievances continued to influence Philippine–US relations (such as the issue of full jurisdiction over American and Filipinos on US bases), but these did not threaten the basic texture of the bilateral relationship. To the extent that Beijing appeared intent on subjugating Taiwan, strategic concerns further multiplied in Manila. With the assumption of the presidency by Ramon Magsaysay, the Philippines consequently sought explicit assurances for its independence and security from Washington and ultimately joined the Southeast Asia Collective Defence Treaty (Manila Pact) in September 1954.

To secure its position in the Western camp, Thailand had pragmatically ceded those territories to Britain and France that it had acquired during the war. Bangkok also paid compensation for damages to these states, with the consequence that France became the first country to recognise the administration of Prime Mininster Phibul Songkram. Thai security concerns multiplied with the increasing strength of the Viet Minh, the Communist led nationalist movement that sought the end of French colonial rule. Thai trepidation was reinforced by the occupation of Laos by the Viet Minh in 1953. This made the regime fearful that the Pan-Lao movement might extend their struggle into Thailand's Northeast. These fears were accentuated by further Viet Minh incursions into Laos and Cambodia in 1953 and early 1954. Phibul genuinely believed that communism posed a threat to Thai national identity and sovereignty as well as Buddhism, which the Field Marshal was interested in promoting as a source of political legitimacy to strengthen his domestic political position and his personal stature as a meritorious leader. In the face of the communist struggle, Phibul remained concerned about Chinese economic influence, and dissatisfied with the latter's incomplete assimilation. However, the 1954 Thai proposal for a Buddhist anti-communist bloc failed because France regarded the plan as a threat to the French Union. Thailand thus welcomed instead the inclusion of Laos, Cambodia and territories under the 'free Vietnamese Government' in the treaty area of the Manila Pact (Fifield 1968: 253). Bangkok volunteered to become the seat of the Southeast Asia Treaty Organisation (SEATO), established in February 1955, notwithstanding or rather because of the widespread belief that the US was taking Thailand for granted. When Thailand felt SEATO reacted insufficiently decisively to events in Laos, its frustration culminated in the Joint Statement by Foreign Minister Thanat Khoman and Secretary of State Dean Rusk of 6 March 1962, whereby the US guaranteed the security of Thailand independently of its obligations under the Manila Pact.

Unlike Thailand and the Philippines, Indonesia came to reject partisanship in the ideological and military confrontation building up in Southeast Asia before and after Dien Bien Phu. Jakarta denounced the Manila Pact that created SEATO as an uncalled-for intrusion of the Cold War into Southeast Asia. Indeed, the thought of becoming a pawn in the power game of the superpowers met with abhorrence in Jakarta, not least for fear of endangering the integrity of its recently secured territorial space and of inviting outside intervention into a country beset by problems of economic adversity and public order. The inter-systemic conflict, i.e. the existence of two competing ideologies, was not a problem *per se* from Jakarta's perspective. To Indonesia's leaders the chief problem of world peace appeared instead to be the mutual non-recognition of the legitimacy and identity of ideological foes. Denouncing the reciprocal disqualification of each other by the capitalist democracies and socialist states as an immoral confrontation, Jakarta argued the need for an ideological synthesis. In response, Indonesia aimed in practice for a foreign policy that would be both independent and active, or *bebas-aktif* (Weinstein 1976: ch. 5). According to Dewi Fortuna Anwar, this foreign policy doctrine was 'designed to keep Indonesia's independence to the maximum, by allowing the country to pursue whatever course it deemed best to serve its national priorities, without being tied up to external commitments it could not control' (Anwar 1994: 18). Equally, Jakarta articulated its claim to meaningful participation, respect and more weight in regional international politics, in line with its sense of entitlement, which built on its own revolutionary achievement. In the view of Michael Leifer (1983: 59),

> [T]he revisionist view of the international system articulated by Sukarno had a direct relationship to the prosecution of Indonesia's foreign policy goals. His theory of international relations constituted a moral claim expressed in terms of distributive justice, which had been denied to the Republic.
>
> (Leifer 1983: 59)

Jakarta consequently refused to join pro-Western and anti-communist organisations like SEATO and instead convened the Bandung Conference in April 1955, which was attended by twenty-nine African and Asian countries.[2]

Bandung served three main purposes. First, it articulated pent-up dissatisfaction with the inadequate consultations by the major powers regarding their involvement in Asian affairs in the context of US–PRC antagonism. According to a pro-Western delegate, Indonesia and other Asian countries had made an 'effort ... to regain their personality and international dignity and [it] was an assertion of their personality vis-à-vis the West' (cited in McTurnan Kahin 1956: 38). Second, it laid the foundations for peaceful and friendly relations with the PRC, which appeared to many to be a dissatisfied power, given its support for the Viet Minh and for the subversion of Southeast Asian countries by local communist parties. And, third, it created an environment in which it would be more difficult, or at least embarrassing, for China to abandon its pledges to conform to the principles and norms of international society, i.e. to create a moral constraint against direct or indirect interference and aggression. It was apparently believed that the more frequent China's pledge to observe the basic principles of international society, and the wider the audience, the clearer would be the moral interdiction to violate the principles at stake (McTurnan Kahin 1956: 8).

In the event, Indonesia's objectives were partially realised and partially frustrated. What is important for our purposes is that, in both content and language, the Ten Principles of the Bandung Declaration reflected, as might be expected, not Indonesia's vision of regional order, but a compromise that accommodated the very favourable stance by Manila and Bangkok towards the idea of collective self-defence. Moreover, commitments to basic principles of international society notwithstanding, the Declaration also failed to hide the reluctance by participant countries to recognise unequivocally the regimes of those espousing a different political ideology and socio-economic forms of organisation than their own. Bandung thus failed to bridge the divide between the divergent identities that had been growing across Southeast Asia. The clash of claims to identity became even more serious after Malaya gained independence in 1957. Notably, this clash of claims to identity is at the heart of the failure of early designs of regional co-operation and increasing alienation between regional leaders.

Frustrated regionalism

The strong anti-communist orientation in Kuala Lumpur and Manila undermined an early initiative for regional organisation in the form of the Southeast Asian Friendship and Economic Treaty (SEAFET), proposed by Malaya's prime minister, Tunku Abdul Rahman, in January 1959. Bangkok was generally supportive of the attempt to safeguard national security by promoting intra-regional trade and prosperity. And so were the Philippines.

Although the Tunku was at pains to dissociate his proposal for regional economic co-operation from notions about the formation of a defence or collective security pact outside SEATO, the proposal was met with suspicion in some other regional capitals. While this suspicion was fuelled in part by the anti-communist rhetoric coming out of Manila, the Tunku himself also bore responsibility for this. As Jorgensen-Dahl put it, '[the Tunku] displayed an unfortunate tendency to mention regional economic and cultural cooperation in the same breath as he lamented the evils of communism and encouraged an ever-vigilant opposition to it' (Jorgensen-Dahl 1982: 15). It was this penchant for public espousal of fervent anti-communism that led the Indonesian president, Sukarno, to suggest that an inherently unwelcome regional bloc had been in the making. While the Tunku soon came to realise that anti-communism would have to be de-emphasised if the proposal was to gain wider regional acceptance, Filipino leaders, in view of events in Laos around this time, continued to stress precisely their anti-communist credentials.

In the event, Indonesia never joined what became the Association of Southeast Asia (ASA), founded on 31 July 1961, as its perceived association with anti-communism could not be remedied. Nor could the unattractiveness of the corporate identity be overcome by the general endorsement given to Thanat Khoman's advocacy that its form of co-operation should be informal and the degree of institutionalisation minimal so as to accentuate the importance attributed to members' sovereignty. Bangkok's proposal had stood in contrast to the treaty form and the creation of an elaborate organisational structure for the European Community, emulation of which had initially been mooted in Kuala Lumpur and Manila (Jorgensen-Dahl 1982: 20–2). By 1963, however, ASA had ground to a halt, and this form of regionalism could not be revived, let alone broadened, before 1966. At issue was the serious regional instability that arose from the downturn of three dyadic relationships.

The Philippines–Malaysia

The suspension of regional co-operation in the framework of ASA resulted from the dispute over Sabah between Manila and Kuala Lumpur (Leifer 1968). The Philippines' claim to Sabah originated against the background of attempts by the administration of the then president, Diasdado Macapagal, to rid the country of its stigma as the 'little brown brother' who was not 'in the mainstream of Asian nationalism' (Leifer 1972: 127). This struggle for recognition had been activated when, after having previously felt a sense of superiority over its neighbours, the Filippino elite, as a result of its staunch anti-communism and bilateral defence pact with the US, saw its country branded a US 'puppet'.[3] Carlos Rómulo, then ambassador to the United Nations (UN), expressed well the moral dynamic underpinning Philippine nationalism when he said that '[w]e do not want to be a pariah in Asia and no self-respecting nation wants a pariah for an ally' (quoted in G. Taylor 1964: 255). From the perspective of Malaya's leaders, however, the Philippines unrealistically and naively believed it possible to make a claim to Sabah while promoting ASA and maintaining normal relations with the new state of Malaysia, which was to encompass Malaya, Singapore and the northern Borneo territories of Sabah and Sarawak (Abdullah Ahmad 1985: 68). In addition to claiming Sabah, and thus questioning the territorial configuration of Malaysia, Manila also provided moral support for the challenge to Malaysia's legitimacy put forward by Indonesia. When the Philippines withheld diplomatic recognition of the Federation of Malaysia official ties between Manila and Kuala Lumpur were severed on 17 September 1963, and they were not restored until 3 June 1966.

Konfrontasi: *Malaysia–Indonesia*

When Malaya became independent in 1957 Indonesia immediately recognised the new Malay state and, represented by Prime Minister Juanda,

capital of Malaysia

even concluded a treaty of friendship with Kuala Lumpur in 1959. Five years on, however, Indonesia had embarked on a course of confrontation against Kuala Lumpur, including hostile acts such as infringements of Malaysia's territorial integrity by way of armed incursion by Indonesian 'volunteers', and diplomatic vilification. Many reasons have been identified for the onset of *konfrontasi* (Mackie 1974; Gordon 1966; Poulgrain 1998), and they need not be extensively reproduced here.[4] For our purposes it suffices to note that *konfrontasi* was a particular expression of a struggle for recognition and security underlying Indonesian–Malaysian foreign-policy interaction. As regards the struggle for recognition, it cannot be divorced from the broader historical context at the time, and in particular Sukarno's attempt to overcome the last vestiges of colonialism. As regards the struggle for security, Sukarno insisted on the termination of leases on military bases in the region. This demand must be appreciated against the backdrop of Indonesian leaders' experience of foreign intervention and a sense of vulnerability that stemmed from the distended nature of the archipelago, which had already prompted Jakarta to issue its Archipelago Declaration of 13 December 1957.

president of Indonesia *(th)* *PM of Malaysia*

Whereas Sukarno sought to expunge all vestiges of colonialism from Southeast Asia, the Tunku harboured no such intentions because of his perceptions of threats. Sukarno had sought to synthesise diverse trains of religious and political thought (Islam, Marxism and nationalism) in opposition to colonialism and to balance the attendant domestic political forces. By contrast, the Tunku was convinced that communists and true Malays could never co-exist (Gullick 1967: 38). This was a conviction based on his meeting the leader of the Malayan Communist Party (MCP), Chin Peng, in Baling in December 1955. Beyond differences between Indonesia and Malaysia over how communism and colonialism, respectively, affected the security and identities of countries in Southeast Asia, other identity-based perceptions also engendered mutual alienation. For instance, priding itself in having gone through an identity-defining revolutionary and bloody struggle to attain independence, Indonesia's leadership was less than impressed with the way in which Malaya's 'feudal-aristocratic elite' achieved its release into the world of sovereign states.

Nevertheless, it would appear that Sukarno was willing to give sovereign Malaya a chance to 'prove' itself. Thus, within a week of joining international society Kuala Lumpur was expected to give full support to Indonesia's attempts to integrate West Irian into Indonesia. In Sukarno's opinion, resolving this issue in his favour was 'a question of colonialism or independence' (quoted in Leifer 1983: 52). Significantly, the Tunku failed to reciprocate as desired. This irked Sukarno. To ideological incompatibility thus was added rivalry and personal alienation. From the perspective of the Tunku, however,

[Sukarno] was afraid that a strong and economically flourishing Malaysia could be a threat to Indonesia's claim to primacy in the Malay World and Sukarno was particularly afraid that Sumatra might want to join Malaysia. Sukarno also had never liked me; he did not like anyone, a Malay in particular, who was better than him.

(quoted in Abdullah Ahmad 1985: 39)

Indonesia's dual struggle for security and recognition became more acute after the Tunku tabled a proposal for the merger of Malaya with Singapore, Sabah and Sarawak (both of which border Indonesia directly) in a federal 'Malaysia' in May 1961. Brunei was originally included in the merger proposal but opted out (D. Singh 1984: 138–48). Malaysia's proposed conception as a federal state activated bitter memories for Indonesians, who tended to perceive the former as a colonial ploy. The reason for this was that Malaysia would maintain, if not expand, defence links with its colonial mentor, the United Kingdom, as outlined in the London Agreement of 9 July 1963. As Mackie argued, '[o]ne reason for Indonesia's eleventh-hour opposition to the British presence in 1963 was the realization that extension of the 1957 agreement to cover Malaysia might entail an indefinite prolongation of the British military arrangements there' (Mackie 1974: 33). The assumption by the British of 'responsibility' for other areas beyond those of Malaysia also registered Jakarta's disapproval.[5] Sukarno was further incensed at another clause of the London Agreement which stipulated that Malaysia would definitely be founded on 31 August 1963. In his view, this would make a mockery of the ascertainment of opinion on merger in the Borneo territories, agreed in Manila in July 1963, because its outcome would only be known in September, after the proposed formation of Malaysia. In the event, Jakarta also withheld diplomatic recognition as Malaysia was born, so that official relations were severed.

Whereas to Sukarno the subsequent pursuit of *konfrontasi* provided a sense of purpose and national dignity, it was an affront and a serious security challenge to the Tunku. And the Tunku was not prepared to yield to Sukarno. As he later explained:

We had to fight him [Sukarno], though reluctantly, to uphold our honour and sovereignty. We are Malays like him who value honor. 'Biar putih tulang asal jangan putih mata': a Malay saying if rendered in English means something like this – we would rather perish than have our honour trampled upon.

(Quoted in Abdullah Ahmad 1985: 45)

Malaysia–Singapore

It was the fear of the consequences of an independent Singapore embracing communism, from the Tunku's perspective, and Lee Kuan Yew's need to attract new industries to avert mass unemployment and political instability which, in 1961, had finally convinced the two leaderships to merge. However, the continued significance of these interests soon paled against the intensity of the antagonisms that developed thereafter. Singapore's hopes for a functioning common market proved futile. With *konfrontasi* to deal with, the Tunku took offence at the apparent unwillingness of Singapore to spend more on Malaysia's defence if this did not simultaneously imply improving the defence of Singapore. In the event, the question of Singapore's financial contribution to central Malaysian coffers was secured only at the expense of 'wounds inflicted on the relationship [that] failed to heal' (Turnbull 1977: 287). Matters were not helped when UMNO was comprehensively defeated, some might say routed, in the 1963 general election in Singapore even in what were Malay-majority constituencies. However, two other developments brought the tension to a head: first, the PAP's goal of a 'Malaysian Malaysia', which implied a multi-racial Malaysia in which all ethnic communities would enjoy equal privileges; second, a string of violations of what the Tunku considered to be respectful behaviour.

As regards the first of these points, the PAP decided to contest a number of peninsular constituencies in the 1964 elections in order to present itself as an alternative to the Malaysian Chinese Association (MCA), the Chinese junior partner of UMNO in the Alliance. The approach adopted involved lodging verbal attacks directed at the Malaysian Chinese Association and its president Tan Siew Sin, who was accused of being the 'eunuch' of UMNO. The Tunku regarded the PAP's assault on the MCA as an attack on UMNO and consequently on Malay political supremacy. If the objective of the PAP was to enter into some sort of working partnership with the Tunku, or even to enter the cabinet in Malaysia, its strategy backfired. The assertiveness of the PAP, which also labelled the Malay dignitaries 'feudalistic' or 'naive' angered so-called Malay 'ultras' and led them in turn to denigrate the PAP government in Singapore. The Singapore race riots of 1964 developed in this context, raising the spectre of widespread communal violence across the Peninsula. The following year, in 1965, the Malaysia Solidarity Convention was formed, which sought to unite opposition parties against Malay supremacy under the slogan of a 'Malaysian Malaysia', thus accentuating the threat to the survival of the regime in Kuala Lumpur.

As regards the second antagonism, the Tunku found Lee Kuan Yew's personal combative style in advocating a non-communal and meritocratic Malaysia to be not only abrasive, undignified and disloyal, but also in violation of the norm of a public search for compromise, conciliation and consensus. Alienated by the 'verbal overkill' from Singapore, he argued, moreover, that the notion of 'Malaysian Malaysia' meant (that) what the Malays had the Chinese wanted a share of but what the Chinese had they wanted to keep to themselves' (quoted in Abdullah Ahmad 1985: 94). Significantly, he was also quite annoyed by what he perceived to be the unfair or incorrect representation of Malaysia (and himself) by the foreign media. As the Tunku put it, the foreign press 'are trying to build up the image of Lee Kuan Yew [while] they at the same time are belittling us' (quoted in Boyce 1968: 28). In particular, the Tunku found objectionable foreign governments' inclination to treat Lee Kuan Yew, who to him was just the leader of the biggest opposition party, 'as an equal partner in the Government of Malaysia', contrary to the idea that '[i]n a nation there can only be one national executive head' (quoted in Boyce 1968: 29).

In the end, the Tunku gave unambiguous expression to the moral grammar informing his stance on Singapore, showing Lee Kuan Yew the door out of the Federation.[6] Its break-up in August 1965 left Singapore's leaders in a state of shock, mistrust and, above all, with a feeling of innate vulnerability. Henceforth, Singapore would refer to itself as a 'poisoned shrimp' or as 'Israel in a Malay–Muslim sea', terms that strengthened its neighbours' distrust and which they considered characteristic of Singapore's arrogance.

Having outlined how a struggle for security and recognition generated considerable alienation among various regional leaders, the final part of this chapter seeks to reconstruct the main contours of the final phase of the dialectical process following of estrangement that is the genesis of the 'ASEAN way': mutual recognition and reconciliation.

Reconciliation as a foundation for ASEAN political and security co-operation

The process of mutual recognition and reconciliation manifested itself in two interrelated developments: the end of *konfrontasi* and the founding of ASEAN. It built on the emergence of the political will to deal with the negative fallout of the intra-regional disputes and personal antagonisms among regional leaders. This relied in part on the willingness and success of third-party mediators. Thailand, in particular, was to advance as the main theatre for reconciliation. However, reconciliation – or at least accommodation – also required the emergence of new leaderships. President Sukarno lacked the political will to seek reconciliation, and arguably so did the Tunku as long as Sukarno was in power. Similarly obdurate during his term in office was Philippine President Macapagal. With the rise in Indonesia of Lieutenant-General Suharto, to whom executive powers were transferred from Sukarno on 11 March 1966, the influence of a new group of emerging leaders in Malaysia and President Ferdinand Marcos in Manila, the process of reconciliation was facilitated.

Ending konfrontasi

By 1964 the limits of Sukarno's 'exercise in political pyrotechnics', as Michael Leifer (1983: 99) once referred to *konfrontasi*, were starkly obvious.

Not only had this policy not succeeded in undermining the legitimacy of Malaysia in international society, but, as an exponent of the New Emerging Forces that was fighting against the Old Established Forces, Indonesia had also alienated several Western governments in the process of implementing confrontation. Equally, Jakarta had undermined its position as a founding member of the Nonaligned Movement, not least because Indonesia's hostility towards Malaysia increasingly stood in startling contrast to its position, so clearly formulated at Bandung, on the non-use of force in international relations. In effect, the policy of *konfrontasi* prevented Indonesia from winning recognition as a regional leader in Southeast Asia and beyond in the non-aligned movement. Later, President Suharto would argue that Sukarno's *konfrontasi* had also violated Indonesia's *bebas-aktif* principle in foreign affairs, whereby Jakarta was to pursue an independent and active foreign policy, which implied avoiding an alignment with any one bloc.

Equally significant for a reassessment of *konfrontasi* were Indonesia's economic demise and the neglect of development, which had been one of the key immediate post-independence goals. When Sukarno privileged relations with communist regimes over those with Western donors in the wake of Indonesia's struggle against the exponents of the 'established order', he had effectively jeopardised any real prospects for an economic upswing. The severity of the country's economic decline led Franklin Weinstein to observe that 'domestic imperatives which had become the focus of political rhetoric were undermining the legitimacy of confrontation itself' (Weinstein 1969: 70). In addition, Indonesia's armed forces were apprehensive of a shift in the domestic balance of power in favour of the Indonesian Communist Party (PKI). Significantly,

> the doubts [expressed by the army over the Crush Malaysia campaign, which was formed by Sukarno as late as February 1966] did not signify any questioning of Sukarno's analysis of the unjust manner in which Malaysia was formed; rather, they were indicative of apprehension about the viability of confrontation as a means of advancing Indonesia's foreign policy goals and, most important, about the impact of confrontation on the development of the political situation in Djakarta.
>
> (Weinstein 1969: 9)

Nevertheless, given that *konfrontasi* had become such an important element in defining Indonesia's identity, the process of abandoning it was considered less than easy, especially as the possible domestic consequences were not immediately obvious. Sukarno himself vigorously denied rumours of the abandonment of *konfrontasi* (Anwar 1994: 40–1).

Two questions in particular still needed to be addressed for Indonesia to step away from confrontation. First, how could President Sukarno's original protestations in relation to the inclusion of Sabah and Sarawak in the Malaysian Federation be accommodated? This was, in essence, an issue of how to allow Indonesia to save face in view of Sukarno's demand at the time that an expression of popular will in North Borneo acceptable to Jakarta precede the formal act of recognition. The second question focused on how to reintegrate Jakarta into the mainstream of Southeast Asian international politics.

As regards the first point, Malaysia and Indonesia signed the so-called Bangkok Accord, which gave way to an 'improved version', the Jakarta Agreement, signed by Tun Razak and Indonesia's foreign minister, Adam Malik. It was this agreement that finally ended confrontation, on 16 August 1966. The Bangkok Accord still committed Indonesia to recognise Malaysia diplomatically without the precondition of a prior poll in Sabah and Sarawak. This was rejected by Jakarta because Sukarno, who had been elected president for life, was at the time still perceived to enjoy a measure of domestic political support from Islamists, the Nationalist Party of Indonesia and parts of the armed forces.

Seeking to avoid a settlement that might be interpreted as an embarrassing capitulation by Indonesia and a public humiliation for Sukarno, the New Order regime continued to work for a compromise agreement. Ultimately, it was agreed that Malaysian–Indonesian relations would be normalised, but no exchange of Ambassadors (diplomatic representation) was to occur until after an ascertainment of the public will in the Borneo territories.[7] In the end, elections in April 1967 sanctioned the status quo. On this basis, full diplomatic relations were restored on 31 August 1967, three weeks after the founding of ASEAN.

A manifest symbol of Jakarta's reconciliation with its neighbours was the founding of ASEAN. As Dewi Fortuna Anwar noted, 'the urgency for Indonesia to co-found ASEAN was primarily to restore the country's regional and international standing' (Anwar 1994: 4). And, as she further put it, the point was also to 'exorcize the ghost of confrontation' (Anwar 1994: 45). In the event, Indonesia's participation in this regional association proved to be neither easy nor quick, reflecting deep-seated suspicions of its neighbours. In late 1965 the Philippines, with an eye to extending its membership to Jakarta, advocated a revival of ASA, whose activities had ceased in 1963. The other members, Malaysia and Thailand, concurred, so that the Association was officially active again by March 1966. However, when Thanat Khoman sought to issue an invitation to Jakarta to join ASA in 1966 Malaysia opposed this. When Kuala Lumpur itself extended such an invitation to Jakarta only in February 1967, the latter, while agreeing that institutionalised co-operative relations would be congenial to advancing its domestic and foreign policy agenda, failed to endorse ASA. Instead, the New Order regime submitted a counterproposal for a new regional organisation.

This proposal was driven by at least two factors, intimately linked to considerations of identity. First, joining ASA, given its anti-communist but also anti-Indonesian associations, would, from the Indonesian perspective, be tantamount to a loss of face, particularly given that ASA had not escaped Jakarta's scathing criticisms in the past. Suharto would thus only consent to a new regional organisation in which Indonesia would be a founding member of equal status and rights and whose image would be compatible with Indonesia's independent and active foreign policy. Second, proposals within the influential Army Staff and Command College focused on a confederation of Southeast Asian countries that would also include Burma, Laos, Cambodia, and Vietnam as additional members (Anwar 1994: 126–30). Burma and Cambodia had previously both rejected ASA's credentials.

Initially, the Tunku, pointing to Indonesia's track record on multilateralism, failed to be persuaded about Indonesia's motives for rejecting an extended ASA, which, after all, was 'his brainchild first and foremost' (Jorgensen-Dahl 1982: 35). Indeed, he thought a revitalised ASA good enough for Indonesia to join. His fresh suspicions about Indonesia's intentions abated somewhat, however, especially after a meeting with Adam Malik in May 1967. Earlier suspicions had in part been allayed in the course of the visit by a delegation of eight high-ranking Indonesian officers from the Crush Malaysia Command (KOGAM), headed by Brigadier-General Soenarso, to Tunku Abdul Rahman in May 1966.[8] Another reason for insisting on ASA, at a time when the New Order regime had already indicated its disfavour, was a proposal circulated by the Thai Foreign Ministry for the creation of a Southeast Asian Association for Regional Co-operation (SEAARC).

At issue was a passage that assigned to the resident states of Southeast Asia primary responsibility to ensure regional stability and security. It also stated that foreign bases should be temporary, and should not be used to subvert the independence of regional states, just as collective defence arrangements were not to serve the interests of the major powers (reprinted in Jorgensen-Dahl 1982: 36). Thailand's foreign minister, Thanat Khoman, succeeded in convincing the Tunku not to persist in formulating strong reservations about the wording in public, as he feared that this might jeopardise the reconciliation process with Jakarta. Interestingly, he did so by resorting to what would later become an important part of the ASEAN confidence-building program: 'golf diplomacy'. As Boyce put it, the Tunku–Thanat Khoman bond of confidence was 'consolidated from time to time on the golf course' (Boyce 1968: 229).

Underscoring Indonesian tenacity on this point, however, the Indonesian re-draft of what would be the Bangkok Declaration again contained a passage almost identical to that included in the SEAARC proposal and, before that, in the official documents released in Manila in late July 1963.[9] Historical memories entrenched in the public mind about subversive American activities *vis-à-vis* Indonesia that were launched from US bases in the Philippines and about the involvement in internal rebellions of British forces stationed in

Singapore appear to have been of significance in this regard. Not surprisingly, this draft again met with serious reservations, particularly by Manila, which preferred to have no reference to security matters, and Singapore (Chan Heng Chee 1969: 182–4). Manila relied on its defence arrangement with Washington for external security, while Singapore was interested in keeping Western states, particularly the United States, engaged in the region as an insurance against a possible unpalatable local hegemony.

In contrast to previous occasions, however, a mutually acceptable compromise subsequently emerged. The key passage, according to which 'the arrangements of collective defence should not be used to serve the particular interest of any of the big powers', was deleted. In its stead the following was inserted into the preamble of the Bangkok Declaration:[10]

> Affirming that all foreign bases are temporary and remain only with the expressed concurrence of the countries concerned and are not intended to be used directly or indirectly to subvert the national independence and freedom of States in the area or prejudice the orderly processes of their national development.

(ASEAN 1967)

This paragraph implied that Indonesia was prepared to recognise the existing defence links of neighbouring states as integral characteristics of their respective political identities. By implication, Jakarta would no longer challenge the legitimacy of neighbouring countries that relied on external powers for their defence and deterrence. At the same time, other ASEAN members clearly committed themselves not to challenge publicly Jakarta's long-term vision of a more autonomous regional political and security order in Southeast Asia. It was recognised that Jakarta was committed to this vision on the basis of Indonesia's *bebas-aktif* principle, which had been formulated under Sukarno but which was also invoked, albeit in a different form, by the New Order and on which its legitimacy was in part based. In other words, while Suharto shared with his predecessor a sense of regional entitlement, he believed that the recognition of Indonesia as the political core of Southeast Asia should be attained in ways other than by confrontation. The aggressive nature of Indonesian nationalism would thus be superseded by a policy of self-abnegation, with developmental nationalism becoming the key focus of the New Order. In this context, Indonesia's new rulers sounded the call of AMPERA (*Amanat Penderitaan Rakyat*) – the message of the people's suffering. It argued that the provision of the population's basic needs had been disregarded. Suharto also put forward a new security doctrine – *Ketahanan Nasional*, or National Resilience. He defined this as 'the ability of a nation to cope with, endure and survive any kind of challenges or threats she meets in the course of her struggle to achieve her national goals' (quoted in Leifer 1983: 190, fn 3; Also see Anwar 1996). At the personal level, moreover, 'a flamboyant and heroic style of leadership' was exchanged 'for one of quiet dignity' (Leifer 1983: 112). These factors proved essential in achieving reconciliation between Kuala Lumpur and Jakarta but also allowed for overcoming stresses and strains in other bilateral relationships.

As regards Kuala Lumpur and Jakarta, the process of reconciliation was facilitated by ensuing practical security co-operation between the two sides. A joint commission for defence and security had already been established, in August 1966. In March 1967 the two sides concluded a formal 'Security Arrangement', intended to allow for joint counter-insurgency operations along their shared border in Northern Borneo against ethnic Chinese communist forces. This limited but significant form of security co-operation was extended, in revisions to the arrangement in April 1972, to include joint maritime surveillance and naval exercises.

There was also co-operation on questions of maritime jurisdiction (Leifer 1978). In November 1969 Jakarta and Kuala Lumpur exchanged ratification notes of an agreement that delimited the continental shelf between the two countries in the Strait of Malacca and in the South China Sea. The following March, President Suharto paid a state visit to Malaysia, with a view to developments in Indochina. The two sides reaffirmed the basic principles of the UN Charter and the Ten Principles of Bandung. In particular, they vowed to observe the principle of non-interference 'in any way whatsoever, in each other's internal affairs' (Indonesia–Malaysia Joint Communiqué 1970). A bilateral treaty that aimed at delimiting the territorial sea boundary between the two countries in part of the Strait of Malacca was also signed on this occasion. And in November 1971 the two states issued a joint statement whereby the legal status of the Straits of Malacca and Singapore as international straits was declared moribund, provoking protests from maritime powers interested in the unhindered passage of their commercial and military vessels. Although environmental concerns guided this co-operation too, the wider significance of the issue of maritime jurisdiction was a function of Indonesian leaders' sense of vulnerability, which derived from the country's geographical fragmentation, and which, as we have seen, had already prompted Indonesia to declare the archipelago principle on 13 December 1957.[11]

Malaysia–Philippine accommodation

Several keys were required to unlock the door of accommodation (rather than full reconciliation) between Kuala Lumpur and Manila. One of these keys appeared to be the change in leadership, as the bilateral relationship at first improved somewhat after Ferdinand Marcos was elected president of the Philippines in November 1965. Yet his accession to power was neither instrumental in a reconsideration of the Philippines' foreign policy, nor would it provide the basis for reconciliation. Sukarno's courting of the PKI, his alignment with the People's Republic of China and the violent confrontation with Malaysia had more than mitigated Manila's eagerness to stand by Jakarta in the pursuit of its own quest for greater regional recognition – even before the accession to political power by Marcos. Malaysia, meanwhile, had great difficulty in bringing about reconciliation with Manila, given that Marcos too did not want to prejudice the Philippine claim to North Borneo. Still, with Marcos as president, Kuala Lumpur and Manila re-established diplomatic relations on 3 June 1966, against the background of the revival of ASA the previous March, notwithstanding objections by Sukarno.

In the event, the Sabah dispute was carried over into ASEAN. Nevertheless, bilateral relations seemed to be improving when President Marcos paid an official visit to Malaysia in January 1968. But the Tunku deemed Marcos a 'braggart', and hopes for reconciliation were crushed when, in March, revelations about the so-called Corregidor Affair appeared, which involved an apparent attempt by the Philippines to infiltrate Sabah. Malaysia issued a sharp diplomatic protest and demanded that Manila unambiguously affirm its recognition of Malaysia's sovereignty over Sabah. Manila did not comply, but instead expressed reservations over Malaysia's competence to represent Sabah diplomatically. The Malaysian government was especially frustrated by what it saw as Manila's failure to clarify the legal nature of its claim and the premature foreclosing of possible avenues for conflict settlement other than arbitration by the International Court of Justice, which Kuala Lumpur would not accept.[12] When the Philippine government passed the Base Line Act, which expressly reaffirmed Manila's claim to the territory, diplomatic relations between Manila and Kuala Lumpur were suspended and Ghazali Shafie warned that by upholding the claim to Sabah Manila risked destroying ASEAN (Muhammad Ghazali Shafie 1968/1987). Owing to the mediation by Indonesian President Suharto, relations were restored a year later, however, even though the dispute continued to fester. Significantly, Manila agreed not to raise the Sabah issue at future ASEAN meetings. This agreement was crucial to the emergence of the norm that bilateral disputes should not involve the Association.

True reconciliation between Manila and Kuala Lumpur was hampered by, among other things, Malaysia's alleged material and logistical support of Muslim rebels in Mindanao (Tilman 1976). Indicative of the problem was that the Marcos regime suggested that Manila would renounce the claim to Sabah only if the Malaysian government provided assurances that Sabah, under the administration of Tun Mustapha, would not be a sanctuary to Muslim dissidents. In the end an agreement of sorts was attained, whereby

> [t]he policymakers act as if they have agreed that Malaysia will refrain from supporting Philippine Muslims but will not stop Tun Mustapha's assistance to them; the Philippines will continue to attack the Muslim separatist movement but will refrain from action against Sabah or from

direct public criticism of Malaysia; the Philippines will not press its claim to Sabah but will assert its right to the waters around the Sulu archipelago.

(Noble 1975: 453)

More than ten years later Prime Minister Dr Mahathir Mohamed still described the Philippine claim to Sabah as a bone 'stuck in the throat, painful to swallow and difficult to remove' (quoted in Antolik 1990: 70). Just how problematic this issue proved for Malaysia–Philippines relations is illustrated by the fact that for many years to come the Malaysian head of government refused to pay Manila an official state visit.

Singapore's slow reconciliation with its immediate neighbours

In the immediate aftermath of the parting of the ways with Kuala Lumpur in August 1965, reconciliation between the leaderships in Kuala Lumpur and Singapore seemed quite elusive. In Singapore the leadership was determined to entrench – particularly *vis-à-vis* Malaysia – recognition and ready acceptance of a sovereignty about which there was hypersensitivity (Leifer 2000: 25). Leaders in Kuala Lumpur, meanwhile, were 'reluctant or unprepared to accept the existence of an equal and independent entity across the Causeway and Singapore' (Lau Teik Soon 1969: 159; also see Chan Heng Chee 1971).

In the event, numerous controversies emerged between the two sides over issues such as the feasibility of a common market, the common currency or the control of defence bases and facilities in Singapore. Singapore leaders were also troubled by the secretive circumstances surrounding the end to *konfrontasi* (Leifer 2000: 58).

Significantly, in the years immediately following the Singapore–Malaysia de-merger bilateral relations tended to demonstrate a complete lack of regard for principles which would later form the core of ASEAN's diplomatic and security culture, particularly the norms of respect and quiet diplomacy, contradicting respective assurances previously given. This left their diplomacy awash with accusations and counter-accusations of interference in their respective internal affairs. By early 1968, half a year after the establishment of ASEAN, 'the two sides were at the point of treating each other in terms and policies more alien than their attitudes towards other countries' (Lau Teik Soon 1969: 155). Respect for the principle of non-interference improved after the 1969 race riots in Malaysia, as leaderships in both capitals clamped down on local press coverage bent on rousing another diplomatic exchange of blows.

Meaningful accommodation became possible only once the Tunku had left the political scene and Tun Razak, and later Hussein Onn, assumed the premiership in Malaysia. That said, a visit by Lee Kuan Yew to Kuala Lumpur arranged for August 1970 had to be postponed until 1972 because of the political fallout arising from overzealous Singapore immigration officials having cut the hair of three Malay youths entering the city-state. Also, Singapore was strongly opposed to Malaysia's proposal to neutralise Southeast Asia (see Chapter 3). Lee Kuan Yew's relationship with Dr Mahathir Mohamed was, at least initially, better than with any of his three predecessors. However, even then Singapore did not at any time overcome its sense of innate vulnerability, which, in terms of relations with Kuala Lumpur, has been manifested, *inter alia*, in the strong dependence on potable water.

Official relations between Indonesia and Singapore were established on 6 June 1966, even though the New Order continued to regard the city-state as an economic parasite and a bastion of colonialism given the retention of defence links with Britain. Bilateral ties deteriorated sharply, though, when Lee Kuan Yew's government rejected a personal plea for clemency by President Suharto to spare the lives of two Indonesian soldiers sentenced to death for economic sabotage during *konfrontasi*. Singapore's leaders ignored the plea in part to assert the rule of law and in part to assert Singapore's sovereignty and independence by a manifestation of strength. President Suharto resisted pressure from the Indonesian public and from within the armed forces to strike militarily against Singapore, and heeded the advice of the foreign minister, Adam Malik, not to suspend diplomatic relations. Jakarta also decided against involving ASEAN in the conflict. To be sure, bilateral confidence-building and reconciliation suffered a serious setback, as illustrated by Jakarta's subsequent attempt to reduce its economic independence on the city-state in retaliation for the humiliation inflicted.

The subsequent process of reconciliation between the two countries and leaderships was slow. It developed in tandem with Singapore's early moves to repair bilateral relations and adopt a more constructive attitude within ASEAN. In 1971 Singapore decided merely to take note of a passage authored by Jakarta and Kuala Lumpur whereby 'the Straits of Malacca and Singapore are not international straits' and which had the potential to restrict maritime access to the city-state. A breakthrough in reconciliation was attained when in May 1973 Prime Minister Lee Kuan Yew visited Jakarta to sign a treaty demarcating the territorial sea boundary between Singapore and Indonesia. Crucially, he used the opportunity to sprinkle flowers on the graves of the two executed marines, an act which, though not comparable in its historical significance, was reminiscent of the unprecedented act of atonement by Willy Brandt in Warsaw.

Suharto responded positively to the symbolism, not least by arranging with Lee a direct and private discussion of key regional and international issues, which allowed a pragmatic relationship to gain more depth and warmth. Given the expressed concerns about the PRC, the Suharto regime appreciated in particular Singapore's undertaking to establish a political identity separate from Beijing and not to establish diplomatic relations with the PRC before Indonesia had done so. Lee Kuan Yew had, moreover, already proved his personal non-communist credentials to the New Order by his resolute action against the political challenge and agitation of the Barisan Socialis at more or less the same time that the PKI was being destroyed in Indonesia.

Arguably, bilateral confidence-building also benefited from Singapore's policy of anti-communalism, ethnic integration and pacification to deal seriously with the problem of vestigial ethnic chauvinism. Of course, Singapore's anti-communalism was not designed purely as a policy to assuage outsiders, but also as an important policy to instil into Singaporeans a sense of communal solidarity or *asabiyya*, as S. Rajaratnam (1987) – drawing on the fourteenth-century Arab philosopher Ibn Khaldoun – would have it. Such solidarity was regarded as a prerequisite to averting the possibility of the long-term social, economic and political decline of Singapore. Also, Singapore's conscious rejection of a self-regarding nationalism, while in itself perhaps still a rejoinder to past criticisms of Sukarnoist foreign policy, helped placate those within Indonesia with lingering anti-Chinese suspicions. Singapore's leaders' attempt to imbue a new meaning into nationalism from an 'anti-colonial philosophy towards a philosophy of national development', i.e. towards 'regionalism and internationalism' (Rajaratnam 1987) was generally well regarded in Jakarta. This was the case even though Foreign Minister Rajaratnam argued that 'the nationalism which was appropriate in the fight for freedom is inappropriate to deal with problems of independence' (Rajaratnam 1987: 139, 140). But he was careful not to disparage historical memories of neighbouring leaderships by paying homage to the value of the 'old nationalism, which … [a]fter all … helped [Southeast Asian countries] to win independence, [and] to bring back self-respect to their people' (Rajaratnam 1987: 141).

Finally, but related to the second point, Singapore's focus on national development identified a common platform of concern in all ASEAN countries, given the political consequences of economic adversity brought about by confrontation. According to one scholar, 'ASEAN regimes came to share an almost religious belief in the effects of rapid economic growth in diffusing the sources of social and political discontent within their societies' (Acharya 1992: 153).

The emergence of the 'ASEAN way'

As the above account demonstrates, ASEAN's diplomatic and security culture was, by the early 1970s, increasingly respected as a framework for intramural relations. Member states not only observed the principle of the non-use of force, but also increasingly complied with the exigencies of the norms of sovereign equality, non-interference, the norm of not calling on ASEAN to address bilateral disputes, as well as the principles of quiet diplomacy, respect and tolerance. This respect was illustrated in a variety of ways. These included the continued shelving of bilateral disputes, restraint in commenting upon developments in other member states and a decline in the more raucous elements of diplomatic conduct, some occasional disparaging remarks notwithstanding. Other relevant expressions included relatively tight control of the local press, a penchant for private meetings between leaders and the maintenance of quiet channels of communication. Compared to normative frameworks governing previous forms of regionalism, the 'ASEAN way' set the foundation for more intensive communication among ASEAN regimes and much greater attention to the exercise of restraint and respect for national sensitivities or the idiosyncratic sensitivities of leaders. As such, it marked a conscious attempt to address perceptions of threat and override the moral grammar of social conflicts.

ASEAN's diplomatic and security culture was decisively reinforced within only a few years, primarily as a consequence of events in Indochina. As early as the 1960s ASEAN leaderships had shared a commitment to facing off the challenge of communist insurgency.[13] In the mid-1970s they resolved to stand firm in the face of communist victories in Vietnam, Laos and Cambodia. By signing the Treaty of Amity and Co-operation (TAC) in February 1976, at the first ASEAN Summit, and later ratifying it, the Association cast in legal form some of the norms that had begun to shape intramural relations, particularly sovereign equality, the non-use of force and non-interference/non-intervention (ASEAN 1976a). Interestingly, the TAC contained within it (in ch. IV) a challenge to the 'ASEAN way' in the form of a proposal for an ASEAN High Council, put forward by the Philippine foreign secretary, Carlos Rómulo. The proposal, which aimed at ASEAN mediation of bilateral disputes, challenged the principle whereby ASEAN should not become involved in such disputes.

The High Council, charged with taking cognisance of conflicts between members and recommending appropriate means of settlement, was to be composed of representatives of all member states at ministerial level. Significantly, however, the challenge of the ASEAN High Council to the 'ASEAN way' was attenuated, if not de facto dislodged, by the additional provision that all parties to a conflict would be able to veto their involvement. In other words, member states of the Association would thus only be in a position to actually offer assistance to address conflict among other ASEAN states if all sides concerned would consent to such mediation. Moreover, conflicting parties were only called upon to be 'well disposed' towards any offers of mediation. Not surprisingly however Malaysia's leadership was concerned that the proposal for an ASEAN High Council constituted an attempt by Manila to draw in third parties to press the Philippines' case on the issue of Sabah. At the time of writing, the High Council has yet to be constituted.

Indeed, the proposed establishment of the ASEAN High Council only did not undermine an element of the 'ASEAN way', but addressed a theoretical problem that had arisen in connection with ASEAN's discourse on the establishment of a Zone of Peace, Freedom and Neutrality (ZOPFAN).

As we shall see in more detail in the Chapter 3, the ZOPFAN Declaration suggested that resident countries in Southeast Asia should autonomously manage regional order, not least through respect for international principles and norms. The problem was that such respect by ASEAN countries could not exclude the possibility of intramural conflict. Were conflict to arise among ASEAN countries, they might be tempted to call on the assistance of foreign powers, a development that would directly contradict the idea of ZOPFAN. By embracing the idea of the establishment of a dispute-resolving mechanism, ASEAN's earlier reluctance to identify an institutionalised approach to intramural dispute resolution would – in theory – be repaired. With the provision in place, outside powers would also be denied any reason to interfere in ASEAN affairs.

Conclusion

This chapter has expanded the argument that the genesis of ASEAN's diplomatic and security culture is best conceived of as both a nationalist struggle and the outcome of a longstanding struggle for recognition and security. It showed, in particular, how processes of reciprocal recognition of the political identity among regional elites were particularly crucial to the emergence of the 'ASEAN way' as a framework to mediate estrangement and insecurity. The next chapter returns to the discussion on ZOPFAN, among other things, in an attempt to examine to what extent ASEAN has sought to extend its diplomatic and security culture to the wider Southeast and East Asia.

3   ZOPFAN and the ASEAN Regional Forum

The extramural dimension of ASEAN's struggle for security and recognition

At a time when ASEAN's diplomatic and security culture had not yet attracted significant respect by members in their intramural relations, the Association was also faced with major strategic change in East Asia. The war in Indochina proved unwinnable for the United States, and the incoming Nixon administration decided to effect a military disengagement that was designed not to embarrass Washington. According to the Nixon Doctrine, first enunciated in July 1969 in Guam, victims of aggression were henceforth themselves expected to provide the necessary manpower. This led to the 'Vietnamisation' of the Vietnam War. Meanwhile, ties between Moscow and Beijing had deteriorated to the point of military exchanges along the Ussuri River, cross-border penetrations into Xinjiang and Soviet proposals to target China's nuclear capability. The Nixon administration exploited the opportunity and successfully worked towards a relaxation in ties with the PRC. This rapprochement soon became an alignment that saw Beijing and Washington co-operate to meet the perceived Soviet threat in the context of tripolarity. Notably, the Nixon Doctrine had already been preceded by Britain's decision to withdraw from East of Suez. It was against this background that questions about regional order and respect for basic norms of international society by the major powers arose with some urgency for ASEAN governments.

This chapter examines the ways in which the Association has sought to win a commitment by other regional states to norms associated with the 'ASEAN way', primarily the norms of sovereign equality, non-intervention and non-interference and the principle of the non-use of force. It covers not merely the early period of ASEAN's institutional existence, but extends into the post-Cold War period, during which sustained attempts to extend aspects of ASEAN's diplomatic and security culture have been directed at China, Japan and the United States. The chapter is divided into four sections. The first explores the origins and purpose of the 1971 ASEAN proposal for a Zone of Peace, Freedom and Neutrality. It examines how ZOPFAN, although a unilateral declaration, aimed at winning respect for norms associated with the 'ASEAN way' to protect the emerging framework for interstate conduct in Southeast Asia and establish a broad normative context for relations between regional states and East Asia's major powers. As will become clear, as an approach to enhance regional security and to engage the regional major powers, ZOPFAN was thus very different from the initial Malaysian proposal to neutralise Southeast Asia, which had triggered the search for the compromise that was the Kuala Lumpur Declaration. The second section examines the post-1971 development of ZOPFAN. It discusses how ASEAN states clarified the meaning of ZOPFAN, how they sought to apply the latter *vis-à-vis* North Vietnam, and how the failure of this effort led to the signing of the Treaty of Amity and Co-operation and the Declaration of ASEAN Concord. The third section examines the effects on ZOPFAN of the different political priorities in Hanoi and the ASEAN capitals, as illustrated by Vietnam's invasion of Democratic Kampuchea, and how, ultimately, ASEAN–Vietnam reconciliation was achieved by Hanoi's willingness to honour the very norms that it had rejected years earlier. Finally, I examine to what extent processes of norm-elaboration taking place in the ASEAN Regional Forum are derived from ASEAN's attempt to promote at least certain aspects of its diplomatic and security culture as a framework for political and security co-operation in East Asia in the post-Cold war period.

The origins of the ZOPFAN proposal

Intramural accommodation and reconciliation still remained in doubt when ASEAN governments expressed their determination 'to exert initially necessary efforts to secure the recognition of, and respect for, South East Asia as a Zone of Peace, Freedom and Neutrality, free from any form or manner of interference by outside Powers.' The Kuala Lumpur Declaration of November 1971 (ASEAN 1971) did not, of course, mark the first time that ASEAN member states referred to what might be conceived of as an extramural dimension of the 'ASEAN way'. Indeed, the first ASEAN document to indicate that some of the norms guiding ASEAN's intramural relations ought equally to have validity for the entire Southeast Asian region was the Bangkok Declaration (ASEAN 1967). The preamble of that Declaration contained an unambiguous call by ASEAN leaders to the major powers to organise relations between Southeast Asian countries and extra-regional (meaning East Asian and Asia-Pacific) powers on the basis of the principle of non-interference.[1] Such references should not be taken to imply, however, that the ZOPFAN Declaration was the product of long-term strategic planning by all ASEAN leaders, or that it has been the only expression of an attempt to formulate an extramural application of ASEAN's diplomatic and security culture. Rather, ZOPFAN, like other major documents and agreements signed by ASEAN leaders, emerged as the outcome of a process of diplomatic interaction focused on consultation and a search for consensus among member states, a process that has itself been identified as part of the 'ASEAN way'.

The compromise that is ZOPFAN was forged in an attempt to satisfy diverse, if not competing, national and regime security interests, as well as contending identity claims. Its genesis lay in the original proposal for Southeast Asia's neutralisation, which dates back to 23 January 1968 and was put forward by Tun Dr Ismail, then a backbencher in Malaysia's *Dewan Rakyat* (Lower House). The proposal by Tun Dr Ismail, who would re-enter the government under Premier Tun Razak, was in effect an attempt to identify a cost-effective and integrated solution to Malaysia's security challenges, both domestic and foreign. It came just after the announcement by Prime Minister Wilson on 16 January that British forces would be withdrawn from Malaysia by the end of 1971, rather than 1975, as previously anticipated. Britain's withdrawal from East of Suez implied the termination of the Anglo-Malaysian Defence Arrangement (AMDA).[2] Debates also took place in New Zealand and Australia about reducing their forces in Malaysia. The implicit challenge for ASEAN security inherent in such deliberations was further reinforced by the Nixon Doctrine, spelled out in the 1969 Guam Declaration, whereby American troops would in future not be committed to fighting regional wars on the Asian continent. Sopiee (1975: 136) described the emerging strategic context thus: 'the British lion no longer [had] any teeth, the Australian umbrella was leaking and the American eagle was winging its way out of Asia' (Sopiee 1975: 136).

In substance, Malaysia's neutralisation proposal sought to ensure a neutral Southeast Asia that was free from big power entanglements, from external threats and from external subversion (Hamzah 1992). The proposal required the major powers to accept and respect Southeast Asia as an area of neutrality. Several elements were involved: first, the exclusion of the region from major power competition by international agreement; and, second, the establishment of supervisory means to guarantee Southeast Asia's neutrality (Alagappa 1991: 272). The signing of non-aggression pacts was also put on the agenda.

The Malaysian premier, Tunku Abdul Rahman, was perhaps less keen to embrace Tun Dr Ismail's neutralisation idea than the then vice-premier, Tun Abdul Razak, the next premier and then Special Representative of Malaysia and permanent secretary for foreign affairs, Ghazali Shafie. Both endorsed the proposal, as they viewed Malaysia's security environment as having become more complex and potentially more dangerous. The Vietnam War had spread to Laos and Cambodia, and the fighting in the months of March and April 1970 generated significant concern, not only among Malaysian political leaders, but also in other ASEAN capitals. Against the background of events in Indochina and Western disengagement, the possibility that Hanoi might eventually seek political if not military domination of Southeast Asia could not be discounted. Vietnam had spoken for resistance movements in Laos and Cambodia at the 1954 Geneva Conference and appeared to harbour the goal of rebuilding an Indochinese federation.

However, a certain degree of restiveness among Malaysian leaders also pertained in view of the uncertainty concerning the prospect of rising Chinese influence in Indochina.

Arguably, the neutralisation proposal constituted, above all, an attempt by Malaysia's incoming leadership to address the security challenge emanating from the PRC and to limit its regional influence. China not only continued to churn out a barrage of revolutionary propaganda in the direction of ASEAN, including exhortations to overturn domestic political orders, but also seemed very interested in removing US influence from mainland Southeast Asian countries, particularly Thailand, Laos and Cambodia. Some feared that Beijing and Hanoi might *both* encourage national liberation movements in Southeast Asia (Gurtov 1970: 13).

To remove the greatest obstacles to neutralisation, the new administration was determined to grant the PRC not only diplomatic recognition, but also recognition as a major power. In return, the Malaysian government expected China's recognition of the legitimacy of the ruling coalition in Kuala Lumpur and respect for the norm of non-interference. Such recognition was important given the sizeable ethnic Chinese population in the country and the perceived potential for a repeat of the May 1969 race riots if Beijing were to exploit the pro-China sentiments among Malaysian Chinese.

Tan Sri Ghazali Shafie declared neutralisation to be Malaysia's official policy at the Preparatory Non-Aligned Conference in Dar es Salaam on 17 April 1970. The proposal was reiterated by Tun Abdul Razak in his then capacity as deputy prime minister at the Summit Meeting in Lusaka the following October. It was also introduced to audiences at the Commonwealth Heads of Government Conference and the United Nations General Assembly. Although the proposal arose against the backdrop of a changing security context, its support by Tun Abdul Razak was not driven merely by security considerations. Identification with the proposal was also designed to lift Malaysia's regional prestige. Indeed, as Bilveer Singh (1992: 42) has argued, Malaysia's proposal was guided by the feeling that Southeast Asia and Malaysia had been denied their proper role in world politics. Beyond that, it was meant to foster an identity in international relations that would be clearly distinguishable from Prime Minister Tunku Abdul Rahman's pro-American stance (Wilson 1975: 8). Having explained the neutralisation concept to leaders in Indonesia and Thailand in person, Tun Abdul Razak and his colleagues hoped that ASEAN would support it.

The ASEAN debate on ZOPFAN

Malaysia's public argument in favour of neutralisation was very straightforward: the lesson of Vietnam (particularly the involvement of major powers in the Second Indochina War) made neutralisation necessary. Malaysian leaders made several caveats, however. The most important one, no doubt, was that the proposal could not be pursued so long as the war in Vietnam continued. Another was that neutralisation would only amount to a successful security strategy if Southeast Asian governments set their own houses in order by addressing more comprehensively the needs and grievances of their citizens and, more generally, by seeking to overcome their regimes' legitimacy deficit. Greater bilateral and multilateral co-operation was seen as useful in and necessary to achieving this aim. A further caveat by Malaysian leaders was that ASEAN was to clarify that the legitimate interests of the major powers would not be adversely affected by Southeast Asia's neutralisation. Such provisos notwithstanding, decision-makers in Kuala Lumpur clearly believed that neutralisation could be attained.

Even though the widening of the Vietnam War was a focus of grave concern for other ASEAN countries, at the root of which 'foreign interference' was seen to lie, not a single other member government wholeheartedly supported Malaysia's neutralisation initiative. The Thai government, for instance, attributed the crisis in Indochina to the designs of what it perceived as a predatory regime in Hanoi and the Vietcong. In the view of Bangkok, neutralisation would not address the threat posed by these actors. Moreover, differences of opinion had crystallised within the governing Thai administration on the issue of China. Thailand's then prime minister, General Thanom Kittikachorn, cast doubt on China's credentials as a possible guarantor power and strongly opposed China's material support to communist insurgents in Thailand. The foreign minister, Thanat Khoman, on the other hand, favoured some kind of rapprochement with China, a view perhaps also attributable in part to irritations over perceived interference in Thailand's internal affairs by US media and members of Congress.[3] Having allowed US bases in Thailand to be used to prosecute the war against Vietnam, a development deeply resented by the leadership in Hanoi, the Thai leadership generally expressed a preference for a regime of armed neutrality over one of guaranteed neutrality. This led them to argue in favour of strengthening ASEAN's intramural political co-operation (Wilson 1975: 76).

President Suharto of Indonesia, who had been miffed by the official launch of the neutralisation idea taking place without him having first been consulted on the issue, also came out against the Malaysian proposal for major power guarantees to maintain peace and stability in Southeast Asia. The Indonesian leadership feared that the exercise of major powers' guarantees would provide, rather than forestall, opportunities for interference. Attendant major power rivalry, so Jakarta believed, would also undermine the stability of regional states. In this context, the Suharto government had already noted with dismay the inability or unwillingness of outside powers to prevent wider Indochina slipping into war. To counter this development, Indonesia had convened the Djakarta Conference on Cambodia in May 1970, albeit without much success due to the unwillingness to attend of China, North Korea, North Vietnam and India. Second, both for security and domestic political reasons, Indonesia's armed forces rejected the implicit idea underlying the neutralisation proposal, the normalisation of relations with the PRC, which Indonesia's Foreign Ministry had edged toward (Sukma 1999: 106–10). Moreover, Malaysia's neutralisation proposal irked

Indonesian leaders because it could only be realised at the expense of Jakarta's aspirations to achieve at least Middle Power status. Given Jakarta's aspirations and concerns for regime legitimacy, the New Order regime sought to persuade regional governments to let Southeast Asians assume primary responsibility for regional security – in effect an effort to modify substantially Malaysia's neutralisation proposal. In this context Indonesian leaders advocated the building of socio-political and economic strength, or national resilience (*ketahanan nasional*) in each member state.[4]

Singapore also signalled caution and reservation in relation to the possible neutralisation of Southeast Asia. A major reason for this was lingering apprehension about a possible sub-regional Malay hegemony. This fear had been revived by the Malaysian–Indonesian declaration in 1971 that they would no longer recognise the Straits of Malacca and Singapore as international straits (Leifer 1989: 60–1). The proposed neutralisation scheme further reinforced such anxiety, as it would de-legitimise *all* major power involvement in Southeast Asian affairs, on which Singapore had, to a large extent, banked its security. Indeed, a possible exit of the United States from Southeast Asia was deemed undesirable for both deterrence and economic reasons, as Singapore's aspiration to become a global city also depended, in particular, on American investments. Rather than publicly express these misgivings, Singapore's leadership emphasised the potential pitfalls in Malaysia's neutralisation proposal. Among other things, it was suggested that China's foreign policy still remained 'in the evangelistical phase' (Lee Kuan Yew 1970: 10). Singapore's leadership also raised extremely pertinent questions about whether the scheme might be undermined if the guarantor powers were locked into disputes either among themselves or with zonal states (Wilson 1975: 27–8). It was further suggested that alternative scenarios to the neutralisation scheme, such as alliance arrangements or alert diplomacy, might be more effective in meeting ASEAN members' security objectives.

Like Singapore, the Philippines sought to avert both Southeast Asia's legal neutralisation and the withdrawal of America's naval presence. However, the Philippine position was characterised by ambivalence. On the one hand, Kuala Lumpur's proposal was opposed because the Philippines, as a member of SEATO, greatly benefited from its defence ties with Washington generally and US bases in particular, both economically and in terms of an enhancement of its national security (Hänggi 1992: 125–7). On the other hand, Manila was tempted to undercut its security dependence on Washington for nationalistic reasons. In the end, however, considerations against political support for the Malaysian proposal weighed stronger, not least because of the likely consequences of neutralisation for the pursuit of Philippine territorial claims to Sabah (Alagappa 1991: 273).

In the event, Malaysia's neutralisation proposal was not repudiated, but modified. ASEAN moves for a compromise accelerated against the back-drop of two related developments: the impending admission of the PRC to the United Nations Security Council and the July 1971 announcement by Washington and Beijing that President Nixon would visit the PRC.[5] The announcement raised the prospect of an alignment between Washington and Beijing, which some ASEAN governments feared might lead to Southeast Asia being carved up into different spheres of influence. To nip in the bud any such outcome, viewed as unpalatable by all members, ASEAN foreign ministers agreed on a collective response at an extraordinary meeting in Kuala Lumpur in November. This response built on a draft declaration for a 'zone of peace, freedom and development' prepared by Thanat Khoman, who had been relieved of his post as Thai foreign minister, but nevertheless represented his country as the Special Envoy of the National Executive Council of Thailand.[6] Significantly, the revised Thai draft, later adopted as the Kuala Lumpur Declaration, followed Indonesia's objections to the original neutralisation proposal in that it sought not legal guarantees but political pledges to attain a zone of neutrality. The political character of the document was reflected in the lengthy preamble to the Kuala Lumpur Declaration, which otherwise contained only a short operational part emphasising the significance of national development and regional co-operation. ZOPFAN nevertheless stood for a two-pronged approach to shaping regional order. One the one hand, ZOPFAN was an attempt to establish a legitimate normative framework that was to guide future interstate interaction. On the other, ZOPFAN embraced the argument that national security could be enhanced through the pursuit of practical intra-regional co-operation.

Although it was a compromise, which revolved around a shared commitment to the norms of sovereign equality and non-interference, the Kuala Lumpur Declaration perhaps best articulated Indonesia's foreign policy position, in terms of Jakarta's struggle for security and recognition. If one looks at the process of arriving at this compromise kindly, it represented a major achievement on the part of the ASEAN countries given their wide-ranging and, in part, antagonistic security interests. Indeed, Amitav Acharya labelled it 'a classic example of the emerging ASEAN Way of compromise, consensus building, ambiguity, avoidance of strict reciprocity, and rejection of legally binding obligations' (Acharya 2001: 55). Interestingly, technically this first major attempt to externalise the 'ASEAN way' was actually launched outside the scope of regular ASEAN activities.[7]

Significantly, none of the members believed that the chosen formulations would impact negatively on their foreign policy or security interests. Indeed, by the time the ZOPFAN Declaration was released, Kuala Lumpur, for instance, had, upon the abrogation of the bilateral defence accord with Britain, become a member of the Five Powers Defence Arrangements (FPDA). While the FPDA was a consultative mechanism, Malaysia's security was nevertheless enhanced thereby, and was further boosted by virtue of New Zealand and Australia retaining military forces on the Peninsula (Jackson 1971). Arguably, then, these security links made it easier for

Malaysia's ruling coalition to join Indonesia in advocating the normative framework inherent in the Kuala Lumpur Declaration. Nevertheless, the efforts undertaken to win adherence to the norms of sovereignty, non-interference and mutual respect by non-ASEAN countries *vis-à-vis* the Association helped its members, over time, to reinforce the acceptance and intramural regard for those norms.

We shall now focus on how ASEAN, under the de facto leadership of Jakarta, further elaborated on the ZOPFAN Declaration. This will help us to appreciate that ZOPFAN, if not from the beginning then increasingly as time went on, represented an (ambitious) attempt to externalise certain norms associated with ASEAN's emerging intramural diplomatic and security culture and, as such, became ever more removed from the original neutralisation proposal.

ZOPFAN's development

The line from the Bangkok Declaration to the Kuala Lumpur Declaration, where it said that 'interference will adversely affect its freedom, independence and integrity' (para. 6), has already been noted. It would therefore appear that the two dynamics that we encountered in relation to the origins of the Bangkok Declaration also informed the process of seeking to actualise ZOPFAN: the struggle for security and recognition. As we have already seen, the focus on the principle of non-interference in the process of defining the component concepts making up ZOPFAN was designed to address problems of security confronted by ASEAN leaderships, including concerns about societal security. Beyond that, the stress on the principle of non-interference also implied a moral injunction, in the sense that interference was perceived to be a violation of member states' rights as sovereign entities in international society. The extent to which these two dimensions informed the attempt to make ZOPFAN the normative platform for regional interstate relations becomes clear when one examines the individual elements of the concept. It is for this reason that the definitions of ZOPFAN's individual component concepts, as agreed by the ASEAN's Senior Officials Committee in July 1972, are reproduced here in full:

> A zone of peace, freedom and neutrality exists where national identity, independence and integrity of the individual States within such a zone can be preserved and maintained, so that they can achieve national development and well-being, and promote regional co-operation and solidarity, in accordance with the ideals and aspirations of their peoples and the purposes and principles of the United Nations Charter, free from any form or manner of interference by outside powers.
> Peace is a condition where the prevalence of harmonious and orderly relations exists between and among States; no reference is hereby made

to the internal state of affairs in each of the zonal States. A situation of ideological, political, economic, armed or other forms of conflict either among the zonal States themselves, between one or more zonal States and outside powers, or between outside powers affecting the region, is not a condition of peace.

Freedom means the freedom of States from control, domination or interference by other States in the conduct of their internal and external affairs. This means the right of zonal States to solve their domestic problems in terms of their own conditions and aspirations, to assume primary responsibility for the security and stability of the region and their regional and international relations on the basis of sovereign equality and mutual benefit.

Neutrality means the maintenance of a state of impartiality in any war between other States as understood in international law and in the light of the United Nations Charter; in the context of the Kuala Lumpur Declaration, however, it means that zonal States shall undertake to maintain their impartiality and shall refrain from involvement directly or indirectly in ideological, political, economic, armed or other forms of conflict, particularly between powers outside the zone, and that outside powers shall not interfere in the domestic or regional affairs of the zonal States.

(quoted in Hänggi 1992: 211–14)

As enunciated by ASEAN's senior officials, ZOPFAN, given the emphasis on non-interference over any legal commitments, stands firmly in the tradition of Asian neutralism and nonalignment, unlike Malaysia's original neutralisation proposal. This point is, *inter alia*, also corroborated by the reference to the 'Declaration of the Promotion of World Peace and Co-operation' in the Preamble of the Kuala Lumpur Declaration itself. Hänggi has persuasively referred to the conceptual and intellectual roots underlying ASEAN'S notion of neutrality in ZOPFAN as an expression of a 'postclassical, modern neutrality' (Hänggi 1992: 220–1). Arguably, the fact that ASEAN members subscribe to ideas of ideological neutralism reaffirms the argument presented whereby a dual motivational force underpinned ZOPFAN. The importance of a struggle of recognition in this regard, has been highlighted by Peter Lyon (1969, 1963), who pointed out that in the context of the new Asian states neutralism has been 'just another name for nationalism' (Lyon 1969: 165).

Rhetorically, the moral grammar of nationalism is made most explicit by the invocation of the component concept of freedom in the ZOPFAN formula. Freedom here is associated with the right of the state to adopt, develop and retain particular systems of governance, rather than with notions of personal autonomy and attendant political and civil rights. The adoption of this particular understanding of freedom by ASEAN senior officials would indicate that the struggle for ASEAN members' acceptance in international society was not over for Southeast Asian leaders after their attainment of legal independence. Indeed, by linking freedom and non-interference in the concept of neutrality, the senior officials rearticulated a sense of grievance experienced by ASEAN leaders in view of their inability to control events affecting their respective countries. As President Suharto put it at the Conference of Non-Aligned Nations in Lusaka in October 1970, 'We are indeed fully saturated with deplorable experiences of subversion and outside interference in our internal affairs' (Suharto 1970: 11). Or, as Tun Abdul Razak formulated it a year later, there was 'no wish to be a pawn in any game the big powers play' (Razak 1971: 7). Thanat Khoman had earlier expressed a similar view. As he put it, 'the inert practice of letting far-away nations dominate our lives and shape our national destinies in a manner which does not take into account our interests but seeks to satisfy their own benefits should be a thing of the past' (Khoman 1970a: 3). Significantly, the stress on freedom and neutrality by some the larger ASEAN countries on the basis of their historical achievements and international law was matched by the stress placed on the norms of non-interference and sovereign equality by the smaller ASEAN members.

The major powers did not endorse the project of a zone of peace, freedom and neutrality in Southeast Asia. Nor did they commit themselves to the inherent normative framework centred upon the norms of sovereign equality, non-interference and the non-use of force, as ASEAN had suggested they should. Consequently, ZOPFAN emerged not as a 'possession goal' involving the actual realisation of a zone of peace, freedom and neutrality, but as a 'milieu goal', in the sense that observance of the norms identified might generate conditions conducive to regional peace and stability in Southeast Asia.[8] In view of the major powers' reluctance to underwrite ZOPFAN in a meaningful way, ASEAN's attention quickly focused on whether ZOPFAN would be acceptable to the government in Hanoi as a basis for a framework for regional co-existence. In the Kuala Lumpur Declaration the ASEAN foreign ministers and the Special Envoy from Thailand had already agreed to encourage other Southeast Asian countries to associate themselves with the objectives and aspirations expressed.

ASEAN, Vietnam and ZOPFAN

Neither South nor North Vietnam had been enthusiastic about ZOPFAN when the Kuala Lumpur Declaration was released. This was, in part, because of a lasting concern with the original neutralisation proposal. The Thieu regime, for instance, believed the proposal would be unworkable in the absence of a genuine major power commitment to Southeast Asia's neutrality and doubted whether the necessary exercise of restraint by these powers in an unstable war situation would prove feasible. In other words, the Saigon government believed that a situation marked by the region's neutrality would in any case amount to a disturbance of the regional balance of power and facilitate communist aggression (Nguyen Manh Hung 1973: 140). The leadership of the Vietnamese Communist Party (VCP) was equally unimpressed. At the time of ZOPFAN's adoption, Vietnam was a country at war and Hanoi also relied on external material support. Acceding to the normative framework embedded in ZOPFAN would effectively have deprived Hanoi of the opportunity of unifying Vietnam by force. Not surprisingly, ASEAN thus failed to enlist North Vietnam's support for ZOPFAN even though the Vietnam War was drawing to a close. From Hanoi's perspective, however, the nationalist objective of reunification was not the only obstacle to winning a public commitment to the norms of sovereign equality, non-interference and the non-use of force.

Indeed, a gulf of distrust had opened up during the Second Indochina War between ASEAN members and North Vietnam as a consequence of direct or indirect acts of intervention on the part of individual ASEAN countries against the National Liberation Front of South Vietnam (Thayer 1990: 138).[9] Under the leadership of its general-secretary, Le Duan, the VCP described the Association as an 'imperialist invention' and an 'insidious proxy', whose essence was likened to that of SEATO. Angered that ASEAN leaders had sought to deny Vietnam what they themselves claimed for their own countries, namely unification and independence, the VCP leadership was extremely reluctant to recognise ASEAN as a legitimate diplomatic player in Southeast Asia. Indeed, Hanoi expressed support for the 'struggle of the peoples of the Southeast Asian nations for independence, democracy, peace and social process' which insurgents were at the time waging in several ASEAN member states. As noted, ASEAN countries, in turn, found disturbing this revolutionary fervour and the apparent inclination to interfere in their domestic affairs.

Following the Paris Peace Agreements of 27 January 1973, ASEAN offered to respect the political identity of the Democratic Republic of Vietnam in return for Hanoi's respect for ASEAN members' sovereignty and territorial integrity. In this context, ASEAN governments noted approvingly the similarities between the Agreement on Ending the War and Restoring Peace in Vietnam and the ZOPFAN Declaration. It was held that here were two documents that focused on the significance of the principle of non-interference by outside powers. This was interpreted and represented in terms of a convergence of ideas about how to organise international relations in Southeast Asia. ASEAN essentially proposed that the whole of Southeast Asia could be turned into a Zone of Peace, Freedom and Neutrality (ASEAN 1973). Hopes to find agreement on a basis for legitimate forms of regional interstate conduct proved illusory, however. The underlying reason was not the somewhat paltry contribution to the reconstruction of Indochina States that the Association had proposed, even if this indicated differences within ASEAN on Indochina policy.

At issue, instead, was the unwillingness of the North Vietnamese to participate in a multilateral endeavour that was controlled by countries that

Hanoi still considered proxies of the United States and which might seek to liberalise Hanoi's political system of government in line with ASEAN's understanding of 'freedom'. At the heart of this reluctance was the problem of opposing political identities, as mentioned above, and a pursuant Vietnamese unwillingness to extend recognition to those who had in the past sought to frustrate its rightful nationalist struggle. Hanoi consequently rejected invitations to attend ASEAN's annual ministerial gathering in the proposed capacity of observer in both 1973 and 1974.[10]

Plans to make ZOPFAN a framework expressing the two sides' mutual recognition as legitimate political players soon became even less likely to come to fruition. Military victories against South Vietnamese forces ultimately led to the quicker than expected fall of the Thieu regime (Brown 1991). And in the aftermath of its final moral, political and military victory over the United States, the battle-hardened VCP leadership espoused an even stronger sense of entitlement to respect and regional influence than before the Second Indochina War. This sense of entitlement made it quite difficult, if not impossible, for ASEAN to commit the Democratic Republic of Vietnam (DRV) to its proposed blueprint for regional interaction. Indeed, Vietnam felt both inclined and in a position to challenge not only the norms espoused by ASEAN, but also the Association itself. In this context, Hanoi particularly welcomed the accession to power of an ideologically compatible government in Laos.[11] Soon thereafter, Le Duan and the leader of the Lao People's Revolutionary Party, Kaysone Phomvihan, stressed their support for communist insurgencies in Southeast Asia. The reluctance of the DRV to seek accommodation with ASEAN and its rejection of ZOFPAN as a shared normative platform on which to base their relations proved disconcerting to ASEAN leaders.

The question of which norms should underpin the emerging regional order in Southeast Asia became so acute that by November 1975 the ASEAN Committee of Officials on Neutralisation proposed four immediate steps in order to realise the zone of peace, freedom and neutrality in Southeast Asia. One proposal aimed at upgrading to treaty form ASEAN's own regional code of conduct, hitherto explicitly elaborated in the Bangkok and Kuala Lumpur Declarations and the ZOPFAN guidelines. A draft had already been submitted to the Eighth ASEAN Ministerial Meeting in May 1975, within a month of the fall of Saigon. A second proposal called for the passing of a UN resolution that would declare Southeast Asia a zone of peace, freedom and neutrality. A third proposal aimed to seek international agreement for Southeast Asia's denuclearisation. And, fourth, it was proposed that non-aggression pacts be signed with external powers (Hänggi 1992: 151). In the event, ASEAN heads of state and government earnestly pursued only the first of these four proposals. This led to the signing of the Treaty of Amity and Co-operation (TAC) (ASEAN 1976a) and the Declaration of ASEAN Concord (ASEAN 1976b) on 24 February 1976.

The TAC and the Declaration of ASEAN Concord represented another milestone in ASEAN's ability to work out important compromises. The two documents also brought into the open and sanctioned a deepening of what hitherto had been tacit ASEAN intramural political and security co-operation. Moreover, the TAC outlined in treaty form a clear set of norms that had regulated, and was meant to continue to regulate, the relations among ASEAN members. As such, it amounted to a formal affirmation of the sanctity of existing boundaries in Southeast Asia as well as of the norms and practices associated with the 'ASEAN way'. For some smaller members like Singapore, the reaffirmation of the norms of the non-use of force and non-intervention, in particular, appears to have had special significance, not least in view of Jakarta's intervention in East Timor in late 1975. Singapore may have appreciated that the ostensible purpose of that intervention was to deny outside powers a possible strategic foothold within the perimeter of the Indonesian archipelago (Leifer 1983: 154–60),[12] but its anxiety then was manifested in its critical voting behaviour in the United Nations General Assembly (Koh 1998: 1–9).

Nonetheless, by this time ASEAN was generally confident about the usefulness and legitimacy of the constitutive elements of the 'ASEAN way', both as a process and a normative framework governing intramural relations. Some observers argued, therefore, that respect for the 'ASEAN way' at the intramural level had created an atmosphere that proved conducive to overcoming various diplomatic hitches and to managing disputes in bilateral relations (Wanandi 1979: 52–3). This was illustrated by the fact that contentious issues such as contraband trade or the status of the Straits of Malacca and Singapore had not derailed an emerging process of mutual confidence-building. Nor had intramural dissension over the locality and function of the ASEAN Secretariat, an issue ultimately resolved in Indonesia's favour (Indorf 1984: 68).

The lack of any fallout pursuant to Malaysia's 1974 diplomatic recognition of Beijing, in the form of sustained alienation or otherwise, also underscores this assessment, especially as '[d]espite the formula of agreeing to disagree, there was little doubt that Malaysia had broken ranks, exposing the limits of political co-operation within ASEAN' (Leifer 1989: 63). Jakarta viewed Malaysia's initiative as having transgressed the norm of solidarity on a question deemed vital for national and regional security by a fellow member. Importantly, the significance attached to the substance of ASEAN's diplomatic and security culture was not put in doubt by this. Indonesia's leadership recognised that, after all, Malaysia had acted within its prerogative as a sovereign state. Moreover, Jakarta itself had wanted a pledge from China in relation to the non-interference principle, that the latter would not sponsor the revival of the PKI, on the basis of a distinction between government-to-government and people-to-people relations.

Continuities and discontinuities

By codifying and highlighting again the significance attributed to norms of international society both the TAC and the Declaration of ASEAN Concord reaffirmed the basic premises of ZOPFAN as a proposed framework for intra-regional relations. However, the Declaration also effectively redesigned the operational part of the Kuala Lumpur Declaration. Here, ASEAN leaders articulated the conviction that their countries' true independence, as well as their prosperity, critically depended on their internal political stability, which in turn depended on external powers refusing to take up opportunities for intervention. At their first summit in Bali in 1976 ASEAN leaders emphasised that domestic and political regional stability would emerge only if ASEAN governments succeeded in improving the livelihood of its citizens, which would foster national and regional resilience. National resilience, as the Indonesian foreign minister, Professor Mochtar Kusumaatmadja, explained, would serve 'to enhance the capability and ability of each member country and its people in all fields of national endeavour, in order to withstand and overcome all kinds of outside interference and adverse influence' (quoted in Wannamethee 1992: 97). Once national resilience was achieved across ASEAN through intra-regional co-operation in 'all fields' (Declaration of ASEAN Concord: Article 12), so the further argument put forward by ASEAN leaders, regional resilience, could also be attained. In this way, as Michael Leifer reasoned, ZOPFAN would henceforth be 'a regional condition ... which individual ASEAN states could work toward by pursuing a common approach whereby development-induced political stability would give rise to regional effect' (Leifer 1989: 67). The regional effect aspired to would primarily find expression in a reduced likelihood of unwanted interference by other Southeast Asian countries and their backing by any major powers. Hence, it would reduce the chances of armed conflict at the intramural level. National resilience, it would appear, was also meant to become a substantial source of respect for ASEAN members by non-ASEAN countries within Southeast Asia and beyond.

Significantly, the formalisation of the 'ASEAN way' as a regional code of conduct in the TAC and ASEAN's willingness to enter into broader and deeper co-operation with one another constituted only two of three avenues to regional order pursued by the Association. The third avenue concerned ASEAN's support for and reliance on external security and defence links. Thailand and the Philippines retained their bilateral alliances with the United States, while Singapore and Malaysia remained members of the FPDA. Considerable continuity thus characterised the approach to security embedded in the ZOPFAN Declaration and the documents signed in Bali, notwithstanding the differences mentioned. In both 1971 and 1976 ASEAN appeared to suggest that national and regional security could both be enhanced by adherence to basic norms of international society even if respect for these norms constituted only one facet of a comprehensive approach to security. The second point of conti-nuity concerned the positive practical effects of development and the third, if the worst came to the worst, entailed reliance on the provision of external security.

We now ask whether ASEAN's display of diplomatic activism and soli-darity at Bali proved successful in winning the Indochinese states' endorsement of ASEAN's diplomatic and security culture as a framework for sub-regional order. From ASEAN's perspective, adherence to the legal-political norms but also to the norm of respect was particularly important given concerns over possible communist subversion. As Acharya put it, '[r]egional order could not be maintained without an agreement on the fundamental importance of regime security anchored in the principle of non-interference' (Acharya 2001: 58). The next section will explore the continuing disagreement over the norms of non-interference and non-inter-vention between ASEAN capitals and Hanoi following Vietnam's reunification, and its implications for ZOPFAN, as well as the reasons that ultimately allowed the disagreement to be overcome.

Vietnam and ASEAN on ZOPFAN: from antagonism to agreement

When Vietnam proposed the establishment of a 'zone of peace and friendly co-operation' in February 1976, Hanoi seemed to indicate an interest in placing its relationship with ASEAN on a new footing. After Vietnam's reunification in July 1976, however, it was clear that this would not be the case. The Socialist Republic of Vietnam (SRV), in its first foreign policy initiative, made an offer to ASEAN members whereby relations with them would be established on the basis of the five principles of peaceful co-exis-tence as well as genuine independence, peace and neutrality (Gilks 1992: 158). The emphasis on genuine independence suggested Hanoi was more concerned with launching a 'just struggle' against ASEAN than with securing a mutually acceptable normative framework for regional co-exis-tence and co-operation. In a blatant demonstration of this policy, Laos and Vietnam pointedly rejected ASEAN's prescription for regional order by blocking mention of the ZOPFAN formula in the final communiqué at a conference of the non-aligned heads of government, held in Sri Lanka in August 1976 (Leifer 1989: 74).

Though some ASEAN leaders continued to harbour hopes for mutual reconciliation between Vietnam and the Association, these were only inter-mittently revived. Hopes arose, in particular, in the context of Vietnam's formidable problems of national reconstruction and development in the aftermath of reunification. Moreover, Hanoi's apparent efforts to discourage the attendance of the communist parties of Indonesia, Malaysia and the Philippines at the Fourth Party Congress of the VCP in December 1976 appeared to be designed impress individual ASEAN governments. By

December 1977 Hanoi had established diplomatic ties even with its histor-
ical rival Thailand, spasmodic obstacles created by the anti-Vietnamese
disposition of the Thai premier, Thanin Kravichien, notwithstanding.[13]
This development was paralleled by a diplomatic offensive *vis-à-vis*
ASEAN in the form of a spate of regional visits undertaken by Foreign
Minister Nguyen Duy Trinh in late 1977 and Foreign Minister Vo Dong
Giang (hitherto deputy foreign minister) in early 1978. It was at this point
in time that Vietnam appeared to be prepared formally to endorse
ZOPFAN.

Notwithstanding these developments, it is doubtful whether the ameliora-
tion of ties between ASEAN states and Vietnam up to this point, already
amounted to a commitment to ASEAN's diplomatic and security culture.
Indeed, it may be argued that Vietnam's efforts toward accommodation were
not genuine, but insincere and highly instrumental. Hanoi clearly needed to
overcome its problems of post-war economic reconstruction, and ASEAN's
dialogue relations with the industrialised world attracted Vietnam to the
Association. At the time Hanoi also required political, if not military,
support because Vietnam and the PRC were headed toward an imminent
crossing of swords over the ethnic Chinese problem in Vietnam and
Democratic Kampuchea (DK). Vietnam's regional diplomacy thus implied
less a willingness to recognise ASEAN's political identity and purpose than
an attempt to improve its chances to win the United States as a strategic
counterweight against a possible China-led encirclement and to enhance its
economic prospects. Aware of such considerations, ASEAN remained suspicious of the SRV, including Hanoi's apparent interest in acceding to the
TAC (Williams 1992: 71).

Within a year relations between ASEAN countries and Vietnam faltered.
This was due to the latter's military intervention in DK and the installation
of a client government in Phnom Penh, actions that were flagrantly at odds
with ASEAN's attempts to win endorsement for core norms associated with
the 'ASEAN way' as a framework for intra-regional relations.[14] In response,
ASEAN members re-evaluated their defence policies (Huxley 1984).
Vietnam's military presence in the People's Republic of Kampuchea (PRK)
was officially classified as an 'impediment' to the realisation of ZOPFAN
until Hanoi's troops were withdrawn, which occurred in the autumn of
1989.

ZOPFAN in the 1980s: development or stasis?

When ASEAN's diplomatic and security culture failed to emerge as the
accepted normative foundation for ASEAN–Indochina relations because of
Vietnam's challenge to its key norms and ASEAN's diplomatic manoeuvres
to reverse Hanoi's intervention in Cambodia, some ASEAN members
pressed for the further development of ZOPFAN's operational aspects. A
key instance in this regard was Indonesia's attempt to reinforce its

Archipelagic Principle,[15] which regards Indonesia's land area and waters as indivisible. Indonesia edged closer to international recognition of this principle with the 1982 United Nations Convention on the Law of the Sea (UNCLOS), which made allowance for archipelagic states, but at the time it had not come into force. In the event, Jakarta induced ASEAN to revive the Association's Working Group on ZOPFAN (WGZOFPAN) in order to study the feasibility of a Southeast Asia Nuclear Weapons Free Zone (SEANWFZ) as a component of ZOPFAN, an aspiration noted as early as 1971.

The proposal served both political and military security objectives. As regards the former, Indonesia was seen to pursue a stance of non-alignment by distancing itself from the rivalry between the two superpowers. In military security terms, Indonesia hoped to guard itself against the possibility that any incipient force modernisation and development of nuclear capabilities might lead to unwelcome regional powers steaming through the Indonesia archipelago (Kusuma-Atmadja 1993). In a sense, therefore, SEANWFZ thus served to reinforce the Archipelagic Principle. The SEANWFZ project did not elicit a positive response from the majority of ASEAN states, however. Members, like Thailand, Singapore and the Philippines, whose defence arrangements involved foreign powers or who otherwise had a particular interest in US deterrence were reluctant to antagonise Western nuclear states by promoting a proposal whose realisation might damage their security interests in more ways than one. The proposal was also seen as suffering from other limitations.

Insofar as the SEANWFZ proposal was designed to create a new reference point for making Indochina and Burma embrace ZOPFAN, it was irreconcilable with ASEAN's long-term insistence on the illegitimacy of the PRK (Alagappa 1987b). Moreover, the objective of establishing and winning respect for Southeast Asia as a nuclear weapons free zone by the major powers was even more ambitious than winning their respect for a firm commitment to what, after all, were only basic norms of international society. The United States, in particular, remained adamantly opposed to the proposal and argued that it would undermine its nuclear deterrence posture without constraining the Soviet Union. Following largely unsuccessful efforts to make significant headway on this issue, the Third ASEAN Summit Meeting, held in Manila in 1987, adopted an ASEAN Programme for Action concerning the implementation of ZOPFAN and SEANWFZ, even though many specifics, such as verification or compliance, had not been clarified. It was only in 1995 that ASEAN states, the Indochinese countries and Myanmar signed a treaty on the establishment of a regional nuclear weapons free zone. Significantly, the Association even then failed to win the necessary support for the zone from the nuclear powers. On the other hand, the treaty on SEANWFEZ illustrates once again the ability of Southeast Asian countries to arrive at broad compromises.

Vietnam–ASEAN reconciliation

The approach of the end of the Cold War induced Vietnamese leaders to seek reconciliation with ASEAN and develop co-operative relations with the grouping on the basis of the normative framework Hanoi had rejected a decade earlier. The first steps in Vietnam's foreign policy reorientation occurred a year after the Sixth National Party Congress of the VCP in December 1986, at which party leaders had decided to embark on a policy of *doi moi*, or renovation. Vietnam's strategic readjustment of its foreign relations, apparently decided in secret by the politburo in 1987 (Thayer 1999: 2–4), was subsequently, in May 1988, officially labelled 'multi-directional foreign policy'. This policy was subsequently revised at the Seventh National Party Congress in June 1991 to one of being 'friends with all countries' so as to better address the pressing problem of economic reconstruction and transformation. As noted, this problem had arisen as a consequence of Vietnam's costly military intervention in Cambodia and was further compounded when the Soviet Union scaled down the economic and financial support previously extended. Amicable relations with neighbouring states, so went the apparent official reasoning at the time, could help procure the requisite foreign investment that Vietnam depended on as a catalyst for the country's domestic reform process.

In the eyes of the Vietnamese government, moving closer and ultimately joining ASEAN would provide Vietnam with an opportunity to accede to the Asia-Pacific Economic Co-operation (APEC) Forum, formed in 1989, and to the General Agreement on Tariffs and Trade/World Trade Organisation (GATT/WTO).[16] GATT membership would imply the granting of Most Favoured Nation Status to Hanoi by Washington, a development coterminous with lower tariffs on Vietnamese exports to the United States and an end to trade discrimination for political reasons.[17] This was seen to entail trade diversion effects in Vietnam's advantage as well as better prospects for foreign direct investment (FDI) and technology transfer. At the same time, membership in ASEAN was desirable because ASEAN members' economic success and developmental strategy were worthy of at least partial emulation. Boosting socio-economic development was designed to help strengthen Vietnam's political system (and to secure the rule of the VCP), a project that Thaveeporn Vasavakul termed the 'third wave of state building in Vietnam since 1945' Vasavakul (1997). Vietnamese leaders also attached importance to embracing or joining the regional grouping as this would raise Hanoi's diplomatic prestige and transform its image. Finally, Vietnam also sought close ties with ASEAN to stymie Thailand's bid for sub-regional leadership in continental Southeast Asia in the early post-Cold War period.

Moving closer to ASEAN and invoking the latter's norms was also viewed as a double normative shield. On the one hand, this shield was to help protect Vietnam against criticisms by the United States on the human rights and democracy front. On the other hand, it was meant to protect against the continued external security threat that was seen to emanate from the PRC. The Chinese leadership had pursued a 'bleeding white strategy' towards Hanoi during the Cambodian conflict that it vowed to terminate only on the terms of the Chinese Communist Party (CCP). When the Cold War ended, China not only maintained military pressure on Vietnam's northern border, but also militarily confronted the Vietnamese navy in the Spratlys. This surprised some Vietnamese who had expected the bloody suppression of the street protests in China in 1989 to lead to a revival of an ideological alliance between the two sides.

There is no need to chronicle in detail here the process of rapprochement and reconciliation between the Association and the SRV.[18] It suffices to note that one important prerequisite for this development was Thai Premier Chatichai Choonhavan's new sub-regional policy, which stressed 'turning the Indochinese battlefields to marketplaces'. Still, ASEAN remained divided on the merits of closer ties with Vietnam for some time. However, a breakthrough occurred after the signing of the political settlement, which ended the Cambodian conflict. Hanoi acceded to the TAC on 21–22 July 1992, thereby winning immediate observer status in the Association. A number of unresolved issues then delayed Vietnam's accession to the Association, among which were disagreements over whether Hanoi's economic and political systems would have to undergo a fuller transformation. Other concerns centred on Vietnam's likely economic performance, its contribution to organisational stability and the possible implications for relations with China (Hoang Anh Tuan 1993: 287–8). The process formally ended with Hanoi's admission to ASEAN on 28 July 1995.

Hanoi had no objections to embracing ASEAN's diplomatic and security culture, particularly the legal-political norms, as the Cold War came to an end. To the extent that insecurity and estrangement between Vietnam and ASEAN remained, both could be mediated through the norms that had been accepted as the guide for interstate and interpersonal relations at leadership level within the Association. Given members' good overall record on adhering to the norms of sovereign equality and non-interference, VCP leaders had every right to expect that relations with Hanoi would be conducted on the same lines. Most of all, a commitment by ASEAN to its diplomatic and security culture *vis-à-vis* Vietnam implied that the Association would neither want to nor be in a position to pressure Hanoi into changing the nature of the governing regime. By the same token, of course, the commitment by Vietnamese leaders to the same norm was also understood to translate into their acceptance that it would no longer be politically feasible for them to challenge the legitimacy of the Association and the various political regimes of its member states. Vietnam's commitment to the TAC was thus the first major step in the process of reconciliation that was concluded with full membership.

As we have noted, in giving organisational expression to its reconciliation with Vietnam along these lines, ASEAN leaders decided to give preference to the process of expansion of the Association over the alternative idea of creating a separate regional construct in Southeast Asia alongside ASEAN (Hänggi 1992: 196–7). Some within the Association with a strong interest in quickly developing regional economic co-operation and integration had favoured proposals for an organisationally autonomous mechanism that might not involve an expansion in ASEAN membership. It is significant that those who instead favoured the option of replicating the experience of the early ASEAN years, focusing on confidence and consensus building as had been done in order to incorporate Indonesia into Southeast Asian regionalism, ultimately won the argument. As regards the economic dimension of ASEAN co-operation, the ASEAN governments agreed that all new members would be obliged to respect the provisions for an ASEAN Free Trade Area (AFTA), albeit on different timetables.[19] Significantly, even before ASEAN's rapprochement and reconciliation with Vietnam and Laos proceeded apace, developments in the wider East Asia also needed attention. Increasingly, problems of regional order could no longer be conceptualised only with reference to Southeast Asia. In this context, the question arose as to how ASEAN would relate to the major powers in the emerging post-Cold War world.

ASEAN's response to the strategic context of the post-Cold War period

The major strategic change perceived by ASEAN leaders as the Cold War unwound was US disengagement from Southeast and East Asia.[20] This was significant insofar as the United States had for some years acted as a benign hegemon in the region. In particular, during the latter Cold War period the US had proved a reliable provider of external security for the ASEAN states. The withdrawal of US forces and the closure, for different reasons, of American bases in the Philippines seemed to lead to a possible strategic vacuum in East Asia. To the extent that an American forward military presence in the Western Pacific remained in place, doubts were voiced over its sustainability and credibility (da Cunha 1993). Moreover, some doubts over whether the US would continue to protect essentially pro-American governments in Southeast Asia (ASEAN-6) were raised as a result of Washington's much stronger promotion of democracy and human rights than before the end of the Cold War. (ASEAN-6 refers to the first six members of the Association. In view of ASEAN's successive enlargement, one distinguishes ASEAN-5, ASEAN-6, ASEAN-9 and ASEAN-10.)

In the context of Washington's perceived disengagement from the region, the increased strategic latitude of the PRC posed the key challenge for ASEAN leaderships within the context of an apparent shift in the balance of power. China had become increasingly assertive in pursuing its territorial and jurisdictional claims in the South China Sea, which ASEAN countries found to be at odds with a call for joint development there made by Premier

Li Peng during his visit to Singapore in August 1990. China's ties with Thailand and Myanmar also raised disquiet among some Southeast Asian leaderships. As regards Thailand, the creation of a Chinese-supplied arms stockpile in Thailand suggested a possible continuation of the Sino–Thai special relationship after the end of the Cambodian conflict. China's close political and military relations with the widely ostracised military regime Burma/Myanmar also indicated Beijing's growing influence in continental Southeast Asia. Several ASEAN governments felt that China should clarify its regional intentions, while simultaneously making known their views.[21] Most significant, in this regard, were perceived encroachments by the PRC into the South China Sea.

Japan was also the subject of ASEAN concerns. These also arose in the context of what ASEAN leaders perceived as US disengagement from East Asia. They centred, in part, on the possibility of Japan's military rearmament. One reason for this was that Tokyo was regarded as having an increasing interest in protecting regional international shipping routes in the event of an American strategic withdrawal, as its economy was entirely dependent on them. Another reason for heightened concern stemmed from the assumption that Japan might seek to play a more assertive security role in the Pacific in the event of US disengagement. Tokyo's participation in peacekeeping activities of the UN Transitional Authority in Cambodia (UNTAC) was seen as evidence for Japan's growing assertiveness in regional security, even if its part in this operation was low key. Lee Kuan Yew, in particular, argued that Japan's role in UNTAC might lead to the shedding of its self-imposed restraint. Such a development was widely regarded as likely to accentuate Sino–Japanese rivalry and initiate an arms race ('chain reaction' hypothesis).

Notably, concern over the contours of a future pan-regional order grew as the perceived strategic shifts were also accompanied by an apparent shift in the distribution of economic power in the East Asia-Pacific region. Not least owing to the conclusion of the North American Free Trade Area (NAFTA), US economic interests in East Asia were regarded as on the decline, while Japan's economic performance appeared to be sparkling. In this context, analysts also noted growing trade frictions between the US and East Asian countries that were pursuing export-led economic development and thus depended on access to the US market, leaving the former to demand 'managed trade'. In the view of some, especially in Singapore, Washington's relative lack of success in opening up East Asian markets on its terms further accentuated apprehension about a possible US strategic disengagement.

In view of the need to address the problem of regional order, it is not surprising that some within ASEAN should have turned to the ZOPFAN concept as a possible framework guiding interstate relations in East Asia. Significantly, some momentum in favour of ZOPFAN had built up in the preceding years. Soviet leader Mikhail Gorbachev had unreservedly endorsed ZOPFAN, as well as the establishment of a nuclear-free zone, at the time of the 1987 ASEAN summit. He had also offered to pull out of the Camh Ranh base in return for the closure of American bases on the Philippines (Buszynski 1992c). Reacting to domestic and Indonesian pressure to pursue a more non-aligned foreign policy, the newly elected president, Corazon Aquino, and her foreign minister, Raul Manglapus, seemed by 1987 to have moved the Philippines somewhat closer to embracing ZOPFAN than was the case under the Marcos regime. This was linked to strong domestic pressure to remove the neo-colonial vestige of American bases that many regarded as reinforcing the image of Philippine weakness (Simon 1989; Solidum 1988; Buszynski 1988: 82–5). Moreover, the complete withdrawal of Vietnamese troops from Cambodia in the autumn of 1989 eliminated much of what ASEAN had consistently referred to as the 'impediment to the early realization of ZOPFAN'. Despite these developments, the notion that ZOPFAN could provide the basis for a wider regional order was in many ways a non-starter.

The post-Cold War ASEAN 'debate' on ZOPFAN

One of the reasons the concept of ZOPFAN was debated at all by ASEAN leaders was that not to do so would have been tantamount to a loss of face for the Malaysian and Indonesian governments, which had hitherto ardently subscribed to the ZOPFAN formula. To the extent that ASEAN members had – at least in declaratory terms – sought to insulate Southeast Asia from the travails of the major powers when the Kuala Lumpur Declaration was passed, this idea was rejected by all ASEAN countries at the end of the Cold War. Even Kuala Lumpur and Jakarta proposed the 'actualisation' of ZOPFAN. This implied that rather than insulating Southeast Asia from major power interference the latter were to be engaged. Also, the 'actualisation' of ZOPFAN was to be compatible with ASEAN members' security and defence links and co-operation (Muhammad Ghazali Shafie 1992: 40, 42). Foreign bases would henceforth only be rejected if their control entailed extra-territoriality. In other words, security co-operation with friendly powers was to be fully endorsed. It is noteworthy in this context that Malaysia, which increasingly regarded itself as the new 'frontline state' in view of Chinese actions in the South China Sea, suddenly announced previously unreported security co-operation with the United States since the 1970s and 1980s (Buszynski 1992a: 846; also see J. D. Young 1992). It also expressed satisfaction with the utility of the FPDA (Najib Tun Razak 1995: 49–52). And it accepted that Singapore's offer to Washington of moving a command task force responsible for repair and resupply of the American Seventh Fleet from Subic Bay to Singapore did not violate ZOPFAN premises. Notably, Jakarta endorsed the legitimacy and utility of ASEAN states' 'places, not bases' strategy, particularly because of the perceived contradictions between Beijing's declaratory policy and its efforts to reclaim territory and jurisdiction in the South China Sea.

Singapore's decision-makers had perhaps the strongest reservations about the revival of ZOPFAN. This is not to say that Singapore's leaders no longer wished to win respect for ASEAN norms integrated into the ZOPFAN formula. Indeed, Singapore regarded compliance with international norms such as the non-use of force, sovereign equality and non-interference as an element in its security strategy for the city-state. Yet in this regard the ZOPFAN Declaration was not of much value as it did not involve any commitments by the major powers. To Singapore, moreover, a reinvigoration of the ZOPFAN discourse, especially given its widespread association among scholars, journalists and extra-regional decision-makers with the termination of a foreign military presence, was thus seen to be counterproductive. Its leaders wanted the United States to remain engaged in the region, not least to avert an unpalatable local hegemony.

The Paris Peace Accords of 23 October 1991 failed to breathe much life into the intramural debate on ZOPFAN.[22] Indeed, the accords ironically linked Cambodia's internal and external neutrality in a way that revealed more parallels with the approach to realising Malaysia's original neutralisation formula for Southeast than with ZOPFAN. Enthusiasm for ZOPFAN was not revived when China endorsed it at the 1992 ASEAN Ministerial Meeting. Indeed, by this time the early post-Cold War developments and the perception of threat that these generated within ASEAN made implausible any notion of the groupings' yearning for an autonomously managed regional order. This raises the question of how ASEAN dealt practically with the strategic uncertainty and security challenges of the early post-Cold War period.

Addressing changes in the regional balance of power

As we have seen, ASEAN decided to expand its membership to include Vietnam as the first Indochinese entrant into the Association in the aftermath of the collapse of the Soviet Union. While this step was a move towards less instability for Southeast Asia and had the potential to increase ASEAN's wider regional clout, it was nevertheless insufficient. As Michael Leifer argued at the time:

> A structure of intra-mural conciliation may be widened, and a collective diplomatic voice may be strengthened. These are desirable outcomes in themselves but they do not necessarily provide the building blocs for a new regional order in the post-Cold War era.
>
> (Leifer 1993: 276)

The problem of regional order as it presented itself to ASEAN was essentially one of creating a stable balance of power between the principal states in East

Asia that would not disadvantage ASEAN. Or, as Indonesia's foreign minister, Ali Alatas, put it, an 'equilibrium among them [the major powers] and between them and Southeast Asia' (quoted in Acharya 1993: 57). The under-lying thinking in terms of the balance of power was perhaps most visible in the thinking of Singapore decision-makers. Not dissimilar notions of equidis-tance were also very much shared by the Malaysian prime minister, Mahathir Mohamed, and Indonesia's President Suharto (Leifer 1999b; Acharya 1999a). The perceived need for a stable balance of power was predicated on the under-standing that the post-Cold War era was unlikely to presage an end to major power rivalry in East Asia. ASEAN leaders also recognised that Southeast Asia could not be isolated from any rivalry among East Asia's major powers. In this context, two options presented themselves. One was to strengthen intramural security and defence co-operation in ways that would raise ASEAN's standing as a political-military power. The other centred on extending the model of ASEAN's interactions with the wider region.

Intramural multilateral security co-operation

From the establishment of ASEAN until the end of the Cold War, security co-operation within the Association had been primarily limited to bilateral border security activities. Singapore's prime minister had called for multilat-eral military exercises among ASEAN members in the early part of the Cambodian conflict, but this proposal had been rejected. In view of the post-Cold War strategic and security context and the challenge this posed for regional order, the idea of an ASEAN defence arrangement attracted considerably more attention than in the past. The Philippines, for instance, advocated the creation of an ASEAN defence committee or regional secu-rity forum because it lacked a credible defence capability. Various distinguished members of Indonesia's foreign policy and security establish-ment made similar proposals.

In the event, ASEAN leaders reacted to shifts in the regional balance of power by modernising and enhancing their respective military capabilities (Chin Kin Wah 1987; Acharya 1994) without developing closer military ties at multilateral level. Indonesia's then foreign minister, Ali Alatas, opposed the idea of an ASEAN military pact or similar, as both Malaysia and Singapore viewed such a proposal with suspicion. Malaysia's lack of enthu-siasm for multilateral, or even trilateral, defence co-operation among the states that Donald Emmerson called a 'provisionally emerging regional secu-rity core' (Emmerson 1996a: 83) was built on apprehensions that such a development might undermine Malaysia's special relationship with Indonesia to Singapore's advantage. Malaysian leaders at the time were already intensely suspicious of Singapore after an alleged spying incident in 1990, which led to the temporary suspension of the two countries' bilateral defence co-operation. Kuala Lumpur suggested as an alternative to broader intramural defence co-operation the introduction of more extensive bilateral

security co-operation among ASEAN states and emphasised its commitment to the FPDA. Singapore leaders meanwhile worried that the
establishment of an ASEAN defence mechanism might lead to an unpalatable surrender of sovereignty to the grouping in general and to Indonesia, as
ASEAN's informal leader, in particular. For its part, following its experiences during the Cambodian conflict Thailand's military had less than full
confidence in the sustainability of multilateral ASEAN defence co-operation
and preferred to rely on a continued American security presence.

Ultimately proposals in favour of an ASEAN defence arrangement did
not formally founder on the rocks of intramural suspicion. Rather, those
who contended that the formation of a quasi-alliance would impede rather
than promote a constructive dialogue with China won the public argument. Moreover, it was argued that if China perceived that ASEAN
wanted to counterbalance or contain Beijing it would be less likely that
China would respect the norms of non-interference and non-use of force
as well as restraint in resolving disputes. Also, few of the ASEAN countries that had just established or normalised relations with the People's
Republic – such as Singapore and Indonesia – were reluctant to put the
relationship with Beijing at risk, both for economic and political reasons.
The question thus became how to practically engage the major powers in a
way that would help create a stable balance of power among them while
simultaneously allowing ASEAN to enhance its regional influence and
security.

Locus and framework for East Asian security co-operation

Singapore, above all, has been credited with forging a structure for a multilateral security dialogue which is meant to uphold the 'regional distribution
of power through political means' (Leifer 2000: 135). This goal clearly
served the interests of Singapore, but to the extent that the establishment of
such a dialogue was designed to reinforce or accentuate ASEAN's regional
diplomatic role, it also drew support from other member states, particularly
Indonesia.

ASEAN governments announced at the 1992 ASEAN Summit in the
Singapore Declaration that to strengthen the effort of promoting external
dialogues on enhancing regional security the Association would 'intensify its
external dialogues in political and security matters by using the ASEAN
Post-Ministerial Conferences (PMC)' (ASEAN 1992). In doing so, they took
up a proposal from the Institutes of International and Strategic Studies in
ASEAN states (ASEAN–ISIS 1991) that the existing structure of the
ASEAN PMC would be the forum best suited for this purpose. The utility of
the PMC structure was proven and useful, not least because it brought
together key Pacific Rim states and the grouping would be able to influence,
if not control, the agenda and the ground rules of interaction of the security
dialogues.

This was neither the first time the PMC had been put forward as an adequate setting to engage in dialogue with other regional states, nor indeed the first proposal from within East Asia that a regional political-security dialogue should take place. In June 1989 Ali Alatas had suggested an expansion of the PMC (Buszynski 1992b: 102). Also, Japan's foreign minister, Taro Nakayama, had proposed the establishment of a forum for political dialogue at the 1991 PMC. Significantly, the major powers accepted ASEAN's proposal, with the United States giving it an enthusiastic response. By coincidence, it fell to Singapore, as the chair of the ASEAN standing committee for the period from July 92 to July 93, to flesh out the mandate given by ASEAN heads of state/government the previous January.

In the event, Singapore proposed that a meeting bringing together the most senior foreign ministry officials from the ASEAN states and the Association's dialogue partners be organised before the annual meeting of ASEAN foreign ministers in July 1993. With the blessing of both Washington and Jakarta this proposal was then altered to include in this meeting senior officials from Vietnam, Laos and Russia (Leifer 2000: 135). The Senior Officials' Meeting (SOM) was a unblemished diplomatic victory for Singapore insofar as the officials agreed that '[t]he continuing presence of the United States, as well as stable relationships among the USA, Japan and China, and other states of the region would contribute to regional stability' (quoted in Leifer 1996b: 24). This consensus paved the way for a diplomatic effort to engage all major regional powers simultaneously through a structure of interaction that was to be modelled on ASEAN's own experience. At the subsequent ASEAN Ministerial Meeting in Singapore foreign ministers inaugurated the ASEAN Regional Forum (ARF) as the future venue for regional security dialogues.[23] The ARF convened for its first working session in July 1994.

The ARF's proposed normative framework

Singapore officials had not presented a lead on the terms of reference for the interactions of ARF members when a decision on the latter's inauguration was taken. Such proposed terms were only spelled out in the 1995 ASEAN Regional Forum Concept Paper (ARF 1995) put forward in the name of the then chair of the ASEAN Standing Committee (ASC), Brunei Darussalam, even though the final draft had been prepared in Singapore. The ASEAN Concept Paper for the ARF stressed the gradual evolution of security co-operation from confidence building via preventive diplomacy to the elaboration of approaches to conflicts. It appealed to all ARF members to associate themselves with the TAC. As regards the latter, ASEAN had notably managed to win an endorsement of the TAC 'as a code of conduct governing relations between states and a unique instrument for regional confidence-building, preventive diplomacy, and political and security co-operation' in the first ARF ministerial meeting in Bangkok (ARF 1994). Significantly, the Concept Paper also highlighted the importance of developing confidence among regional countries and furthering preventive diplomacy on the basis of ASEAN's diplomatic culture, as stipulated in its Annex A.

In effect, this meant that ASEAN was seeking respect for basic norms of international society as the foundation for political and security co-operation in East Asia more generally, and as the terms of reference for the immediate workings of the ARF more particularly. There were probably several reasons for emphasising these norms. First, ASEAN states considered respect for these norms to be important for peaceful and stable relations among regional states, not least because of the number of existing conflicts. According to Amitav Acharya, underlying ASEAN's initiative 'was an assumption that its norms, such as the non-use of force, consultations and consensus, and the ASEAN Way of socialisation could be adopted and employed as the building block of a regional security community in the wider Asia Pacific region' (Acharya 2001: 166–7).

Respect for norms such as sovereign equality and non-interference have also been seen as delegitimising challenges to the distinct political identities of individual ASEAN states. The calculation was no doubt that to the extent that ASEAN could win firm endorsements to these norms and related diplomatic processes by the major powers, the political costs of the latter not adhering to them *vis-à-vis* ASEAN countries would significantly increase. Singapore had already been concerned for some time about a transparent and agreed normative framework for the interactions between ASEAN and the regional major powers. This was illustrated by its earlier proposal that the five Permanent Members of the UN Security Council sign the TAC. However, with an eye to the provisions on the ASEAN High Council in the TAC, Indonesia had at the time resisted this proposal, for fear of *inviting* interference by the major powers in the internal affairs of the Association or its member states.

By deciding to organise multilateral security dialogues along the lines of previous ASEAN intramural experience and central features of the Association's diplomatic and security culture, it rejected in practical terms proposals to replicate the institutional experience of the Conference on Security and Co-operation in Europe (CSCE) (P. Cronin 1992). Such proposals had been associated with Soviet President Mikhail Gorbachev and Australia's foreign minister, Gareth Evans. These proposals, however, were viewed as essentially too structured and formalistic, not least because they went against the grain of ASEAN's diplomatic and security culture and were perceived as eclipsing the role and significance of the Association to the advantage of the major powers. ASEAN did, however, embrace and develop the concept of co-operative security that had been proposed as a new approach to Asia-Pacific security by Canada's foreign minister, Joe Clark.

As the foregoing discussion has demonstrated there are at least two significant differences between the ZOPFAN concept and the ARF process, the joint emphasis on basic international norms notwithstanding. First, the ARF explicitly seeks the inclusion and presence of the major powers in Southeast Asia, whereas ZOPFAN stood for the detachment of Southeast Asia from major power rivalry and interference in any manner or form. Second, the ARF process has been about the successful involvement of the regional major powers in practical regional norm-elaboration processes that have built on norms associated with ASEAN's diplomatic and security culture. ASEAN had completely failed on this score in the 1970s.

Significantly, what in the ZOPFAN Declaration was the second operational objective – enhanced regional economic co-operation – has in the post-Cold war period also been pursued with more vigour than at any time previously. By the early 1990s, ASEAN had decided between three proposals, a proposal for a Common Effective Preferential Tariff (proposed by Indonesia), an ASEAN Economic Treaty (supported by the Philippines) and an ASEAN Free Trade Area (AFTA). The last idea had been revived by the Thai prime minister, Anand Panyarachun, and was supported by both Goh Chok Tong and Dr Mahathir Mohamad, the latter having earlier proposed an East Asian Economic Grouping (EAEG) that would also have included Japan, China and Korea as a counterpoint to APEC.[24] In the event, Thailand's proposal for the creation of AFTA was accepted at the 23rd ASEAN Economic Ministers Meeting in October 1991. One purpose of AFTA was to avoid allowing existing market forces to draw ASEAN economies too close to the economies of Northeast Asia, given the potential for the outbreak of economic conflict, especially between Japan and the United States. By establishing AFTA, ASEAN hoped to further improve its competitiveness to remain a platform for exports. AFTA thus had not merely an economic, but also a security objective, as economic security was seen as reinforcing political security. Intensified economic co-operation would also strengthen ASEAN's struggle for recognition and influence as a grouping in the wider region.

The nagging security problem

Although the establishment of the ARF has involved an attempt to push a particular normative framework to underpin regional political and security co-operation, there has been evidence of disillusionment among ASEAN countries about the likelihood of its full acceptance.[25] In December 1995, for instance, Indonesia signed an unprecedented security agreement with Australia that betrayed a limited trust in prospects for China's socialisation as a regional good citizen who would respect the core norms of the 'ASEAN way'.[26] Other ASEAN countries similarly emphasised the value of their bilateral or multilateral external security links, such as the FPDA (P. Young 1997; for a previous assessment also see Chin Kin Wah 1991). This shows the limits of ASEAN's struggle for security through winning respect for basic norms. Michael Leifer (1999a) argued that to conceptualise the 'ASEAN way' as a model of security was to commit a 'category mistake'. Notably, even if ASEAN governments themselves do not ascribe a sufficient deterrence function to norms of the 'ASEAN way' in their external relations, these norms continue to be viewed as a framework that serves to mediate insecurity and estrangement and in which political and security co-operation can and should occur.

Conclusion

This chapter has argued that, certain passages in the Bangkok Declaration notwithstanding, ASEAN leaders' first major attempts to win respect from the major regional states for the principle of non-interference were linked to changes in the strategic environment in the late 1960s and early 1970s. The emergence of China in particular had given rise for concern. Malaysia's neutralisation proposal was conceptually transformed into the ZOPFAN Declaration, whose meaning was then further explicated over the years. Notably, neither the regional major powers nor the Indochinese countries, albeit for different reasons, initially endorsed ZOPFAN as a framework for political and security co-operation with the ASEAN states. In the post-Cold War period ASEAN no longer focused on ZOPFAN to respond to the question of how to engage, if possible, the major powers. However, the normative framework embedded within ZOPFAN and later rearticulated in the TAC served as the foundation for the process of reconciliation between Vietnam and ASEAN. It was also transferred to proposals of how participants in the ARF should interact. Significantly, ASEAN has not relied on respect for the 'ASEAN way' to safeguard its external security against the potential threats emanating from changes in ASEAN's strategic environment. Throughout its existence its members have relied on the United States as the chief provider of regional security. While this chapter has been about how ASEAN has endeavoured to win respect for aspects of ASEAN's diplomatic and security culture beyond the confines of the original membership, it has also noted that regional conflict emerged when Vietnam's sense of entitlement collided with ASEAN's struggle for security and recognition. We shall return to this relationship in Chapter 4 with reference to the conflict in Kampuchea/Cambodia. As we shall see, the dual struggle for security and recognition may both reinforce and challenge the 'ASEAN way'.

4 The Cambodian conflict and the 'ASEAN way'

The struggle for a pristine interpretation of principles

On 25 December the People's Army of Vietnam (PAV) and the Kampuchean People's Revolutionary Armed Forces invaded Democratic Kampuchea. Synthesising scholarly work on this issue, three reasons appear to have particularly salient. First, Democratic Kampuchea engaged in sustained political and military provocations against Vietnam, involving territorial incursions, the killing of perhaps hundreds, if not several thousand, Vietnamese, and the destruction of arable land and harvests. In part, these provocations by the Khmer Rouge derived from longstanding grievances against perceived territorial annexations of land considered integral to Cambodia and from a resurgent (but manipulated) sentiment that the Vietnamese Communists sought to enslave, if not annihilate, the Khmer people. The second reason stemmed from a prevailing sense of strategic vulnerability on the part of the leadership of the VCP that was accentuated as perceptions of Vietnam's encirclement by China and Democratic Kampuchea became more and more pronounced (Gilks 1992; Chang Paomin 1985). Third, the Khmer Rouge and VCP leaders failed to agree on proper relationships between themselves and with others because of their different models of revolution, worldviews and divergent security interests. Arguably, Hanoi's leaders had not abandoned the historically entrenched notion of an Indochina Federation under Vietnamese leadership.

The Vietnamese ousting of the Khmer Rouge and the installation of a client government, the Kampuchean People's Revolutionary Council, shocked ASEAN governments. Indeed, the Vietnamese invasion engendered among ASEAN leaders a pronounced sense of betrayal. This happened especially because of the prime minister, Pham Van Dong's, reassurances that he would respect the independence, sovereignty and territorial integrity of each Southeast Asian country only weeks prior to his country's armed intervention in Cambodia (Leifer 1989: 90; van der Kroef 1979: 165–6). The depth of ASEAN consternation and outrage at Vietnam's armed intervention was probably intensified by the embarrassment of having incorrectly calculated that Hanoi's future influence on Southeast Asia would likely be benign by virtue of Hanoi's expected preoccupation with the formidable challenge of her post-war economic reconstruction (Jackson 1982: 127–8).

shows weakness

Given that Vietnam's 'betrayal' also constituted a brazen violation of Article 2(4) and Article 2(7) of the UN Charter, the Association's immediate response to events in Kampuchea proved relatively restrained.[2] In a statement issued on behalf of the ASEAN Standing Committee, Indonesia's foreign minister, Mochtar Kusuma-Atmadja, expressed regret at the escalation and enlargement of the conflict between 'the two states in Indochina'. He also called on both parties to respect each other's independence, sovereignty, territorial integrity and political system, and to refrain from using or threatening to use force (ASEAN 1979a). Two days after the establishment of the People's Republic of Kampuchea (PRK), ASEAN 'strongly deplored the armed intervention against the independence, sovereignty and territorial integrity of Kampuchea' and called for the 'immediate and total withdrawal of the foreign forces' from Kampuchean territory (ASEAN 1979b). The call was repeated following the signing of the 25-year treaty of friendship, peace and co-operation between the PRK and the SRV and the launching by China in February 1979 of a 'punitive attack' on Vietnam. These pronouncements marked the beginning of more than ten years of sustained and intense diplomatic activity by the Association with the aim of securing the withdrawal of Vietnamese troops from Kampuchea and the right of the Cambodian people to self-determination free from external interference and coercion. ASEAN was particularly successful in mobilising international opinion and votes in the UN General Assembly against the intervention. This ultimately earned it the label of 'diplomatic community' (Leifer 1989: ch. 3), notwithstanding the fact that the final settlement of the Cambodian conflict depended crucially on the political will of the five Permanent Members of the UN Security Council (P5).[3]

The main purpose of this chapter is not to describe ASEAN's contribution to finding a settlement to the Cambodian issue,[4] or to explore any of the problems encountered by the United Nations Transitional Authority in Cambodia after the signing of the Paris Peace accords in 1991.[5] Instead, the chapter seeks to explore to what extent the intervention in Cambodia and the diplomatic efforts undertaken to arrive at a political settlement of the Cambodia issue entailed indirect and intramural challenges to the unambiguous validity of core norms of ASEAN's diplomatic and security culture. In other words, the chapter examines the resilience of the 'ASEAN way' in the context of ASEAN's well-known intramural differences over how to deal with Vietnam's intervention in Kampuchea. 'Resilience' will be understood here as solidarity in upholding an unsullied interpretation of the validity of principles associated with the 'ASEAN way'. ASEAN's ability to sustain in solidarity its insistence on a rigorous and uncompromising application of a pristine understanding of the principles in question (primarily non-use of force, non-intervention) is viewed here as a test of their overall relevance and meaning to ASEAN decision-makers in the conduct of international politics.[6]

The chapter will be divided into five sections. The first examines the reasons why ASEAN members espoused divergent views on Hanoi's intervention in Kampuchea, yet jointly called for the withdrawal of Vietnamese troops from Kampuchea and decried the illegitimacy of the Heng Samrin regime. The second section discusses ASEAN's diplomatic strategy *vis-à-vis* Vietnam and the PRK to reverse the Vietnamese intervention in Kampuchea, and the challenges inherent in Indonesian and Malaysian alternative proposals to reach a political settlement with Vietnam. The third section examines why Indonesia and Malaysia effectively deferred to the Thai–Singapore stand on Kampuchea until the mid-1980s, when Jakarta began to pursue vigorously the idea of informal talks between the Cambodian parties without preconditions. The fourth section examines to what extent Jakarta's pursuit of cocktail diplomacy represented an intramural challenge to an unsullied interpretation of core principles linked to ASEAN's diplomatic and security culture and how other member states reacted to the proposal in the context of emerging major strategic changes. The final section explores to what extent the process and the final outcome of the Paris Peace negotiations still entailed challenges to core principles of ASEAN's diplomatic and security culture.

ASEAN members' reactions to Vietnam's intervention

A complex mix of considerations underpinned ASEAN members' individual responses to Vietnam's intervention in Cambodia. As we shall see, members' reactions were shaped by security concerns, political considerations and a sense of moral outrage engendered by the violation of ASEAN's conception of regional order.

Thai leaders have historically been sensitive to land-based threats to their country's security. Indeed, preserving both (parts of) Laos and Cambodia as (suzerain) buffers had historically registered as a significant theme in Thai foreign and security policy. This was illustrated, for instance, by Thailand's willingness to reassess ties with the United States over the issue of Laos' neutrality in the early 1960s (Nuechterlein 1965: 182–220). Not surprisingly, therefore, Bangkok's military establishment had major concerns about the impact of the invasion of Democratic Kampuchea, given that the two countries shared a 798-kilometre border. However, the fear of invasion did not rank as the most pressing concern for the Thai military at the time, despite Thai leaders' mindfulness that Vietnam might seek revenge for Thailand's involvement in the Vietnam War, as then Commander-in-Chief General Chavalit Yongchaiyuth later stressed. Bangkok had a formal military alliance, and it also sought security guarantees from China to deter an attack on the kingdom (Leifer 1989: 137). As Muthiah Alagappa has argued, the primary security threat arising from Vietnam's invasion of Cambodia was instead to Thailand's political and social stability (Alagappa 1987a). The violation of Thailand's strategic environment also had political ramifications, however, since removing Cambodia as a buffer carried symbolic significance unpalatable to the Thai politico-military establishment in the context of the historical rivalry with Vietnam.

To the extent that the invasion of Democratic Kampuchea posed further sustained security problems, these related more to the exodus by tens of thousands of Cambodian refugees into northeast Thailand, including members of the anti-Vietnamese resistance.[7] This raised the possibility of direct fighting between Vietnamese and Thai forces on Thai soil.[8] Such fears were justified, as subsequent Vietnamese strikes at sanctuaries and supplies of the Khmer Rouge resistance forces in Thailand would show (Tongdhamachart 1982: 78). However, these incursions were also a direct response to what Michael Leifer termed Thailand's 'practice of flawed neutrality' (Leifer 1982: 20), expressed, among others things, in the transit of arms shipments from the PRC to the Khmer Rouge.[9] In addition, some decision-makers similarly worried about the security threats emanating from the presence of several thousand Hmong refugees in Thailand. For instance, it was feared that their presence might provoke Lao irredentism towards the Lao-speaking provinces of northeast Thailand and that this might, in turn, serve as a pretext for Vietnam to intervene in Thailand's domestic affairs (Stuart-Fox 1982: 219).

Singapore

While Singapore was not directly threatened by the presence of Vietnamese troops in Cambodia because of its distant geographical location, its leadership found Vietnam's intervention to have seriously impaired regional stability and security. Hanoi's expulsion of the nationalistic Khmer Rouge regime implied the loss of a buffer against what Singapore's leadership saw as Soviet-led expansionist communism (B. Singh 1990). Although the city-state had in the past been supportive of Moscow's presence in Southeast Asia, Singapore's security interests by then strongly militated against enhanced Soviet influence in Indochina. The military alliance between Hanoi and Moscow was viewed not only as shifting the regional balance of power in favour of the Soviet Union, but also as turning Southeast Asia into a cockpit of Sino–Soviet rivalry. This rivalry was bound to play on the Chinese factor, with possible implications for ethnic and bilateral relations in Southeast Asia.

In this context, Singapore's leadership became particularly vocal about the influx from Vietnam of ethnic Chinese refugees into Malaysia and Indonesia. The refugee crisis was perceived as a tool which might potentially accentuate ethnic division and endanger the growing prosperity and socio-political stability of Singapore's Malay neighbours, which could, in turn, spill over into bilateral relations with Singapore (Rajaratnam 1979; ASEAN 1979c; ASEAN 1979d). Singapore had gone to significant lengths to propagate and foster a 'Singaporean' rather than Chinese identity in view of the suspicions harboured by its regional neighbours in relation to the

Chinese living both within and without their boundaries (Hill and Lian Kwen Fee 1995). Foreign Minister S. Rajaratnam gave lucid expression to Singapore's threat perception when he referred to the enormous outflow of ethnic Chinese refugees from Indochina as 'human bombs'. Indeed, the PAP leadership had few qualms in depicting Vietnam as a 'combat state' to highlight the degree of the alleged regional threat emanating from a Moscow-backed Hanoi. Later Rajaratnam would argue that Hanoi's objective had been to see whether the Association was 'mush or steel' (Rajaratnam 1987: 397).

A very important rationale of Singapore leadership's emphatic opposition to Vietnam's intervention in Cambodia concerned the possible ramifications for Singapore's security from Hanoi's intervention in Kampuchea. Indeed, events in Kampuchea demonstrated to Singapore that the use of force and the violation of territorial integrity still played a significant part in international affairs. Acquiescing to Vietnam's intervention would also amount to the recognition of a 'new code of conduct' in Southeast Asia that would give a country the right to invade another country and to set up a puppet government. As Bilveer Singh put it, 'If the Vietnamese and the Soviets were able to get the international bodies to accept Heng Samrin, it would be tantamount to an acceptance that might is right. No small, weak nation would be secure' (B. Singh 1990: 30). Singapore could not accept such a development under any circumstances, even if it had previously not been so harsh a public critic of Indonesia's intervention in East Timor. Whereas special circumstances and the importance of good relations with Indonesia had led Singapore to allow for a strategically less serious infraction of the premises of regional order, it was felt that it could not do the same with regard to the Soviet-backed Vietnamese intervention in Kampuchea. To do so might be to give carte blanche to any potentially aggressive regional government that might seek in the future either to intimidate the city-state politically or to violate its physical integrity.

Indonesia

Indonesia's position on Vietnam's intervention in Cambodia was one of ambivalence, which was attributable to the bureaucratic rivalry of the Ministry of Foreign Affairs (DEPLU) and Indonesia's Armed Forces (ABRI). DEPLU joined the ASEAN chorus of concern over Hanoi's infringement of ASEAN's proposed normative framework for regional co-existence and co-operation in Southeast Asia. The sympathies for Vietnam within sections of ABRI, however, extended from voicing understanding for Vietnam's intervention in Cambodia to comments that Vietnam had a right to unify Indochina under its leadership (Suryadinata 1996: 128) After all, Indonesia had incorporated within its territorial boundaries not only the entire territorial configuration of the former Dutch East Indies, but also the former Portuguese colony of East Timor. Moreover, Vietnam was perceived as a fervently nationalist country despite Hanoi's embrace of Moscow, as illustrated by its long and, in human terms, costly struggle for independence.

Underlying Indonesia's ambivalence were also different perceptions of China's and Vietnam's respective threat potential to Indonesia. Relations between Hanoi and Jakarta had become strained but were not frozen in the aftermath of the 1965 Gestapu affair and the dissolution of the Jakarta–Hanoi–PhnomPenh–Beijing–Pyongyang axis forged under Sukarno. The suspicions some military leaders entertained *vis-à-vis* North Vietnam until 1976 focused in particular on Vietnam's dual-track policy towards Indonesia, which involved support for the remnants of the PKI by the VCP, as well as for the *Frente Revolucionara do Timor Leste Independente* (FRETILIN). With the worsening of the Sino–Vietnamese conflict, however, and Hanoi's reduction of its political support for FRETILIN in 1978, a major easing of bilateral tensions followed (Suryadinata 1991: 335–6). Significantly, any fear on the part of Jakarta's elites that Hanoi might seek to promote communist rebellion never outstripped fears regarding China, which fed on perceptions of the historical expansionism of China during the Yuan Dynasty under Kubilai Khan and those of the ethnic Chinese community in Indonesia (Sukma 1999: 54–8).

Indeed, the historical memories and suspicions of the PRC as an interventionist state had been reactivated in the late 1950s over the question of the treatment of overseas Chinese, Beijing's support for the PKI and China's alleged role in the 1965 attempted coup. They had again been accentuated by China's 'punitive' strike against Vietnam in February 1979. China's retaliatory invasion of Vietnam in February 1979 demonstrated once again to Jakarta Beijing's preparedness to use force in international relations. China's intervention was well understood as a riposte designed to offset some of the damage thought to have been inflicted on its regional stature by its inability to prevent the eviction of the Khmer Rouge. However, in Indonesian eyes the CCP leadership had resorted to force although such action stood to gain nothing but an entrenchment of the Vietnamese position in Cambodia and the import into Southeast Asia of Sino–Soviet rivalry. In this context, Indonesia's leadership felt that ASEAN's support for Beijing's strategy of attrition against Vietnam would primarily benefit China, especially if the military assistance provided to Pol Pot's forces through and by Thailand provoked a military clash between Hanoi and Bangkok in northeast Thailand. For Jakarta, one unwelcome scenario was that in such a situation Beijing might make good its pledge to defend Thai interests (Porter 1981: 6). This would then lead to the further solidification of China's influence in Southeast Asia. Not surprisingly, China's military intervention proved a factor in subduing attempts by DEPLU to normalise relations with Beijing.[10]

Malaysia

The initial reaction by Malaysia's leadership to Vietnam's invasion of Cambodia and the establishment of the PRK was also 'sympathetic rather than agreeable' (C. Y. Chang 1983: 539). Such forbearance seems, in part, to have stemmed from a feeling of admiration for Vietnam's nationalism, previous moves by Kuala Lumpur actively to promote closer ties with Hanoi and a genuine desire to keep Vietnam out of the Sino–Soviet conflict. At the same time, Malaysian leaders agreed with their Thai counterparts that Kampuchea should be neutral and act as a buffer between Bangkok and Hanoi.

[handwritten margin note: in disagreement with ASEAN]

However, broadly sharing Jakarta's strategic perspective of threat, Malaysian uneasiness over China's intentions towards Southeast Asia had not dissipated, not least because of Vice-Premier Deng Xiaoping's refusal to renounce party-to-party links with the Communist Party of Malaysia while on tour in several Southeast Asian capitals in November 1978. As Tan Sri Ghazali Shafie put it, 'this is a policy of rotten fish being served in the specialised recipe of a sweet and sour dish' (quoted in Lee Poh Ping 1982: 519). Deng had also irritated his Malay hosts by referring to ethnic Chinese in Malaysia as 'second class citizens' (Lee Lai To 1981: 68).

Malaysia's position on Vietnam's intervention in Cambodia was, moreover, guided by apprehensions that China might seek to gain a foothold in Southeast Asia. In this context, Malaysian leaders wanted Chinese influence in Thailand, in particular, to be kept to a minimum (Stuart-Fox 1982: 218–19; Leong 1987). While Premier Hussein Onn remained circumspect in voicing concerns about the PRC, the Mahathir administration would later openly declare China to be a threat to Southeast Asia.

Despite these threat perceptions Kuala Lumpur's sympathies for Vietnam faded somewhat as Malaysia soon confronted an enormous influx of Indochinese refugees. The arrival of ethnic Chinese (Hoa) 'boat refugees' in hotbeds of Malay nationalism such as Kelantan and Trengganu provoked repeated outbreaks of violence and hostility. Indeed, the refugee issue quickly became susceptible to political manipulation by domestic forces which claimed that these refugees were accorded better treatment by the government authorities than were indigenous Malays (Zakaria Haji Ahmad 1979; Richardson 1982: 103–6).

Other ASEAN members

The Philippine government did not share the other ASEAN members' feeling of threat concerning either China or Vietnam. Instead, President Ferdinand Marcos remained preoccupied both with the consequences of the lack of political legitimacy enjoyed by his regime and with an economic downturn. Security challenges emanated, in particular, from the Moro National Liberation Front and the insurgency mounted by the reconstituted Communist Party of the

Philippines.[11] At the time Manila was also concerned with solidifying its entitlement to the Kalayaan Island Group, also claimed by both Vietnam and China. Fifield (1980: 203) has described the Philippine stance toward both Beijing and Hanoi as 'evenly critical', but it is perhaps also possible to argue that Manila's stance was one of semi-detachment. Consequently, President Marcos did not adopt a separate stand on the Cambodian issue, but preferred to follow the ASEAN consensus. Brunei Darussalam did the same after joining the Association in 1984, although the Sultanate appears to have been closer to the Indonesian and Malaysian position.

ASEAN's endeavours to enforce principles associated with the 'ASEAN way'

ASEAN's initial strategy to reverse the situation in Kampuchea was one of confrontation rather than accommodation, although the latter became more ascendant as the former proved increasingly bankrupt. The strategy of confrontation, favoured by Thailand and Singapore, had two dimensions: diplomatic and military. In military terms, Bangkok allowed the institutionalisation of a Khmer Rouge presence in its border areas, even though this meant accentuating Thailand's own security problems, as noted above. In addition to the provision of sanctuaries, the Thai government also allowed the transfer of military materiel to the Khmer Rouge, as well as troop training. In doing so, Thailand's leaders forged a de facto military alliance with the PRC, despite a residual perception of Beijing as a long-term threat. China was the obvious candidate for such a partnership, as Japan's Fukuda Doctrine of 1977, which was reaffirmed by Prime Minister Suzuki on a visit to Thailand in 1981, inhibited Tokyo from assuming a military role in Southeast Asia (Sudo 1992). Bangkok's approach thus came to entail active support for Beijing's policy of attrition that was designed to coerce Vietnam into submission, to reverse its occupation of Cambodia and to dismantle the PRK. Meanwhile, Thai decision-makers also sought to revitalise the alliance relationship with the United States.

At the diplomatic level, Thai leaders used ASEAN and the United Nations as vehicles to exert pressure on Vietnam and the Heng Samrin regime, not least by emphasising its role as a 'frontline' state. Significantly, given its reliance on Beijing for supplying the Khmer Rouge with weapons, Thailand's scope for diplomatic manoeuvre would subsequently become inflexible, a development that entailed a measure of friction with the other member states of the Association. It was Singapore, however, that emerged as the key shaper of world opinion on the Cambodian conflict.[12] As Peter Schier has argued, Singapore henceforth attempted to 'make itself indispensable to ASEAN through its role as mediator, initiator and organizer of ASEAN activities' (Schier 1982: 227). Singapore, in particular, emphasised the Soviet–Vietnamese communist threat to Southeast Asia, pointing to the parallels between Moscow's intervention in Afghanistan and its backing for Hanoi's intervention in Kampuchea. By depicting the issue of Kampuchea in terms of a threat of communist world revolution and domination, Singapore could appeal to strong anti-communist sentiments within ASEAN and in the West. Also, such an articulation of threat allowed the city-state to justify calls on the United States to stay engaged in upholding regional order, a persistent goal in Singapore's foreign and security policy. Notably, the anti-communist rhetoric further allowed Singapore to demonstrate its independence from China. At the United Nations – where it was represented by the extremely able, refined and persuasive Professor Tommy Koh – Singapore would take a leading role in drafting resolutions to be adopted by the relevant UN organs. While the Soviet Union vetoed a United Nations Security Council draft calling for an immediate ceasefire and the termination of hostilities in Southeast Asia as well as a speedy withdrawal of all foreign forces in March 1979, the United Nations General Assembly supported ASEAN's position for many years.[13] Singapore also adopted an assertive approach in the Non-Aligned Movement, seeking to prevent Kampuchea's seat from being left vacant or Kampuchea even being replaced by the PRK, as evidenced by the proceedings at the Sixth Summit in Havana in September 1979. In fact, Singapore opposed any moves that might be interpreted as recognising the legitimacy of the Heng Samrin regime or Singapore's belated acquiescence to the violation of principles on whose acceptance its political independence – and perhaps even its survival – was considered to depend.[14]

Singapore's success was extraordinary: for about a decade from 1979 the United Nations General Assembly voted to reject the credentials of the PRK government, while continuing to accept those of Democratic Kampuchea and, as of 1982, those of the Coalition Government of Democratic Kampuchea (CGDK). Notably, Prince Norodom Sihanouk, who assumed the presidency of the CGDK, had himself initially proposed that the Cambodian seat should be left vacant (Schier and Schier-Oum 1985: 69–80). The success was also extraordinary because the non-recognition of the Heng Samrin regime by the industrialised West and large parts of the developing world brought with it a number of interesting legal developments. While Britain, France and Australia, for example, accepted the credentials of Democratic Kampuchea in the United Nations, these countries did not maintain bilateral relations with the country. The British government, for instance, contrary to its and other states' normal practice, also continued to deny recognition to the PRK despite the latter's later effective control over Cambodia (Peterson 1997: 35, 158).

Singapore, moreover, managed to nip in the bud Vietnam's attempts to justify its invasion of Democratic Kampuchea as, in part, a humanitarian intervention in a domestic power struggle between rival Cambodian factions.[15] Singaporean policy-makers believed that international law should not condone an intervention even for alleged humanitarian purposes, as other militarily more powerful states might in future take advantage of this to the detriment of smaller neighbours.[16] Perhaps not least to prevent international public opinion being swayed by the humanitarian argument, and because Hanoi was a direct party to the conflict, Singapore therefore exposed Vietnam, rightly or wrongly, as a hegemonic state. To make the point that, rather than humanitarian concerns, predatory designs had underpinned Vietnam's disposition towards Democratic Kampuchea, Singapore's top officials skilfully and ruthlessly exploited what were perceived to be inconsistencies in Vietnam's position on the PRK. In terms of method, Singapore embarrassed Vietnam with its repeated argument that Vietnam had descended from being a 'heroic' state to one that was aggressive and expansionist.[17] Professor Tommy Koh said on the rationale of such attempts: 'I believe that no country is immune from the pressure of world opinion, although I recognize that some governments are more concerned about their self-respect and how others regard them than others' (Koh 1998: 22).

Singapore's strategy became more complicated to implement as various findings, such as those of the UN Sub-Commission on the Prevention of Discrimination and Protection of Minorities on atrocities in Democratic Kampuchea, entered the public domain,[18] leading some Western governments to register reluctance to give Democratic Kampuchea continued support. However, Singapore insisted that recognition of the Heng Samrin government could not be an alternative since such a step would sanction Vietnam's invasion of Kampuchea retroactively. When arguments nevertheless appeared in favour of the admissibility removing Pol Pot from power by force, some Singaporeans retorted that a government's repressive policies did not warrant an armed foreign intervention by an outside power. Still, Singapore had to forestall the possibility of continued non-recognition of Heng Samrin and simultaneous de-recognition of Khmer Rouge, which might also be seen to undermine its foreign policy objective of asserting the sanctity of the principles of sovereignty, non-intervention and the non-use of force. Singapore thus accepted the need to broaden the political base and to adjust the political face of Democratic Kampuchea, and led ASEAN's search for a political 'third alternative', not least by convening a meeting of resistance fighters in the city-state in September 1981. Ultimately this quest culminated in the formation of a tri-partite Coalition Government of Democratic Kampuchea, which was officially invested on 22 June 1982.[19] As for Singapore, the city-state continued to deny the PRK any legitimacy. Singapore followed this course in an undeterred way even after Prince Sihanouk's remark that Cambodians would again 'choose Vietnamese protection against the horrors of Pol Potism' (quoted in Klintworth 1989: 8), which suggested that many Cambodians in fact tacitly supported the Heng Samrin regime.

In practice, a cornerstone of ASEAN's initial attempt to 'enforce' compliance with principles associated with the 'ASEAN way' had been the proposal for an International Conference on Kampuchea (ICK). That conference was meant to bring together Vietnam, the Soviet Union, the PRC and all other 'interested parties'. By insisting on this proposal, Singapore and Thailand also rejected earlier Vietnamese proposals, which aimed for non-aggression pacts with ASEAN states, a demilitarised zone and a limited troop withdrawal. From their perspective, agreeing to the latter would have been tantamount to accepting Hanoi's military intervention and the legitimacy of the Heng Samrin regime. Vietnam and the PRK in turn rejected the ICK proposal and put forward a counterproposal for an ASEAN–Indochina conference. Meanwhile Hanoi argued that the Cambodian conflict constituted a domestic power struggle only and portrayed Vietnam's military involvement as the result of a relevant invitation by the Heng Samrin regime. In the event, ASEAN failed to secure Vietnam's participation at the conference, which was eventually organised in July 1981.

Notably, ASEAN's ICK draft declaration – which was drawn up on the initiative of Singapore's Lee Kuan Yew and had been designed to assuage both Thai and Vietnamese security concerns as well as to deny China any pretext to intervene in Southeast Asia – was significantly amended owing to major power opposition. ASEAN's draft had called for the disarming of all Khmer factions, the dispatching of UN peacekeeping forces and the establishment of a temporary UN administration in Kampuchea pending free elections that were to be held under UN supervision. Unexpectedly, however, the draft declaration met serious resistance both from China's Deng Xiaoping, who had adopted a furiously anti-Vietnamese stand that paralleled the unflinching diplomatic position of the fratricidal Khmer Rouge, and from Washington, with the Americans playing the 'China card' against the Soviet Union. As a consequence, the ICK declaration could only be passed after passages relating to the disarmament of the different Cambodian factions and the organisation of the interim administration had been severely watered down (Chanda 1986: 386–9).[20]

ASEAN's partial political defeat at the ICK in the face of combined US–China opposition caused resentment within ASEAN circles, not least because Lee Kuan Yew had – apparently mistakenly – perceived Deng Xiaoping to have indicated political support to ASEAN's proposed political settlement during a visit to Beijing in November 1980. Making the best of a less than ideal situation, ASEAN would nevertheless henceforth regard the ICK declaration 'as the legal and moral basis for a settlement in Kampuchea' (Thayer 1990: 150). Malaysia and Indonesia were quite dissatisfied with both ASEAN's performance and China's strong-arm approach, in particular as ASEAN's diplomacy was aimed at promoting certain members' specific agendas rather than at a determined effort to find a settlement of the Cambodian conflict as such, as Gareth Porter (1981: 4) has pointed out. There were, he argued, questions about the extent to which Vietnam's proposal to effect a withdrawal from Kampuchea upon the cessation of the Chinese threat was at any time seriously explored. Martin

Stuart-Fox has noted that Singapore and Thailand seemed significantly less interested in Vietnamese military and political control over Laos (Stuart-Fox 1982: 219). That control had taken the form of the deployment of about 50,000 Vietnamese troops and several thousand resident Vietnamese experts, and the conclusion of a treaty of friendship and co-operation.

Nevertheless, when the formation of a Kampuchean coalition government, in which ASEAN and in particular Singapore had invested a lot of political capital, ran into trouble owing to intra-factional squabbling, Malaysia's foreign minister sought to involve himself, not least to save ASEAN's initiative. In the event, Tan Sri Muhammad Ghazali Shafie convinced the president of the Khmer People's National Liberation Front (KPNLF), Son Sann, to agree to coalition terms that particularly suited the interests of the Khmer Rouge and the PRC. Importantly, no significant political breakthrough followed the establishment of the CGDK until 1987. Still, Malaysia's diplomatic efforts in this episode, as well as an earlier spurned proposal for a phased withdrawal by Vietnam, raise the question of to what extent those within ASEAN who had demonstrated understanding for Vietnam's predicament fully supported the Thai–Singapore line of finding a political settlement of the Cambodian conflict. More specifically, the question is whether Malaysia and Indonesia put forward proposals for a political solution of the Cambodian conflict that could be interpreted as being more flexible with regard to the validity of the principles of non-intervention and the non-use of force than those submitted by Singapore and Thailand.

Malaysian and Indonesian views and proposals: towards an intramural challenge?

Malaysia and Indonesia both subscribed to ASEAN's objectives of achieving a withdrawal of Vietnamese troops from Kampuchea and allowing for that country's self-determination without foreign interference or coercion. Not only Indonesia's DEPLU but also the Malaysian Foreign Ministry hence declared support for ASEAN's position to be 'one of principle' (Ahmad Rithaudeen 1979: 207). However, given their perception of China as a security threat, leaders in Kuala Lumpur and Jakarta had little interest in seeing the armed hostility in Cambodia become protracted and hence they sought to promote a political settlement that would respect Vietnam's security interests in Indochina. Even where rival establishments held different views on whether at issue was a problem between Vietnam and China or between ASEAN and Vietnam, as was the case between ABRI and DEPLU in Indonesia, all agreed that ASEAN would be well placed to help Vietnam regain standing in international society. Indeed, prospects for a political settlement of the conflict were generally considered fair since Vietnam's strong nationalist credentials suggested that Hanoi's tilt towards the Soviet Union was unlikely to endure.

The first instance of an attempt by Malaysia and Indonesia to promote a political solution that took into account Vietnamese security interests was when President Suharto and Prime Minister Onn Hussein agreed on and announced the so-called Kuantan Doctrine in late March 1980. The Kuantan formula suggested that ASEAN recognised that Vietnam had legitimate security interests in Indochina. Equally, it suggested that the major power influence of both the Soviet Union and China should be expunged from Indochina, a step that would also suit the security interests of both Malaysia and Indonesia. A further underlying idea was to win Washington's active support for the independence and national reconstruction of Vietnam because such a development would lessen Hanoi's dependence on Moscow (Porter 1980: 6). Given that Singapore had expected that the Kuantan summit would endorse Lee Kuan Yew's idea of an early summit meeting on Cambodia, the formula caused considerable offence in the city-state, as the Kuantan Principles implied a possible justification of Vietnam's invasion of Cambodia in terms of an alleged China threat. Singapore's leadership remained adamant that no such justification for the breach of the norms of non-intervention and the non-use of force could be accepted. Although the Kuantan formula was meant to reduce the communist threat and to strengthen the US commitment to Southeast Asia, it was rejected by Singapore, which also lobbied against US recognition of Vietnam (Quinn-Judge 1980: 1). As mentioned above, ASEAN instead opted to convene an international conference, a diplomatic effort that was doomed to failure in view of the combined opposition clearly consistently expressed by the three Indochinese states months earlier.

In the aftermath of the failed International Conference on Kampuchea, Indonesia and Malaysia both reluctantly subscribed to the ASEAN position as formulated by Singapore and Thailand. As noted, Malaysia in particular played a major role in securing the establishment in June 1982 of a tripartite coalition involving the Khmer Rouge, KPNLF and FUNCINPEC, a coalition which Singapore especially had promoted and which was first agreed in September 1981. Malaysia's support of ASEAN's policy to the advantage of the Khmer Rouge and its Chinese backers should not be viewed as contradicting what this chapter has argued were perceptions held in Malaysia and Indonesia. Rather, it should be understood as evidence that Kuala Lumpur would not allow ASEAN to fail diplomatically in attaining a political solution to the Cambodian conflict. Interestingly in this context, Jakarta went so far as to criticise the Singapore foreign minister, S. Dhanabalan, publicly 'for giving the wrong impression to the world that ASEAN as a whole was trying to arm the non-communist Khmer resistance' (quoted in C. Y. Chang 1983: 543).

Indonesia and Malaysia nevertheless both sought to explore further the possible middle ground between Hanoi and Phnom Penh, on the one hand, and Bangkok, Singapore, the CGDK and Beijing, on the other. The 1983 ASEAN Appeal[21] and Malaysia's subsequently proposed 'five-plus-two' policy framework, which aimed at bringing to the table the ASEAN-5 states as well as Vietnam and Laos, testified to this. Vietnam repeatedly rejected ASEAN's 'Appeal' for the restoration of Cambodia's independence of September 1983, not least during Nguyen Co Thach's visit to Jakarta in March 1984, while Beijing repudiated the 'five-plus-two' formula. The Indonesian foreign minister, Mochtar Kusuma-Atmadja, then proposed a five-year plan for the resolution of the conflict in May 1984. Significantly, while it was contrary to ASEAN's position on economic assistance to the SRV and the question of US-SRV normalisation, the plan was not at odds with the basic principles for regional order espoused by ASEAN. This was so because it merely demanded that Vietnam withdraw its troops from Kampuchea and did not address the question of representation. Notably, the plan again built on remarks by General's Benny Murdani in February 1984 in which he unequivocally articulated ABRI's sympathies by terming Vietnam's invasion of Kampuchea an act of national survival.

A further intervention testing ASEAN's consensus position on Kampuchea occurred in the aftermath of the very successful Vietnamese dry-season offensive of 1984/5, which saw the loss of army bases of all three factions of the CGDK. This time, at an unofficial ASEAN Foreign Ministers' Meeting during the thirtieth anniversary of the Asian–African Nations Conference organised in Jakarta in April 1985, Malaysia's foreign minister, Tengku Ahmad Rithaudeen, proposed 'proximity talks' that would see negotiations between representatives of the PRK and the CGDK take place via a mediator-negotiator. That proposal was in line with Ghazali Shafie's apparent belief that 'the Heng Samrin administration must be the core of any future regime in Cambodia, and that Malaysia wants only to broaden it, not replace it' (Porter 1982: 6). The proposal went to the heart of the principles defended staunchly by Singapore and Thailand as it seemed to involve the legitimatisation of the government now led by Hun Sen. Not surprisingly, the CGDK rejected the idea of proximity talks. At the insis-tence of its hard-line states ASEAN therefore quickly rehashed the idea by proposing instead that negotiations should be held between the SRV and the CGDK, with the possibility of the PRK forming part of the Vietnamese delegation (ASEAN 1985). The Vietnamese leadership saw this move as a calculated insult to the PRK.

Following ASEAN's designation of Indonesia's foreign minister, Mochtar Kusuma-Atmadja, as the Association's official interlocutor of Vietnam, both DEPLU and the Indonesian armed forces pursued initiatives that further tested ASEAN's official consensus. General Murdani, for instance, repeated his controversial statements about Vietnam not posing any threat to Southeast Asia. Also, the Centre of Strategic and International Studies in Jakarta organised the Second (informal) Indonesia–Vietnam seminar to promote a further exchange of views between Vietnam and Indonesia.[22] Thereafter, Indonesia began to pursue the idea of a 'cocktail party', an idea previously proposed by Norodom Sihanouk in late 1985 to allow the Khmer groups to hold informal discussions about how to overcome the diplomatic deadlock. In a positive response to this proposal the PRK stressed its willingness to commence negotiations with 'opposition Khmer individuals or groups' if this excluded the 'Pol Pot clique'. The CGDK, meanwhile, rejected such a development. The latter's Eight-Point Proposal of 17 March 1986 instead advocated the idea of a quadripartite coalition government of Kampuchea. At the same time the CGDK refused to hold talks with the PRK president, Heng Samrin, if this implied the recognition of the PRK. In doing so, the CGDK repelled firmly not only the idea of accepting Vietnam's violation of the principle of non-intervention in any form, but also any notion of the Kampuchean conflict being internal in nature. ASEAN members repeatedly endorsed the Eight-Point Plan in the following months (ASEAN 1986b) even while Singapore's foreign minister suggested amendments along the lines of ASEAN's 1981 ICK draft, the disarming of the Cambodian factions and the establishment of an international peacekeeping force.

Indonesia officially revived the 'cocktail party' proposal in May 1987. In focusing on a quadripartite gathering of the four Khmer factions to the exclusion of Vietnam, China, ASEAN and the Soviet Union, Jakarta clearly sought to move towards a practical and realistic solution to the conflict, in line with Sihanouk's wish to initiate informal talks with leaders in Phnom Penh. Vietnam's supportive remarks on this issue made to Romania's Nicolae Ceauescu in early 1987 appeared to warrant the pursuit of this initiative, which had hitherto been prevented by the CGDK and the governments in Beijing, Singapore and Bangkok. These governments shared the CGDK's concern that if the coalition were to accept the proposal for intra-Khmer talks without the participation of Hanoi 'it would commit suicide by abandoning its status as the sole legal and legitimate Government of Kampuchea' (quoted in Raszelenberg and Schier 1995: 109).

Jakarta's proposal effectively to divorce the issue of the withdrawal of Vietnamese forces from the process of how to achieve intra-Khmer reconciliation placed it at odds with those ASEAN countries that had hoped Vietnam's economic problems would lead Hanoi to submit to their demands. It was also the most explicit indirect challenge yet to the principles associated with the 'ASEAN way' in the context of attempts to find a political solution to the Cambodian conflict given the diplomatic positions of Bangkok and Singapore. In short, the proposal for 'cocktail diplomacy' was different in character from previous Indonesian interventions, most of which had centred on making other ASEAN members appreciate the perceptions of threat held in Hanoi and Jakarta.

The question to be addressed in the following section is why Indonesian and Malaysian leaders effectively deferred to the Thai–Singapore stand on Kampuchea for the number of years that they did. Indeed, was Indonesia not 'fed up' with ASEAN, finding the latter's policy over Kampuchea not only symptomatic of ZOPFAN's elusiveness, but also in direct contradiction to it, as Michael Leifer (1989: 139) argued? The following section will then explore the strong reactions to the proposal by other ASEAN members.

Understanding ASEAN's solidarity and commitment to principles associated with the 'ASEAN way'

ASEAN solidarity on the question of Cambodia has been thought to involve members' shared commitment to attaining a political settlement that would reverse Vietnam's violation of Kampuchea's sovereignty and allow Thailand – as the frontline state – to veto, if it considered it necessary, ASEAN's strategy towards Hanoi and Phnom Penh (Paribatra 1987: 4). Indonesia's and Malaysia's solidarity with ASEAN despite their misgivings over the Cambodia strategy pursued by Singapore and Bangkok may be understood to have rested in part on the realisation that China's unrelenting policy of 'bleeding Vietnam white' would not elicit an unbearable threat to regional security. In a sense the display of solidarity was also a product of their judgement that Vietnam too had to make concessions for a mutually acceptable compromise to be attained. Leaders in Jakarta and Kuala Lumpur considered the external pressure on Vietnamese rulers as potentially making the SRV more amenable to such a compromise, and to that extent they supported it. These points do not provide the only keys to understanding the solidarity exhibited by member states, however. Indeed, the solidarity exhibited worked overwhelmingly to Thailand's particular strategic advantage, not least in Indonesian eyes. Arguably, we may understand ASEAN's solidarity even better if we invoke the notion not merely of a struggle for security, but also of a struggle for recognition.

The dual struggle for security and recognition underpinned ASEAN's attitude towards Vietnam from the very beginning. Thailand both was apprehensive about and resented the implications of Vietnam's violation of sub-regional order through the establishment by military conquest of a perceived puppet regime in Phnom Penh in the apparent attempt to re-establish an Indochinese federation.[23] The removal of Kampuchea as the buffer between Vietnam and Thailand signalled to Bangkok that it was being placed in an inferior position *vis-à-vis* Hanoi in the context of their historic rivalry (Leifer 1989: 90–1). Similarly, Singapore's leaders felt very strongly about Hanoi's blatant disregard for its own and ASEAN's prescription for regional order, the purpose of which, from Singapore's perspective, was to ensure sovereign equality and survival of small states in Southeast Asia. Singapore's leaders also resented Vietnamese attempts to stir up anti-Chinese feeling in ASEAN states by labelling Singapore a 'mouthpiece' of Beijing. Ghazali Shafie also gave voice to the dual struggle when he formulated Malaysia's position as follows:

When Vietnam projected the idea of an Indo-China solidarity it could have been accepted without much [sic] qualms. When Vietnam attacked Pol Pot it could have been treated with equanimity if the exercise was purely punitive and limited since everyone in this region had recognised the misdeeds of Pol Pot by his subversion of the Khmer Krom and the military attacks on South Vietnam. But when Vietnam occupied the whole of Kampuchea and worse still shows determination not to make concession but to stay, there is justification enough for ASEAN to view Vietnam's action with misgivings and a growing concern. Such action was no more in pursuance of security and an exercise in the eradication of fear but rather the fulfilment of a committed dream to unite Indo-China under one political control as a prelude to turn the rest of South East Asia into a sort of Vietnamese comecon.

(Muhammad Ghazali Shafie 1980/1982: 319)

Perceptions of Vietnamese intransigence

The point about the moral grammar of conflict is useful to better understand how Vietnam's diplomacy and actions could frustrate and alienate even those ASEAN governments that had initially been sympathetic to Hanoi's security predicament and genuinely committed to working towards a political settlement that would protect Vietnamese interests. Indeed, the timing of many of Vietnam's actions in Kampuchea and the generally uncompromising nature of its diplomacy frequently limited the room for diplomatic manoeuvre by countries like Indonesia. In other words, what from ASEAN's perspective were considered to be Vietnamese provocations left Vietnam unable to exploit ASEAN's intramural divisions and to avert a strengthening of ASEAN's consultative mechanisms.

Hanoi's track record of perceived diplomatic provocations *vis-à-vis* ASEAN began almost immediately after Vietnamese troops had invaded Democratic Kampuchea. Then Hanoi's permanent representative to the United Nations, Ha Van Lau, suggested to his Singapore counterpart, ambassador Tommy Koh, that international society would forget the Kampuchea problem within two weeks of the intervention. The remark was viewed as offensive as it carried yet another frontal assault on the cherished principles of sovereignty, non-intervention and the non-use of force, and also seemed to bespeak an unacceptable arrogance on the part of Hanoi (Leifer 1989: 100–1). Subsequently, Vietnamese leaders would anger ASEAN by insisting that the PAV presence in Kampuchea had come about at the request of the People's Revolutionary Council in Kampuchea and was consistent with the principles of the United Nations Charter and the Non-Aligned Movement. The SRV and the PRK further infuriated the Association by referring to discussions about the situation in Kampuchea in the United Nations General Assembly, which were spearheaded by ASEAN, as 'illegal' or as 'gross interference' and by describing the situation in

Kampuchea as 'irreversible'. In response ASEAN rejected proposals to sign bilateral or multilateral treaties between Thailand and the Indochinese states in which the two sides were to pledge non-aggression and non-interference in each other's internal affairs and refuse any other country use of their respective territory as a base against other countries. From the perspective of ASEAN leaders, such proposals merely aimed to justify and perpetuate Vietnam's military presence in Kampuchea. The theme of the 'irreversibility' of the situation in Kampuchea, in particular, annoyed the newly formed moderate government of Prime Minister Prem Tinsulanond and provoked within Thailand what Quinn-Judge (1980: 7) termed 'visceral nationalism'. There was also a personal dimension. Indeed, Thailand's Foreign Minister Sitthi 'had nursed bitter feelings toward Thach from earlier meetings at which the Thai foreign minister felt Thach was both harsh and conde-scending' (Porter 1982: 4). Vietnam's perceived intransigence and arrogance made Thailand lean ever closer towards the PRC and the Khmer Rouge.

In addition to blandly reinterpreting ASEAN's proposed basic principles for regional order to suit its strategic and political objectives, the VCP also showed little understanding of, or interest in pursuing, the initial alternative proposals to address the Kampuchean conflict put forward by Indonesia and Malaysia. For instance, by flatly criticising the Kuantan formula, Vietnam's leadership embarrassed the sponsors of the Kuantan principles, Malaysia's prime minister, Datuk Hussein Onn, and Indonesian President Suharto. The proposal – described by Donald Weatherbee as a reiteration of the ZOPFAN formula applied to the Kampuchean context because it sought to remove undue major power influence from Vietnam (Weatherbee 1985: 12) – was designed to meet the long-term security interests of Hanoi. Indeed, it was precisely for this reason that Thailand's then incoming prime minister, General Prem, and the foreign minister, Air Chief Marshal Siddhi Savetsila, had both rejected the initiative. Rather than adopting a concilia-tory or ambivalent stance, however, Vietnam too rejected the proposal for its failure to mention the United States as a superpower whose presence was unwelcome in Southeast Asia (Leifer 1989: 106–7). Hanoi's rejection may well have stemmed from irritations arising from the two ASEAN leaders' apparent suggestion that Hanoi was a mere satellite of Moscow, an unac-ceptable notion to Hanoi's pride in its nationalist past, but this failed to lessen Vietnam's perceived provocation.[24]

Indonesia's and Malaysia's willingness to challenge – in Vietnam's favour – the position on Cambodia taken by Singapore or Thailand was further undercut when Vietnam initiated a major retaliatory incursion into refugee camps in Thailand that were holding non-communist refugees. Vietnam engaged in cross-border military action on 23 June 1980, for instance, following the repatriation of some refugees by the Thai government, an act Hanoi leaders had interpreted as an 'unfriendly' move to replenish the ranks of the Khmer Rouge. The timing of the Vietnamese assault, which occurred during a visit by the foreign minister, Nguyen Co Thach, to

Jakarta, just prior to the ASEAN Ministerial Meeting organised for 26–30 June 1980, was viewed by all ASEAN states as warranting a harsh diplomatic response. As noted by Michael Leifer, '[f]rom that point, ASEAN became more explicit in its challenge to Vietnam' (Leifer 1989: 108), demanding nothing less than a total withdrawal of Vietnamese forces and rejecting the Indochinese proposal to alleviate Thai–Cambodian border tensions.

The routine affirmation by the foreign ministers of the Indochinese states of the nature of the Cambodian conflict as a 'civil war' and their similarly routine avowal of their 'militant solidarity' further reinforced the image of Hanoi's leadership as utterly intransigent. Vietnam's counterproposal to ASEAN's plan for an International Conference on Kampuchea, which focused on convening a regional conference between ASEAN and the Indochina states rather than an international one, did not attract support within the Association. In return, Vietnam did not participate in the ICK and dismissed ASEAN's call for the disarmament of all Cambodian factions and the creation of an interim administration pending free elections. For many years to come Hanoi would contend that ASEAN's demands were engineered to allow the Khmer Rouge to regain power. Certainly Thailand's own intransigence toward Vietnam was a product of its attempt not to endanger its alliance-type relationship with the PRC. In the eyes of Thai leaders, this was a possibility if ASEAN followed Vietnam's demand to table the Sino–Vietnamese conflict as a legitimate issue for discussion against Beijing's wishes.

As we have seen, concerns about the evolving stalemate made Jakarta and Kuala Lumpur undertake further intensive intramural lobbying as well as launch new initiatives to attain a diplomatic breakthrough. Significantly, most of these initiatives foundered because Hanoi continued to reject them rather than to treat them as a potential basis for compromise. In June 1983, for instance, ASEAN no longer demanded that Vietnam withdraw its troops from Cambodia unconditionally and signalled that it would seek to prevent the Khmer Rouge from returning to power by the use of force. Vietnam rejected the so-called 'ASEAN Appeal'. In 1984 Vietnamese leaders failed fully to appreciate a remark made by General Benny Murdani, who explicitly repudiated the idea that Vietnam posed a threat to Southeast Asia. This became apparent when President Suharto received the Vietnamese foreign minister, Nguyen Co Thach, in Jakarta in March 1984. Then Suharto tabled a proposal that offered Vietnam a part in any peacekeeping activities in Kampuchea and invited Hanoi to organise West Irian-type elections. While the first proposal was designed to allay Vietnamese security fears, the second would have legitimised Vietnam's presence in the PRK. The Vietnamese foreign minister rejected both proposals out of hand, however (Suryadinata 1996: 129–30).

Suharto appears to have deemed such inflexibility both offensive and embarrassing. As Michael Leifer explained, 'Nguyen Co Thach's apparent repudiation of this formula provoked Suharto's personal annoyance, because it had been made without consultation with ASEAN counterparts' (Leifer 1989: 130). Indonesia's self-assumed diplomatic leeway towards the SRV was further undercut by the major dry-season offensive undertaken by the Vietnamese People's Army in 1984/5, which was ostensibly designed to achieve military predominance and involved military incursions into Thailand. During this offensive, Vietnamese forces destroyed a large number of border camps of the non-communist resistance, without, however, obtaining decisive military victory. In response to these developments President Suharto found it necessary to reassure ASEAN foreign ministers of Indonesia's continued solidarity on Cambodia. Significantly, a joint appeal for an international supply of arms and material support was made in favour of the CGDK, and the retired Adam Malik proposed a major military exercise on the Thai–Cambodian border (Acharya 2001: 89). Apart from being embarrassed by Vietnam's leadership, there were other reasons, also linked to its struggle for recognition, why Jakarta, despite its disillusionment with ASEAN's Kampuchea strategy, time and time again rejoined the ASEAN consensus forged around the more hard-line position adopted by Singapore and Thailand.

Indonesian decision-makers perceived membership in ASEAN to have significantly raised Jakarta's international stature both regionally and internationally (Anwar 1994: 196–224). This had been a key original purpose in the establishment of the Association. Indonesia's standing would be reduced, however, if Jakarta openly rejected or no longer supported the ASEAN consensus on key principles that also formed the basis of the 'ASEAN way'. Bearing in mind that the Association was built on a process of reconciliation, any abandonment or questioning of these principles and of ASEAN's regionalism were perceived as leading to grave suspicions of Indonesia by its immediate neighbours, with attendant repercussions for regional instability. The Indonesian government also required diplomatic support from fellow ASEAN states in dealing with international criticism on East Timor so as to legitimise Jakarta's military intervention and annexation. Indonesia also had economic reasons for demonstrating solidarity with Thailand. In the minds of Indonesian leaders ASEAN had proved itself a relatively useful vehicle for bargaining with the developed world on trade matters, economic co-operation and development assistance, from which Indonesia's economy benefited. It was apparently believed that if Indonesia were to oppose ASEAN on the issue of Cambodia relations with the United States and other Western countries, international financial institutions and international investors might be impaired.

Despite the difficulties and frustration experienced in dealing with Vietnam, Indonesia's leadership did not abandon attempts to find the basis for a compromise between the parties. Just how relevant the notion of a struggle for recognition was in this respect has been clarified by Andrew Macintyre, with reference to the work of Franklin Weinstein

(1976: ch. 5, esp. p. 189). Macintyre (1987: 528) has explained Indonesia's diplomatic activism on the Cambodia issue in terms of Indonesia's self-esteem and the attendant commitment to an 'independent and active' foreign policy. Indeed, the Suharto government found it difficult simply to defer to the Singapore–Thai line and to accept the deadlock in negotiations of the conflicting parties for more than short periods. In other words, Indonesian leaders' sense of themselves made them propose new initiatives to be undertaken to break the impasse whenever the situation would warrant it.

This argument can also be substantiated with regard to Indonesia's promotion of 'cocktail diplomacy'. At a time when Vietnam had signalled its preparedness to revise its position in the wake of the international developments described above, Thailand's hard-line approach to Cambodia no longer seemed justifiable. Indeed, some sections of Thailand's (military) elite appeared to be more interested in defending vested interests in drawing out the conflict than in aiming for a real solution to it.

Arguably, the Suharto regime, which had since the late 1960s demonstrated considerable restraint in the international affairs of Southeast Asia, felt that its sense of regional entitlement and struggle for regional and global prestige deserved greater recognition precisely because of the changes in global and regional international politics. That said, Indonesia's uneasiness about the de facto military alliance between Bangkok and Beijing had increased, as indications of Sino–Soviet détente emerged, coupled with the growing presence of the People's Liberation Army Navy (PLAN) in the South China Sea.

The next section examines to what extent Jakarta's pursuit of cocktail diplomacy represented an intramural challenge to an unsullied interpretation of core principles linked to ASEAN's diplomatic and security culture, and how other member states reacted to the proposal in the context of emerging major strategic changes.

'Cocktail diplomacy': an indirect challenge to principles linked to the 'ASEAN way'

Indonesia's proposal to indulge in 'cocktail diplomacy' encountered strong resistance from Bangkok and Singapore. Indeed, initially it appeared as if Thailand and Singapore would again force Jakarta to backtrack on a proposal for a political solution to the Cambodian conflict. This seemed to be the outcome of the Twentieth ASEAN Ministerial Meeting, which was held in Singapore in June 1987 (ASEAN 1987a). The position then adopted by ASEAN called for the restoration of the sovereignty, territorial integrity and independence of Cambodia. Not surprisingly, this left both Indonesia's foreign minister and the Vietnamese government dissatisfied. Also, in response to this development the PRK prime minister, Hun Sen, stated his support for Indonesia's proposal of organising two-stage negotiations. And the SRV leadership again tacitly suggested an encounter between Sihanouk and Hun Sen, leading the Indonesian government to pursue further the idea of informal 'cocktail diplomacy' with Prince Sihanouk. The latter then informed Jakarta that he hoped – through such informal contacts without preconditions – to circumvent PRC influence on the Khmer Rouge. In light of these developments and the major domestic political changes within both the Soviet Union and Vietnam, which – at least in Moscow – had opened up avenues for a new approach to the Cambodian conflict, Indonesia's foreign minister, Mochtar Kusuma-Atmadja, visited Vietnam between 27 and 29 July 1987. There he won Nguyen Co Thach's agreement to an informal meeting of the antagonists, to be held on equal footing, without preconditions and with no political labels. While a first stage of the process was only to involve the Cambodian protagonists, the subsequent stage would see the participation of other countries, including Vietnam (*Joint Press Release on Indonesian Foreign Minister's Visit to Vietnam* 1987).

The Thai and Singaporean leaderships were deeply disturbed by this move. Significantly, the outcome of a hastily convened special ministerial meeting on 16 August 1987 to review Indonesia's 'cocktail proposal' was once again a revised compromise formula that reflected more closely the positions of Thailand and Singapore. ASEAN members thus agreed that the informal meeting, initially among the Kampuchean parties, was to be followed immediately by the participation of Vietnam. Also, the CGDK's Eight-Point Proposal was again supposed to form the basis of the discussions in the cocktail meeting (ASEAN 1987b: paras 3 and 4). By reinterpreting the Mochtar–Thach agreement in this way, the indirect challenge to the 'ASEAN way' was repulsed in part. However, Vietnamese leaders made it plain that they regarded the understanding of 27 July as binding on ASEAN and argued that Indonesia had a duty to implement the agreement. Moreover, the PRK issued a five-point Declaration on the Political Solution to the Kampuchean Problem on 8 October 1987, in which it endorsed the idea of national reconciliation and a willingness to negotiate with the CGDK, albeit not with Pol Pot and his 'close associates' (Peou 1997: 32). Notably, the declaration also embraced positively the notion of a future 'coalition government'.

In spite of ASEAN's official statements, the ASEAN special ministerial meeting had not brought about a full meeting of minds in favour of Singapore and Thailand. Indeed, ASEAN's joint exploratory note prepared for proceedings at the 1987 UN General Assembly once again saw ASEAN converge more closely around Indonesia's position (Snitwongse 1988: 284). According to Justuf van der Kroef it was

> for the sake of making a gesture of unity towards its own official 'interlocutor' with Vietnam, Indonesia's Mochtar Kusumaatmadja, and in order to undercut any waverers among potential supporters of

another ASEAN resolution on Cambodia, ASEAN now seemed to be more fully endorsing the Mochtar–Thach 'cocktail' concept at last.

van der Kroef (1988: 310)

From the perspective of the PRK, however, ASEAN's draft resolution remained 'erroneous and fallacious' because it failed to give formal recognition to Phnom Penh. In spite of this criticism, Indonesia's 'cocktail party' proposal had contributed to a momentum that soon saw an informal meeting between Hun Sen and Prince Sihanouk take place in Fère-en-Tardenois, in France, on 2–4 December 1987 and again the following January. In the event, the two meetings made little progress, not least because Sihanouk's position within the CGDK at the time was too weak to allow him to ignore the criticisms of the Khmer Rouge, the KPNLF and their political backers, China and ASEAN. His demands, *inter alia*, for the dismantling of the PRK and the formation of a provisional government prior to general elections clashed with those of Hun Sen, who called for the elimination of the Khmer Rouge and wanted to allow the formation of a provisional government to occur only after elections.

Building on the idea of 'cocktail diplomacy', two Jakarta Informal Meetings (JIM) followed – organised in July 1988 and in February 1989 – both of which failed to achieve a diplomatic breakthrough.[25] From a symbolic point of view, JIM-1 was a breakthrough in that as the Cambodian parties first met in the morning and were only later joined by ASEAN, Laos and Vietnam. In terms of substance, the meeting was designed to forge a comprehensive political settlement that aspired to link the timetable for Vietnamese withdrawal to the elimination of the Khmer Rouge and focused on power-sharing arrangements as well as peacekeeping. It foundered in part because of Vietnamese and Phnom Penh intransigence on such points as the size and function of a UN peacekeeping force. Another key reason was the refusal of the Khmer Rouge to accept the PRK's proposal to establish a national reconciliation council, which would include all four Khmer factions but exclude Pol Pot and his close associates. The Khmer Rouge also insisted on a 'total and unconditional withdrawal of Vietnamese troops from Cambodia' first. JIM-2 also failed to move ahead the peace process because Phnom Penh and Hanoi rejected concessions on two issues: an interim government and the question of the mandate and size of the international force, on which the non-communist resistance and the Khmer Rouge had by then agreed.

Singapore's reaction to 'cocktail diplomacy'

For Singapore, above all, the Mochtar–Thach agreement clearly marked a major revision of ASEAN's previous position and thus represented a serious diplomatic defeat on an issue of principle on which the city-state had for years demonstrated (co-)leadership within ASEAN. In particular the agreed format of the 'cocktail talks' appeared to imply that at the root of the Cambodian conflict was a civil rather than international war, as Hanoi had contended all along. Even though it realised that it could not force Jakarta's hands, Singapore's government, even in 1988, remained combative in tone.

Two points in particular were emphasised. First, it was noted that because 'cocktail diplomacy' was at variance with ASEAN's longstanding diplomatic efforts in the United Nations, as expressed in multiple United Nations General Assembly resolutions, ASEAN's diplomatic standing in international society would be impaired. Second, it was argued that disregard for the principles of non-intervention and the non-use of force would further undermine regional security. In this context, it should be said that in order to demonstrate its attachment to these principles and its moral credibility Singapore had also opposed the US-led intervention of Grenada in 1983.

Re-emphasising both themes of a struggle for recognition and security, Singapore's foreign minister perhaps most clearly articulated Singapore's concerns. Writing in *Contemporary Southeast Asia* in the aftermath of JIM-2, S. Rajaratnam (1989) suggested that 'cocktail diplomacy' amounted to extending de facto recognition to the PRK, which was to play into Vietnam's hands. Playing to remnant fears of communism – within and beyond ASEAN – Rajaratnam portrayed Vietnamese foreign minister Nguyen Co Thach as 'the friendly neighbourhood tiger', who allegedly was still anxious to build a 'new Indo-Chinese empire' (Rajaratnam 1989: 345). Alluding to the 'break' with ASEAN principles and protocol at the Second Jakarta Informal Meeting, Singapore's foreign minister argued sarcastically that, 'It was the psychological décor and geomancy of seating arrangements at JIM II in Jakarta which enabled Mr Co Thach to pull off his political three-card-trick' (Rajaratnam 1989: 347). The foreign minister did not fail to remind readers what Hanoi should have done in his view, namely to apologise for and reverse its error of violating the basic tenets of both international society and the 'ASEAN way'. And he warned of the dangerous precedent set: 'So should a member of ASEAN fall victim to a future aggressor, it need only refer to any ASEAN "Cambodian solution" that directly or indirectly condones aggression' (Rajaratnam 1989: 360).

Singapore's exasperation with 'cocktail diplomacy' was, of course, an expression of its own geopolitical predicament. Significantly, Indonesia's indirect challenge to the 'ASEAN way' by dint of 'cocktail diplomacy' had come at a time when Singapore became aware once again that it could not take its survival for granted. Although there was no immediate threat to Singapore's well-being or independence, a certain degree of anxiety had developed against the backdrop of what in 1987 proved to be less than fully cordial and comfortable bilateral relationships with both Indonesia and Malaysia.[26] As regards Indonesia, Singapore's leaders worried about the degree of future commitment of ABRI to ASEAN. Such uneasiness may well have been the consequence of the apparent differences over Cambodia between the Department of Defence and Security (DEPHANKAM) and ABRI, on the one hand, and the Foreign Ministry, on the other. It was probably reinforced when, in March 1986, Jusuf Wanandi, Executive Director of the Centre of Strategic and International Studies in Jakarta, made comments about what he alleged to be a less enthusiastic commitment of younger officers to the Association (Anwar 1994: 157–8). Looming changes in Indonesia's international and domestic politics also made Singapore's government wary of any reduction in the significance of the 'ASEAN way'.

For example, in advance of the 1987 ASEAN Summit Indonesia had argued strongly for a change to ASEAN's institutional structure. While Indonesia may have pursued this course of action primarily to enhance its ability to defend its economic interests *vis-à-vis* other Pacific Rim states and beyond, Singapore's leaders seem to have believed that the undertaking could have led to a renewed attempt to build a more centralised ASEAN. The city-state had previously considered such plans as a potential liability in its attempt to remain fully independent. Finally, Singapore's insistence on the continued validity of the principles of the 'ASEAN way' must also be viewed against the background of growing disagreements with Indonesia over the role of the United States. Indonesia had amassed a number of grievances against the United States in the 1980s (such as Washington's lack of support for a New International Economic Order or the Law of the Sea Convention as well as protectionism in the textile industry, in particular). Jakarta's leaders were also agitated by Washington acquiescence in the removal of President Marcos. Significantly, President Suharto felt shunned by Washington's foreign policy elite because the US paid only 'minimal attention to consultation with Indonesia as its "regional manager"', while playing the 'China card' (McMichael 1987: 17). To summarise, Jakarta favoured a more 'autonomous' regional approach to international politics and security. Singapore, on the other hand, especially because of concerns about its neighbours' growing assertiveness, articulated unambiguous support for the continuation of a United States military presence in the region (Abin 1991; Desker 1991). As regards developments in Indonesia's domestic politics, uncertainty over the presidential succession had emerged. Also, political Islam appeared to be on the rise in Indonesia, a trend expressed in the founding of the Indonesian Muslim Intellectuals' Association in 1990 (Ramage 1995). The increasing influence of political Islam also raised questions about the future foreign policy across the causeway in Malaysia (Shanti Nair 1998).

Singapore's apprehensions over Singapore–Malaysia relations at the time were stark. The 1986 visit to Singapore by Israel's non-executive president, Chaim Herzog, had placed the bilateral relationship under significant strain, as attested by the withdrawal of their ambassadors by Kuala Lumpur and Jakarta. The strain in relations with Malaysia continued as Singapore banned four foreign Islamic preachers from entering Singapore in 1987, in an apparent attempt to avoid politics under the cloak of religion. What were perceived to be tactless remarks by Brigadier-General Lee Hsien Loong on the 'unsuitability' of Singapore Malays for the Singapore Armed Defence Forces also complicated relations with Singapore's immediate neighbour to the north. In sum, perceptions about an uncertain regional future had convinced Singapore that the 'ASEAN way' should not be tinkered with.

Bangkok's reaction to 'cocktail diplomacy'

The government in Bangkok had initially reacted in a very similar manner to Singapore. However, unlike their counterparts in the city-state, Thailand's new leaders, under Premier Chatichai Choonhavan, accentuated the Indonesian challenge to the 'ASEAN way', plunging the Association deeper into crisis.

Thailand had unswervingly stood by Singapore and the CGDK on the non-recognition of the PRK regime. Above all, however, it was the Prem government's reliance on China for deterrence against Vietnam that ensured policy continuity on this point for many years. However, by 1988 Thailand had performed a volte-face on this issue. This policy shift has been attributed, in particular, to talks between Prime Minister Prem and the Soviet leadership in late May 1988 (Evans and Rowley 1990: 264–5). It would appear that this meeting brought Prem's thinking in line with that of General Chavalit, the army's Supreme Commander, who had as early as November 1987 described the Cambodian conflict as a 'civil war' between two Cambodian communist factions. The policy shift was then translated into a practical initiative following the election of Chatichai Choonhavan as prime minister in August 1988. It was perhaps best illustrated by Siddhi Savetsila's historic call on his Vietnamese counterpart in Hanoi in the following January and the invitation issued to PRK Premier Hun Sen (as a private guest) to have direct talks in Bangkok in January 1989 (Pibulsonggran 1989). The sudden reversal of Thai policy, effected without serious prior consultation with its ASEAN counterparts, stunned them.[27] Indeed, Bangkok generated considerable anger by embracing a distinction that Thai decision-makers had for years resisted in a tone of moral outrage, namely between a *de jure* and de facto policy position *vis-à-vis* the PRK.[28]

Thailand's about-face on Cambodia was prompted by perceptions of the significance of a number of international developments. Initially these included Mikhail Gorbachev's 'new thinking', US–USSR rapprochement, the impending Sino–Soviet summit of May 1989 and increasing friction in Thailand's bilateral commerce with the United States (Um 1991; Innes-Brown and Valencia 1993; Buszynski 1994). At the sub-regional level, Laos had normalised relations with China in 1987 and the PAV had begun to withdraw its troops from the PRK. The developments led the administration of Prime Minister Chatichai Choonhavan to conclude that if Kampuchea was no longer going to be a stumbling block in relations among the major powers, it should not be a stumbling block in the pursuit of Thailand's regional and economic interests (Sirikrai 1990: 256–7). The notion of *Suwannaphum*, or golden peninsula, which the Chatichai administration initially reactivated, also betrayed a struggle for recognition, however. The project of building bridges in the battlefield of Indochina would clearly imply regaining a pre-eminent role for Bangkok in the post-Cold War period. Thailand also sought an end to the Kampuchean conflict and the role of gateway to Indochina for economic reasons. Indochina was to become both Thailand's market and the supplier of its natural resources. The objective of turning Indochinese battlefields into marketplaces was also to serve the business interests of members of Chatichai's Chart Thai Party. Significantly, Bangkok's response to Indonesia's role in initiating 'cocktail diplomacy' in turn triggered a very negative retort from other members. Ironically, however, the disagreements resulted in the re-establishment of a consensus regarding the continued intramural validity of core principles associated with ASEAN's diplomatic and security culture.

Reactions to Bangkok's challenge to ASEAN's diplomatic and security culture

The depth of Singapore's resentment over Thailand's sudden reversal of its stand *vis-à-vis* Indochina is difficult to exaggerate. In Singapore's view Chatichai's policy had failed to pay any regard to the significance of the norms of sovereignty and non-intervention for security building within ASEAN and to their inherent symbolic value. Indeed, Bangkok had effectively made a case for the relative validity at best of key aspects of ASEAN's diplomatic and security culture. Apart from the possible security implications such a development might have, Singaporean leaders worried about the potential fallout for ASEAN in terms of any damage to its international credibility and regional prestige. In Singapore's view, the Thai premier did not seem to recognise that his about-turn might embarrass and the Association and render it meaningless in the eyes of Western dialogue partners. Singapore's foreign minister, S. Rajaratnam, for instance, argued that in indulging in this policy shift Thailand had failed, among other things, to understand that Vietnam was using ASEAN members merely as bait to lure foreign investments from Western countries. As he bluntly remarked: 'What passes for economic activity in Vietnam today is economic parasitism and ASEAN businessmen should be aware of this' (Rajaratnam 1989: 352). And sarcastically he added, 'It would be a pity, therefore, were ASEAN solidarity to be bartered away for the sake of a few beads and trinkets dangled before it by a smiling tiger' (Rajaratnam 1989: 361).

Jakarta's anger at Premier Chatichai's policy swing matched that of Singapore. Notably, while Jakarta displayed clear signs of impatience with other ASEAN members in promoting 'cocktail diplomacy', the proposal had not been meant to undermine the validity of the 'ASEAN way'. As in the intervention of East Timor, Indonesia had only been prepared to challenge the principles of the 'ASEAN way' indirectly, by not ascribing to them the status in relations with non-ASEAN countries that they enjoyed at the level of intramural relations. As we have seen, Foreign Minister Mochtar's proposal of December 1985 to initiate a process of 'cocktail diplomacy' amounted to an attempt at finding a regional rather than broadly international solution to the Cambodian conflict.

Jakarta was particularly outraged at the Chatichai government because it was also felt that Indonesia had, out of a sense of commitment to ASEAN, long subordinated key political and security interests to Thai advantage. As Foreign Minister Mochtar argued, 'ASEAN cohesion and political solidarity ... was dealt a rude blow by Thailand's turn-around on the Kampuchea question' (Kusuma-Atmadja 1990: 166). However, Indonesian resentment appeared not to be primarily the result of Thailand having challenged the absolute validity of the 'ASEAN way', which Jakarta itself had challenged, albeit less controversially. Instead, Indonesia's leadership appears to have been at least as concerned over the practical efforts of Bangkok to mediate between Hun Sen and Prince Sihanouk. If successful, such efforts would have undercut Indonesia's own diplomatic striving to attain a negotiated settlement. Indonesia's leaders had long resented the lack of recognition for their deferral to Bangkok on the issue of Cambodia and had, moreover, increasingly disliked the 'shift in the political centre of gravity of the Association from Jakarta to Bangkok' (Leifer 1989: 101). In the event, Bangkok was seen as bearing some responsibility for the failure of JIM-2 and the 1989 Paris Peace Conference, in that Thailand's new posture was viewed as again having bolstered the intransigence of Phnom Penh and Hanoi. Indeed, even as the efforts to end the Cambodian war progressed, the Indonesian leadership appears to have found quite unpalatable Chatichai's apparent personal quest to outperform Indonesian diplomacy, as testified by his keenness to see Cambodia's Supreme National Council convene for its first meeting in Bangkok (Tan Lian Choo 1991: 293).

The fourth section has demonstrated that the pursuit of 'cocktail diplomacy' provoked serious concern in Singapore, as the former appeared to suggest acquiescence to a major violation of the framework for interstate and intra-regional conduct that Singapore had laboured to preserve in the most pristine form possible. It has also showed that the challenge inherent in the pursuit of 'cocktail diplomacy' was amplified by Thailand's Indochina policy under Premier Chatichai Choonhavan. This policy posed a threat not only to the relevance of the 'ASEAN way', but also to the Association, against the backdrop of an uncertain post-Cold War period. Perhaps paradoxically, this development helped ASEAN to demonstrate solidarity on the relevance of the principles once more at stake.

The diplomatic endgame to the Cambodian conflict and the 'ASEAN way'

Against the background of the changing international environment, described in Chapter 3, and the Thai volte-face that posed a challenge not only to the principles associated with the 'ASEAN way', but also to the organisation itself, Singaporean and Indonesian leaders joined forces to protect ASEAN's diplomatic position.[29] This was illustrated by Jakarta's support for ASEAN's position, at the First Paris Conference, that the nature of the Cambodia war was an international conflict.

Still, Indonesia remained engaged in attempts to arrive at a political settlement of the Cambodian conflict. In February 1990 Indonesia's new foreign minister, Ali Alatas, organised the First Jakarta Informal Meeting on Cambodia (IMC) in his capacity as co-chairman of the Paris Conference and as ASEAN's interlocutor of Vietnam. At this meeting the Khmer factions agreed on the establishment of a 'supreme national body' vested with sovereignty, but differed on how it should be composed. A Second Informal Meeting on Cambodia was held in Jakarta in September 1990. Here, the Cambodian parties agreed on a composition of the Supreme National Council (SNC) whereby six of its twelve members were to come from the State of Cambodia (SOC), with another six from the *Front Uni National pour un Cambodge Indépendent, Neutre, Pacifique et Coopératif* (FUNCINPEC), KPNLF and the Khmer Rouge. The thirteenth member was to be the SNC president. This agreement followed the consensus on a Framework Document at which the P5 arrived in August 1990 (see p. 110). It was ultimately left to the coercive diplomacy of the P5 to secure respect for their August 1990 Framework Document, which would culminate in the Cambodia Peace Accords of October 1991.

Meanwhile Singapore, in particular, clearly played for time to allow the non-communist resistance to develop into a credible alternative to Hun Sen's PRK. It has been suggested that as the peace process evolved certain ASEAN members encouraged intransigence on the part of the Sihanoukists and the KPNLF and sought to avert special deals between Hun Sen and Prince Sihanouk that might involve the recognition of the Phnom Penh regime. They were seen as having done so not least by advocating the need for a 'comprehensive and durable political solution' (Evans and Rowley 1990: 287–92). Faced with the reality that the PRK (as of April 1989 the SOC) was not about to collapse even after the final withdrawal of Vietnamese troops, ASEAN governments joined China in demanding at the Paris 1989 Conference on Cambodia that the SOC be dismantled. Moreover, ASEAN governments did not object to attempts by the Khmer Rouge to dislodge the SOC by military force. Ironically, however, the fighting within Cambodia in the spring and summer of 1989 demonstrated that at this stage the Cambodian conflict was at heart a 'civil war' between the CGDK and the SOC. Ultimately, Singapore's total defence of the principles of sovereignty and non-intervention failed as the P5 states edged toward a compromise on a power-sharing arrangement for Cambodia which they subsequently pressured their proxies to accept.

The demise of ASEAN's longstanding official position was predestined when Washington declared in July 1990 that it could no longer support the CGDK in the UN. The administration of George Bush justified the decision by arguing that it sought to prevent the Khmer Rouge from returning to power, a position adopted already in 1989, and that this step did not involve recognition of the PRK. At the same time, Washington supported the formation of an interim coalition government. Meanwhile Beijing still called for the dismantling of the SOC. On 28 August 1990, however, the P5 agreed on a Framework Document, which included provisions for the establishment of the SNC. This was to be a unique legitimate body and source of authority, in which, throughout the transitional period, before elections national sovereignty and unity would be enshrined. To arrive at this compromise, China had made two major concessions: first, Beijing no longer insisted on the dismantling of the SOC; second, she no longer insisted on the formation of a quadripartite government prior to elections in Cambodia (Peou 1997: 139). Consequently, the SOC could advance as a legitimate player in the peace process and be represented on the SNC, as were the Khmer Rouge and the KPNLF. Meanwhile it was also decided to leave intact the administrative structures of the SOC, although finance, foreign affairs, national defence, public security and information were later to come under the responsibility of the United Nations Transitional Authority.

Further compromise on the details of the comprehensive political settlement to be pursued became possible against the background of the normalisation of Sino–Soviet relations as well as other developments. For example, in bilateral talks between June and October 1991 Vietnam and China agreed on the inclusion of the Khmer Rouge and a minimal interim role UN presence. Previously Vietnam, which had not been a party to the Framework Document, had objected to a large-scale UN intervention force and again demanded the exclusion of the Khmer Rouge. After the signing of the Framework Document Washington exerted pressure on Vietnam to use its influence in Phnom Penh, which had also rejected the P5 compromise, suggesting that the normalisation of US–Vietnamese relations could be jeopardised if Vietnam failed to comply. Hanoi complied, having previously reiterated that it was up to the Cambodian factions to agree on a solution. The door to the 1991 Paris Conference and its Final Act was thus open.

Singapore and the other ASEAN countries were in no position to play down or reinterpret these developments, especially as regards the question of representation of the Khmers in the new power-sharing arrangement. ASEAN's, or rather Singapore's, principled position collapsed with China's acceptance of Hun Sen 'as an authentic Cambodian representative and not as a Vietnamese puppet', which was made entirely clear when they invited him to China for a Supreme National Council meeting in July 1991 (Yahuda 1996: 269).

Conclusion

This chapter has offered insights on how ASEAN's diplomacy *vis-à-vis* Vietnam and the PRK in the 1980s was influenced by a dual struggle for security and recognition that found expression in, among other things, the adamant defence of principles associated with and constituent of the Association's diplomatic and security culture. ASEAN displayed impressive solidarity in its stance toward Hanoi and Phnom Penh, serious intramural differences notwithstanding. Indonesia's forbearance with ASEAN on this issue up to 1987 was shown to have depended on several factors, including Jakarta's economic interests and the provocative manner in which Vietnamese leaders repulsed the initiatives for a political settlement of the conflict put forward by ASEAN member states. Ultimately, however, it was inconceivable for Jakarta to defer to Bangkok and to remain a passive player in the international politics of Southeast Asia. Both Jakarta's self-conceived political identity and its changing international circumstances militated against this.

The idea of embarking on 'cocktail diplomacy' to find a political solution to the conflict proved very controversial, as it seemed to sacrifice a pristine interpretation of the norms of non-intervention and non-use of force. To Singapore, this development indirectly threatened the absolute validity long accorded to the same legal-political principles, not least as elements of the 'ASEAN way'. In the event Jakarta's challenge was accentuated in a more direct form by the incoming government of Premier Chatichai. In contrast to the Indonesian challenge, the Thai challenge was regarded as highly detrimental to ASEAN so that Singapore and Indonesia reaffirmed the validity of the principles of the non-use of force and non-intervention. Ultimately, however, all of ASEAN had to bow to the pressure of major powers and accept the political compromise on Khmer representation on the SNC, as the repository of Cambodia's sovereignty. A compromise that reflected Cambodia's political reality and that did not require the SOC to be dismantled.

Chapter 5 focuses on the extramural challenge posed by one of the major powers to ASEAN's diplomatic and security culture in the post-Cold War era: China's challenge.

5 China's relations with ASEAN

Challenging or reinforcing the 'ASEAN way'?

China's relations with Southeast Asia have undergone significant development since the end of the Cold War. Routine high-level exchanges have become part and parcel of Beijing's ties with ASEAN as a grouping, as well as of her bilateral ties with individual member states of the Association. Trade ties have expanded considerably and picked up again quickly after an interim decline linked to the Asian financial crisis. Also, China and ASEAN have co-operated ever more closely on an increasing number of issues in an array of international forums, such as the ARF, the Asia–Europe Meeting and the so-called ASEAN Plus Three process, which brings together ASEAN-10, Japan, South Korea and China. Notwithstanding these developments, various ASEAN leaders have continued to signal – albeit for different reasons – that they are not confident about China in regional international society. They worry about the potential of a serious deterioration in Sino–US and/or Sino–Japanese relations as Beijing seeks to cement regional, if not global, major power status and the likely implications this could have for the Association. Many regard China as a major economic competitor. And some fret that ASEAN or individual members could yet become embroiled in an armed confrontation with China over competing claims to sovereignty and territorial jurisdiction in the South China Sea. Consequently, ASEAN states have by and large embarked on a dual approach of integrating China into the fledgling institutions of regional international society while also hedging against the possibility that this approach might not deliver the results hoped for.

It is within this broader context that this chapter examines whether China has challenged or reinforced ASEAN's diplomatic and security culture in the post-Cold War era. Reaching conclusions on this question is of considerable importance, for at least two reasons. First, at stake is whether ASEAN has been successful in winning from a major regional power a commitment to respect for norms associated with its diplomatic and security culture and which ASEAN countries also regard as important in their ties with Beijing. Second, establishing whether China challenges or promotes the 'ASEAN way' (or both) in the international politics of East Asia is important for any assessment of the evolving PRC–ASEAN relationship in the context of relations between the major powers in East Asia. Notably, to the extent that this chapter finds that China supports the 'ASEAN way' as a framework for regional security co-operation, it will further explore whether such support is given merely for tactical purposes or out of a genuine commitment to its core principles.

The chapter will be divided into four sections. The first identifies the nature of China's challenge to the Association and the 'ASEAN way'. For reasons of historical perspective, this will be done very briefly for the Cold War period and then in more detail for the post-Cold War years. The second section explores China's challenge to ASEAN's diplomatic and security culture in relation to the processes of norm-elaboration in the ARF. The third section examines how China challenges an extension of the 'ASEAN way' to the South China Sea conflict, with particular emphasis on China's record of adhering to the norms of the non-use of force and restraint. The fourth section looks at the extent to which China has reinforced or challenged norms or practices associated with the 'ASEAN way' in the aftermath of the Asian financial crisis.

Identifying China's challenge to the 'ASEAN way'

If one only compared the norms associated with ASEAN's diplomatic and security culture with the Five Principles of Peaceful Co-existence espoused by China, one might wonder how the PRC could ever have be said to have challenged core principles of the 'ASEAN way'.[1] The explanation, of course, is to be found in the insight that foreign policy performance extends beyond the rhetorical invocation of principles to include how they are practised in a specific context. And the fact is that China's foreign policy practice towards Southeast Asia has at times been guided by considerations and motives that have not been fully compatible with the Five Principles of Peaceful Co-existence.

The Cold War period

At the height of the Cold War the CCP supported communist parties in Southeast Asia in a revolutionary bid to undermine regional governments and to overturn the global *status quo* (van Ness 1970; Gurtov 1971). Beijing's intermittent acts of interference (in the form of protests, propaganda or repatriation) on behalf of ethnic Chinese living in Southeast Asia further reinforced regional suspicions of the PRC (Suryadinata 1985). More diffuse fears of China's political hegemony also played a role (Yahuda 1986; Wanandi 1988: 180–1). Some of these built on memories of the Middle Kingdom's historical interactions with what was formerly referred to as the 'Nanyang' (literally 'Southern Seas'), when China was 'treating foreign countries as all alike but unequal and inferior to China'

(Wang Gungwu 1968: 61).[2] China's sheer size and geographical proximity has been another factor.

Significantly, PRC violations of legal-political principles like the non-use of force or non-interference in the Cold War period did not necessarily qualify as a wholesale challenge to the 'ASEAN way'. First, as mentioned above (see chapter 3), ASEAN states had sought to win acceptance by regional major powers for the sanctity of basic norms of international society through a unilateral declaration, but China took years to endorse ZOPFAN. Second, the governments in Beijing and the ASEAN capitals disagreed profoundly over the validity of justifying material and financial support for communist insurgents in Southeast Asia on the basis of party-to-party relations. Yet, at least under Deng Xiaoping, the PRC stressed her commitment to the norm of sovereignty, of which non-intervention and non-interference are corollaries. Also, China did not seek to influence individual ASEAN governments to become involved in the internal affairs of other member states.

Finally, to the extent that China posed a limited challenge to an attempt to have norms associated with the 'ASEAN way' also guide China–ASEAN interaction, this challenge eased significantly between the late 1970s and the end of the Cold War. For instance, China expressly supported ZOPFAN as of 1978. Thereafter, Beijing passed citizenship laws, which gave legal expression to a commitment undertaken by the PRC in 1954, namely to rule out dual nationality and to compel Chinese in Southeast Asia to choose between their local citizenship and that of the PRC. And, not least in order to win ASEAN's unflinching support in reversing Vietnam's intervention in Cambodia, the Chinese government reduced provisions for communist insurgents loyal to Beijing. Examples included the emergence in Beijing of Chin Peng to disband the MCP (Buszynski 1995: 166, 169). Notably, the communist leadership also began to prod the Khmer Rouge into accepting a political solution for Cambodia. These actions helped re-establish to some extent China's credibility and reputation in Southeast Asia, even if they were clearly also motivated by international ostracism after the violent suppression of large-scale street protests in Beijing in early June 1989. These steps paved the way for the resumption of diplomatic ties between Beijing and Jakarta, followed by the initiation of the former's diplomatic relations with Singapore and Brunei Darussalam. As a prominent analyst argued, diplomatic recognition of China by these countries symbolised 'the Association's confidence in its ability to deal with major powers whose motives may still be viewed with suspicion' (Simon 1990: 87). Still, it should be noted that in view of the confrontation between China and Vietnam in the South China Sea at the time, some ASEAN leaders increasingly worried less about any disregard of the norm of non-interference than the possibility of China using force of arms against ASEAN claimants. Importantly, not all member states of the Association perceived this challenge to be of equal significance at the time.

The post-Cold War period

China's post-Cold War challenge to principles associated with the 'ASEAN way' as a code of conduct for relations with ASEAN tends to be linked to two diplomatic efforts undertaken by the Association. First, ASEAN has been keen on making China participate in and abide by the norm-elaboration processes through political dialogue in the areas of confidence building and preventive diplomacy that take place in the ARF. As elaborated in the ASEAN Concept Paper for the ARF, ASEAN governments have also been keen to engage China to agree on a set of principles that would guide relations among countries, not only in Southeast Asia, but also in the wider East Asia region. As the Concept Paper makes clear, ASEAN has also been interested in seeing China, as an ARF participant, associate itself with the TAC. Allowing the major powers to accede to the TAC has for some time been proposed by Singapore, but before 1995 Indonesia had rejected this, as had China incidentally, on the grounds that it was a Northeast Asian country (Lee Lai To 1999: 29).[3]

Second, although ASEAN members seemingly failed in the late 1980s to appreciate in equal measure the implications of China's policy in the South China Sea, particularly in the Spratlys, the Association thereafter developed a more cohesive outlook on the issue. Indeed, for some years now ASEAN has been intent on winning Beijing's explicit endorsement of the principles first outlined in the 1992 Declaration on the South China Sea (also known as the Manila Declaration). The latter objective was rearticulated in 1995, following the discovery of Chinese structures on Mischief Reef, and again in the Concept Paper, where it explicitly stated that such endorsements of the Declaration would serve 'to strengthen its political and moral effect' (ARF 1995). More recently ASEAN has sought a commitment to working out a regional code of conduct for areas of the South China Sea. There would appear to be at least two norms linked to the 'ASEAN way' that China is seen particularly to be challenging in relation to the South China Sea: the norm of the non-use of force and the corollary norm of restraint.

The following two sections seek to clarify to what extent China has really been challenging ASEAN's efforts to externalise modes of behaviour modelled on the 'ASEAN way' as a cornerstone of a framework for their interaction and co-operation in the post-Cold War era. The question will be addressed in two ways. The first section will examine China's participation in regional multilateral security dialogues and attendant norm-elaboration processes. Of interest here is whether Beijing has undertaken the commitments in the areas of confidence building and preventive diplomacy proposed in the ASEAN Concept Paper for the ARF or subsequently agreed by ARF participants. In a further section the paper will then assess China's position in relation to processes of confidence building and preventive diplomacy relating directly to the South China Sea.

China's View of and Participation in ARF Activities

Initially China's leadership viewed the idea of regional multilateral security dialogues in the ARF with a measure of trepidation. The primary reason for this was that they suspected that it would allow Tokyo to win recognition as a political and, possibly, military power. Another was that the Forum would become a one that sought to internationalise existing bilateral disputes (Garrett and Glaser 1994). Other concerns in relation to the ARF focused on the possibility that the United States and its regional allies might seek to manipulate such dialogues in order to contain China or 'smother' China.[4] Indeed, early calls for greater military transparency and related confidence-building measures by some Western ARF participants were interpreted as an attempt to stymie the modernisation of China's armed forces (Tian Zhongqing 1995: 47). Chinese decision-makers even appear to have been suspicious that Washington might attempt to pressure China to renounce publicly the use of force in relation to Taiwan, or advocate the admission of Taiwan to the multilateral security dialogues as part of a long-term strategy to promote Taiwan's independence. The background to such fears was that Sino–US ties had deteriorated markedly in the aftermath of events in June 1989 and threatened to descend into a new Cold War. Fear of such a threat arose primarily in response to an apparently irreconcilable conflict over international norms (Yahuda 1996: 282),[5] particularly in relation to the norm of non-proliferation that Beijing had subordinated to the principle of sovereignty.[6] This was completely unacceptable to Beijing, running counter to its attempt finally fully to restore the sovereignty and territorial integrity of China.

Notwithstanding these concerns, and despite the fact that it did not have a significant track record in multilateral security dialogues if one discounted its experience and somewhat ambiguous record in the United Nations and certain non-proliferation regimes (Kim 1994; Johnston 1996), the PRC participated in the ARF. She did so because Chinese leaders believed that, on balance, their country's presence in the ARF might prevent damage to national interests. She also sought the forum's membership because its leadership considered it inappropriate for China, as a rising power, not to be represented. Expressed in more positive terms, China pursued a triple agenda in participating in the regional security dialogues and the attendant norm-elaboration processes. These were, first, to defuse perceived attempts at containment by the US, Japan and their Southeast Asian security partners; second, to promote multipolarity while giving China a voice in regional security dialogues and averting decisions affecting her interests being taken in Beijing's absence; and, third, to improve overall relations with ASEAN. Beijing's initial motivations in joining the ARF were thus expressive of China's broader struggle for security and recognition (Wu Xinbo 1998).

The PRC view of evolving ASEAN-led multilateralism in security matters

In the course of its involvement in the ARF the People's Republic has found reassuring the methods by which the Forum operates. Indeed, through the first few ARF meetings China has grown fairly confident that her position will not simply be overridden, despite repeated attempts by some members to do just that on alleged or actual majority views. That positive attitude has not been affected by fluctuations in Sino–US relations, as when, for example, the US granted the Taiwanese president, Lee Teng-Hui, a visa to visit his alma mater in 1995, contrary to previous policy. One reason for this is the principle of consensual decision-making that has allowed Beijing in the ARF to deal with the United States on the basis of formal equality, irrespective of the true weighting of their power equation. In effect, the consensus rule has also accorded Beijing a veto power that she has not been reluctant to use. ASEAN-sponsored multilateralism in security affairs has, moreover, offered China a chance to question the United States' leadership role in the Asia-Pacific region, to attempt to play ASEAN off against the US, and to argue against Japan assuming a more prominent regional political-military role. When Beijing confronted allegations of the 'China threat', especially in the wake of its missile tests to influence political processes on Taiwan, the ARF provided a forum to refute this theory (Tian 1995: 50; Gao Jiquan 1996; Zhang Jialin 1994).

Beijing has also appreciated the practice of ending ARF meetings, not with declarations or resolutions, but with short statements by the respective chair as an acknowledgement of the complexity of many (latent) regional conflicts and members' recognition that at best long-term solutions can be found for them (Leifer 1996b: 40, 42). Obviously, by supporting ASEAN in its role as the ARF's driving force, Beijing has in its own view contributed to strengthening the trend of multipolarity, which in itself is clearly a Chinese foreign policy objective. After an initial 'wait and see' attitude China has assumed an increasingly proactive stance in the ARF. Significantly, Chinese leaders have found both ASEAN's role in the Forum and the normative framework in which regional multilateral security co-operation is embedded so congenial and conducive to China's national interest that they have been hailing the ARF as beneficial to regional peace and stability. As we shall see again later (p. 136), China has gone so far as to promote the pursuit of co-operative security through the ARF as a substitute to formal defence alliances between regional countries and the United States.

First, however, the chapter turns to the question whether China has actually committed itself to the activities proposed and norms advocated by ASEAN. Thus the next subsection analyses the extent to which China has responded positively to the proposals contained in the ARF Concept Paper.

Beijing and confidence building

The ASEAN Concept Paper for the ARF (ARF 1995) identified confidence-building measures as the first stage of security co-operation.[7] It outlined nine proposals to enhance confidence among ARF members that could be adopted in the short term. These measures concerned the development of a set of basic principles, the adoption of comprehensive approaches to security, a dialogue on security perceptions, the publication of defence publications, the participation in the UN Conventional Arms Register, enhanced contacts, exchanges between military academies, observers at military exercises, and seminars for defence officials and military officers.

With respect to confidence building through greater military transparency, Beijing's early compliance with the Concept Paper was initially derided as a propaganda effort. In particular, the PRC's first ever White Paper on arms control and disarmament provoked much scorn among the majority of Western officials and academics as it provided only limited (if any) valuable information (*Arms Control and Disarmament* 1995).[8] This again raised suspicions about the extent to which China was prepared to participate meaningfully in regional confidence-building measures, suspicions which Chinese academics quickly sought to dispel (Krepon 1997; Liu Huaqiu 1995). On balance, the judgement in question may have been too harsh, especially as it should also be noted that the first White Papers submitted by the ASEAN countries were not necessarily more revealing. It is also a fact that at the time in question the precise criteria for composing defence policy statements were still being drawn up, not least within the Council for Security Co-operation in the Asia-Pacific (CSCAP) (Choi and Wattanayagon 1997: 84). This concerned such key points as comprehensiveness, balance and mutual supportiveness, precision and reliability, consistency and standardisation, as well as availability of data. China was not a member of CSCAP at the time.

That China has not been opposed to confidence building *per se*, even in the military sphere, has been demonstrated by a number of agreements entered into at the time, including the Shanghai Agreement of April 1996, which paved the way for the mutual reduction of forces along the Sino-Russian border.[9] Following the initial tentative stance, China's embracing of the proposed confidence-building measures, spelled out in Annex A of the ARF Concept Paper, has also clearly illustrated this. Beijing has, for example, submitted reports to the UN Conventional Arms Register, and since 1997 Chinese representatives have attended the ARF meetings of senior defence and military officials and of the Heads of National Defence Colleges. Indeed, the fourth such meeting was organised in the PRC in September 2000.

Significantly, Beijing has not only demonstrated the political will to participate in confidence-building measures in the context of the ARF, but has also gone so far as to adopt a proactive stance in this respect. As early as 1996/7, for instance, the PRC assumed the joint chairmanship of the Inter-sessional Support Group on Confidence-Building Measures (ISG –CBM), during which ARF members were invited to Beijing to observe military exercises. However, the relevant ARF inter-sessional meeting, hosted by Beijing in March 1997, ended on a note of discord as China attacked the notion of the US–Japan alliance as the cornerstone of regional security (Winters 1998: 227–8). According to Chinese policy-makers at the time, co-operative security should not merely complement bilateral military alliances but ultimately supersede them.

Still on the more proactive side, Beijing has introduced various proposals for confidence-building measures, on issues such as co-operation on defence conversion. This proposal followed the dissolution of the joint Sino–US commission on conversion that had been established only in 1994. At the time, China had, for instance, asked for assistance to transform China's military flight-control system into a civilian one while simultaneously improving its safety standards (Möller 1998a: 105). US Secretary of Defence William Perry had initially endorsed the idea, but the US Congress decided to dissolve the commission, with Republicans in particular worried about China reaping a military advantage from the use of US technology. The issue was further pursued by the ARF at Beijing's request, as illustrated by a recent seminar organised at expert level.

Moreover, the PRC has suggested that academic research be undertaken in the fields of military medicine and military law. Incidentally, this last proposal was included in a list of possible new ARF confidence-building measures endorsed by members at ARF 5 (ARF 1998d). In October 1999 China organised an ARF Professional Training Programme on China's security policy. She also offered to set up the ARF Regional Maritime Information Centre. Its participation in multilateral discussions on disaster relief management may also be noted as an exercise in regional confidence building.

Interestingly, Beijing has pursued its own brand of confidence building. In this context, it has stressed omni-directional and multi-level forms of military diplomacy. Such military diplomacy has seen visits by Chinese naval vessels to the US, Thailand, the Philippines and Malaysia, some of which were unprecedented. It should further be noted that to Beijing the numerous high-level exchanges with ASEAN states, primarily the Philippines, Vietnam, and Malaysia, involving the establishment of committees and working groups to discuss overlapping jurisdictional claims, also qualify as instances of confidence building and preventive diplomacy, again at the bilateral level.[10] So did the offer of a loan of US$2–3 million for military purposes, made to Manila in February 1997 by China's defence minister, Chi Haotian (*CHINA aktuell*, February 1997: 8).

While these are perhaps small steps in the field of confidence building, China has nevertheless demonstrated goodwill and proactivity. At the time of writing there are no indications that ASEAN governments feel that China needs substantially to reinforce its commitment to such confidence-building measures. More important to the majority of ASEAN governments are certain commitments that they wish China to make publicly and unambiguously. These commitments fall into or overlap with the realm of preventive diplomacy.

Beijing and preventive diplomacy

The ASEAN Concept Paper for the ARF identified the development of preventive diplomacy as the second stage of regional security co-operation. Significantly, Beijing has not been altogether keen to embrace preventive diplomacy in the context of the ARF, and has argued that it remains appropriate to focus on confidence-building measures to improve the climate of relations between regional countries (Liu Huaqiu 1995; Shi Chunlai 1999). In particular, Beijing has excluded the possibility of the ARF chair or other parties engaging in preventive diplomacy autonomously. China has merely accepted that there may well be an overlap between confidence building and preventive diplomacy.

From China's perspective, debates on preventive diplomacy have been problematic for at least two reasons. First, discussions on preventive diplomacy at both Track I and Track II levels[11] have usually had as a starting point the definition of preventive diplomacy proposed by former UN Secretary-General Boutros Boutros-Ghali. According to his definition, preventive diplomacy comprises 'action to prevent disputes from arising between parties, to prevent existing disputes from escalating into conflicts and to limit the spread of the latter when they occur' (Boutros-Ghali 1992: 475). China has contested vehemently the adequacy and appropriateness of this definition. Chinese officials have particularly scoffed at the idea that the 'action' to be undertaken as preventive diplomacy could range from diplomatic, through economic to military responses by a variety of actors. Because of the unpalatable implications that might arise for Beijing (especially as regards Taiwan) were such a definition to be generally accepted, Chinese officials have insisted on the need for ARF members to reach a common understanding of the term 'preventive diplomacy'. As China's foreign minister, Tang Jiaxuan, argued at ARF 5:

> The Chinese Delegation holds [that] ... it is necessary to lay down the guiding principles for building confidence and conducting security dialogue and cooperation in the Asia-Pacific region. At the same time, the ARF should continue to make timely exploration of the overlapping subject matters of confidence building measures and preventive diplomacy as well as the ways and means of addressing them. When conditions are ripe, we can probe the theories and approaches of preventive diplomacy which are suited to regional features. We believe

that under the guidance of correct principles, ARF's dialogue and cooperation will be more fruitful.

(Tang Jiaxuan 1998)

Despite China's strong misgivings about preconceived notions of preventive
diplomacy that would potentially carry unpalatable implications for Beijing,
and in line with Tang's remarks, China's stance on preventive diplomacy has
not been one of ruthless blockade. Having reiterated its consent for the ARF
to explore the overlap between confidence-building measures and preventive
diplomacy, Beijing has, in particular, not rejected the proposal that the
ISG–CBM examine the good offices role of the ARF chair. Of the measures
identified in 1999 (ARF 1999) as falling into the area of overlap between
confidence-building measures and preventive diplomacy (an enhanced role
of the ARF Chair, an ARF register of experts/eminent persons, a voluntary
Annual Security Outlook (ASO) and voluntary background briefings on
regional security issues), China has implemented two. First, China voluntarily contributed an assessment of the regional security situation to the
ASO compiled by Thailand as the seventh ARF chair. Second, China
provided a voluntary briefing on defence matters in Beijing in November
2000. This compares to similar contributions from just two ASEAN states,
Thailand and Singapore.

As regards the norm-elaboration processes leading to preventive diplomacy, therefore, China has clearly moved in step with the majority of
ASEAN governments. Indeed, ASEAN governments have also been wary
of some interpretations of the concept of preventive diplomacy, and they
also wonder how it would be implemented and by whom. In short, the
extent of ASEAN's participation in the area of overlap between preventive
diplomacy and confidence-building measures suggests, among others, that
it cannot be argued that from ASEAN's viewpoint China poses an unacceptable challenge to the evolution of preventive diplomacy within the
ARF context. Like a number of the new entrants and even some of the
earlier member states of the Association, China hopes to proceed more
slowly with preventive diplomacy than Western ARF members would like
to. That the fundamental fault lines lie between China and Australia/United
States rather than between China and ASEAN is also evident from the
evolving consensus on the concept and principles of preventive diplomacy
that Singapore has been drafting (ARF 2000b). Singapore's paper did
incorporate an amended definition of preventive diplomacy as originally
given by Boutros-Ghali. However, in terms of its principles it stressed that
preventive diplomacy is meant to be about diplomacy, and that it is non-
coercive, voluntary, building on consultation and consensus and requiring
trust and confidence, while being in accordance with recognised norms of
international society such as sovereignty and non-interference. Contrary to
the wishes of CSCAP, for example, the Singapore 2000 Draft Paper also
limited preventive diplomacy to conflicts between and among states. It is,

moreover, notable that the ARF Chairman's Statement (ARF 2000) high-lighted that progress on this issue would have to be at a pace comfortable for all, that decisions on preventive diplomacy would be made by consensus and that the ARF's focus on confidence-building measures would 'remain key'. All these points suggest that new practices on the preventive diplomacy front will take time to develop. Importantly, even though most ASEAN other than Singapore, Thailand and the Philippines have – like China – not exactly demonstrated an unambiguously positive commitment to the development of an ARF consensus on preventive diplomacy, ASEAN countries generally do not deem China's response as wholly satisfactory. The reason is that while norm-building in relation to preventive diplomacy serves a common purpose for reasons of regime and national security, China has been perceived as exploiting ASEAN's weaknesses in the South China Sea conflict. We shall examine this point in relation to what Aileen San Pablo-Baviera (1998: 223) has called the 'mother of all disputes'.

The South China Sea

The conflict on overlapping claims to islands, islets and reefs in the South China Sea, as well as that derived from these in relation to territorial jurisdiction is extremely complex and no attempt will be made here to outline the merits of individual claims. Suffice to say that analysts generally believe that the dispute has the potential to lead to serious conflict if mismanaged. As was mentioned above (p. 115), China would appear to challenge ASEAN's efforts to win an explicit endorsement of two norms: the norm of the non-use of force and the norm of restraint.

The challenge to the norm of the non-use of force

The first dimension of China's challenge to the 'ASEAN way' concerned the possibility that China might resort to the threat or use of force to enforce territorial and jurisdictional claims in the South China Sea against ASEAN claimants. Arguments emphasising the possibility of such behaviour are usually built on one or more of the following points:

- China has historically resorted to force when its leaders have perceived severe threats to its national security or its territorial integrity;
- in 1985 the Chinese leadership decided on a revised defence strategy emphasising regional contingencies and limited wars under high-tech conditions (Godwin 1996; also see Lewis and Xue Litai 1994);
- Beijing clashed violently with Vietnam in the Spratlys in 1988;
- some within China's ruling circles apparently considered the failure to oust other claimants from occupied territory in the South China Sea in the years between 1986 and 1988 as a 'lost chance' (Sheng Lijun 1995a: 12);

- China has been intent on a major military modernisation, not least of the People's Liberation Army Navy (PLAN);[12]
- China's punitive campaign against Vietnam in 1979 served as a recent reminder that China was prepared to initiate armed conflicts, at significant military costs;
- China has been reluctant to spell out clearly the differences in the nature of her claim to 'unalienable sovereignty' over Taiwan and that to 'indisputable sovereignty' to the South China Sea. As regards Taiwan, Beijing has of course refused to rule out the use of force should certain contingencies arise;
- China's leaders have depended increasingly on assertive nationalism rather than communism or socialism as a legitimating ideology (Whiting 1995);
- the People's Liberation Army (PLA), which is seen to have a penchant for resorting to confrontational tactics to press territorial claims, is regarded as enjoying significant influence over the decision-making processes of China's leadership (Lam 1999: ch. 4).

The challenge to the norm of restraint

China has also been seen as continuing to challenge the norm of restraint, treated here as a corollary of the norm of the non-use of force. It has done so despite the urgings for restraint by ASEAN since 1992 in the aftermath of Beijing's occupation of a series of features located in the Spratlys and the passage of a Law on the Territorial Sea and the Contiguous Zone in February 1992. From ASEAN's perspective it has been regretful that China would appear to have committed herself to respect the norm of restraint, without in practice having lived up to her words. Indeed, from ASEAN's viewpoint China still has unequivocally to endorse the 1992 ASEAN Declaration on the South China Sea. At the time China apparently claimed that it had informed the Philippine foreign secretary, Roberto Rómulo, that the principles of the Declaration were largely identical to China's position (Lee Lai To 1999: 28–9). However, Chinese officials apparently pointed out that Beijing could not formally endorse the Declaration on the grounds that at the time not all claimants were ASEAN members (Vietnam was not).

For ASEAN, the issue of restraint was again raised in stark form when it emerged, in early 1995, that the PRC had occupied Mischief Reef, also claimed by the Philippines. Beijing's record of gradually seeking to expand its physical presence in the South China Sea has since increasingly been referred to as China's 'creeping assertiveness' (Garver 1992; Chanda, Tiglao and McBeth 1995; Leifer 1995b; Valencia 1996; Storey 1999). The Mischief Reef incident prompted ASEAN to release a joint statement expressing serious concern about peace and stability in the South China Sea (ASEAN 1995). However, a number of incidents have since occurred involving Chinese navy vessels or fishermen. Not all incidents have taken place in the

Spratlys. Some have transpired around Scarborough Shoal or near the Vietnamese coastline. In March 1997, for instance, China proceeded to explore the seabed very close to Vietnam's shoreline. A Chinese rig involved in the exploration was removed only about a month later, following an ASEAN ambassadorial meeting in Hanoi. Vietnam's foreign minister, Nguyen Manh Cam, was later reported as having said that during three-day expert-level talks on this issue in Beijing between 9–11 April 1997 Chinese negotiators had refused to discuss the core issue of sovereignty and had not produced any evidence to back their claim (*Reuters*, 14 April 1997). Near the end of 1998, when ASEAN states faced serious economic dislocation and resultant political adversity, China proceeded to upgrade the facilities on Mischief Reef. This suggested that Beijing was indeed intent on 'capitalising on opportunities' (Ang Chen Guan 2000: 202) in different parts of the South China Sea. Significantly, beyond acting without restraint, it would also appear that China has invoked international law only for the purpose of strengthening its maritime claims and deliberately evaded justifying its own position. Relevant developments have reinforced fears that China is not commited to acting with restraint in the South China Sea, let alone interested in seeking a solution to the territorial and jurisdictional conflict.

In May 1996, for instance, Beijing declared baselines for measuring its territorial sea adjacent to the mainland and around the Paracel Islands, stating that the remaining straight baselines of the territorial sea of the PRC would be announced at another time. The declaration of baselines expanded the area claimed by Beijing as falling under its jurisdiction from 370,000 square kilometres to about 3,000,000 square kilometres. Not surprisingly, the declaration provoked protests and requests for clarification from Indonesia, Malaysia, the Philippines, Vietnam and others. Initially, it was believed that in setting these baselines China had – without proper basis – invoked the status of an 'archipelagic state'. However, the PRC has since clarified that the declared straight baselines are not claimed on this basis. It would appear that China now claims the waters inside the baselines as 'internal' waters.[13]

In June 1998 China adopted a Law on the Exclusive Economic Zone (EEZ) and the Continental Shelf that declared the PRC's EEZs with reference to the disputed straight baselines declared two years earlier. From the perspective of other claimants to the South China Sea, the significance of this particular legislation lay in the reaffirmation of China's historical entitlements (*lishixing quanli*) in the South China Sea (Nguyen Hong Thao 1998). As regards the timing of the new legislation, Chinese analysts argued that this particular law had been in the pipeline for many years and that its enactment had previously been delayed in order not to upset ASEAN and to avert negative international opinion (interview with analyst from Institute of Asia-Pacific Studies, Shanghai Academy of Social Sciences, Shanghai, 21 July 1998). However, given its timing in the aftermath of the Asian financial crisis and considerable disarray within ASEAN, China's explanatory remarks failed to deflect concern in ASEAN capitals over its position and ultimate intentions as regards the South China Sea. From the Chinese perspective of course the argument is increasingly that since other claimant states invoke those provisions of international law that best suit their national interest, China should and will do the same.

What has irked ASEAN officials, in both formal and informal settings (such as the Indonesian-initiated and Canadian-funded Managing Potential Conflicts in the South China Sea workshop series), is that China has consistently refused to specify the Chinese claims to the South China Sea. In particular, ASEAN diplomats and scholars have been miffed at Beijing's failure to explain the purpose, meaning and nature of the nine undefined dots making up a 'historical' claim-line on a Chinese map produced in 1947. Beijing's attempt to avoid concretising the co-ordinates of the 'dotted' claim-line in the South China Sea has left ASEAN claimants uncertain about whether China is claiming 'only' the islands, rocks and reefs, or the whole sea enclosed by the dotted line. The question of jurisdiction is further complicated by China's use of the term 'adjacent seas', a term which does not find mention in the United Nations Convention on the Law of the Sea. Not surprisingly, Beijing has also been reluctant to specify what it understands by 'joint development', in which it purports to be interested. China has, for example, not proposed to ASEAN the delimitation of any zone to be jointly developed among the claimants, leading ASEAN claimants to continue to suspect that China seeks joint development, if at all, then only on a bilateral basis. The biggest uncertainty, however, prevails over whether Beijing will also draw straight baselines around the Spratlys, whereby China would arrogate to herself vast tracts of sea as internal waters and territorial sea, as well as the right to suspend innocent passage of foreign vessels or transit of foreign aircraft.

The 'other' side of Beijing's record in relation to the South China Sea

Despite Beijing's initial reluctance even to discuss disputes about sovereignty and jurisdiction in the South China Sea, the fact is that its leaders and officials have, over time, accepted that this issue would be broached and tabled in various multilateral settings. For instance, following the Mischief Reef occupation, Chinese senior officials agreed to an informal discussion about the Spratlys in April 1995, before the first official ASEAN–China SOM. In this encounter ASEAN succeeded in allaying the remaining fears of the Chinese about the purpose of ASEAN's multilateral venture and in making clear that the Association does not appreciate being exposed as a paper tiger. Various scholars have noted China's positive response to ASEAN's collective criticism in the wake of the Mischief Reef incident (Leifer 1996b: 38, 55).[14]

At the second ASEAN–China SOM in June 1996 Beijing reaffirmed its readiness to settle questions of maritime jurisdiction in accordance with international law. It was also reported that China at least proposed to initiate an exchange of views among experts in this regard. A discussion of relevant PRC legislation took place at expert level between China and Indonesia in 1997. As of the third ASEAN–China SOM, in Huangshan in April 1997, the South China Sea dispute emerged as a formal agenda point for consultations. These have since been complemented by exchanges on the South China Sea among senior officials of ARF members. In the last few years China has incrementally allowed discussions on the Spratlys to deepen further across different institutional settings. Of particular note is the fact that substantive progress on preventive diplomacy has been in the making, in the form of a regional code of conduct.

Regional code of conduct

ASEAN foreign ministers first called for a regional code of conduct for the South China Sea in 1996 (Ang Chen Guan 2000: 209). At the time China rejected this, insisting that only bilateral codes of conduct between the PRC and another ASEAN claimant were possible. At the Sixth ASEAN Summit, in Hanoi in late 1998, the Philippines were, however, tasked to draft a regional code of conduct that would be acceptable to Beijing. This followed the perceived violations by the latter of the principle of restraint in relation to Mischief Reef, following China's decision to fortify existing structures apparently damaged in the wake of storms. 'Repairs' seemingly included the installation of anti-aircraft artillery and further military communications facilities (Cossa 1998). Manila had responded to these events by accusing Beijing of violating the spirit of the 1992 ASEAN Declaration, the China –Philippine Agreement of August 1995 and the ASEAN–PRC Joint Statement of December 1997, but to no avail. According to official PRC sources, relevant parties had been informed beforehand of the 'repair work' (Embassy of the PRC 1998). In subsequent weeks and months the Philippines impounded Chinese fishing vessels, detained their crews and resorted to a series of threats, without being able to make China budge (*SÜDOSTASIEN aktuell*, November 1998: 456; Richardson 1998c). A regional code of conduct, long favoured by other regional diplomats, was deemed the best way to exert pressure on China. Talks on the subject at the 1999 ASEAN–China SOM failed to produce a breakthrough, however.

In the event, Manila relaunched a proposal for a regional code of conduct for the South China Sea in April 1999, after various members of the Philippine government and Congress went on a diplomatic offensive against the PRC at the Sixth ASEAN Summit and the ministerial meeting of the 1999 Asia–Europe Meeting (ASEM). China still rejected the idea, but it was agreed that an ASEAN–China working group on a regional code of conduct would be set up. This group set out to explore issues such as the safety of navigation, search and rescue, the advocacy of self-restraint and the undertaking not to resort to the use or threat of force to settle competing claims. The Philippine authorities then provoked Beijing by sinking Chinese fishing boats in May and July 1999, without further political effect. In the meantime, however, the urgency of having a regional code of conduct acquired further significance when Malaysia built a two-storey structure with a helipad on Investigator Shoal and Vietnamese gunners on Tennent Reef aimed at a Philippine reconnaissance plane.[15]

However, China–ASEAN talks encountered difficulties over the geographic spread of the proposed code. These centred on Vietnam's insistence that the code of conduct should also apply to the Paracels, a demand that Beijing has adamantly rejected. In the event, the Philippines' attempt to bridge the gap by introducing into the draft a formulation whereby the code would cover 'disputed areas claimed in the South China Sea by more than two claimant states' was unsuccessful (*Philippine Daily Inquirer*, 16 March 2000: 2.). That said, the ASEAN–China Working Group on the Code of Conduct decided on a consolidated working draft in May 2000, which was to serve as a common basis for further consultation by the Working Group.

The finalisation of the draft has continued to elude officials.[16] Also, the Philippine navy continued to engage Chinese fishing vessels in Scarborough Shoal in early 2001. However, this does not detract from the fact that there is broad agreement that the proposed code should provide guidance on how to handle disputes, build trust and confidence, promote co-operation on marine issues and environmental protection, as well as modes of consultation. Indeed, at the time of writing there is considerable optimism on all sides that an agreement on a regional code of conduct can be reached.

Contextual assessment

Writing in the mid-1990s, Jusuf Wanandi pointed out the potential of engaging China in regional security dialogues and quiet diplomacy:

> It should be recognised that she [China] has been isolated for so long and therefore needs a lot of understanding and patience. This should not mean 'kow-towing' to her or joining the Chinese 'bandwagon' to secure a relationship with China for the longer future when she becomes a real great power. The problem is how to make her realize when she made mistakes. If it is being done in a friendly way, and not in public, she might listen. This could take some time to have an effect, because it might not be understood by her or her face is at stake or simply due to her cumbersome layers of bureaucracy.
>
> (Wanandi 1996: 13–14)

Despite his optimism China did not consistently react with restraint in the South China Sea. As a consequence, as Ang Cheng Guan has suggested, ASEAN claimant states would continue to have good reason to suspect that Beijing still hopes to 'capitalise on opportunities' (Ang Cheng Guan

2000: 202). This suspicion is all the more understandable as ASEAN's uncertainty about China's intentions and future behaviour also continues to feed on a historically informed appreciation of the past effects of interdependence on China (Huxley 1998: 15; Yahuda 1997). On the other hand, if one is to evaluate fairly Chinese behaviour *vis-à-vis* ASEAN on the South China Sea, one must bear in mind that Beijing might have good reason to be less than fully forthcoming on all demands made by ASEAN claimants on this issue.

At least three arguments appear pertinent. First, Beijing has an economic and strategic interest in defending its claim to maritime jurisdiction in the South China Sea, like other claimants. As her modernisation proceeds and both external trade and energy requirements rapidly expand, China is increasingly dependent on secure sea lines of communication. Given its status as a net importer of oil, Beijing clearly also has an interest in the exploitation of possible hydrocarbon resources in the South China Sea. Second, what is at issue for the People's Republic in the South China Sea is an issue of sovereignty. Sovereignty may often be taken to be only a legal concept, but it involves a *moral* claim that exists independently of legal title, in this case relating to the rightful ownership of territory. China's policy-makers and academics have widely been genuinely engulfed in moral outrage at what for China amounts to a policy of 'island-snatching' pursued by some ASEAN countries in the Spratlys. Chinese anger may be comprehensible if one appreciates that the legal claims of certain other claimant states, which often only date back to the 1970s, are not immune to challenge either (Sheng Lijun 1995a: 2–6; Möller 1998a: 136–9). Indeed, what was then North Vietnam had for more than two decades explicitly recognised the legitimacy of the long-standing Chinese claims to the Spratlys.[17] By 1997, however, Vietnam had occupied more islets, reefs and banks in the South China Sea than all the other claimants together.

Moreover, while ASEAN and Beijing have not made significant progress on the South China Sea issue, Beijing has been prepared to allow itself to be drawn into bilateral discussions concerning the validity of competing claims and various multilateral talks. Professor Ji Guoxing has explained China's ambivalence in dialectical terms as a 'contradiction', the principal part of which remains the 'pursuance of good-neighbourly relations with Southeast Asian countries' (Ji Guoxing 1998: 101).[18] In other words, just as several ASEAN countries do not wish the South China Sea disputes to take hold of China–ASEAN relations, so the People's Republic does not wish these disputes to become a stumbling block to the overall improvement in relations.

In any case, despite all the ambiguity China has demonstrated in the South China Sea, she has exercised a greater measure of restraint than she is usually given credit for. That restraint has been quite marked in the face of repeated perceived provocations by Vietnam and the Philippines, involving, for instance, the destruction of Chinese sovereign markers, the sinking of fishing vessels, and the arrest and detention of Chinese fishermen. It is too early to say whether this restraint indicates China's willingness to adhere to self-inhibiting norms on an issue of significance or whether it is simply the product of calculations about the potential opportunity costs. Equally, it seems too early to reach definitive conclusions about whether China's restraint in the face of provocations flows from the view that sustained non-compliance with the normative framework promoted by ASEAN might endanger its pursuit for recognition as a responsible major power. Although China does not unequivocally adhere to the norm of the non-use of force and its corollary, the norm of restraint, ASEAN nevertheless seems more confident now than in the early and mid-1990s that a non-violent solution to the Spratly conflict can be reached. Moreover, while the territorial and jurisdictional disputes remain a serious concern for ASEAN, they do not necessarily stand in the way of improved relations with China conducted within ASEAN's normative framework. The question thus becomes whether, and to what extent, Beijing has in other ways recently challenged the normative framework for regional co-operation proposed by the Association. The following section will explore this question in the context of China–ASEAN relations in the second half of the 1990s.

China's recent challenges to the 'ASEAN way'

When China's prime minister, Li Peng, visited Malaysia and Singapore in August 1997 shortly after the onset of the region's financial crisis, he put forward five principles to guide China's policy towards Southeast Asia (*CHINA aktuell*, October 1997: 986). These were mutual respect and equality; non-interference in each other's domestic affairs; the promotion of an increased level of dialogues and consultations, including summit meetings; mutually beneficial economic development; and enhanced co-operation in forums such as the UN, APEC, ASEM and the ARF. In December 1997, on the occasion of the Second Informal ASEAN–China Summit in Kuala Lumpur, China and ASEAN signed a joint statement that marked the culmination of almost two years of consultation and negotiation over the feasibility of issuing a joint political declaration. Proposed by China at the second ASEAN–China SOM in Bukittingi in 1996, the statement reaffirmed among others things the validity of the norms of the non-use of force and the peaceful settlement of conflict, as well as the norm of restraint. These norms have since been repeatedly re-emphasised by both sides in their routine bilateral diplomatic discourse as the normative staple to guide inter-state relations and interpersonal ties among leaders. Still, in view of the purpose of this chapter it is necessary to examine whether in practice Chinese leaders and officials have challenged either some of the norms said to guide China–ASEAN relations or their underlying rationale as seen from ASEAN's perspective. In the next section we shall examine this point in relation to the norms of sovereign equality and non-interference.

Recognition in ASEAN–PRC relations

In the context of ASEAN's intramural relations, smaller members especially have promoted the norm of sovereign equality. The norm has been similarly emphasised by ASEAN states in their relations with China. This can be understood against the backdrop of China's apparent 'Middle Kingdom complex' and its attempt

> to place itself at the top of a new hierarchical pyramid of power in the region – a kind of new 'tribute system' whereby patronage and protection are dispensed to other countries in return for their recognition of China's superiority and sensitivities.
>
> (Shambaugh 1996: 187)

Significantly, for ASEAN the issue of recognition in ASEAN–PRC relations extends beyond efforts by ASEAN countries to be treated as sovereign equals. Members of the Association have long sought Beijing's recognition of their distinct political identities. ASEAN leaders have collectively also sought recognition from the PRC as one of the poles in the emerging regional order. To evaluate to what extent China has been prepared to extend the desired recognition to ASEAN leaderships, it is useful to analyse how the PRC–ASEAN relationship has been conceptualised.

Conceptualising PRC–ASEAN relations

From China's perspective, PRC–ASEAN relations matter and have been analysed in the broader context of Chinese analysts' thinking on the 'international pattern' (*guoji geju*), which is the structure formed by the interactions among the major powers. Up to the Asian Crisis the consensus position on the future development of global politics was that the continued existence of conflict, limited wars and civil strife notwithstanding, the current era of peace and development would see the emergence of a multi-polar world following the ongoing transitional period. In this context, Chinese analysts and decision-makers focused on the development of major power relations which they conceptualised in geometric terms as four power triangles, with the United States at the centre (G. Chan 1999: 96–112; Dittmer 1997: 17). Apart from the United States, Chinese analysts identified Russia, Japan, the Europe and the PRC as the core actors, or 'international strategic forces', in world politics. Except for the EU, the same countries were seen as forming the four poles in East Asia. ASEAN has thus not been regarded as forming a pole. Indeed, even after its enlargement most Chinese analysts viewed ASEAN as merely representing a 'potential pole', not least because the Association has been considered to lack strong comprehensive power, especially economic and military power.

This line of analysis was reflected in China's adoption of a new discourse in the second half of the 1990s on building 'partnerships' (*huoban guanxi*).

This form of relationship was meant to convey a measure of significance superseding that of ordinary diplomatic relations. 'Partnerships' were conceptually delineated across three dimensions: temporal, modal and local. They were all meant to last well into the twenty-first century, with constant consultation designed to reinvigorate personal relationships and intensive economic co-operation designed to create an important foundation for a strong and stable relationship (Weggel: 1998: 820–3). In the event, Beijing's pursuit of 'partnerships' proved diplomatically cumbersome even though she eventually managed to sign or issue relevant documents with all the major centres of power.

Beijing and Moscow, for example, agreed to foster a 'strategic co-opera-tive partnership' (*zhanlüe xiezuo huoban guanxi*) of equality, mutual confidence and mutual co-ordination in April 1996, in the declared attempt to establish a new international order characterised by multipolarity and the rejection of hegemonism (Garver 1998; J. Anderson 1997). In May 1997 the PRC and France issued a joint declaration in which both agreed to build a 'comprehensive co-operative partnership' (*quanmian xiezuo huoban guanxi*). And in October of the same year China and the United States agreed to forge a 'constructive strategic partnership oriented toward the 21st century' (Chen Peiyao 1998). In April 1998, at the first EU–PRC Summit in London, Commission President Jacques Santer stressed that Brussels would forge a 'comprehensive co-operative partnership' with China and organise regular summits. And during the first ever visit of a Chinese head of state to Japan, in November 1998, Beijing also reached agreement with Tokyo on a 'part-nership of friendship and co-operation'.[19]

China and the Association have also invoked the concept of 'partnership' to describe their ties. Significantly, the partnership in question is a 'partner-ship of good neighbourliness and mutual trust' (Joint Statement 1997: 3). The fact that the partnership does not have the label 'strategic' or 'compre-hensive' indicates that Beijing believes ASEAN lacks strong comprehensive power, especially economic and military power. Nevertheless, from Beijing's perspective the use of the concept of 'partnership' *vis-à-vis* ASEAN appears to be designed to signal that the Association and its members do matter to Beijing, even if ASEAN is regarded as something of a weak player in the international politics of East Asia. From ASEAN's perspective the concept of a partnership of neighbourliness and mutual trust reflects members' collective appreciation of China's regional significance and continuing concerns as about the prospect of China becoming a fully established good citizen in regional international society. It is also far from clear that ASEAN would have wanted the label of strategic partnership attached to its relations with the PRC, given its members' reliance on the United States for external security.

Still, it seems reasonable to argue that by describing ASEAN–China ties as a 'partnership' Chinese leaders sought to convey the point that they recog-nised ASEAN as an important regional player in the broader international politics of East Asia. To be sure, this recognition did not imply that ASEAN was regarded as a political-strategic weight equal to the PRC or the other major powers. That could not be, as China has herself pursued what Sheng Lijun (1995b) has referred to as a policy of 'status enhancement'. The PRC's own struggle for recognition as a global power, is in part derived from China's traditional understanding of its own centrality (Kirby 1994), imbued with ideas about liberalism applied to the state (Hughes 1995). But, like to the modern national history of the ASEAN states, it also marks a response to the multiple violations of identity-claims that China experienced from the nineteenth to the late twentieth century.

Interference and human rights

Beijing has consistently denounced perceived attempts at 'Western' interference in China's affairs, especially under the pretext of human rights. Nevertheless, the Chinese leadership has found it increasingly impossible not to allow human rights as a valid subject of international dialogue and international law, albeit within strict boundaries (Seymour 1998). In the early 1990s ASEAN countries supported China's diplomatic campaign for the continued validity of the norm of non-interference and the promotion of the principle of mutual economic benefit that was meant to deflect criticisms of its human rights record and delegitimise a linkage between human rights and economic relations (Chen Jie 1993: 235). Key ASEAN member states also joined forces with Beijing to defend their common stance in the run-up to and during the UN-sponsored World Conference on Human Rights, held in Vienna in June 1993.

As the social order deteriorated in Indonesia in the spring of 1998, involving riots, looting and the killing of Indonesians of ethnic Chinese descent, China faced the delicate problem of whether to speak out against these events. The problem derived not merely from the scale of the atrocities and the number of dead, but also from the fact that the disturbances were apparently orchestrated by elements within Indonesia's armed forces that have generally been very apprehensive of the PRC. Beijing initially refused to be drawn into public criticisms of the Suharto regime (Suryadinata 1998). Indeed, at the time of his visit to Jakarta in April 1998 China's foreign minister, Tang Jiaxuan, stated unambiguously that China considered the mounting social unrest and racial violence a domestic matter in which China would not interfere. The evident purpose was not to jeopardise relations with Indonesia, which had just been lifted to a new high by Tang's visit and his promise of financial assistance worth US$300 million (Richardson 1998a). This reaction stood in marked contrast to the 1994 expression of concern voiced by a Chinese foreign ministry spokesman in response to social unrest and violence that targeted the ethnic Chinese community in Medan in north Sumatra (Sukma 1994). That comment had drawn an adverse Indonesian reaction.

As the security situation in Indonesia deteriorated, however, China's embassy, in mid-May, assisted in the evacuation of Chinese nationals. Following the resignation of President Suharto, a PRC government spokesperson also expressed the hope that the Indonesian government would take effective measures to protect the lives and properties of all its minorities, including the ethnic Chinese (quoted in the *Bangkok Post*, 22 May 1998: 5). Meanwhile, China affirmed that it was not interfering in Indonesia's affairs. Yet on the sidelines of the 1998 ASEAN post-ministerial meetings, Tang Jiaxuan voiced concern over the plight of ethnic Chinese Indonesians and asked Jakarta to adopt 'earnest measures' to address the situation (*Straits Times*, 30 July 1998: 2). By 3 August 1998 the Chinese government had issued a declaration in which it called on the Indonesian authorities to punish the perpetrators of the murders and rapes to which ethnic Chinese Indonesians had been subjected during the May riots.[20] The question is whether this stand is best interpreted as a diplomatic one-off or perhaps as the beginning of a return to more routine interference by China in the affairs of ASEAN states.

Two things are important to an understanding of China's belated unofficial and official involvement in Indonesia's domestic politics. First, once knowledge about the rape and killing of ethnic Chinese Indonesians had become common currency in mainland China – it took several weeks for the information to filter through the state media – an increasing number of Chinese citizens expressed outrage at the events. Under these circumstances inaction on the government's part would have constituted a politically embarrassing silence on the abuse of the basic rights of people of Chinese origin. In the event, protests by students and others were tolerated within certain limits, as evidenced by demonstrations staged in Beijing on several occasions, not least on Indonesia's national independence day (*CHINA aktuell*, August 1998: 801). Second, and more importantly, the CCP-led government did not deem it feasible to take a backseat on the violations of the human rights of ethnic Chinese, even though they had foreign citizenship, if this allowed the Taiwanese authorities to score political points against Beijing. Taipei's official public reaction was much more aggressive than Beijing's stance (Zha 2000). Notably, Vice-Premier Qian Qichen still expressed concern about 'Chinese Indonesians' at the 1998 National Day reception organised by the State Council's Office of Overseas Chinese Affairs. In view of these considerations and the embarrassment linked to the riots, the Indonesian government did not register public indignation at what constituted an infraction of the principle of non-interference, but many within Indonesia no doubt found Beijing's stance disturbing.

Despite this episode in recent Sino-Indonesian relations, the CCP leadership would not appear generally to have shifted ground on the norm of non-interference in its relations with the Association. Following the accession to political power of Abdurrahman Wahid in October 1999, a new tone in the diplomatic language used between Jakarta and Beijing suggested increasingly friendly, albeit pragmatic, relations that stress the norm of non-interference. Arguably, Beijing's continued commitment to the basic norms of ASEAN's diplomatic and security culture was also testified to by the signing or issuing of bilateral framework agreements on future co-operation with ASEAN countries.

Frameworks for future bilateral co-operation

As Derek da Cunha argued, 'Asean states are today far more dependent on policy coming out of Beijing than they have been for the past decade or so' (da Cunha 1998). At the height of the Asian economic crisis this was the view held in Bangkok, in particular. Beijing's contribution to the country's international financial rescue package, Chinese assurances that the yuan would not be devalued, and promises to absorb more Thai exports all indicated to Thai analysts China's rising capacity as an economic and financial power. In part to acknowledge its gratitude and in part to promote Thailand's longstanding objective of becoming a hub for the economic development of Indochina and southern China, Bangkok proposed to spell out its long-term co-operative agenda with Beijing. In February 1999 this took the form of a Joint Statement on a Plan of Action for the Twenty-First Century. This was to be the first of ten joint statements signed or issued from February 1999 to December 2000 by the PRC with all ASEAN countries on their future bilateral co-operation.[21]

The substance of joint statements

The details of the joint statements vary, but it is possible to identify several common features. First, the statements identify the areas in which bilateral co-operation is to be explored or enhanced. While future relationships between China and ASEAN member states are qualified as 'all-directional', the emphasis on co-operation in the areas of trade and investment is conspicuous. A second objective listed in the statements is the advancement of political co-operation through close and frequent contacts between leaders and officials. Where feasible and desirable, China and the ASEAN members have, moreover, agreed to fine-tune diplomatic positions in various international forums such as the ARF, APEC, ASEM, ASEAN Plus Three and the United Nations. Third, several framework agreements explicitly mention co-operation in security and defence.[22] Fourth, most framework agreements register a consensus – albeit one that varies – on the aspired regional order. For instance, while the China–Singapore statement bears no reference to 'multipolarity' or the establishment of a 'new just and equitable international political and economic order', Malaysia and the Philippines agreed to a formulation stressing the promotion of a new 'equitable and rational' political and economic world order. The Indonesia–China statement is by far the most assertive in tone, calling as it does for a 'just and more balanced new international political, economic *and security* order'.[23]

As regards the principles that are to guide relations between China and ASEAN member states, most statements make reference to the principles of the UN Charter, the Five Principles of Peaceful Co-existence (FPPC), the principles of the TAC and other recognised principles of international law. The China–Indonesia statement also invokes the Ten Principles of the Bandung Declaration. In other words, both the PRC and the various ASEAN governments have again formally committed themselves to respecting the basic principles of international society in their bilateral relations. The question is whether the commitment is more than just rhetorical.

From Beijing's perspective at least three developments highlighted the need to reinforce the claim to the validity of principles such as sovereign equality and non-interference in the context of its relations with ASEAN. One relevant development concerns Taipei's efforts to enhance its international stature in Southeast Asia. Particularly after the Taiwan Straits Crisis of 1995–6, Taiwanese leaders redoubled their efforts, seeking to win political capital by offering to assist crisis-stricken Southeast Asian countries, not least by investing in them.[24] In view of such overtures, Beijing believed it needed to be circumspect about the potential for economic distress to make ASEAN countries punch even small nails in what from Taipei's perspective is the coffin of Beijing's one-China policy.

In the event, Chinese leaders warned ASEAN states not to let their economic and financial plight get in the way of good bilateral relationships with the People's Republic. Beijing pointed out that while she had behaved responsibly by not devaluing her currency, Taipei had done exactly the opposite and in precipitate fashion, too. Also, Beijing sought to quell debates about possible closer ties with Taiwan, like those held, for instance, in some circles in Manila against the background of the Sino-Philippine dispute in the South China Sea, despite the opposition to such ideas by the country's Department of Foreign Affairs. Beijing has thus focused on winning clear commitments to the one-China principle in the texts of the joint statements. This has been achieved. Taiwan is variously described as a 'part of China' (Singapore), an 'integral part of Chinese territory' (for instance, Thailand and the Philippines), or an 'inalienable' part of China. In return for their continued commitment to the one-China policy, Beijing has expressly vowed to respect the independence, sovereign equality and territorial integrity of ASEAN countries.

A second reason for Beijing to reaffirm the basic principles of international society and the 'ASEAN way' arose from the perceived need to endorse the continuation of ASEAN's prerogative role in the ARF. This compulsion stemmed from the weakening of ASEAN's political influence and bargaining power which had accompanied the decline of members' economies since July 1997. Importantly, Chinese decision-makers regarded, not merely ASEAN's economic malaise, but also the attendant loss of standing incurred in international society as undermining international receptivity to ASEAN's claim to remain the ARF's driving force. This assessment bore particular relevance insofar as Western powers had previously sought to apply pressure on ASEAN regarding the future agenda, character and control of the ARF. These issues are closely linked to the ARF's normative framework, which is itself based on ASEAN's diplomatic and security culture.

Third, although the ARF cannot be credited with playing a major part in promoting the improvement in Sino-US relations,[25] Chinese leaders have viewed its multilateral security dialogues as an opportunity for China's foreign minister to propound ideas close to the heart and interests of Chinese leaders. This has extended to building up moral pressure on issues of particular significance to Beijing. Indeed, Beijing has used the ARF as a platform on which to advocate its 'new concept of security'. This emphasises, among other things, respect for the Five Principles of Peaceful Co-existence, the peaceful settlement of conflicts, and the promotion of mutual trust and understanding through security dialogues and co-operation in the security and economic fields (*China's National Defense* 1998; Finkelstein and McDevitt 1999). China has also endeavoured to foster a regional foreign policy mood among other ARF members that is antithetical to the idea of seeking to guarantee security by an increase in arms capabilities or through military alliances. For the Chinese leadership, the idea enlarging military blocs and strengthening military alliances runs counter to the tide of the times (*China's National Defense* 1998). Beijing has also hoped to win support for its position that Japan should not assume a more assertive military role within East Asia.

Significantly, as the Asian crisis unfolded and Western ARF members' criticisms of the forum multiplied, China's regional analysts expressed doubts that ASEAN would continue to command a position from which the Association would be able and willing to practise equidistance *vis-à-vis* East Asia's major powers. Indeed, concerns emerged that ASEAN leaderships might side with one major power against others in order to pursue the Association members' own national interests.

In practice, China has stressed the importance of the following points in relation to the ARF:

* participation on an equal footing;
* reaching unanimity through consensus;
* seeking common ground while reserving differences;
* proceeding in an orderly way and step by step.

Expressing this position consistently has served to protect China's own interests and promote the continued acceptance of ASEAN norms as an underlying framework for regional co-operation. Indeed, insisting on these norms has allowed the Chinese government to play a key role in addressing regional security concerns and enhancing the legitimacy of the PRC as a responsible major power.

Indeed, Beijing's endorsement of norms associated with ASEAN's diplomatic and security culture in defining bilateral frameworks for future co-operation with ASEAN countries must also be seen in the context of extra-regional developments. Most important in this regard was the bombing campaign initiated by the North Atlantic Treaty Organisation (NATO) against the Federal Republic of Yugoslavia in March 1999 without authorisation from the United Nations Security Council. The Beijing leadership condemned the campaign, ostensibly initiated for humanitarian purposes, as 'barbarism'.[26] The accidental bombing of its embassy in Belgrade in early May accentuated China's criticism of NATO's intervention, exacerbating the crisis in Sino-American relations, and its insistence on the validity of longstanding international political-legal principles.[27] As China's foreign minister chose to put it:

> Facts have proven, and will continue to prove that China–ASEAN friendly relations and cooperation based on the Five Principles of Peaceful Coexistence are firmly founded and widely endorsed, and promise tremendous potentials and broad prospects. There are big and small countries in the world. And they may vary from one another in historical background, social systems, level of development, cultural traditions, and values. However, so long as they respect each other, treat each other as equals, seek common ground while shelving differences and conduct mutually beneficial cooperation, they will be able to coexist in harmony and achieve common development. This is useful experience gained in the ever-growing China–ASEAN relations, and it serves the fundamental interests of people of all countries, contributes to regional peace and stability, and can facilitate the establishment of a new, just and rational order of peace and cooperation. Observance of the Five Principles of Peaceful Coexistence, the purposes and spirit of the UN Charter as well as the principles enshrined in the Treaty of Amity and Cooperation in Southeast Asia is the soul of China–ASEAN relations. It is also of vital significance to the international relations and international order in the 21st century.
>
> (Tang Jiaxuan 1999)

Conclusion

ASEAN has not been able to make China abide by the entire proposed framework for governing intra-regional relations to which it has sought adherence by the major powers. While ASEAN has been fairly successful in delegitimising the use of force to settle unresolved territorial conflicts, it has failed to get China to commit explicitly and unequivocally to the principle of restraint. In the wake of the Asian financial and economic crisis a paradoxical situation has arisen, in that Chinese analysts and decision-makers have appeared to view ASEAN's importance in shaping regional order as having diminished. At the same time, the Association's significance for the PRC, primarily in terms of the former's advocacy of the continued importance of basic norms of international society associated with the 'ASEAN way', has increased. This is a direct consequence of the deterioration of Sino-US bilateral relations in the late 1990s. To shield against 'hegemonism' and 'power politics', which China has officially declared to be the main sources of threats to world peace and stability, China has advocated an international order and an attendant new security concept that build on norms also espoused by ASEAN. It is thus possible to argue that China has reinforced the argument in favour of the continued validity of norms like sovereignty and non-interference, hitherto at the heart of ASEAN's diplomatic and security culture. Beijing has also supported the practice of quiet diplomacy and intensive consultations. But this does not imply that China supports all principles and practices of the 'ASEAN way'. As we have seen, the Chinese leadership challenges ASEAN's pursuit of its underlying struggle for security and recognition in fundamental respects, especially in relation to the South China Sea dispute, but also in relation to its quest to become a regional pole of equal stature.

The next chapter will examine to what extent the United States has challenged ASEAN's diplomatic and security culture.

6 The US challenge to the 'ASEAN way'

Since the end of the Second Indochina War Washington has focused far less on Southeast than on Northeast Asia. This is particularly true for the post-Cold War period, as illustrated by Washington's efforts in the 1990s to engage or constrain China, not least to avert armed conflict in the Taiwan Strait, as well as those designed to address conflict on the Korean peninsula (particularly its nuclear dimension). The United States has also invested significantly in revitalising its alliance relationship with Japan. Notwithstanding some adjustments, Washington has retained its forward-deployed forces in Japan and the Republic of Korea.

ASEAN states have long regarded the United States as a benign power. This was the case during the Cold War and is, by and large, again the case in the post-Cold War period, notwithstanding the fact that since 1999 ASEAN has comprised all ten Southeast Asian countries. At least five reasons can be identified why ASEAN states actively welcome the presence of the United States in the region. First, Washington has provided ASEAN states with generous access to American markets. This has greatly helped ASEAN regimes successfully to implement export-led strategies of development, which have not lost their attractiveness, as illustrated by the policies of earlier and new member states of the Association in the aftermath of the Asian financial crisis. Second, Washington has also provided external security to ASEAN members. Thailand and the Philippines have for many years been alliance partners of the US. Other ASEAN countries have for years engaged in various forms of military and security co-operation with Washington. In view of these ties, most ASEAN states have probably been able to invest fewer resources in military spending than one might reasonably have otherwise expected. Third, the US Navy has ensured the safety of regional sea lines of communication that are vital to the economic survival of the ASEAN economies. Fourth, unlike other regional major powers, Washington has no territorial or jurisdictional claims in Southeast Asia. Finally, at least some ASEAN countries also believe that the US regional presence in the form of forward-deployed troops in the wider region and frequent naval visits has served to prevent the emergence of what to them might be an unpalatable local balance of power in maritime Southeast Asia.

All ASEAN members moreover agree that the US presence is also instrumental in upholding a favourable configuration of power in Northeast Asia.

While it is perceived by ASEAN countries as a benign power, the United States has also clearly been the region's hegemonic power. A clearly visible structure of hierarchical relations between Washington and its allies and friends in Northeast and Southeast Asia has been the logical consequence. As a pre-eminent power in East Asia, Washington has been able to use the provision of security or market access as leverage to promote more or less gently its particular interests. However, as Bruce Cumings has argued, in a hegemonic project 'the hierarchy is by no means one of domination, subordination, direct dependence, closed opportunities for others, or a matter of winning all the time' (Cumings 1999: 205). This is precisely the reason ASEAN has been so supportive of Washington. Still, as Cumings has further pointed out, the exercise of hegemony implies efforts by the hegemon to establish 'outer limits on the behaviour of those within the hegemonic realm' (Cumings 1999: 205).

There have been various examples of such endeavours in relation to US–ASEAN ties, and most would appear to have been successful. For instance, when Washington pursued the containment of Moscow, it pursued a hard-line position at the ICK in 1981 that thwarted even ASEAN's limited diplomatic opening to Vietnam. Also, when proposals for multilateral security dialogues in the Asia-Pacific region first emerged, the administration of George Bush reacted negatively to preserve its advantage *vis-à-vis* the Soviet Union. Up to the time of writing, Washington has refused to sign the protocol to the Treaty on the Southeast Asian Nuclear Weapons Free Zone. Obviously the United States also opposes developments in China–ASEAN relations that might undermine Washington's position as East Asia's hegemonic power.

In this context, the purpose of this chapter is to examine whether the United States has challenged the 'ASEAN way' and what form any challenges may have taken. Significantly, by posing this question the chapter is not asking whether the United States at any time violated principles of international society in engaging Southeast Asia. Of course, the United States clearly did violate basic principles of international society on numerous occasions during the Eisenhower, Kennedy, Johnson, Nixon and Reagan administrations in their respective relations with Southeast Asia (McTurnan Kahin and McTurnan Kahin 1995; Kolko 1985; Brown 1991; Schwab 1998; McNamara 1995; Scott 1996: 82–111). However, it makes little sense to speak of a formidable US challenge to the 'ASEAN way' in the Cold War period. Several ASEAN states supported the United States diplomatically or practically in its battle against the expansion of Moscow's military influence. In view of its Cold War struggle against Moscow, Washington had no or little compunction about supporting authoritarian leaderships in Southeast Asia and paid only limited attention to intra-ASEAN ties. Despite what has already been said, ASEAN and Washington were partners seeking to reverse

Vietnam's military intervention in Cambodia, which implied broad diplomatic support for the interpretation of norms associated with ASEAN's diplomatic and security culture as espoused by Singapore and Thailand. To the extent that the United States challenged an underlying purpose of ASEAN's diplomatic and security culture, it did so by ignoring ASEAN's stress on the autonomous management of regional order inherent in ZOPFAN. However, as Chapter 3 demonstrated, ZOPFAN was in abeyance for the latter part of the 1970s and the 1980s.[1]

How, then, should one think about what constitutes the US challenge to the 'ASEAN way' in the post-Cold War period? For the purposes of this book, a challenge to the 'ASEAN way' by the United States obtains to the extent that American administrations have sought to undermine the significance of norms deemed central as a terrain mediating the security and estrangement of Southeast Asian governments. In other words, a challenge exists if there is evidence that the United States has sought to alter the approach that ASEAN members adopt towards each other or towards those states that are signatories to the TAC. Empirically, such a case would arise if the US had attempted to nudge ASEAN governments to propose or adopt modes of intramural behaviour that are at odds with expectations linked to collective understandings of the Association's diplomatic and security culture. A challenge will also be seen to obtain to the extent that the United States has opposed the extension of ASEAN's diplomatic and security culture as the terms of reference for the ARF and the interactions between Southeast Asia and the regional major powers.

In line with this conceptualisation of what constitutes an US challenge to the continued validity of ASEAN's diplomatic and security culture developed above, this chapter will be divided into two sections. The first section explores the US challenge to the 'ASEAN way' in the context of Washington's policy toward Myanmar, not least the extent to which ASEAN countries have resisted US pressure for more openly confrontational policies toward Myanmar. The second section explores whether Washington poses a challenge to the 'ASEAN way' in the context of the ARF and the evolving norm-elaboration processes, particularly with respect to confidence building and preventive diplomacy in the East Asia-Pacific region.

US foreign policy and Burma/Myanmar in the post-Cold War period

Just months before the collapse of socialist regimes in Eastern Europe made President George Bush celebrate the arrival of a New World Order – which it was believed would usher in the spread of liberal democracies and market economies across the globe – the State Law and Order Restoration Council (SLORC) assumed power in Burma. This followed the political violence of August and September 1988 (Lintner 1990).[1] Ever since, the SLORC, relabelled for public relations purposes as the State Peace and Development

Council (SPDC) in 1997, has seen its political legitimacy challenged by the United States, the European Union and various other countries. That challenge was considerably accentuated when the military regime refused the formation of a government on the basis of the May 1990 elections, comfortably won by the National League for Democracy (NLD).[2] Thereafter, Washington's Burma policy focused on an end to the repression of the 'democratic opposition' and the start of a meaningful dialogue with the NLD under Nobel Peace Prize laureate Daw Aung San Suu Kyi and the countries' ethnic minorities (US Department of State 1999). Over the years Washington has applied increasing pressure on the ruling military regime in Yangon to comply with American exhortations. The State Department, for instance, has downgraded US representation in Myanmar from ambassadorial to chargé d'affaires level and imposed visa restrictions for senior officials of the military regime and their families. An arms embargo was put in place and Washington barred all anti-narcotics assistance to the ruling council (Lintner 1994). The United States then suspended economic aid and disqualified Burma from the General System of Preferences and Overseas Private Investment Corporation programmes. In 1997 the US imposed economic sanctions on Myanmar, the purpose of which was to stop new investments by American businesses (US Department of State 1997), which were only to be lifted if major progress in human rights was achieved. In response to significant pressure exerted by international human rights groups, successive US administration have also continued to oppose financial assistance to Myanmar from international financial institutions in the absence of progress towards genuine democratisation (Cook and Minogue 1997: 185–6). Remaining wedded to the so-called 'hostage model', Washington has equally sought to put its weight behind the condemnation of both the lack of freedom of association for workers and the use of forced labour by the military regime. This is supplemented by US multilateral diplomacy at the United Nations General Assembly and the UN Human Rights Commission, where the United States has taken an active role in pressing for strong human rights resolutions on Burma.

While US policy has generally been lauded as an example of how to deal with a 'pariah regime', Washington's stance toward the SLORC/SPDC has not been entirely free of ambiguity (and controversy). For example, although US policy towards Myanmar has been couched in hostile terms, the Clinton administration never altogether ignored Myanmar's enormous resource wealth. Even while they were deciding on sanctions, economic and business considerations were clearly borne in mind by US decision-makers, as illustrated by the Clinton administration's opposition at one point to a bipartisan coalition that pressed for immediate, mandatory economic sanctions against Burma.[3] It is safe to assume that, notwithstanding the emphasis on human rights in US foreign policy towards Burma, geopolitical considerations have also underpinned Washington's unflinching support for Daw Aung San Suu Kyi. From a geo-strategic perspective, Myanmar is an important buffer against increasing Chinese military and economic influence in this part of Southeast Asia and the Indian Ocean (Malik 1997; Liang 1997). From Washington's perspective, a government led by Aung San Suu Kyi could be expected to be very close to the United States, not least out of gratitude for long-term political support. As Robert Rotberg has argued, a 'freed Burma would need large-scale and sustained international friendship and assistance, as well as committed new corporate investment' (Rotberg 1998: 7). Irrespective of the weighting one should ascribe to the different motivations underlying US policy toward Burma, however, Washington has pursued de facto the removal of the military regime in power. It is in this context that the chapter will now discuss to what extent the United States has challenged ASEAN's diplomatic and security culture.

The US challenge to the 'ASEAN way' over Burma/Myanmar

Building on the argument developed so far, US involvement in the domestic affairs of Myanmar is not regarded here as constituting a challenge to the 'ASEAN way' *per se*, irrespective of whether one agrees with Washington's official contention that this has not implied contravening basic principles of international society.[4] However, such a challenge might be seen to reside in US protestations over ASEAN's collective diplomatic approach *vis-à-vis* Myanmar, conceptualised as 'constructive engagement', particularly the decision to admit Yangon into the Association, and other members' stance towards Myanmar thereafter.

Historically, ASEAN's practice of 'constructive engagement' developed as the prolongation of a Thai foreign policy stance of accommodation towards Myanmar that helped, above all, to satisfy particular Thai business interests. Some have suggested that it amounted to a policy of appeasement because it allowed the Burmese armed forces (*tatmadaw*) and ethnic minority fighters loyal to Yangon to conduct military operations against anti-government forces operating on the Thai–Burma border, leading to occasional infringements of Thailand's territorial integrity (Buszynski 1998: 291–6). 'Constructive engagement' was formally adopted as ASEAN's collective approach *vis-à-vis* Myanmar in 1992. Reasons why ASEAN members other than Thailand supported this move varied. Some, like Indonesia, endorsed 'constructive engagement' of Myanmar as a conscious counterbalancing of Myanmar's increasing economic and military dependence on China, in the belief that ties between Yangon and Beijing would further improve only if the former were ostracised. Others appear to have been interested in using 'constructive engagement' as a platform that would facilitate economic competition with Thailand over the spoils to be reaped in Myanmar. At least some ASEAN members may also have believed that, in terms of method, 'constructive engagement' was superior to strategies of condemnation and confrontation to help bring about a political relaxation of sorts within Burma insofar as it did not seek to isolate or embarrass the military regime. That said, ASEAN's diverging interests in Myanmar effectively crippled a coherent diplomatic approach towards Yangon and gave 'constructive engagement' a bad name. The Philippine foreign secretary, Raul Manglapus, for instance, visited Yangon on an unofficial human rights mission in December 1991, but promoting human rights and furthering democracy was a minority interest within ASEAN then and would remain so for some time. This is evidenced by, among other things, the discourse on Asian values that sought to legitimise authoritarian regimes across Southeast Asia.[5] Also, while some members dissented from steps whose symbolism they considered politically unacceptable, ASEAN sent clear signals that it aspired to one Southeast Asia. In the event, Myanmar's membership in ASEAN proceeded along the fast track.

Having only been invited as a guest to participate in the ASEAN Ministerial Meeting processes in 1994, Myanmar acceded to the TAC the year after, which, *interalia*, proscribes its signatories from meddling in each other's internal affairs. In December 1995 the SLORC's nominal leader, Senior General Than Shwe, attended the Fifth ASEAN Summit in Bangkok. There, ASEAN leaders declared themselves in favour of the 'speedy realisation of an ASEAN comprising all ten Southeast Asian states'. The following year Yangon was granted observer status in the Association and became a member of the ARF. Full membership of the Association was attained in July 1997.

Washington was intensely dissatisfied with these developments. From an American viewpoint, 'constructive engagement' proved an ineffective, if not counterproductive, exercise because it failed to generate compliance by the SLORC/SPDC with Washington's demands. When Myanmar joined the ARF without extensive consultations with other ARF members, the Clinton administration reacted angrily. ASEAN countries dismissed US censure and, in justifying the lack of consultation, somewhat cheekily noted the Association's leading role in the Forum. ASEAN governments, moreover, stuck by the argument that closer ties with Myanmar were more likely to improve that country's domestic political situation and contain China's influence in the country than would a policy of confrontation.

Senior General Than Shwe had indeed privately promised Dr Mahathir to work towards domestic political progress. Contrary to such promises, however, the SLORC engaged in sustained crackdowns on Myanmar's domestic political opposition in October 1996. Faced with more arrests of student demonstrators in December 1996, upon which NLD leader Aung San Suu Kyi again called for the imposition of sanctions, the White House imposed visa restrictions on those associated with the military regime (Than and Than 1997: 212–15).

With Myanmar's impending admission into the Association practically sealed at the 1996 ASEAN Informal Summit, Washington (and other Western countries, particularly the European Union) nevertheless still sought to persuade ASEAN governments to defer Yangon's entry, if not to attach political conditions to the prize of membership. Having sent two special envoys to ASEAN capitals to argue unsuccessfully its case against Myanmar in 1996 (Ott 1998: 74), the year after the Clinton administration exerted renewed political pressure on ASEAN by having Madeleine Albright write to all ASEAN heads of government to postpone Myanmar's admission. President Clinton also signed an Executive Order that prohibited new American direct foreign investment in Myanmar. Having argued that Myanmar should not be rewarded by membership 'in one of the most prestigious and important pan-Asian organisations' (Nicholas Burns, cited in Pretzell 1997: 325) yet failed to make political impact, the US Secretary of State went into attack mode at the subsequent ministerial meetings in Malaysia.

Madeleine Albright launched a particularly vigorous challenge at ARF-4 in July 1997 and the subsequent Post-Ministerial Conference, where she termed Burma 'an anomaly within ASEAN' (Albright 1997). Moreover, Secretary Albright added insult to criticism in her challenge to Myanmar's credentials for ASEAN membership by comparing Burmese leaders to Fidel Castro and Saddam Hussein in the now traditional artistic presentations at the end of the ARF meeting (*SÜDOSTASIEN aktuell*, September 1997: 370), where ARF foreign ministers engage in a song and dance session, notable for its sarcasm and open criticism, all wrapped up in funny lyrics sung to well-known tunes. Other attempts to highlight the illegitimacy of the Yangon government focused on the reference 'Burma' rather than 'Myanmar', although the latter has been, since 1989, the official name recognised by, among others, ASEAN and the UN.[6] In subsequent years the US also vigorously protested what officials in Washington and elsewhere saw as violations of Aung San Suu Kyi's freedom of movement and assembly (Albright 1998). In 1999 Madeleine Albright again used the ARF as a platform to argue forcefully that Myanmar continued to pose a threat to regional security (Albright 1999).

Was US criticism of 'constructive engagement' a challenge to the 'ASEAN way'?

The question is whether Washington's challenge of 'constructive engagement' indeed constituted a challenge to ASEAN's diplomatic and security culture. This might be denied – for instance, with reference to the fact that 'constructive engagement' was introduced several years before Myanmar's ASEAN membership in 1997. As such, 'constructive engagement' was a collective ASEAN policy, but not one applied in an intramural context.

However, several arguments support the argument that the US did challenge the 'ASEAN way' over Myanmar. ASEAN's practice of 'constructive engagement' built on modes of interaction associated with the 'ASEAN way' insofar as these emphasised respect for both the political-legal and socio-psychological norms. ASEAN thereby hoped to 'socialise' the military regime in Yangon. Interestingly, ASEAN's emphasis on quiet diplomacy was complemented by increased trade and to some extent deeper military-to-military ties, developments that also replicated to some extent the experience of intramural relations among the Association's original members. Not least for these reasons, 'constructive engagement' has also been designated as a policy of 'restraint' (quoted in Acharya 1995: 175). However, to the extent that 'constructive engagement' marked an instance of externalising the 'ASEAN way', it was admittedly nevertheless an approach aiming to apply broadly rather than rigorously a strict interpretation of ASEAN's intramural diplomatic and security culture. In other words, 'constructive engagement' was, despite its ineffectiveness, still characterised by design and in practice by a degree of ASEAN involvement in Myanmar's domestic political process that went beyond what then was considered to constitute legitimate involvement by member states in each other's domestic affairs. The same argument, albeit with a different and more cynical drift, was also made by Acharya, who noted that 'constructive engagement' was a 'particular kind of interference in support of the regime' (Acharya 2001: 113). Significantly, when ASEAN countries continued to practice 'constructive engagement' after Myanmar's accession to the Association, they inadvertently introduced new possible parameters for the practice of standard intramural norms like non-interference.

It should be noted that the widening of these parameters is attributable to the different positions held on Myanmar by the various ASEAN member states. Both the Philippines and Thailand communicated to fellow members that the domestic politics of Myanmar should be a factor when considering the timing of Yangon's membership of ASEAN. Yet, leaders from both countries deferred in solidarity to Jakarta and Kuala Lumpur, where the incumbent governments had pressed strongly for the admission of Myanmar into the Association on the basis of the Association's four established criteria.[7] These were: adhering to all ASEAN agreements, such as the Bangkok Declaration and the TAC; paying an equal share of the expenses of the ASEAN Secretariat and ASEAN funds; establishing diplomatic representation in all member states of the Association; and satisfying the AFTA criteria. While the Association hence refused to consider political criteria for membership, ASEAN foreign ministers collectively, and some ASEAN leaders individually, announced that they would pile more pressure on Yangon to alleviate the country's human rights problems once Myanmar had joined (Funston 1999: 208). Notwithstanding this indication, given that Myanmar was seen as a political liability and an acute diplomatic embarrassment for ASEAN well before its admission to the Association, the question is why ASEAN members – collectively – largely resisted this US chalenge to the 'ASEAN way', particularly the norm of non-interference, before the outbreak of the Asian financial crisis.[8]

Understanding ASEAN's reluctance to give in to US pressure

A number of reasons underlie ASEAN's decision to endorse and proceed with 'constructive engagement' as well as to admit Myanmar into the Association. First, even those within ASEAN who, like the Philippines, were more or less consistently critical of the SLORC's human rights record had doubts about the wisdom of America's confrontational stance *vis-à-vis* the military regime. Attempts to embarrass and politically isolate the ruling elite in Yangon were largely considered ineffective because of Myanmar's previous isolationist track record. Also, while Myanmar's economic situation had for some time been quite precarious, ASEAN leaders were not convinced that economic sanctions would make the military regime more pliant to external pressure.

A second reason for resisting the US challenge on 'constructive engagement' was linked to the way in which the US exerted pressure on other ASEAN states over the issues of human rights and democracy. Most ASEAN leaderships had hoped for a more partner-like and more equal relationship with the United States in the post-Cold War period, at least as a grouping, particularly in view of their economic success in the 1980s and mid-1990s, their respective reliance on Washington for military deterrence notwithstanding. Contrary to such hopes, however, even staunch supporters in ASEAN of a strong presence of and role for the US in East Asia had advanced as targets for public US criticism on the democracy and human rights front. The resulting obvious discomfort led ASEAN officials to ask Washington to 'hold back threats of sanctions, public scoldings, and pressure tactics that, in Asian minds, do not fit with such a new level of equality and cooperation' (Hitchcock 1997: 3–4). Notably, even Malaysia's then deputy prime minister, Anwar Ibrahim, argued that

> to allow ourselves to be lectured and hectored on freedom and human rights after 100 years of struggle to regain our liberty and human dignity, by those who participated in our subjugation, is to willingly suffer impudence.
>
> (quoted in Mauzy 1997: 212)

As ASEAN moved towards 1997, a third reason for resisting the abandonment of 'constructive engagement' became increasingly important, namely the opportunity to realise the vision of ASEAN's founding fathers of one Southeast Asia. It has been suggested that the pursuit of this vision can be understood as 'regional nationalism', in the sense of ASEAN forming 'a bulwark against overweening foreign influence in Southeast Asia' (Ott 1998: 74). This kind of 'pan-nationalist' feeling has, of course, been particularly associated with Indonesian and Malaysian leaders, including Dr Mahathir Mohamed (Khoo Boo Teik 1995). Indeed, Malaysia's prime minister, who at one point was very critical of Myanmar for having persecuted the Rohingya Muslims, had become quite keen to allow the admission of all CLM countries (Cambodia, Laos and Myanmar) to ASEAN for the Thirtieth ASEAN Ministerial Meeting. This meeting was to be held in Malaysia, and the formation of ASEAN-10 was regarded as an opportunity for Dr Mahathir to raise his own as well as his country's prestige.

The fourth reason for not giving in to the US challenge is linked to increasing irritations between President Suharto and the Clinton administration. These had arisen in the context of attempts to spell out and implement a US foreign policy that would simultaneously promote American strategic interests in Southeast Asia and economic and business interests in Indonesia, while improving human rights and spreading democracy there (Emmerson 1996b). Washington had, for instance, advised Jakarta on the need for reform of the electoral system, the institutionalisation of rights of due process, and the freedoms of expression and association. Indeed, during his visit to Indonesia to attend the 1994 APEC Informal Leaders' Meeting in Bogor, President Clinton had informed President Suharto that relations between the US and Indonesia would not reach their full potential unless significant progress was attained in all of the above areas.

Washington also co-sponsored resolutions in the UN Human Rights Commission to protest human rights violations in East Timor. To obtain improvements in labour rights, the US undertook a formal review of Indonesia's eligibility for US$600 million in Generalised System of Preferences trading privileges and intervened on behalf of then imprisoned labour leader Muchtar Pakpahan. The US government, moreover, expressed its support for the Indonesian Human Rights Commission and gave generously to relevant non-governmental organisations. In 1995 the Republican-dominated Congress reinstated the restoration of International Military Education and Training (IMET), which had been suspended in the wake of, in particular, the 1991 Dili incident in East Timor, but only after adding a human rights curriculum to the programme. The United States also made the delivery of nine F-16s subject to progress in the human rights field (Suryadinata 1996: 142–3).

Defying US criticism of ASEAN's position on Myanmar, President Suharto, in February 1997, travelled to the CLM countries in a widely publicised visit to endorse the rapid admission of the applicant states (*SÜDOSTASIEN aktuell*, May 1997: 198). There, President Suharto had a highly symbolic meeting with former Burmese leader General Ne Win, indicating clearly that ASEAN would not allow itself to be intimidated or dictated to even by friendly states on the substance of ASEAN's diplomacy *vis-à-vis* Yangon. When only a few weeks were left before Myanmar's full membership in ASEAN, Suharto's frustrations with Washington's lobbying efforts and human rights criticisms peaked. At this point the foreign minister, Ali Alatas, cancelled both Indonesia's participation in the IMET programme and the deal to buy the nine F-16s (*International Herald Tribune*, 7–8 June 1997: 1, 5; McBeth 1997).

Pointedly, Alatas argued that Indonesia had wanted to save President Clinton from further embarrassment.

Finally, some ASEAN governments considered US criticisms on the lack of effectiveness of 'constructive engagement' to amount to possible threats to their own regime security. Regime security had become an increasingly strong concern in the mid-1990s as an underlying sense of vulnerability became more pervasive among most ASEAN governments, the apparent achievements towards greater national resilience notwithstanding. This sense of vulnerability was the product of anxiety about the possible social and political consequences of rapid industrialisation and modernisation. Governments also feared that the Western rights agenda could ultimately impact negatively on ASEAN competitiveness and lead to a decline in economic growth rates. This was deemed potentially to undermine the performance legitimacy of ASEAN leaderships, which in turn might further exacerbate existing social and ethnic tensions. ASEAN governments thus took a more differentiated view of the project of enlarging the realm of market democracies and promoting human rights than was expressed, for instance, by Strobe Talbott, who argued that

> [d]emocracy is a powerful resource in our common quest for stability. The historical record is clear: democracies are less likely to squander the lives of their people in wars of aggression; they are less likely to practice terrorism, or to peddle narcotics or to produce refugees.
>
> (Talbott 1994)

In the context of their domestic vulnerability, it should also be stressed that ASEAN governments had serious reservations about the tactics employed by Daw Aung San Suu Kyi in her political struggle against the military regime in Yangon. While some ASEAN leaders do appear to have sympathised with the struggle of the Nobel Prize laureate, she has generally been viewed as being too confrontational and too pushy.[9]

This section has demonstrated that there has been a sustained American challenge to the policy of 'constructive engagement' of Myanmar and, indirectly, on certain norms associated with the 'ASEAN way', especially non-interference and quiet diplomacy. However, as Michael Leifer has argued, 'regional states in the main tolerate and cope as best they can with Washington's intrusive agenda for world order, however appealing may be the logic of upholding common standards of engagement [for both the US and the PRC]' (Leifer 1997a: iv). This suggests that the nature of ASEAN's response to the US challenge is shaped by the benefits – on balance – for national and regional security that arise from the American military presence in East Asia. We shall now examine whether Washington's approach to regional security and multilateral security co-operation also harbours a challenge to the 'ASEAN way', and how ASEAN has responded to any such challenge. At issue are the norms that ASEAN would like to underlie regional co-operation and for which ASEAN has sought acceptance in the ARF.

The US challenge in the context of the ARF

As is well known, the US stance towards regional multilateralism in security co-operation was one of initial reluctance before becoming considerably more sympathetic during the first term of the Clinton era (Cossa 1996). Even then, however, the administration designated the ARF dialogues as but a 'complement' to the San Francisco Treaty System, Washington's established system of bilateral alliances (with Australia, Korea, Thailand, Japan and the Philippines) and its network of security partners. Despite the Clinton administration's positive attitude, American enthusiasm for the ARF and its actual or potential contribution to regional security waned almost as fast as it had developed, before picking up again, public expressions of diplomatic support throughout notwithstanding.

Within three years of its initiation, decision-makers and analysts in the United States essentially let it be known repeatedly that the ARF in and of itself was unable adequately to address US security interests in Northeast Asia. In 1994 and afterwards, for instance, the US administration contrasted the ARF's lack of action in tackling the Korean nuclear crisis with its own robust stance towards the Democratic People's Republic of Korea (DPRK), with the latter ultimately yielding the US–DPRK Agreed Framework. The United States was also critical of the ARF's response to the 1995/6 Taiwan Strait Crisis in view of its conspicuous silence on China's resort to coercive diplomacy *vis-à-vis* Taiwan, which led to the deployment by Washington of two aircraft carrier battle groups.[10] Perhaps to convey the message that multilateralism in regional security co-operation would stand to gain if it was not led by ASEAN, the United States has intermittently revived a proposal to replace the ARF as the main forum for multilateral security dialogue. Then US Secretary of Defence William Perry, for example, spoke out in favour of formal multilateral security discussions in the context of APEC on the occasion of the latter's 1995 Osaka meeting. On the quiet, proposals have also been mooted for changing 'ASEAN Regional Forum' to 'Asian Regional Forum'.

Beyond these longstanding criticisms relating to the relevance of the ARF and ASEAN as its primary driving force, it is possible to identify at least two further dimensions to the US challenge to the 'ASEAN way'. The first revolves around US ambivalence towards, if not opposition to, ASEAN-style confidence building and preventive diplomacy or, more accurately, the slow pace in moving from stage one to stage two in the ARF process. Especially with respect to preventive diplomacy, the US challenge, which is not separate from but accentuates that of other ARF members like Australia, is still primarily located at the level of conceptual discussion and norm-elaboration. It ensued because some ASEAN governments have considered at least certain aspects of preventive diplomacy to be incompatible with ASEAN's diplomatic and security culture which members have sought to extend to the ARF. Of particular significance in this regard are the norms of non-interference and consensus as corollaries of the norm of sovereignty. The second dimension is linked to recent American attempts to multilateralise existing bilateral defence co-operation with its alliance partners and friendly states.

US ambivalence about ASEAN members' thoughts on and practice of confidence-building measures and preventive diplomacy

In the ASEAN-drafted Concept Paper for the ARF the Association suggested short-term as well as medium and long-term measures for confidence building and preventive diplomacy. Among other things, the Concept Paper identified the formulation of a set of principles to ensure a common understanding and approach to interstate relations in the region as an objective for confidence building.

Confidence-building measures

In the area of confidence-building measures, which the ASEAN Concept Paper for the ARF identified as the first stage of security co-operation, the United States soon challenged ASEAN's focus on building mutual trust among members first and foremost on the basis of dialogues and exchanges among participants. Whereas ASEAN's notion of confidence-building measures involved first making participants comfortable with one another and overcoming mutual suspicions, the US emphasised the significance of pursuing military transparency, in line with ASEAN's advanced proposals for advanced transparency-related measures (ARF 1995). In this context, Washington had a particular interest in questions such as force structure, defence strategy, military doctrine, threat perceptions, national security decision-making and civil–military relations. Although the proposed focus on military transparency in the ARF accorded with Washington's general interest in increased military transparency, it would appear that insistence on the urgent implementation of the proposed measures was designed, above all, to address the perceived lack of military transparency of the PRC.[11] Proposals to enhance confidence building through greater transparency have constituted a challenge not merely to the PRC, however, but also to ASEAN experts and politicians. ASEAN leaders not only understood the Chinese argument whereby transparency is the friend of the strong and the enemy of the weak, but also felt uneasy about pursuing the measures contained in the Concept Paper given their intramural circumstances. Indeed, ASEAN governments have generally not exchanged sensitive military data in an intramural context because of lingering mutual suspicions.

That said, as early as 1997 the majority of the ARF and some ASEAN members had submitted Defence Policy Statements and churned out Defence White Papers, albeit of different quality. Also, the ASEAN-6 states, like the People's Republic of China, participated in the UN Conventional Arms Register, and by 1997 Malaysia, the Philippines and Thailand had circulated their respective submissions (ARF 1998b). Malaysia has been involved in working out details regarding the further production of defence policy documents. Greater transparency has also resulted from the diverse bilateral and multilateral security dialogues at the official or Track II level, including the first meeting of heads of ARF members' defence colleges and institutions, organised since 1997. A new list of confidence-building measures, six of which were defence-related, was agreed in 1998 (ARF 1998c). By 2001 these confidence-building measures had essentially been completed.

ASEAN foreign ministers have also accommodated the US demand to secure a meaningful role for defence officials in forum proceedings, despite misgivings about the possible diminution of their own influence. They accepted the argument that if a key purpose of the ARF was to gain insights into other members' strategic intentions, and to reduce both the pressure to engage in arms competition and the chances for miscalculation, defence officials should be allowed to join the ARF process. The Fourth ARF Ministerial Meeting in Malaysia in 1997 marked the first such occasion. While that meeting still saw less than half of the ARF members include defence officials in their delegation, a dramatic increase in defence participation has since occurred in meetings of the working groups. The half-day defence transparency component at the meetings of the ISG–CBM introduced in 1998 has so far also proved symbolically valuable.

Preventive diplomacy

As regards 'suggestions for preventive diplomacy measures', ASEAN had listed the development of a set of guidelines for the peaceful settlement of disputes, taking into account the UN Charter and the TAC. Equally, it was proposed that non-ASEAN countries endorse the ASEAN Declaration on the South China Sea, which emphasises the non-use of force and the exercise of restraint (see Chapter 5). For the medium and longer term, suggestions focused on exploring ways and means of preventing conflict, including through a Special Representative who might undertake fact-finding missions or possess a 'good offices' role, and even a Regional Risk Reduction Centre.

Significantly, on the release of the ARF Concept Paper its suggestions on preventive diplomacy raised expectations about both the timescale and the direction of security co-operation within the ARF. Both sets of expectations failed to be met. This was a direct consequence of resistance by both ASEAN and, particularly, China to the perceived challenge inherent in preventive diplomacy to the principles of sovereignty and non-interference, the non-use of force, the practice of shelving disputes and quiet diplomacy. This will be briefly demonstrated in relation to the definition, objectives and tools of preventive diplomacy.[12]

The first aspect of the US challenge in relation to preventive diplomacy concerns the invocation as a starting-point for the definition of preventive diplomacy as put forward by former UN Secretary-General Boutros Boutros-Ghali in his 1992 *An Agenda for Peace*. According to him preventive diplomacy is 'action to prevent disputes from arising between parties, to prevent existing disputes from escalating into conflicts and to limit the spread of the latter when they occur' (Boutros-Ghali 1992: 11).

This definition allowed for a number of interpretations that were deemed potentially unpalatable by ASEAN governments. First, the definition left unclear whether both interstate and intra-state disputes and which security challenges would be covered. Although the definition was meant to be comprehensive, the ambiguity was clearly problematic from the perspective of ASEAN states, as such an understanding, if accepted as legitimate, would open the door to possible unwanted and unwarranted interference in their domestic affairs. It suggested, second, that preventive diplomacy encompassed crisis management, including such instruments as the preventive deployment of forces and possibly even the use of force. Indeed, as regards the possible use of force, a former senior US government official had suggested that 'for preventive diplomacy to work, it must be backed by the credible threat of military force and the willingness to use it' (Gates 1996). This was unpalatable not only to China, but also to those ASEAN states which emphasised respect for the non-use of force and rejected the notion of coercive measures as constituting legitimate preventive diplomacy measures.[13] Also, the definition did not clarify who would authorise and who would be entrusted with implementing preventive diplomacy measures.

The third aspect of Washington's challenge with respect to preventive diplomacy focuses on the ARF's initial emphasis accorded to preventive diplomacy measures such as norm building, as spelled out in the ARF Concept Paper. Successive US administrations have criticised the ARF and implicitly the Association for not progressing sufficiently quickly with institution building and practical preventive diplomacy measures. The US National Security Strategy, for example, 'endorsed' the ARF's engagement in conflict prevention and resolution (White House 1997: 24), tasks not pursued at the time of the report's publication. In other words, Washington has clearly been of the view that norm building would ultimately not suffice to avoid regional conflict. In a time of scarce resources American policy-advisers and policy-makers, moreover have become increasingly interested in exploiting the advantages of more advanced and effective preventive diplomacy measures before conflicts turn into shooting wars or involve mass violence. The United States has particularly supported Australian proposals to establish a 'good offices' role for the ARF chair. With the controversial 1997 ASEAN Troika in Cambodia serving as a possible exemplar, the Clinton administration further supported the idea of allowing ARF members to call on the ARF chair for assistance in dealing with disputes, even if mediation would occur only on a voluntary basis (Albright 1999). For ASEAN countries, meanwhile, the question has once again been whether preventive diplomacy measures such as early warning, fact-finding and good offices could potentially be perceived as interference in the internal affairs of ARF member states. Clearly, the question of consent arose too.

The third, related, aspect of the US challenge concerns the question of who would de facto be able and/or tasked to initiate and implement preventive diplomacy, and whether this decision was one that could be imposed. In part, the challenge put to ASEAN focuses on whether the ARF chair should be alone in having to deal with a largely expanded role beyond his given organisational responsibilities. In this context, the United States has quietly supported Australia in promoting an idea for an 'ARF troika', whereby the ARF chair would be supported in its activities by the immediate past chair, along with a non-ASEAN ARF member, based on a rotational system.

Indicative of this stance is perhaps the suggestion by the US administration that ASEAN should no longer be able effectively to veto new forms of security co-operation in the Asia-Pacific region, given that its membership is outnumbered in the ARF. As Assistant Secretary Stanley Roth put it: 'ARF's non-ASEAN members now outnumber its ASEAN creators, and so some means must be devised to reflect this, perhaps by permitting an equitable sharing of the privileges and responsibilities of the chairmanship' (Roth 1998). For ASEAN countries, however, this raised the prospect of non-ASEAN members being able to have a significantly stronger influence on whether and what kind of preventive diplomacy might be explored in the event of any emerging crisis. The challenge has also been to consider which other actors might be involved in preventive diplomacy, especially third-party mediation (such as non-governmental organisations (NGOs), eminent persons or governments). On this point, Washington has quietly endorsed Canberra's call for finalising and drawing on the ARF Register of Experts. For ASEAN, the challenge has thus been twofold: first, to establish a preventive diplomacy framework that would in general be compatible with the norms of the Association's diplomatic and security culture; second, to reach an agreement with the non-ASEAN ARF states on whether its members would be able to influence any decision as to who would engage in preventive diplomacy if the circumstances were such that the ARF was to agree that it was advisable or necessary.

ASEAN's response

It is perhaps not surprising that Singapore has been at the forefront of ASEAN efforts systematically to work towards a consensual understanding of the concept and principles of preventive diplomacy.[14] Singapore authored the ARF Concept Paper containing the initial suggestions for preventive diplomacy. Its officials have always been aware of the discrepancy between preventive diplomacy as practised by ASEAN prior to 1995 and that deemed desirable by non-ASEAN ARF members. Consequently Singapore researchers and officials have sought to bridge the divide on preventive diplomacy, as illustrated not least by their input over several years into the ISG–CBM as co-chair or otherwise and, more recently, by their repeated submission of a draft document on the concept and principles of preventive diplomacy.

From Singapore's perspective, steering a middle path in developing regional norms on preventive diplomacy without losing the support of the major powers for the process of norm-elaboration has been crucial. Given its innate vulnerability, Singapore has had a longstanding interest in securing a meaningful US presence and commitment to Southeast Asia. This commitment has never been taken for granted, especially because, in the eyes of Washington, East Asia's strategic environment was more or less benign in the first years of the post-Cold War period, despite China's chal-lenge to ASEAN in the South China Sea. However, to Singapore the chief implication of East Asia's security environment since the end of the Cold War has been that, while the United States no longer needs Asian allies as it did during the Cold War, ASEAN still has to rely on America for the provi-sion of security guarantees. Meanwhile, Singapore's leadership has for some years now been keen to give Beijing a stake in the process of evolving regional security co-operation. This has implied the need to accommodate Chinese objections to proposed ways of developing preventive diplomacy within the ARF. Several of these objections have been shared by ASEAN states, and Singapore has duly noted this.

In more concrete terms, steering a compromise between the two broad camps on preventive diplomacy has involved defining in concrete terms the boundaries between legitimate involvement by ARF members and unwar-ranted interference and intrusion in the affairs of another member. The starting-point for this effort has been to recognise the continued meaning to many ARF members of the norms of sovereign equality and non-interfer-ence, in particular, as core elements of a normative framework for the mediation of regional estrangement and insecurity. At the same time, it has proceeded from the recognition that very defensive interpretations of the norms in question no longer claim absolute authority in international law or international society.[15]

As regards the move from confidence building to preventive diplomacy, ASEAN agreed to lead the consensus at ARF 2 to consider these two issues in tandem, not least because the distinction between them was considered blurred, as some confidence building measures could well be considered integral to preventive diplomacy. Under the chairmanship of the Malaysian foreign minister, Abdullah Badawi, in 1997 ARF 4 produced a ministerial agreement to endorse recommendations made at the preceding

ARF SOM to identify areas in the overlap between confidence-building measures and preventive diplomacy.

In 1998 ASEAN states accepted the recommendations of the co-chairmen of the ISG–CBM for 1997–8, Brunei Darussalam and Australia, to explore the overlap between confidence building and preventive diplomacy in relation to four areas. These focus on an enhanced role for the ARF chair, particularly the idea of a 'good offices' role, the development of a register of experts or eminent persons among ARF participants, an annual security outlook, and voluntary background briefings on regional security issues (ARF 1998a).

After the onset of the Asian crisis Thai officials, in particular, expressed fewer inhibitions about accelerating the development of preventive diplomacy. However, Thailand too remained obliged to tread a fine line between the promotion of its national interests and those of other ASEAN members, many of whom have recently been beset by pressing domestic issues, including social unrest, ethnic and religious violence, and separatist struggles. In the event the ISG–CBM for 1998/9, co-chaired by Thailand and the United States, failed to achieve a major breakthrough, especially as regards the adoption of a set of 'guiding principles' in the use of preventive diplomacy. Consequently, the Sixth ARF instructed the ISG–CBM to explore further the overlap between confidence-building measures and preventive diplomacy, *inter alia* the development of the concept and principles of preventive diplomacy.

In the second half of 1999 momentum was regained on this issue, not least in view of the events in East Timor (see Chapter 8). For instance, the first tentative steps were taken by Thailand, as ARF chair, to establish informal links between CSCAP and the ARF, and to promote interaction between the ARF and other international organisations. The Seventh ARF also endorsed an agreement reached by the ARF SOM in May 2000 whereby the proposed Register of Experts/Eminent Persons (EEPs) would be made available on a voluntary basis.

A lot of effort also went into reaching a common understanding on the concept and principles of preventive diplomacy. In 2000 Singapore submitted to the ARF Ministerial Meeting on behalf of ASEAN a draft paper on the concept and principles of preventive diplomacy that had gone through a major revision process since the previous year, building on work by CSCAP Singapore and extensive regional consultations (ARF 2000b). In the event the draft was welcomed as 'a basis for the ARF's evolving consensus on this subject' (ARF 2000a). Singapore subsequently submitted further drafts to the ISG-CBM in Seoul in November 2000 and Kuala Lumpur in April 2001. However, divisions among ARF members proved difficult to overcome, as illustrated in the language of the consensus paper submitted to and approved by the Eighth ARF Ministerial Meeting in Hanoi in 2001 (ARF 2001a).

Two other redrafts were also approved by the ARF foreign ministers in Hanoi in July 2001. One concerned a Paper on the Terms of Reference for the Experts/Eminent Persons (EEPs), submitted by South Korean and Malaysian officials. The other spelled out the principles, procedures and mechanisms in relation to an Enhanced Role of the ARF chair, submitted by Japan.

Significantly, both documents remain consistent with norms linked to ASEAN's diplomatic and security culture. The proposed terms of reference for EEPs, for instance, stress the non-binding nature of their advice on matters of preventive diplomacy, and the right of ARF states to veto proposals to activate them for in-depth studies or as resource persons in ARF meetings on issues of relevance to their expertise (ARF 2001b). Meanwhile, the precise nature of the enhanced role of the ARF chair in the areas of good offices and co-ordination in between ARF meetings remains subject to an evolving consensus (ARF 2001c).

In another area of overlap between confidence-building measures and preventive diplomacy, the April 2001 ISG–CBM had, moreover, agreed to recommend to the Eighth ARF SOM in Vietnam that the Annual Security Outlook (ASO) would no longer be treated as confidential. This followed the compilation of the first volume in 2000 by the ARF chair, on a voluntary basis and without editing.

Notwithstanding these caveats, the Association has clearly come a long way in agreeing on and spelling out parameters for implementing measures identified as falling in the overlap between confidence-building measures and preventive diplomacy. The extent to which ASEAN members have moved on the issues, either enthusiastically or reluctantly, becomes apparent if one remembers that in the early 1990s the Association emphasised norm building as the core of preventive diplomacy. This was illustrated by its successful effort to make the UN General Assembly adopt a resolution commending the principles of the TAC as a basis for preventive diplomacy, a position restated in 1995 in the ASEAN Concept Paper for the ARF.

By seeking out within its own membership and from China what further developments in the area of overlap between confidence-building measures and preventive diplomacy are possible, ASEAN has averted the stalling of the exercise in norm-elaboration that is crucial to future regional security co-operation. Since 1999 ASEAN has also become more modest by no longer describing itself as the 'primary driving force' of the ARF as it did in the ARF Concept Paper. Still, the term 'driving force', which is currently employed, suggests that ASEAN continues to oppose proposals, favoured in both Washington and Canberra, for an ARF troika. ASEAN members have clearly felt quite uncomfortable about this suggestion, as its implementation potentially, would allow non-ASEAN countries to reshape the ARF's agenda and further reduce the Association's influence on regional affairs. No doubt ASEAN's position is strengthened by China's reluctance to see this happen. China's position helps ASEAN to insist that the ARF should develop at a pace comfortable for all participants, that decisions be made by consensus, and that the ARF should continue to give primary focus to confidence building, while moving towards the development of the concept and principles of preventive diplomacy.

The United States, meanwhile, like other Western ARF members, remains keen to dispel suspicions among ARF members about preventive diplomacy and to see the evolving consensus of the ARF on this issue develop as quickly as possible in order for an appropriate preventive diplomacy capability to emerge. This is testified by, among other things, its proposal to host a workshop for mid-level ARF civilian and defence officials in the near future. In the meantime, Washington also challenges ASEAN's diplomatic and security culture from another angle: the multilateralisation of US security co-operation with its allies in Southeast Asia.

US proposals for further security co-operation: towards preventive defence?

Since the 1976 Summit in Bali ASEAN member states have expressly endorsed individual members' security and defence ties with external powers. The alliance arrangements forged before then are still in force and many more Southeast Asian countries have since developed a variety of new forms of security co-operation with Washington. Despite the anti-Western and particularly anti-US rhetoric occasionally originating in Kuala Lumpur and elsewhere, the earlier ASEAN members in particular have regarded Washington's continued military presence as essential to regional peace and stability. Consequently, when ASEAN governments decided to engage the regional major powers in multilateral security dialogues building on the concept of co-operative security they at no time suggested that America's ongoing presence be terminated.[16] Indeed, quite the opposite, as it was hoped that the balance of power (or rather the specific configuration of power) on which the regional multilateral security dialogues were to be based would remain unchanged. At the same time, the expectation was that ASEAN's political-strategic standing would be augmented as it managed the process of ARF interactions between the major powers as well as between the major powers and itself.

US strategy towards East Asia has been guided by such objectives as preventing the rise of a regional hegemonic power, preserving the existing alliance system, and preventing regional conflicts and wars (Stuart and Tow 1995). These objectives have lost none of their relevance in recent years given the rise of China as a regional and global power, not least in view of East Asia's increasing economic significance for the United States. As the 1998 East Asia Strategy Report stresses, 'US engagement in Asia provides an opportunity to help shape the region's future, prevent conflict and provide the stability and access that allows us to conduct approximately $500 billion a year in trans-Pacific trade' (US Department of Defense 1998).

Washington's recently refined strategy towards East Asia is one of 'comprehensive engagement'. This essentially implies a commitment to addressing both traditional military security concerns and transnational security threats such as terrorism, environmental degradation, drug trafficking, proliferation of weapons of mass destruction and humanitarian crises. The reasoning behind the decision to engage East Asia in comprehensive fashion is that '[e]ven if US security is not immediately threatened, instability, violence and large-scale human suffering often pose a long-term menace to important US political and economic interests' (US Department of Defense 1998).

Seemingly in a bid to cement its position as the region's hegemonic power, US decision-makers have sought to address both the more traditional and the less traditional security agendas with its alliance partners. Of singular importance in this regard have been efforts to revitalise and broaden the alliance with Japan (Mochizuki and O'Hanlon 1998: 128–9).[17] In Southeast Asia the US has sought to expand security co-operation with ASEAN states as well as military access. US policy-makers have for some time appreciated the point that some ASEAN countries might lean more towards China if they believed that the Washington might reduce its security presence or adopt a strict hands-off attitude in relation to the situation in the South China Sea. Not least for this reason, the US government thought it timely in 1998 to seek to overcome the 'provisional air' of the security arrangements fostered in the aftermath of the US withdrawal from the Philippines (Clad 1998: 247). Clearly this decision must also been seen in the context of widespread perceptions that Washington had reacted too slowly – if not inappropriately – to the onset of the Asian crisis.

Efforts in regional military diplomacy led by the Commander of the US Pacific Command (PACOM), Admiral Dennis Blair, are particularly interesting in this regard. Blair (2000) has outlined a multidimensional package of measures the objective of which is to promote US security interests in East Asia-Pacific. One major element is the merging of existing bilateral military exercises. Starting in 2000, Blair has focused in particular on the adaptation of the bilateral US–Thai Cobra Gold Exercise into 'a more multilateral, regionally focused exercise' (Blair 2000). The immediate objective is to involve both existing and potential security partners of the United States to participate in joint planning, training and exercises with US forces as a first step towards possible joint humanitarian operations, peacekeeping and other missions that entail the deployment of armed forces. Connected to this is the Asia-Pacific Regional Initiative (APRI)[18], which seeks to enhance regional co-operation, military training and readiness, as well as to improve communications and intelligence sharing. A further element is the continued emphasis on foreign military officer education. The ultimate objective, as Commander Blair has argued, is to develop a 'security community' in East Asia, i.e. a community of states that would not be inclined to contemplate the use of force against each other.[19] However, as has also been suggested, the 'multilateralization of the US alliance network is probably the best way to constrain China as China's military capability increases' (Mochizuki 2000).

The nature of the challenge

The attempt to revitalise the San Francisco Treaty System, the parallel stress on comprehensive engagement and the recent focus on proposals to build security communities on the basis of military-to-military diplomacy bear three challenges for ASEAN's diplomatic and security culture. First, while these developments *per se* do not undermine the principles of sovereignty, non-interference or other norms associated with the 'ASEAN way', they do challenge the continued significance of norm building along the lines of ASEAN's diplomatic and security culture in the wider region.

ASEAN states of course accept that the norms that served as a framework for the mediation of insecurity and estrangement within the grouping and which to some extent have been extended to the ARF may only make a partial or even limited contribution to stable interstate relations among the major powers. After all, governments, be it those in Japan and China or Washington or within ASEAN itself, may decide to disregard the norms in the conduct of their foreign relations. Nevertheless, ASEAN governments dispute that ASEAN's diplomatic and security culture is completely inappropriate when dealing with the problem of minimal trust and lack of contact among leaders in the wider East Asian region. From this perspective, military-to-military diplomacy can only supplement efforts to extend respect for norms associated with the 'ASEAN way'.

Second, Washington challenges one of the underlying purposes of the Association with respect to the ARF, which is to entrench greater influence of ASEAN members in regional affairs despite their reliance on Washington as a security provider. From the US perspective, however, measures which have hitherto institutionalised ASEAN's current leadership in the ARF and make the pursuit of US interests more difficult are not easily reconcilable with American leaders' conceptions of themselves (Cronin 1997: 103–4). Indeed, Washington has evidently decided that central decisions pertaining to regional order should really taken by the major powers, and that if there is any lasting proprietary role in leading effective regional security co-operation the US should play that part. In this regard there are clear parallels between the US reaction to ASEAN-led multilateralism of the 1990s and rebuttals of proposals for a more autonomously managed sub-regional order put forward by ASEAN in the 1970s.[20]

Third, the above-mentioned proposed developments in enhanced military-to-military contact stress preventive defence over preventive diplomacy. Participation by ASEAN states in the proposed measures may increase pressure on those involved to respond to any emerging regional conflict or crisis in relatively new ways, which may be incompatible with

ASEAN diplomatic and security culture as traditionally understood. For example, under certain circumstances, to the extent that the preventive diplomacy capability available to the ARF is deemed to be either insufficient or unlikely to be invoked, ASEAN states could potentially be under pressure to endorse more far-reaching measures. In other words, depending on the situation emerging intramural challenges to ASEAN's diplomatic and security culture may well be reinforced by some members' closer security co-operation with the United States. Ultimately, it could imply an acceptance by some of the need for a coalition of the willing to deal with regional threats to security that could undertake much more robust forms of preventive diplomacy under non-ASEAN leadership, even if this involves consent by political blackmail. As Malaysia's prime minister suggested, this was in a way what happened with respect to East Timor. Arguably, the extent of such possible developments is dependent not least on the degree to which the US manages to make ASEAN countries embrace instruments geared in principle towards preventive defence.

ASEAN Members' Response

There is ample evidence that ASEAN governments believe Washington should remain the provider of security in the region, given ASEAN's dependence on secure regional sea lines of communication, the state of intra-regional relations and the likely implications for regional international politics in the event of a strategic withdrawal. When the US government issued the US Statement on the Spratlys in May 1995, in response to the occupation of Mischief Reef, ASEAN members saw this statement as having strengthened ASEAN's own diplomatic intervention to help contain Chinese activities. More recently, ASEAN states have publicly recognised the significance of the US-led alliance system for the security of East Asia.

In view of its endeavour to secure the continued military presence of the United States in Southeast Asia, not least to protect its city-state, Singapore leaders have gone to significant lengths in upgrading the city-state's political-military relationship with Washington. When the Philippines decided not to extend its leases for US military bases beyond 1991, Singapore spearheaded the move among regional countries to offer access to US ships in order to retain an US military presence in Southeast Asia. Since then Singapore has routinely depicted the United States as a positive force for stability and prosperity in East Asia.[21] Singapore leaders have also consistently acknowledged their debt to the US for providing security by dint of the American naval presence, even before the full extent of the Asian crisis became apparent. They appreciate that in future such provision is not free of charge (Jayakumar 1996, 1997b: 4, 14). In 1998 Singapore thus committed itself to allowing US nuclear aircraft carriers and submarines to use a new naval base in the city-state for port visits and maintenance from the year 2000 (*Financial Times*, 16 January 1998: 16). While the city-state has not yet signed a full status-of-forces agreement, since 2000 Singapore has participated in the Cobra Gold military exercise organised annually by Bangkok and Washington. Singapore's Senior Minister Lee Kuan Yew was the first to endorse the proposal by Pacific Commander Admiral Dennis Blair (*Far Eastern Economic Review*, 21 December 2000: 10) for deeper co-operation to meet 'common security challenges' such as drug trafficking, piracy, terrorism, international crime and natural disasters. During a recent visit to the United States, Singapore Premier Goh Chok Tong also reminded George Bush's administration of ASEAN's strategic value in stabilising relations among Northeast Asian countries, as well as an equilibrium between North and Southeast Asia (Goh Chok Tong 2001). For Washington, the extent of US–Singapore political-security co-operation is significant. As James Kelly, Assistant Secretary for East Asian and Pacific Affairs, put it: 'Although not a treaty ally, we have a robust defense partnership with Singapore that facilitates our forward deployment and our overall strategy in the region' (Kelly 2001). Notably, cases of significant improvement in military-to-military ties can equally be made with respect to US–Thailand and US–Philippines relations.

Following its accession to power in 1997, the administration headed by Chuan Leekpai suggested to the United States that it could no longer automatically rely on the use of Thai air and naval bases for transit to the Persian Gulf or Northeast Asia (Simon 1998b: 16). This alarmed the US, as the idea of pre-positioning US supplies had also been rejected – by the first Chuan-led government – in October 1994. However, within a few weeks, as the Thai economy further deteriorated sharply, then Thai Army Commander-in-Chief General Chettha Thanajaro stated that Thailand would not object if the US requested the establishment of a floating base off the Thai coast (cited in da Cunha 1998). In the event, with US assistance to deal with the effects of the Asian crisis forthcoming, the two sides agreed to expand the overall scope and quality of joint US–Thai military exercises, including a de-mining programme on the Thai–Cambodian border and bilateral exchanges on Burma, Cambodia and Indonesia. Washington and Bangkok also negotiated an agreement to establish an international law enforcement academy in Bangkok to train law enforcement officials from all over Southeast Asia to combat transnational crime. American diplomacy and logistics capability also played a major part in making Thailand assume a high-profile role in the peacekeeping activities in East Timor. More recently, US special forces have been training a Thai anti-drug task force on the border with Myanmar. Interestingly, several workshops have also been organised by the Thai and US armies, involving the militaries of around twenty Asian and other nations in late 2000 and early 2001 in order to work out the possibilities of deploying multinational rapid reaction forces to deal with humanitarian crisis situations.[22]

Washington has, moreover, succeeded in raising the level of security co-operation with the Philippines.[23] Given the Philippines' weak force structure and largely obsolete equipment, on the one hand, and China's perceived territorial infringements, on the other, both the Ramos and Estrada administrations had in turn sought to rejuvenate their bilateral security ties with the United States. Indeed, the Philippine government is perhaps one of the most sceptical within ASEAN as regards the contribution to regional order of the ARF's focus on co-operative security and has on occasion implicitly called for a NATO-like institution to balance the perceived Chinese threat. With the signing and ratification of the 1998 Visiting Forces Agreement (VFA), a legal framework is now in place for the resumption of US port calls in the Philippines. A resumption of naval exercises occurred in 2000. The two sides agreed, moreover, to set up an inter-agency working group and initiate an exchange of defence officials to determine the equipment requirements.

As these examples demonstrate, some ASEAN countries that depend on the US for market access, investments, technology and deterrence have gone some way to deepening existing defence and security ties with Washington. Although these ASEAN members continue to pursue by and large a dual strategy of military and normative deterrence to ensure their security, it is clear that the emphasis given to the former in the wake of Southeast Asia's economic and political troubles at the end of the millennium weakened the significance of the latter. This seems particularly valid in the case of the Philippines. James Clad explained this significance attributed to better military-to-military and defence ties in the following terms:

> What keeps the Southeast Asians off-balance is not numbers of US personnel but a sense that the region can never be certain which side of the basic strategic line we might choose – that is, whether the United States might opt to 'give China what it wants' in what the United States might view as parochial sideshow disagreements with Southeast Asia. In return, the United States might seek preservation of a bigger accord with Beijing.
>
> (Clad 1998: 256)

SEANWFZ

An additional implicit challenge inherent in efforts to revitalise US alliances and reinforce its presence in Southeast Asia is connected to SEANWFZ. In Chapter 3 it was argued that the proposal for a nuclear weapons free zone might also be understood as the outgrowth of ideas underlying the 'ASEAN way'. It was also argued that sustained US opposition to accede to the protocol of the Treaty on SEANWFZ, agreed and signed in December 1996, may also be conceived of as a challenge to an element of ASEAN's broader diplomatic and security culture. From Washington's perspective, some of the principles and provisions of the SEANWFZ Treaty represent a matter of serious concern because they are seen to conflict with high seas freedom and would, as such, potentially limit the freedom of movement of the US nuclear submarine fleet.[24] The US has therefore insisted that a key paragraph of the Treaty be deleted. This has posed a dilemma for ASEAN. If ASEAN was to agree to this, the nuclear powers might all sign the protocol, but the Treaty would lose its bite. This is not in the interests of all ASEAN governments. If, on the other hand, ASEAN does not alter the Treaty, the nuclear powers are unlikely to sign the Protocol, rendering the project of a SEANWFZ next to meaningless. ASEAN's 1997 offer to revise the wording of the protocol has not mitigated this aspect of the US challenge (Acharya and Boutin 1998). At the time of ARF 6, the United States was the only regional major power (but not the only declared nuclear state) not to indicate its willingness to accede to the Protocol.[25]

Conclusion

This chapter has primarily examined two aspects of Washington's challenge to ASEAN's diplomatic and security culture. One focused on criticisms of 'constructive engagement' and the related admission of Myanmar into the Association. The other was levelled in connection with the slow advance of security co-operation in the ARF towards preventive diplomacy. The chapter argued that the Association resisted US pressure on ASEAN collective policy *vis-à-vis* Myanmar, some ambiguities notwithstanding. This stand was informed by a strong moral grammar, as the Association found that the US challenge was incompatible with the wish of ASEAN to win respect for its regional identity, its diplomatic methods and its security interests. The chapter demonstrated, moreover, how ASEAN has succeeded in accommodating the US challenge to the 'ASEAN way' in the context of the ARF while retaining its fundamentals and its role as its driving force. Although the US challenge has thus far not seriously eroded the fundamentals of ASEAN's diplomatic and security culture, it is by no means certain that continuing US pressure to allow the ARF a greater preventive diplomacy capability will not in the long term undermine the ASEAN consensus on the 'ASEAN way'. Such pressure is reinforced by recent developments in Washington's evolving East Asia strategy as well as ASEAN's own response to their implementation.

7 The concept of flexible engagement and the practice of enhanced interaction

Intramural challenges to the 'ASEAN way'

As the preceding two chapters demonstrated, ASEAN has found it difficult to secure full respect for important elements associated with its diplomatic and security culture by the major powers in East Asia in the post-Cold War era. It was also illustrated in Chapter 4 how the norms of sovereignty, non-intervention and the non-use of force were indirectly challenged by some member states of the Association over the issue of Cambodia. Notably, for much of the 1990s no similarly powerful and sustained challenge to the so-called 'ASEAN way' emerged from within the Association. However, this changed in the wake of a series of circumstances that developed around the time of ASEAN's thirtieth birthday and the aspired-to realisation of one Southeast Asia (Soesastro 1997). Indeed, against the backdrop of ASEAN's enlargement, the Asian financial and economic crisis, and the political changes which economic adversity brought about, a major intramural challenge to ASEAN's diplomatic and security culture developed.

As regards the enlargement of ASEAN, a possible challenge was expected from the new entrants into the Association, the Indochinese states and Myanmar, regarding their respective acculturation to the 'ASEAN way'. Vietnam was generally viewed as a tough negotiator by ASEAN leaderships but amenable to the 'ASEAN way'. In contrast, they expected the acculturation to be considerably more difficult in the case of Myanmar and Cambodia. Their regimes were hardly attuned to the sensitivities of the existing members and showed little indication that they would fully observe the principle of respect in their dealings with them. The military regime in Yangon and leaders of the Cambodian People's Party had also rejected as unacceptable quiet exhortations by other ASEAN members to soften their respective approach toward the domestic opposition.

In the event, although Vietnam remained a staunch defender of its national interests after Hanoi's accession in 1995, problems concerning the acculturation of Vietnamese leaders and officials to the 'ASEAN way' were limited. As regards Myanmar, its leadership demonstrated a measure of boorishness, recalcitrance and assertiveness, even after joining the Association, that the founding members had not expected. The governments of the original members also found quite unsettling the lack of regard for the negative effects on ASEAN's overall standing in international society and the political fallout with its dialogue partners that resulted from the repressive measures taken against the opponents of the ruling military regime. Cambodia proved to be a different case altogether, as Hun Sen's coup against Prince Norodom Ranarridh in early July 1997 embarrassed the Association so much that it led to the postponement of Cambodia's membership in ASEAN.

If the process of enlargement complicated ASEAN's ties with its most important dialogue partners, the Asian financial and economic crisis generated a host of further problems for the majority of its members. Within months, regional governments witnessed the devaluation of national currencies and the onset of a major recession in their respective countries. The severity of the economic crisis, unprecedented in Southeast Asia, proved too much for some individual ASEAN governments to cope with. Within a year of the floating of the Thai baht on 2 July 1997 two regional governments had collapsed. The first casualty was the administration of Thai Premier Chavalit Yongchaiyudt in November 1997. This was followed by the spectacular political demise of President Suharto after very serious social and political unrest in Indonesia (Aspinall, van Klinken and Feith 1999; B. Singh 2000). Malaysia also experienced political troubles, as testified by the ouster of Anwar Ibrahim as deputy prime minister in September 1998.

At the time both the international media and extra-regional policymakers widely considered the Association to have failed in preventing and meeting the challenges wrought by 'globalisation' and perceived domestic failures and inadequacies such as 'crony capitalism'. The principle of noninterference, in particular, was singled out as having obstructed closer ASEAN co-operation and a more critical engagement with the political economies of regional neighbours. Indeed, for many the financial and economic crisis raised questions as to whether the 'ASEAN way' could remain relevant to ASEAN political leaders in the new circumstances of the closing years of the twentieth century and beyond. It is against the backdrop of the problems linked to ASEAN's enlargement and members' need to overcome the effects of the regional economic crisis that a major intramural challenge to ASEAN's diplomatic and security culture arose.

This chapter examines this challenge to the 'ASEAN way' as posed by Thailand's spurned proposal for 'flexible engagement' and the pursuit of 'enhanced interaction' by some ASEAN members in intramural relations. It asks how regional leaderships in Southeast Asia reacted to these challenges in relation to the way in which ASEAN has for long interacted. The objectives of this chapter are thus twofold: first, to understand the nature of and the reasons for Thailand's formal challenge to the 'ASEAN way'; second, to examine to what extent Dr Surin Pitsuwan's advocacy of flexible engagement and ASEAN members' adoption of enhanced interaction eroded the Association's longstanding norms for the conduct of intramural affairs up to the end of 1998. The chapter is organised into four sections. The first section examines the precise challenges to the 'ASEAN way' inherent in the proposed policy of flexible engagement, as well as Thailand's official discourse to justify its initiation. The second section explores other motivations that appear to have prompted its promotion. This is followed by a discussion of the reasons why other ASEAN members overwhelmingly rejected flexible engagement as a corporate policy. The fourth section then examines how the effects of the practice of enhanced interaction influenced the perceptions of regional decision-makers in relation to the relevance of ASEAN's established diplomatic and security culture in the run-up to the 1998 Hanoi Summit.

Flexible engagement: its origins and nature

The intramural challenge to the 'ASEAN way' of the late 1990s first took shape when Malaysia's then deputy prime minister, Anwar Ibrahim, suggested in July 1997 that ASEAN adopt a policy of 'constructive intervention' (Anwar Ibrahim 1997) to foster a more compassionate side of ASEAN. In principle, the idea was that ASEAN members should invite each others' services to boost each other's civil society, human development, education and national economy in order to avoid the kind of political crises experienced by Cambodia after the signing of the Paris Peace Accords up to 1997. Significantly, Anwar Ibrahim's espousal of constructive intervention did not imply or lead to a reversal of Malaysia's official stand on the issue of noninterference. Nevertheless, support for 'constructive intervention' was apparent as the Philippine secretary of foreign affairs, Domingo L. Siazon, Jr, advocated a 'retooling' of ASEAN to deal more effectively with old and new challenges (Siazon 1997) and described ASEAN's policy of non-interference as a 'policy of benign neglect' (quoted in Lee Kim Chew 1998a). As ASEAN experienced further strains, in the form of the 'haze' and the region's financial and economic crisis, support for a revised policy of noninterference was also signalled by the ASEAN Secretariat (Severino 1998). Representatives of some members of the ASEAN Institutes for Strategic and International Studies (ASEAN–ISIS) even appeared to suggest that rethinking the 'ASEAN way' should include a reassessment of whether an invitation to become involved in the affairs of one another was really required (Wanandi 1998; Hernandez 1998). It is against this backdrop that, in the weeks leading up to the Thirty-first ASEAN Ministerial Meeting in July 1998, Thailand's foreign minister, Dr Surin Pitsuwan, advocated that ASEAN adopt a policy of 'flexible engagement'. In the event, ASEAN foreign ministers, at their informal evening session prior to the Thirty-first ASEAN Ministerial Meeting, decided to rebuff Thailand's proposal, but allowed for a formula that affirmed member states' freedom to pursue 'enhanced interaction' *vis-à-vis* one another (Pitsuwan 1998c).

Although the proposal for flexible engagement clearly emerged as a consequence of disaffection with ASEAN's principle of non-interference, its purpose was ostensibly not to dislodge this principle from ASEAN's espoused framework for interstate affairs once and for all.[1] As Thailand's foreign minister himself repeatedly argued, the principle of non-interference would remain valid even if flexible engagement was adopted (*Straits Times*, 3 July 98: 37). To emphasise this point, the Thai foreign minister even discarded Anwar's concept of 'constructive intervention', which Surin had initially also invoked to promote his ideas, in favour of flexible engagement. On the other hand, it is not easily apparent how the principle of non-interference and flexible engagement could not contradict one another, at least in theory. Flexible engagement involves publicly commenting on and collectively discussing fellow members' domestic policies when these either have regional implications or adversely affect the disposition of other ASEAN members (*Straits Times*, 23 July 1998: 14; *The Nation*, 23 June 98: A7; *Bangkok Post*, 23 June 98: 4). Especially in the ASEAN context, non-interference has been understood in terms of a state's freedom from unsolicited, usually verbal, involvement by foreign state-linked authorities in what are considered its home affairs. Surin's argument that flexible engagement and non-interference would nevertheless be reconcilable in practice has thus depended on the point that while there should be a commitment to non-interference, that commitment should not be absolute but flexible. Arguably, however, the advocacy of a more flexible and less pristine pursuit of the principle of non-interference does not fully capture the Thai challenge to the 'ASEAN way'.

The main point to be made in this context is of course that in spite of ASEAN's espousal of the principle of non-interference, the historical record suggests that it would be a misunderstanding to believe that ASEAN countries have never involved themselves in the domestic affairs of fellow members. The release of a joint statement by ASEAN on the eve of the Third ASEAN Summit in Manila constituted an egregious example in this regard. Without naming the addressees, this statement called on both the then Philippine President Ferdinand Marcos and opposition leader Corazon Aquino to refrain from the use of violence in settling their political antagonism following the country's 1986 election and urged the Philippines to maintain national resilience (ASEAN 1986a). Moreover, it has also not been completely unusual for individual states to become involved in the domestic affairs of other ASEAN members. In some instances, such involvement may even have been welcomed. For instance, two former presidents of the Philippines, Corazon Aquino and Fidel Ramos, no doubt appreciated Jakarta's offer to provide its good offices to arrange meetings between the government in Manila and the Moro National Liberation Front (MNLF). These contacts helped the two sides to their peace agreement in 1996 (Magdalena 1997). In contrast, the Philippine government, not surprisingly, objected to the material and logistical support extended to the Moros during Tun Mustapha bin Datuk Harun's rule as chief minister of Sabah (McKenna 1998: 147–8, 155; Che Man 1990: 140).

Malaysia's past stance on the secessionist Pattani United Liberation Organisation (PULO) in southern Thailand was also generally viewed as constituting interference by Bangkok, notwithstanding the ambiguity involved (Nair 1998). The same can be said of Malaysia's view in relation to MCP camps in southern Thailand. Finally, there have been isolated instances of either unsolicited advice given or disparaging remarks made by ASEAN leaders. Significantly, however, such interference did not undermine ASEAN co-operation or solidarity, primarily because it was not perceived by the target governments to have been designed to set a precedent for a new behavioural norm. As long as this was the case, ambiguities in the practice of the principle of non-interference remained tolerable, even if quiet diplomatic protests may have been issued to sanction the ambiguities involved.

If ASEAN leaderships have been able to tolerate a somewhat sullied policy of non-interference in the internal affairs of other members, the controversy surrounding flexible engagement cannot therefore be seen to have developed only in response to the idea that the principle of non-interference should be practised more flexibly. One should instead assume that Thailand's proposal for flexible engagement encountered hostility among ASEAN's membership because of the view that, once implemented, this challenge to the 'ASEAN way' would pave the way for forms of involvement that governments concerned would find *unpalatable*. This raises questions about which further aspects of flexible engagement challenged ASEAN's hitherto ambiguous practice of the principle of non-interference. Arguably, flexible engagement comprised three challenges to the 'ASEAN way' in addition to challenging the principle of non-interference as such.

The first of these complementary challenges was that flexible engagement appeared to allow member countries to criticise each other's policies *in public*. In other words, flexible engagement challenged the principle of quiet diplomacy that traditionally allowed ASEAN members to subdue any bilateral tension as might exist between them, not least arising from instances of perceived interference. As evidenced by the acrimonious interactions between Singapore and its Malay neighbours over the visit by President Chaim Herzog of Israel to Singapore in 1986 (Leifer 1988), for instance, there have obviously been exceptions to this principle, but these have usually centred on this particular special relationship. Indeed, no other bilateral relationship within ASEAN has been so prone to public and official eruptions of outrage. Second, flexible engagement further challenged the 'ASEAN way' because its proposed adoption as an ASEAN policy suggested that public criticism of member states would henceforth be made under the ASEAN umbrella. The 1986 case of the Philippines notwithstanding, this aspect stood in contrast to the ASEAN practice of not collectively making judgements on the domestic affairs of member states or any bilateral disputes. Third, the concept of flexible engagement also threatened to remove the ambiguitthat had characterised

ASEAN's past practice of the principle of non-interference, an ambiguity that had proved important in allowing ASEAN countries to remain largely tolerant of past instances of perceived interference. Given these challenges posed by flexible engagement, one must naturally assume that Thailand's foreign policy decision-makers should have realised that flexible engagement was unlikely to be approved as an ASEAN policy. This raises the question of why the proposal was advanced at all. We shall first examine the official reasoning, before exploring the issue further.

Why Thailand proposed 'flexible engagement': the official discourse

In the run-up to the Thirty-first ASEAN Ministerial Meeting Thailand's foreign minister outlined the official reasoning underpinning his advocacy of ASEAN embracing 'flexible engagement' in two major speeches. The first was an address to the 1998 Asia Pacific Roundtable in Kuala Lumpur, in which Dr Surin Pitsuwan concentrated on how to address Asia's economic and financial crisis as a strategic challenge that threatened the standing, effectiveness and future regional role of the Association. The foreign minister held that a proper response to the reality of globalisation should see advanced ASEAN members more closely co-ordinate their policies on trade, investment, finance and macro-economic issues, both among themselves and with states outside Southeast Asia. Significantly, he also suggested establishing whether ASEAN's standing and voice were impaired by the governmental structures of member states, a lack of transparency, and members' approaches to human rights and the issue of democracy. In this context Surin urged the Association's new members to reassess their processes of economic and political development. As the Thai foreign minister (Pitsuwan 1998a) argued,

> ASEAN members perhaps no longer can afford to adopt a non-committal stance and avoid passing judgement on events in a member country, simply on the grounds of 'non-interference'. To be sure, ASEAN's respect for the sovereignty of fellow members is one reason why the grouping has come this far and enjoyed such longevity. However, if domestic events in one member's territory impact adversely on another member's internal affairs, not to mention regional peace and prosperity, much can be said in favour of ASEAN members playing a more proactive role. Consequently, it is obvious that ASEAN countries have an overriding interest in the internal affairs of its fellow members and may, on occasion, find it necessary to recommend a certain course of action on specific issues that affect us all, directly or indirectly. Or, to be explicit, we may need to make intra-ASEAN relations more dynamic, more engaged, and, yes, more 'constructive' than before.

> (Pitsuwan 1998a)

Those who hoped that the minister would proceed to articulate his rationale for flexible engagement more clearly may have found Surin's subsequent exposition thereof similarly puzzling. Speaking at Thammasat University, he highlighted the urgent need for processes of individual and collective self-renewal of ASEAN members to address adequately the problems of regional interdependence, investor confidence and societal change. Flexible engagement, Dr Pitsuwan suggested, was necessary because

> [t]he danger lies in the fact that while reform is by and large a domestic process, delays or setbacks in one country can affect the recovery of the region as a whole, especially if that country has extensive trade and investment ties with others in the region.
>
> (Pitsuwan 1998b)

Significantly, Surin stressed in this context that the advancement of democracy and human rights 'is a process that each country must work out for itself, in its own way, at its own pace, in its own time'.

It is not surprising that statements of this nature led other ASEAN governments to request further clarification, leading Thailand to attempt first to elucidate its position further and then to circulate a non-paper to other ASEAN countries in time for the ministerial meeting. Thailand's Non-Paper on Flexible Engagement (1998), while re-emphasising Surin's earlier key points, suggested that flexible engagement should be understood in the context of the ASEAN Vision 2020, to which ASEAN governments had committed themselves in December 1997. That document had built on the vision of one Southeast Asian community (*Towards a Southeast Asian Community*, 1996). In other words, the Thai government emphasised that flexible engagement would be an expression of ASEAN's shared moral responsibility to realise 'a concert of Southeast Asian Nations, outward looking, living in peace, stability and prosperity, bonded together in partnership in dynamic development, in a community of caring societies' (ASEAN 1997). This point was again underscored when the deputy foreign minister, M.R. Sukhumbhand Paribatra, again sought to justify Thailand's proposal for flexible engagement at the Institute of Southeast Asian Studies in late July 1998 (Paribatra 1998).

According to the official discourse, therefore, three key reasons appear to account for Thailand's promotion of flexible engagement. First, flexible engagement was to allow ASEAN to respond to the increasing interdependence faced by the region, as events in one country increasingly affected other countries. Second, flexible engagement was designed to confront new security threats, such as economic disruption and various cross-border security problems including international migration, illegal drugs, transnational crime and environmental degradation. Third, flexible engagement was to enhance democratisation and human rights in ASEAN countries. Apart from remaining short on answers as to how flexible engagement should be practised, Thailand's official exposition of the rationale for its promotion left several questions unanswered, however. For instance, was the rhetoric about individual and collective self-renewal only meant to appease amorphous market forces? If not, who would be the primary addressees of flexible engagement? Equally, which would be the target states of flexible engagement? Surin had explicitly referred to Cambodia in his speech at the Asia-Pacific Roundtable, but was Cambodia the only referent? And, fourth, were there other reasons for proposing flexible engagement? The next section seeks to address these questions.

The context of and subtext to Thailand's proposal for flexible engagement

As is apparent from Thailand's official discourse on flexible engagement, its decision-makers aspired to achieve a speedy financial and economic recovery from the regional crisis by seeking to engage in an individual and collective self-renewal of economic and political institutions relevant to the country's well-being. Importantly, Thailand's recovery was not seen to depend solely on regaining the confidence of international investors. Given that the United States had resisted the establishment of an 'Asian Monetary Fund', Thailand's exercise in societal renewal also had to take into account the demands for financial, economic and political reform of those governments which dominate international financial institutions. In other words, Thailand's economic recovery depended, in particular, on convincing the Clinton administration and the European Union that Bangkok merited the support extended, for instance, by Washington during the prime minister, Chuan Leekpai's, visit to Washington in March 1998. In this context, there was sufficient reason for Thailand's top diplomats to calculate that it would be inadequate merely to take steps aimed at the reform of domestic political and economic institutions. Indeed, perceptions of Thailand within the US and the European Union would almost certainly also be influenced by Thailand's foreign policy.

One aspect of Thailand's foreign policy that had been a particular source of friction in relations with the United States and the European Union before the Asian financial crisis broke was Thailand's policy *vis-à-vis* Myanmar. While Western countries have firmly opposed the legitimacy of the ruling military council in Myanmar and demanded the convening of Parliament as decided by the 1990 elections, Bangkok had adopted 'constructive engagement' as ostensibly the most promising method of bringing about political change in Myanmar. As such, its effectiveness has been quite low. This is not surprising because 'constructive engagement' was originally used by Thailand as a 'diplomatic device … designed to deflect international attention from Thailand's cooperative policy' in relation to Myanmar's military regime (Buszynski, 1998: 290–1). Aiming to make Myanmar's State Law and Order Restoration Council (SLORC, later renamed the State Peace and Development Council, or SPDC) sympathetic to Thai economic and security interests, Thailand also urged ASEAN to adopt constructive engagement, which ASEAN did despite reservations by 1992. Ever since, constructive engagement has tended to be restricted to 'polite' criticisms of the military regime in Yangon by way of quiet diplomacy. Not least for these reasons, neither the United States nor the States comprising the EU have been terribly impressed by Thailand's Burma policy, irrespective of whether their own political strategy towards Yangon, which has focused on support for Aung San Suu Kyi, has fared any better (Siemers 1999).

Western governments were especially critical of Thailand's demonstration of solidarity in support of Yangon's admission into ASEAN in July 1997, in spite of Bangkok's own apparent doubts about the wisdom of such a decision and in defiance of intense outside pressure. As Funston (1998b: 303) pointed out, the US State Department has also accused Thailand of violating human rights provisions in relation to Myanmar. In particular, Thailand was criticised for its failure to protect refugee camps against intruding Burmese forces and for having forced the return of several thousand Shan asylum seekers from Myanmar (US Department of State 1998). Thailand had also been at the centre of difficulties that emerged between ASEAN and the European Union, due to Thailand's adamant insistence on Myanmar's participation in EU–ASEAN dialogue meetings. Reacting to the claim of the former Thai foreign minister Prachuab Chaiyasarn whereby Myanmar had won observer status at the ASEAN–EU Joint Co-operation Committee in November 1997, European leaders cancelled the meeting (*Far Eastern Economic Review*, 13 November 1997: 12).[2] Flexible engagement may thus be interpreted as an attempt to demonstrate greater sensitivity to Western foreign and security policy *vis-à-vis* Myanmar, even though Thailand's officials continue to appreciate the enormity of the political challenges faced by the SPDC in dealing with problems of political stability and national unity.[3]

One would do injustice to Thailand's top diplomats, however, if one regarded the proposal for flexible engagement as nothing but an outgrowth of clever instrumental calculations. Indeed, the proposal for flexible engagement is also illustrative of an earnest struggle for the international recognition of Thailand's democratic credentials. Especially since 1992, Thailand is acknowledged to have had an accomplished record in promoting political stability, civil liberties and human rights through a process of democratisation that led to the promulgation of a new constitution in 1997. The fact that Thailand's regional foreign policy has again provoked questions about Thailand's commitment to democracy promotion has been a cause for concern. This concern appears to have been heightened by ASEAN's lack of democratic credentials – Dr Paribatra once branded ASEAN a 'club of dictators' (quoted in Acharya 1998a) – because the Association is a key pillar in Thailand's foreign relations.

Thai discomfort with views associated, rightly or wrongly, with ASEAN has for some time found expression in Thailand's continuing criticisms of the 'Asian values' debate and, more recently, in the affirmation by Dr Surin Pitsuwan that the further globalisation of democratic and human rights norms is inevitable. In this light, one can understand the proposal to adopt flexible engagement as an attempt by Thailand's foreign-policy-makers to provide ASEAN with more of the trappings commonly associated with a value community such as, for instance, the European Union. Flexible engagement can thus be read as reinforcing the point that 'ASEAN's policy [is] not simply an endorsement of the SLORC regime' (Funston 1998a: 24). In essence, therefore, flexible engagement appears to have also had a moral grammar, the aim being to expunge the national shame of 'constructive engagement' and to win full recognition as a democratic state.

Following this logic, flexible engagement may also be seen as a consequence of the loss of standing the Association suffered in the wake of Hun Sen's coup on 5–6 July 1997 against the former first prime ninister of Cambodia, Prince Norodom Ranariddh. The timing of Hun Sen's removal of an elected government through force of arms, only days before Cambodia's scheduled admission into ASEAN, had seriously embarrassed ASEAN members and led its leaders to suspend Phnom Penh's membership in the Association. As Singapore's foreign minister put it: 'If ASEAN had not acted, the credibility that ASEAN had built over the years would have been damaged' (Jayakumar 1997b). At least equally embarrassing for the Association proved to be Hun Sen's blunt challenge to ASEAN's offer to provide its good offices to the Cambodian parties in an attempt to prevent the ouster of Prince Ranariddh from unravelling ASEAN's perceived chief diplomatic success of the 1980s and early 1990s. Despite the initial positive reaction to ASEAN's offer that was signalled by his then foreign minister, Hun Sen surprised Indonesia's foreign minister, Ali Alatas, and his counterparts from the Philippines and Thailand by referring to ASEAN's mediation efforts as interference in Cambodia's internal affairs (Hiebert 1997). Hun Sen subsequently endorsed the ASEAN troika mission.[4] But by then the question of whether the suspension of Cambodia's admission into the Association and the latter's involvement in Cambodian politics could be squared with the 'ASEAN way' had already been put into stark relief.

Difficulties in justifying ASEAN's involvement in Cambodia had arisen for several reasons. First, the suspension of Cambodia's membership into ASEAN was interpreted in Western countries as the first time that the Association had made political criteria the basis of a decision affecting admission. This missed the point that the primary motivational dynamic underlying the suspension of Phnom Penh's membership was a feeling of outrage which sprang from the embarrassment suffered by ASEAN governments generally and President Suharto in particular as a consequence of Hun Sen's timing of the coup. Significantly, though, this moral grammar could not, for obvious reasons, be translated into official explanations of

ASEAN's suspension of Cambodia's membership, leaving all members to deal with the 'political' interpretation instead. Matters were further complicated, as Michael Leifer (1997c) has noted, because ASEAN had in previous years extolled the principle of non-interference in the domestic affairs, not only of member states, but also of other countries in the region. Even if one disregarded that point, Phnom Penh could no longer be treated as an 'outsider', given that a positive decision on the latter's membership had already been taken (Wanandi 1997a). The need to come up with a justification for ASEAN's involvement in the Cambodian political process further increased when ASEAN assumed, with the blessing of the ARF, a stance of diplomatic activism *vis-à-vis* Cambodia. While promoting ASEAN's troika mission towards Cambodia as helpful, foreign governments and the international media, pointing to ASEAN's more reserved approach of constructive engagement in the case of Myanmar, accused the Association of double standards.

Clearly such rationales as were presented by ASEAN to account for its renewed involvement in Cambodian politics failed fully to convince. Hun Sen had given his 'consent' to ASEAN mediation, it was argued, but ASEAN also clearly forced his hand to engage in 'intervention with approval' (Ching 1997). Other officials stressed both the legality and legitimacy of ASEAN involvement in Cambodia with reference to the 1991 Paris Peace Agreements, given that the Association's members were among Cambodia's guarantors. Nevertheless a measure of uncertainty remained, as the Peace Agreements did not specify what precise involvement was warranted as the result of a coup situation. Some analysts walked the argumentative tightrope, by stressing that ASEAN was not interfering because it was not 'taking sides' but merely 'playing a mediating role' (Abdul Razak Baginda, quoted in Hiebert and Vatikiotis 1997: 18; Wanandi 1997b). In other words, the situation in Cambodia had demonstrated the need for a clarification of ASEAN's non-interference policy. Against this background, flexible engagement was probably conceived to avoid any further charges by outside powers that ASEAN was practising double standards. As regards the intramural dimension, flexible engagement would serve to safeguard the Association from the kind of political embarrassment that emanated from Hun Sen's remark that that he did not need to be lectured by ASEAN on human rights and democracy in Cambodia (*SÜDOSTASIEN aktuell*, March 1998: 71).

Third, the Foreign Ministry's leadership probably also saw flexible engagement as a opportunity to enhance the security situation along some of Thailand's borders. As regards the situation on the Thai–Cambodian border, a significant number of refugees had crossed into Thailand as a consequence of Hun Sen's 1997 coup, with attendant fighting between Hun Sen's government forces and FUNCINPEC loyalists. For a long time armed conflict has also occurred along the Thai–Burmese border. The security situation there deteriorated, especially with the expulsion of the Karen National

Union forces from their headquarters in Mannerplaw by Burmese government troops in 1995. This led to tens of thousands of Karen refugees
seeking refuge on Thai soil. Armed incursions into Myanmar by some of
these refugees in turn provoked Myanmar's armed forces (*tatmadaw*) or its
client organisations, such as the Democratic Karen Buddhist Army, to
engage in cross-border pursuits or in the shelling of suspected opposition
groups, and this further impaired Thai border security. Given that neither
Thailand's pursuit of constructive engagement towards Myanmar nor
Myanmar's entry into ASEAN had decisively improved the security situation along the common border, Thailand's proposal for flexible engagement
can also be interpreted as an attempt to address this issue more forcefully.
Obviously not all those within the Royal Thai armed forces shared the view
that the problems had already attained unacceptable proportions (Interview,
23 June 1998), but some local commanders had plainly become increasingly
intolerant of Myanmar. Taking the view that border areas should be gate-
ways for trade and investment with neighbouring countries rather than
buffer zones, their pacification was increasingly not only a military security
concern, but also an important economic interest (Battersby 1998).

The proposal for flexible engagement, given in particular its association
with openness, might also indicate that Thailand was attempting to restate
its ambition to assume a more prominent role within continental Southeast
Asia, if not ASEAN. Thailand had enjoyed a de facto leadership position
within the Association during much of the Cambodian conflict, as other
members – for reasons of ASEAN solidarity – deferred to the contested
Bangkok–Singapore strategy to prevent international recognition of the
Vietnam-backed regime of the PRK. A disposition for at least sub-regional
leadership had been rearticulated at the close of the Cold War when Prime
Minister Chatichai Choonhavan outlined a plan to make Thailand the hub
of Indochina's economic reconstruction (Um 1991). However, the invocation of the concept of *Suwannaphum*, or 'golden land', in this context
revived among Thailand's neighbours unfavourable memories of irredentist
notions of a 'Greater Thai Empire', associated with Phibul Songkram and,
more pertinently, Luang Wichitwathakan (Suwannathat-Pian 1995).
Importantly, while the rhetoric was subsequently abandoned, the project was
not, as testified by the various forms of evolving regional co-operation and
infrastructure development. Moreover, gaining greater regional influence
has continued to register as a theme in recent Thai foreign policy, irrespective of the party political background of those in positions of state
responsibility (Funston 1998b). The departure in May 1998 of the
Indonesian president, Suharto, by then ASEAN's longest-serving statesman,
and the resultant uncertainty as to who, if anybody, was leading the
Association, clearly offered Thailand's leadership an opportunity of a kind
to reclaim what was perceived as lost influence in the Association.

Finally, there would also appear to be a domestic dimension to the
proposal for flexible engagement. By June 1998 the Democrat-led Chuan

government had attracted criticism over the gap between the declared human rights policy and its actual practice from both the Thai media (Chongkittavorn 1998) and various NGOs, including Thailand-based Burmese pressure groups such as the All Burma Students Democratic Front. Flexible engagement was also an instance of bureaucratic politics in that it was meant to highlight the strengthening of the Foreign Ministry's hand over Thailand's regional policy. In previous years Chavalit Yongchaiyudt in particular had supported accommodation towards Myanmar both as Thailand's army commander and as prime minister. In spite of the acknowledgement that direct channels and dealings between the Thai and other regional militaries remain useful to prevent future conflict, flexible engagement signalled that Thai civilians should determine policy. This conforms to the general trend of curbing the influence of the armed forces in Thai politics, which is also demonstrated by the subsequent appointment of Surayud Chulanont as army commander. Having elaborated on the reasons why Thailand's top diplomats promoted flexible engagement, we shall now look again at why this policy proposal was rejected by other ASEAN member countries.

Reasons for rejecting flexible engagement

With the exception of the Philippines, all other ASEAN governments united in opposition to Thailand's proposal to adopt flexible engagement. The reasons for doing so varied, and only some were openly articulated, such as those on the conceptual problems of flexible engagement. For instance, the implicit contention contained within flexible engagement whereby the Association had been indifferent to members' well-being was on the whole regarded as unfair. Non-interference, it was argued, should not be confused with indifference (*Straits Times*, 25 July 98: 23). Another set of criticisms related to the overall conceptual haziness of flexible engagement. Paraphrased by Yoon, it argued that 'flexible engagement is neither here nor there. If it's flexible, it's not clear, not transparent and far from principled. If it's only "engagement", there can be no commitment' (Yoon 1998: A4). More significantly, however, ASEAN members rejected flexible engagement because Thailand had been unable to demonstrate that the policy could be practised without raising a host of problems.

ASEAN governments, for instance, raised objections against lifting the related proscription to call upon ASEAN or to invoke its mantle in addressing bilateral issues, and supported instead the longstanding policy of sitting on the fence with respect to intramural disputes that did not concern them directly. Thailand's apparent attempt to exert pressure on Myanmar to address the border issue, for instance, was not regarded to be of ASEAN concern. As Malaysia's foreign minister put it, '[p]roblems existing between two countries are best settled at the bilateral level. There is no need to transform such problems to become an ASEAN issue' (Abdullah Ahmad Badawi

1998). Significantly, Malaysia had itself demonstrated this preference for bilateral solutions to bilateral problems when the Indonesian justice minister condemned an incident involving the death of eight Indonesian migrants in a Malaysian detention centre as a violation of human rights. Rather than engage in a spat of public diplomacy, the issue was raised in a meeting between Dr Mahathir and then vice-president B.J. Habibie on the sidelines of the second Asia–Europe Meeting in London (*Berita Harian*, 30 March 1998, in *Summary of World Broadcasts* [hereafter *SWB*] FE/3190 B/4, 1 April 1998). Malaysia's prime minister rejected the Indonesian accusation, and the Indonesian government accepted Malaysia's right to deport illegal immigrants arriving in Malaysia (Antara News Agency, 2 April 1998 in *SWB* FE/3194 B/5, 6 April 1998). Differences about splitting the costs of repatriation remained, but quiet diplomacy had been restored and ASEAN had not been involved. By 15 August 1998 Malaysia had quietly deported 200,000 illegal Indonesian immigrants (*International Herald Tribune*, 25 June 1998: 4).

The third argument advanced against the embrace of flexible engagement also stemmed from Thailand's failure to specify the precise criteria of its application. In particular, it was unclear which, if any, issues might be exempt from public criticism, leading some to fear that the acceptance of flexible engagement might open up a Pandora's box. In this context it was felt that, rather than strengthen corporate unity, flexible engagement could sow mistrust and resentment among ASEAN members. In other words, flexible engagement was viewed as potentially having precisely the opposite effect of an adherence to the 'ASEAN way', to which some ASEAN leaders attributed three decades of peace and stability in Southeast Asia (Jayakumar 1997b). As the Indonesian foreign minister, Ali Alatas, argued,

> [i]f the proposition is to now talk publicly about internal problems we will be back to when Asean was not formed, when Southeast Asia was full of tension, mutual suspicion, and only because Asean was created, we have had more than 30 years of stability, of common progress.
>
> (quoted in *The Nation*, 24 July 1998: 1)

Malaysian officials, too, stressed that flexible engagement, once practised, might endanger or even undermine regional security and the future of regional co-operation. According to the then foreign minister, one 'should not take for granted the stable political environment and positive inter-state relations' of ASEAN countries (Abdullah Ahmad Badawi 1998). That Malaysia's foreign minister had a point was proved not least by the acrimonious exchange of claims and counterclaims between Singapore and Kuala Lumpur at the time over an array of issues, such as the transfer of Customs, Immigration and Quarantine facilities in Singapore.[5] Significantly, the Malaysian foreign minister also did not fail to specify what, in his view, would be the consequence for ASEAN if flexible engagement were embraced without ASEAN members being prepared to pool their sovereignty at the same time, namely setting ASEAN on the path towards eventual disintegration.

Singapore broadly shared this perspective of threat to national and regional security, placing particular emphasis on the possible revival of inter-ethnic or inter-religious tensions, which might in turn be exploited by outside forces. As Singapore's foreign minister put it already at the beginning of the Asian financial crisis,

> [m]ost of us have diverse populations, with significant differences in race, religion and language, all of which are highly emotive issues. The surest and quickest way to ruin is for ASEAN countries to begin commenting on how each of us deals with these sensitive issues.
>
> (Jayakumar 1997)

He advocated, therefore, that ASEAN should stick to 'basics' (Jayakumar 1998; Lee Kim Chew 1998b). Professor Jayakumar may well also have feared that Singapore might at some point find itself on the receiving end of flexible engagement, by becoming a scapegoat for the deteriorating social and economic situation in other parts of Southeast Asia. Such apprehension was not too far-fetched, as Singapore's leaders were acutely aware of the fact that a number of influential officials in Malaysia and Indonesia privately viewed 'Singapore' as having taken financial advantage of the economic distress of its neighbours. Higher interest rates for Malaysian ringgit holdings in Singapore than in Malaysia and the alleged currency transactions of Indonesian rupiah by traders in Singapore had been two issues complicating relations between Singapore and its immediate Malay neighbour. Given the uncertainty of political developments in Indonesia, and in particular the possible future emergence of what Singapore would regard as an unpalatable regime in Jakarta, Singapore's rejection of flexible engagement was also clearly designed to reinforce an existing normative shield to guard the city-state's security.

Notably, Singapore's officials were also concerned about the wider strategic implications that might result from the adoption of flexible engagement if, as its consequence, the Association would subsequently fall into disarray. For Singapore, a weakening of ASEAN cohesion and solidarity carried the danger of divide and rule tactics *vis-à-vis* the Association by the major powers (*Straits Times*, 5 August 1998: 34). For instance, it was thought that China might exploit any ASEAN divisions that might stem from flexible engagement in order to continue its policy of 'creeping assertiveness' in the South China Sea. It was thought that the United States, on the other hand, might take advantage of ASEAN divisions to push more strongly its declared foreign policy objectives, which might entail, among other things, a decrease in ASEAN's influence in regional security co-operation, not least in connection with norm-elaboration processes undertaken within the ARF.

Generally, for Singapore, any intramural tensions as might arise from flexible engagement harboured the danger of diminishing ASEAN's – and Singapore's – influence in shaping the framework for the emerging regional order in East Asia.

Finally, but certainly no less importantly, several ASEAN governments objected to the adoption of flexible engagement as a corporate policy for fear that its practice could undermine regime security. After all, flexible engagement, unlike the 'ASEAN way', was associated with transparency, political reform, the empowerment of civil society and Western approaches to running an economy. When ASEAN governments debated the merits and drawbacks of flexible engagement, the impact of the Asian economic and financial crisis had already begun to erode the performance legitimacy enjoyed by ASEAN states (Alagappa 1995), and most ASEAN governments believed that flexible engagement threatened to reinforce this trend. We shall briefly substantiate this argument with reference to Malaysia, Singapore, Brunei Darussalam, Vietnam, Laos and Myanmar.

In Malaysia national security has generally been interpreted by the leadership as being tied to the economic security of Malays (Nathan 1998). To the extent that threats to economic security induce national demoralisation, these have also been regarded as threatening regime security (Haron 1998: 23). Divisions among the Malay leadership have equally been considered as constituting threats to regime security, as they might open up possibilities for undermining Malay political supremacy. When flexible engagement was proposed in June 1998, precisely the above kind of threats to regime security emerged. First, Malaysia was experiencing a sharp contraction of its economy, as well as a substantial drop in the value of its currency and asset markets, which led to all sorts of problem for the country's entrepreneurs. The economic decline had engendered considerable frustration among the ruling elite and large parts of the wider population. Second, serious political contention had developed between Dr Mahathir and his groomed successor, the finance minister Anwar Ibrahim, over the best strategy for overcoming this accelerating decline in Malaysia's economy. By that time Malaysia was locked in an increasing power struggle, as testified by critical remarks made by representatives of the Anwar camp over aspects of Malaysia's political economy at the UMNO assembly in June 1998. It was striking that Anwar's position enjoyed political support from the West. Allowing for flexible engagement under these circumstances would have legitimated open external criticisms of decisions affecting Malaysia's political economy associated with Dr Mahathir or loyal cabinet ministers, which regional leaders preferred to voice, if at all, only privately. It would thus have been very surprising if those key UMNO officials and government ministers closely aligned with Dr Mahathir had supported flexible engagement. Indeed, had Datuk Seri Anwar Ibrahim not favoured the introduction of constructive intervention only the year before?

Concerns about regime security probably also emerged in Singapore as the possibility could not be excluded that some regional governments might be tempted to contrast their sense of democratic identity with Singapore's alleged authoritarianism. In view of US insistence that transparency and democracy constitute the key to economic revival of the region, flexible engagement also raised the possibility that Singapore might be put on the defensive on the issue of 'good governance'. In the context of the Asian economic crisis, flexible engagement consequently possessed the potential to threaten Singapore's regional and international standing, which in turn could have harboured economic and political risks for the city-state.

Brunei Darussalam's official attitude towards flexible engagement was summed up by the foreign minister, Mohamed Bolkiah, who said, 'I think we still like the Asean as we are now' (quoted in *The Nation*, 24 July 1998: 2). Although there appear to have been no unmanageable threats to regime security in the sultanate at the time flexible engagement was proposed, Brunei's leadership has had to confront growing irritation in parts of the population at perceived government mismanagement of the country's finances and other issues. There have also been criticisms of disparity in income, lack of transparency and circumscribed political freedoms. Non-Malay Bruneians, mostly Chinese, and expatriates from Asia and Europe have also been critical of some of the directives of the Islamic Religious Affairs Department (EIU 1999: 43). In such circumstances the continued espousal by the government of the 'ASEAN way' to help ensure political and social stability is readily understood.

When Vietnam joined ASEAN, the 'ASEAN way' held out the promise to Hanoi that ASEAN governments would not seek to change its distinct political identity. Flexible engagement undoubtedly called this assumption into question, as it was perceived to allow ASEAN countries openly to discuss or even exploit the VCP's existing problems of political legitimacy. These problems had already been quite serious through much of the 1990s (Kolko 1997). And the social unrest in the former VCP stronghold of Thai Binh and the southern province of Dong Nai in 1997 had again highlighted in particularly stark form the regime's vulnerabilities in the face of uneven wealth distribution, land disputes and rampant corruption. Although it was initially shielded from the regional financial crisis to some extent, Vietnam faced reduced commitments in foreign investment hitherto considered vital to achieve the country's developmental objectives as Thailand's baht undercut the Vietnamese dong (EIU 1998: 8–9). In these circumstances the 'ASEAN way' remains as relevant as ever for the VCP leadership.

Against the background of unresolved ethnic and ideological tensions among disparate political groups, problems with its transition economy and the fallout of the regional economic crisis (Freeman 1998; Lintner 1998), the Lao People's Revolutionary Party (LPRP) equally rejected flexible engagement out of concern for regime security. It was argued in the *Vientiane Times* that ASEAN should respect the 'desire of the countries of the region to solve their own problems in their own way and according to their wishes' (*Vientiane Times*, 21–3 July 1998: 6).

Myanmar's State Peace and Development Council (SPDC) had reacted with considerable hostility to Surin's advocacy of flexible engagement well before the Thirty-first ASEAN Ministerial Meeting. It was therefore to be expected that the then foreign minister, U Ohn Gyaw, would affirm his commitment to the 'ASEAN way' as 'the best mechanism for our common endeavour' (Gyaw 1998) in Manila. Flexible engagement threatened to undercut what, at least in the view of the military regime, was the hard-won (if limited) legitimacy within international society derived from Yangon's admission to ASEAN. Such legitimacy was also conferred, albeit probably inadvertently, by ASEAN demonstrating on occasion a measure of solidarity with the SPDC at the expense of smooth relations with its main dialogue partners – the United States and the European Union. Having disliked but tolerated being the target-state of constructive engagement, the Yangon regime rejected flexible engagement. This form of engagement had the potential to subject Myanmar to significantly greater pressure and unwelcome comments by the Association in relation to the military regime's human rights record, its progress on constitutional reform or the question of a dialogue with Aung San Suu Kyi. As it happened the Philippines' foreign minister, Domingo Siazon, made an unprecedented call to the Burmese people to emulate the Philippines' bloodless uprising against former president Ferdinand Marcos as the ASEAN dialogues drew to a close (*The Nation*, 28 July 1998: 1). Notably, this call was flanked by several spectacular car sit-ins organised by the de facto leader of the National League for Democracy, Daw Aung San Suu Kyi, to attract international attention to the restrictions imposed on her activities in Myanmar (Siemers 1998: 385–6).

As this section has demonstrated, ASEAN governments rejected flexible engagement for a variety of reasons. Significantly, though, ASEAN foreign ministers departed from the Manila meeting, allowing members – not least against the backdrop of the principle of sovereignty – to engage in what was termed 'enhanced interaction'. This concept conveyed a compromise reached by ASEAN. On the one hand, ASEAN members could not agree on the introduction of flexible engagement as a legitimate corporate policy. On the other hand, those ASEAN leaders who were opposed to the idea and practice of flexible engagement appreciated that they could not stop other members from pursuing this policy, not least against the backdrop of their continued respect for the principle of sovereignty. While enhanced interaction would in practice therefore be no different from the pursuit of flexible engagement, enhanced interaction would have the status only as a national rather than a corporate policy. Notably, enhanced interaction, like flexible engagement, was considered to respect the principle of non-interference. Dr Surin Pitsuwan was unambiguous in his pledge to pursue enhanced interaction. As the Thai foreign minister put it: 'I feel confident I can raise any issue without fear of being misunderstood or accused of interfering' (*The Sunday Nation*, 26 July 1998: A2).

The two questions the final section of this chapter will therefore now address are whether Thailand or other ASEAN countries have indeed practised 'enhanced interaction' and what consequences this has had for the Association and the validity of the 'ASEAN way'. The analysis will focus, in particular, on how other ASEAN leaders reacted to the political ouster of Malaysia's former deputy prime minister, Anwar Ibrahim.

The practice of 'enhanced interaction'

The dismissal and subsequent detention of Datuk Seri Anwar Ibrahim under the Internal Security Act was met with surprise and considerable outrage within Malaysia. Western governments and ASEAN leaders, too, were shocked at this turn of political events in Kuala Lumpur and appalled when Anwar emerged with a bruised eye at his first court hearing in late September 1998 to face charges of unnatural sex and corruption. The Mahathir administration sought to counter the domestic and international opprobrium in two ways. First, it instituted a major public relations effort that aimed to counter Anwar Ibrahim's attempt to portray himself as the defender of the rights of the Malaysian people. In order to cast doubt on the character of the former deputy prime minister, it was, for instance, implied that Anwar had provoked his detention under the Internal Security Act to demonstrate that the government was acting unfairly. Equally, it was suggested that injuries sustained to his left eye might not have been the product of police brutality, but of his own clever scheming, the purpose of which was ostensibly to shame the Mahathir government in world opinion. Violent street protests by supporters of the reform (*reformasi*) movement were depicted as an attempt by a minority to bring down an elected government through undemocratic means. Second, and more importantly for our purposes, Malaysia defined the boundaries of what it would consider to be legitimate involvement in its internal affairs on this issue. Although Kuala Lumpur had been unable to deny Thailand and the Philippines the introduction of 'enhanced interaction', it was clear that Malaysia's leadership was attaching continued importance to the norm of quiet diplomacy in the context of 'enhanced interaction'. In other words, the government signalled that raising the matter of Anwar Ibrahim constituted legitimate 'enhanced interaction' only to the extent that respective involvement was either restricted to private comments or conveyed through the appropriate channels. As the next paragraphs will show, several ASEAN leaders did not fully heed Kuala Lumpur's exhortations in relation to quiet diplomacy when practising their national versions of 'enhanced interaction'.

'Enhanced interaction' à la Bangkok

Thailand's diplomacy *vis-à-vis* Malaysia in the period from September to mid-November testified to Dr Surin Pitsuwan's apparent position that enhanced interaction and the 'ASEAN way' should lie along a continuum rather than form polar opposites. Bracing itself for a possible upsurge in popular discontent at the extraordinary developments in Malaysia, the Thai government sought to avoid needlessly antagonising the Malaysian government over the Anwar issue. Premier Chuan Leekpai even urged the Thai media to refrain from sensationalising reports on relevant events in order to avoid misunderstandings between the two countries. Thailand also hinted that it would co-operate with Malaysia in accordance with the two countries' border agreement should Kuala Lumpur request that Bangkok monitor travellers crossing the mutual border to prevent fugitive opposition figures from entering into Thailand (*Straits Times*, 1 October 1998). Moreover, when questions were raised about whether Kuala Lumpur was a suitable host for the 1998 APEC Summit, Prime Minister Chuan argued that APEC members should articulate privately any complaints they might have in relation to Kuala Lumpur's human rights record, as Thailand had done (*Straits Times*, 28 October 1998). However, when the diplomatic exchanges between the Mahathir government and others threatened to derail the APEC Summit and affect US relations with Southeast Asian countries, the Thai foreign minister suggested that the Anwar trial was endangering the economic resuscitation of the Association (*Straits Times*, 5 November 1998). Thailand, in other words, mostly practised enhanced interaction in a manner compatible with the 'ASEAN way'. As Surin Pitsuwan argued, it would be other ASEAN leaders whose resort to enhanced interaction went 'far beyond [Surin's] original suggestion or expectation' (*Time Asia*, 2 November 1998).

President Estrada's 'personal diplomacy'

In contrast to Thailand's measured version of enhanced interaction, the Philippine president, Joseph Estrada, reacted to Anwar's political undoing and physical mistreatment by engaging in several rounds of 'personal diplomacy'. Characteristically, in public the president would issue critical remarks about Malaysia's political and judicial processes, only quickly to follow them up with insistent denials that these interventions had occurred in an official capacity. For example, President Estrada strongly raised the possibility of not attending the 1998 APEC Summit because 'they put my good fried Anwar behind bars' (*Straits Times*, 2 October 1998), but then labelled such remarks a mere 'personal opinion'.[6] President Estrada also received Nurul Izzah Anwar, the daughter of Anwar Ibrahim, to accept her expressions of gratitude for the public support Estrada had given to her father. Yet in an apparent attempt to overcome the problem of straying from quiet diplomacy when engaging in enhanced interaction against Malaysia's admonitions, another attempt was made to separate 'personal' from 'official' diplomacy by pointing out that the meeting took place without Estrada's foreign policy advisers. The true nature of such apparent attention to protocol was repeatedly exposed. For instance, in a clear reference to Malaysia, President Estrada had spoken of a 'compelling need for democratic means' in East Asia (Estrada 1998). Significantly, he had also hinted publicly at the possibility of a joint appeal by him and President Habibie to secure Anwar's release from jail. And when the two met in mid-October 1998 they pointedly announced that they had discussed Anwar.

President Habibie's approach

Over the years, Anwar Ibrahim and the Indonesian president, B.J. Habibie, had forged an ideological bond and personal friendship in their common aim to promote civil society and a modern and progressive brand of Islam in their respective countries. This bond had also found expression in the strong ties between Anwar's Institute of Policy Research in Kuala Lumpur and the Centre for Information and Development Studies in Jakarta, headed by Habibie before he assumed the presidency. It is no surprise, therefore, that, like President Estrada, Dr Habibie voiced his concern for Anwar and questioned the motive for his dismissal. Indeed, the president despatched one of his advisers to visit Anwar in the wake of the his political ouster. Significantly, the reactions of Indonesia's domestic political opposition and the wider public to events in Malaysia were starkly negative too. Within days of Anwar's detention, for instance, the Indonesian Committee for Solidarity with Anwar Ibrahim had organised public protests, as supporters of *reformasi* in Indonesia were generally distressed to see the standard bearer of Malaysia's political and economic reform fall victim to a 'political conspiracy'. In early October President B.J. Habibie cancelled a planned visit to Malaysia, which would have been his first official trip abroad since taking office (Richardson 1998b). For a long time, Habibie also remained undecided about whether he would participate in the APEC Summit in Kuala Lumpur. The eventual decision to attend was announced only after Anwar had been released from detention under Malaysia's Internal Security Act (ISA) and held on remand instead. Like President Estrada, Habibie also received Nurul Izzah Anwar 'privately', while his government reaffirmed the validity of the principle of non-interference. Indeed, the Indonesian foreign minister, Ali Alatas, argued that President Habibie's personal statements should not be interpreted as agreement or disagreement with Malaysian policy, nor as lecturing another state, and therefore they could not be considered as intervention in the affairs of another country (*Straits Times*, 5 November 1998).

Malaysia's response

Against the backdrop of the resort to enhanced interaction by Thailand, the Philippines and Indonesia, it depended upon the Mahathir government to ensure that its bilateral relations with these ASEAN neighbours or ASEAN co-operation more generally would not be seriously affected. This was generally to be avoided, not least given the increasing deterioration of Malaysia's economy. Kuala Lumpur was probably also wary of risking a simultaneous major downturn in all its key bilateral relations with ASEAN states given that Singapore–Malaysia relations had already suffered another turn for the worse at about the same time as enhanced interaction began to be practised.[7] Nevertheless, Malaysia demonstrated clearly its reluctance to accept breaches of the principle of quiet diplomacy in the context of enhanced interaction.

As regards Thailand, Malaysia's leadership did take exception to the Thai foreign minister's late intervention prior to the APEC Summit. Malaysia's foreign minister played down the issue, and only an editorial in the Malay daily *Utusan Malaysia* labelled Surin a 'new puppeteer' (*Straits Times*, 7 November 1998). In the case of Indonesia, traditionally a staunch advocate of the 'ASEAN way', Malaysia organised for visits to Jakarta by a government minister and a 'private' visit by former deputy prime minister Tun Ghafar Baba. The latter, in particular, failed miserably in influencing Indonesian public opinion in Kuala Lumpur's favour. In an apparent bid to pre-empt or contain subsequent public expressions of dissatisfaction by President B.J. Habibie at Anwar's ordeal, Malaysia soon turned the tables on Indonesia by raising implicit questions about the Indonesian president's standing and political support. Malaysian leaders argued, for instance, that Habibie's stance on Anwar Ibrahim was 'totally understandable' as the Indonesian leader realised he needed the reform movement on his side to 'legitimise his presidency' (*Straits Times*, 19 October 1998). To this were added warnings about the social and economic cost that would arise for Jakarta if Malaysia did not take in some of the millions of Indonesian economic refugees as temporary labourers, as it had in previous years.[8]

There can be no doubt that in particular President Estrada's public criticisms of the Mahathir administration caused considerable offence in Kuala Lumpur, which may linger for some time. Estrada's attempt to pass off a form of enhanced interaction considered illegitimate by Kuala Lumpur as 'personal' remarks in distinction to his country's 'official' foreign policy was considered unpersuasive by Malaysian leaders. Still, Abdullah Badawi was on occasion so courteous as seemingly to accept the argument (*Straits Times*, 21 October 1998). Initially, Malaysia had reacted to Estrada's criticisms by issuing diplomatic protests. As indignation at President Estrada's diplomatic tactics increased, however, Malaysia's leaders began to attack Estrada personally by seeking, for example, to portray the Philippine leader as a 'new kid on the block' who had not yet quite understood how ASEAN was supposed to function. Malaysia's disaffection with the Philippine leadership was also demonstrated in other ways. In October 1998 Kuala Lumpur postponed a quarterly meeting on joint patrols of the waters between Kuala Lumpur and Manila that was designed to foster bilateral co-operation against arms smuggling, piracy and other illegal activities. Malaysia also rebuffed the request of several Philippine congressmen for an official invitation to Anwar Ibrahim's trial, and labelled 'inappropriate' President Joseph Estrada's plans to visit the former deputy premier in custody during the APEC meeting, as this would 'intimidate' Malaysia's courts. Indeed, Dr Mahathir visibly prevaricated on whether he should even invite the Philippine president to a standard one-on-one meeting during the APEC summit, once the latter had announced his attendance. The Mahathir administration also speculated publicly about whether the intake of foreign labour in 1999 would again include a significant number of Filipinos (on whose remittances the Philippines in part depend). Indeed, it appears there were even threats that Kuala Lumpur might actively interfere on behalf of the Morobangsa in Mindanao if the Estrada administration really were to reactivate the Philippine claim to Sabah (*Straits Times*, 15 November 1998).[9] The Philippine presidential spokesman, Fernando Barican, was seen as having raised this possibility by arguing that the claim to Sabah had previously only been put on ice (*SÜDOSTASIEN aktuell*, January 1999: 15). These comments followed veiled threats by Dr Mahathir that Malaysia might also consider flouting the 'ASEAN way' if other members of the Association did not desist from continuous infringements of its core norms vis-à-vis Kuala Lumpur (*Straits Times*, 1 November 1998).

While President Estrada publicly appeared unimpressed by this unprecedented threat, Malaysia's brinkmanship was nevertheless instrumental in weakening the force of the argument whereby it would be legitimate for some ASEAN leaders publicly to issue critical personal comments about Malaysia that supposedly did not reflect official opinion. Malaysia's warning of potentially more serious strife between Kuala Lumpur and Manila, as well as the implications for ASEAN co-operation as regards the Philippines, was not lost on the Philippine secretary of state, Domingo Siazon, or the former president Fidel Ramos, who had become an advisor to President Estrada. Their assessment of the costs of enhanced interaction, which was shared by parts of the media (Doronila 1998), proved important in avoiding spiralling towards the point of no return. While he did not issue an apology, President Estrada ceased commenting publicly, and that proved sufficient to restore relations with Kuala Lumpur to at least a semblance of normality. However, credit for eventually reconsidering the effects of this recriminatory form of enhanced interaction goes not only to the Philippines. As the following section will show, American Vice-President Albert Gore also played a major part in silencing – at least temporarily – the regional guns aimed at the 'ASEAN way'.

The 'ASEAN way': saved by Al Gore?

At the pre-APEC Business Summit organised in Kuala Lumpur in November 1998 the American vice-president repeated the standard argument that democracy is the key foundation of prosperity because investors put their money and their faith in democracy. Implicitly Al Gore also contended, however, that anti-government protests in Malaysia, which he seemed to endorse, were occurring because the Malaysian government had been unable – by virtue of its authoritarian nature – to end the economic suffering of the Malaysian people. Littered as it was with darts directed at Dr Mahathir's government, Al Gore's speech was received with outrage, even fury, by Malaysian leaders. For example, the then foreign minister, Datuk Seri Abdullah Badawi, accused the US administration of attempting to incite Malaysians to riot in order to topple the government. Al Gore did not just arouse the anger of those who he clearly meant to offend, however. He inadvertently also sparked off a nationalist reaction among many of those Malaysians who had hitherto essentially remained part of the country's silent majority in the struggle by advocates of *reformasi* against the Mahathir camp (Devan 1998). And, more significantly still for our purposes, Al Gore's speech also induced ASEAN leaders to rally around the 'ASEAN way'. There are at least three reasons why this should have happened.

First, the US vice-president overstepped an important psychological benchmark set by ASEAN leaders to distinguish acceptable from unacceptable behaviour by an outside power towards one of their members. Even ASEAN leaders critical of Dr Mahathir agreed that Al Gore's remarks had demonstrated (again) a measure of disrespect for the political and cultural sensitivities of an ASEAN member government. Second, Gore's speech not only highlighted the continued emphasis on the promotion of democracy as a key element of American foreign policy, but also conveyed the impression that the United States remained interested in exporting to Southeast Asia a particular model of liberal democracy. Such an objective would to some extent be at odds with the focus on good governance within the region. Third, the vice-president could be interpreted as having issued a warning that unless regional governments allowed for political change and greater openness there was a distinct possibility that international (American) investors would turn their backs on crisis-stricken East Asia. The substance and the circumstances of the Gore speech suggested that the particular form of enhanced interaction practised by members was beginning to affect the way in which external powers interacted with ASEAN members. Beyond the issue of respect, Al Gore's remarks appear to have given rise to concerns that enhanced interaction, if in breach of the principle of quiet diplomacy, might greatly increase ASEAN members' insecurity *and* terminate ASEAN's quest for recognition as a major player in regional international society. Consequently, what was at least an implicit consensus emerged whereby public expressions of enhanced interaction were, at least temporarily, put on hold by member states. The sense of urgency to stop ASEAN's slide into political irrelevance and poor standing in international society was only reinforced by the imminence of the Association's Sixth Summit in Hanoi in December 1998.

As chair of the ASEAN Standing Committee it was incumbent upon Singapore to forge a consensus on what ASEAN should do to offset increasingly widespread perceptions of ASEAN corporate decline and ineffectiveness. In order to restore ASEAN 'credibility', Singapore advocated that ASEAN leaders demonstrate their united resolve to address some of the root causes of the financial and economic crisis. In practical terms, Singapore argued that ASEAN countries should press ahead with the liberalisation of trade and the opening up of their economies to international investments. Singapore also strongly supported the idea of greater ASEAN transparency in relation to its members' economic and financial data. At the same time, however, its leaders remained interested in reaffirming ASEAN 'basics'. When one looks at the agreements that ASEAN leaders concluded at the Sixth Summit in Hanoi, it is clear that ASEAN members broadly endorsed Singapore's dual strategy, even if that strategy was partially undermined by noticeable intramural divisions over the timing of Cambodia's admission to ASEAN.

The Hanoi Summit

As regards ASEAN's commitment to economic openness, the heads of state and government announced a number of so-called 'bold measures' to stimulate short-term investment and to accelerate the implementation of the ASEAN Free Trade Area. Also approved was the Hanoi Plan of Action (HPA), which outlined how ASEAN intended to set about realising the goals the Association set out in the ASEAN Vision 2020 in the five-year-period from 1999–2004. Significantly, the HPA, by making reference to the TAC, re-stressed the core features of ASEAN's basic code of intramural conduct, including the principle of non-interference. One might assume that this reference to the TAC is in fact also one to the 'ASEAN way', not least because there is no mention of enhanced interaction in the text of the HPA. In consequence, the HPA can also be understood as an implicit reaffirmation of norms such as quiet diplomacy in the context of ASEAN's ambiguous practice of non-interference. As regards the Association's endeavour to win respect for norms associated with the 'ASEAN way' by non-ASEAN states, the HPA pledged to win respect for the TAC as a 'code of conduct governing the relations between Southeast Asia and those outside the region'. In order to succeed in this particular task, ASEAN members also pledged to ratify the Second Protocol of the TAC, which allows non-ASEAN members (principally the Dialogue Partners) to accede to the TAC.

Interestingly, while the message sent at the Hanoi Summit was thus one of continuity in ASEAN's diplomatic and security culture, ASEAN also endorsed greater transparency and regional involvement in economic and financial matters, illustrating their acceptance of further processes of enhanced interaction. Indeed, following on from the Manila Framework

Agreement, whose constituency exceeds the Association's membership, ASEAN finance ministers had in October 1998 endorsed a peer review and information exchange in areas such as interest and exchange rates, as well as capital flows (Tassell 1998). Interestingly, the HPA also committed the Association to formulating draft rules of procedure for the operations of the ASEAN High Council as originally envisaged in the TAC. This indicated a renewed attempt finally to pave the way towards collective intramural conflict settlement, previously something that was to ASEAN like a red rag to a bull. However, the careful wording appeared to suggest that, in contrast to intramural debates about macroeconomic indicators, ASEAN leaders did not view the involvement of the Association in bilateral disputes among members as imminent.

Conclusion

This chapter has demonstrated that the consequences of enhanced interaction, as practised *vis-à-vis* Malaysia after the former deputy prime minister Anwar Ibrahim saw his immediate political future cut short in dramatic circumstances, confirmed the validity of the arguments proffered by ASEAN governments that had been opposed to flexible engagement. In the event, it seems that only by speculating about and threatening the de facto unravelling of ASEAN as a diplomatic and partial security community did the Mahathir government succeed over time in putting a temporary stop to the sustained breaches of the 'ASEAN way' by some of Kuala Lumpur's neighbours. Nevertheless, Thailand's intramural challenge in the form of the flexible engagement proposal did bring about the further development of ASEAN's diplomatic and security culture. This further development focused mainly on extending the range of issues and contexts traditionally defined as internal affairs in which other ASEAN governments were allowed to become legitimately involved. Considerations about regime security, ASEAN cohesion and regional influence did not suggest an imminent or complete abandonment of the 'ASEAN way', however. Also, the likelihood that enhanced interaction would continue to be pursued by ASEAN leaderships did not imply that norms such as quiet diplomacy had already become obsolete. Still, the events of 1997/8 raised questions about how short lived the reprieve was going to be for the 'ASEAN way' and ASEAN itself. Would ASEAN reassess the Hanoi consensus? Would new challenges arise? The final two chapters will address these questions.

8 ASEAN's diplomatic and security culture after the Hanoi Summit

Has 'old' thinking been dominating 'new' practices?

In spite of the declared consensus on the continued salience of ASEAN's diplomatic and security culture, which was rearticulated at the 1998 Hanoi Summit, ASEAN leaders soon revisited the normative terrain of the 'ASEAN way'. The main reason for this was that the reassertion at Hanoi of the validity of ASEAN's longstanding interpretations and practices did not succeed in dispelling continuing doubts over the relevance and purpose of the Association, especially outside the latter's confines, for at least two reasons. First, the divisions over the admission of Cambodia, which had become apparent in the run-up to and during the summit, had shattered the notion of a unified ASEAN. Second, the outcome of the Hanoi Summit could be and was perceived by critics of the Association as a failure to address the one challenge that was regarded as lying at the heart of the crises that swept Southeast Asia: ASEAN diplomatic and security culture. The assumption by ASEAN in Hanoi of a proactive stance on economic, financial and various other forms of co-operation did very little to change the perception that ASEAN had become bogged down by respect for its intramural norms. Nor did the earnest tone in which ASEAN spoke about the long-term objective of creating 'caring societies'. As the respected weekly the *Economist* had put it some months earlier, '[t]he "ASEAN way" no longer works' because 'the organisation's cardinal principle of non-interference has run into the reality of interdependence' (*Economist*, 28 February 1998: 59).

To the leaders of ASEAN member states such an analysis remained flawed. In their view, ASEAN members had appreciated their intramural security interdependence as well as that between Southeast and Northeast Asia. ASEAN leaders had also over many years since the 1970s pursued policies designed to achieve national and regional resilience, in appreciation of interdependence. Moreover, ASEAN member states had knowingly and enthusiastically embraced economic globalisation years before the onset of the Asian crisis – without simultaneously abandoning the 'ASEAN way'. And finally, ASEAN leaders had dealt with intramural challenges to ASEAN's diplomatic and security culture on previous occasions, as well as lived with and condoned considerable ambiguity regarding the practice of norms such as non-interference. Indeed, did not the Hanoi Plan for Action (ASEAN 1998b: ch. VII) indicate that it was ASEAN leaders' intention to explore again the initiation of the hitherto phantasmal ASEAN High Council?

While they understandably felt frustrated at the misconceptions prevalent in significant parts of the international analysis and commentary on ASEAN regarding the purpose and nature of the Association, member governments felt that they could not afford to ignore either the analysis or the op-ed pieces on ASEAN. At best, articles published in the *Economist* merely served to perpetuate the myth that ASEAN's elites stubbornly cling to supposedly ridiculously outdated concepts and practices.[1] At worst, however, such unqualified and undifferentiated remarks could translate into a continuation of the economic misery experienced by ASEAN member states and seal the relegation of the Association to the sidelines of the international politics of East Asia. As Singapore's foreign minister, Jayakumar, warned, '[p]erceptions can define political reality' (Jayakumar 2000).

Within the next two years, first under Singaporean and then under the Thai chairmanship of the ASEAN Standing Committee, four initiatives signalled to ASEAN's critics that its members had reassessed the salience of their diplomatic and security culture. The first of these concerned the initiation of the ASEAN Surveillance Process (ASP), which led to the first meeting of ASEAN finance ministers in March 1999. Although it did not touch directly on political-security issues, the ASP nevertheless seemed to represent a step beyond tacitly agreed collective understandings of the 'ASEAN way' insofar as the ASEAN finance ministers could henceforth raise with each other macroeconomic or financial issues previously considered to be none of their business. As the Asian crisis had manifestly underscored, these had the potential to disrupt regional economic security and intra-regional political stability.

The second initiative, in July 1999, on the eve of the annual ministerial meeting, was the introduction of the so-called 'Retreat', which offers an opportunity for ASEAN foreign ministers to brainstorm on topics of concern in the absence of officials or other aides. Like the ASP, the 'Retreat' suggested that ASEAN was loosening its grip on norms such as non-interference. The third development saw the participation of several ASEAN countries in the International Force in East Timor (INTERFET) and the subsequent peacekeeping activities conducted under the umbrella of the United Nations Transitional Administration in East Timor (UNTAET). This marked another first in that peacekeepers by one ASEAN member state had never before served in a UN mission undertaken in another.[2] When INTERFET gave way to the successor mission of UNTAET, a Filipino and then a Thai general assumed command of the peacekeeping forces in East Timor.

The fourth initiative, formally agreed by ASEAN in July 2000, focused on the endorsement of an ASEAN troika. The official purpose of the troika is 'to enable ASEAN to address in a timely manner urgent and important regional political and security issues and situations of common concern likely to disturb regional peace and harmony' (ASEAN 2000a). It consists of the acting chair of the ASEAN Standing Committee and the preceding and succeeding chairs, unless otherwise agreed.[3] This initiative, too, suggested a decline in the importance attributed by ASEAN leaders to the norm of non-interference and an increasing focus on institutionalising ASEAN procedures.

This chapter examines these four developments with a view to ascertaining to what extent any attendant new practices have superseded previously held collective understandings in relation to the norms of the 'ASEAN way'. The chapter is divided into four sections. The sections examine each one of the initiatives in more detail before canvassing arguments on whether it is necessary to qualify the extent to which they can or should be seen as constituting developments of ASEAN's diplomatic and security culture. This will involve assessing whether new partial collective interpretations of existing norms or new norms have emerged.

The ASEAN surveillance process

The ASP was formally established at the Special Meeting of the ASEAN Finance Ministers in early October 1998.[4] The process has encompassed two aspects: first, the monitoring of global, regional and national economic and financial developments, summarised twice yearly in a surveillance report. The purpose of the monitoring is to avert a relapse into major macroeconomic and financial instability by ASEAN member states with all the attendant negative consequences this would have for societal and regime security, and perhaps even inter-state security.[5] The second aspect of the ASP has centred on a peer review process conducted by the ASEAN finance ministers. This builds on the ASEAN surveillance report, which contains recommendations for the ministers. In the peer review, initiated in March 1999, ministers exchange views and information on specific economic policies and issues of structural reform. Topics discussed include measures designed to stimulate domestic demand, maintain prudent fiscal management, and expedite bank and corporate restructuring. If ministers perceive a potential threat to any member economy the peer review offers an opportunity for finance ministers to suggest to their counterparts that different directions or new measures be tried in the areas of finance and economic policies. Alternatively, they may suggest that ministers jointly consider unilateral or collective action to counter such threats (ASEAN 1998a).

The establishment of the peer review by finance ministers marked a significant development. First, ASEAN finance ministers had previously met only once under the ASEAN format. They had only informal gatherings on the sidelines of IMF, World Bank or Asian Development Bank meetings. Also, to address their specific economic problems the governments of ASEAN member states had previously relied considerably more on other states and institutions than on each other. Second, and more importantly for our purposes, the surveillance process allows for what in the past would almost certainly have been considered interference by ASEAN leaders but which now – as all member governments have endorsed the process – constitutes legitimate involvement.

Significantly, however, the surveillance process does not in itself undermine ASEAN's diplomatic and security culture. While the surveillance process has implied an expansion of the scope of issues in which other ASEAN policy-makers may become legitimately involved, the process also stipulates by inference those areas in which involvement is still not considered legitimate. Thus, while the brief is to monitor and analyse the macroeconomic situation and developments within the region, the process of monitoring *other* areas depends on the approval of the ASEAN Select Committee.[6] Interestingly, governments are also only required to provide baseline data to the ASEAN Surveillance Co-ordinating Unit as supplied to the IMF. ASEAN governments can thus, if they so desire, evade a broadening or deepening of the discussion (Funston 1999: 214). Indeed, individual member countries are permitted not to disclose their own national data and information under certain circumstances. On selected surveillance issues, for example, which may not be relevant to some member countries, the 10 (initially 9) minus x principle may be applied. This principle, introduced in the 1980s in relation to economic co-operation, allows those ASEAN countries interested in pursuing a certain initiative to do so, while those who do not effectively opt out but do not stand in its way. All these points suggest that, while the peer review process can bring pressure to bear on member states, limits to the intrusiveness and scope of the peer review process remain. Not surprisingly, there is no premeditation for collective sanctions against any member, even if that member were to demonstrate continuous disregard of 'good' policies, leading to poor economic performance.

Furthermore, although the process is transparent in terms of its agreed outcome, the actual discussion process leading to the compromise outcome, of course, is not. Also, all data, reports, proceedings and information generated from the ASP are treated confidentially. This builds on the view expressed by some member states that the publication of sensitive data could jeopardise the prospects for full economic recovery. The emphasis on confidentiality, which can be seen as conforming to the principle of quiet diplomacy, of course also makes it less likely that ASEAN leaders will wittingly or unwittingly embarrass fellow leaders. As regards the implementation of the ASP, then, norms associated with ASEAN's diplomatic and security culture still matter. As we shall see in the next section, similar points emerge in relation to the 'Retreat'.

The initiation of the 'Retreat'

When the ASEAN foreign ministers organised the first formal 'Retreat' in July 1999, it was represented as part of 'a continuous process of serious examination of the longer-term issues facing ASEAN' (ASEAN 1999). Singapore's foreign minister, S. Jayakumar, had previously, in even more assertive language, described it as 'a process of constant and critical evaluation and re-evaluation to strengthen ASEAN' (Jayakumar 1999a). In practice, the 'Retreat', having no fixed agenda, has provided ASEAN foreign ministers with an opportunity to brainstorm together and to engage with each other, in the absence of any official and aides, on an array of issues that affect ASEAN's image, credibility and regional significance. In 1999 ASEAN foreign ministers discussed three core issues: the future of ASEAN, the future of the ARF and the future of the PMC and dialogue processes.

On the issue of the future of ASEAN, three points of agreement were reached. These focused on the need to manage intramural differences in a way that would not disrupt co-operation, the need to avoid a two-tier ASEAN, and the continued salience of consensus, consultation and the norm of non-interference. As regards the last of these, Professor Jayakumar spelled out what in his view remained a dilemma for the Association. As he saw it, ASEAN should not necessarily abandon the norms of non-interference, consultation and consensus, but the question was how without abandoning them the organisation and its members could face up to new challenges in relation to governance, democratisation and human rights (Jayakumar 1999b). With respect to the future of the ARF, discussion at the 'Retreat' focused on the question of how ASEAN could retain its leading role while simultaneously bringing about a sense of participation and a sense of ownership of the Forum among non-members of ASEAN. As regards the PMC and attendant dialogue processes, the question concentrated on whether these still had any real relevance. Although conclusive answers to these questions were not reached, the first 'Retreat' received positive reviews, not least by its host. According to Jayakumar (1999b), ASEAN foreign ministers had achieved the objectives of the 'Retreat' by getting together and fleshing out their respective position and, disagreements notwithstanding, managing these in a way that would allow them to move on with co-operation for their mutual benefit.

The assessment in July 2000 of the outgoing chair of the ASEAN Standing Committee, Thailand's foreign minister Surin Pitsuwan, was even more ebullient. The 'Retreat' organised at the Thirty-third ASEAN Ministerial Meeting in Bangkok followed the same basic objective as its predecessor: promoting ASEAN's self-renewal. However, in contrast to the first, attention at the second 'Retreat' converged around finding consensus on a specific proposal, namely the ASEAN troika, a vehicle to address political and security issues, as well as situations of common concern that had the potential to upset regional peace and harmony, which was agreed during the ministerial proceedings. In the event, Thailand's foreign minister described the 'Retreat' as 'splendid' (quoted in Reyes 2000a). This upbeat feeling about the usefulness of the 'Retreat' apparently inspired all ASEAN members to continue the practice. As one regional newspaper reported, 'the past two retreats were so good that the ministers now want more retreats in an informal setting so that they can thrash things out among themselves before the world gets in their way' (*The Nation*, 26 July 2000).

The first inter-sessional informal 'Retreat' of ASEAN foreign ministers was organised in Yangon in late April 2001. The most important topics discussed included the Initiative for ASEAN Integration, which aims to help overcome the gap between the early and later members, and ASEAN's drug policy. Myanmar's foreign minister also appears to have informed his counterparts about the status of the dialogue begun by the incumbent regime wth Daw Aung San Suu Kyi in October 2000. Other topics raised focused on the implementation of the Hanoi Action Plan and the preliminary report of the Eminent Persons Group on how to strengthen ASEAN co-operation (Kulachada Chaipitat 2001).

Given its purpose, the 'Retreat' amounts to a new form of 'enhanced interaction', albeit one that – in contrast to when the latter was practised in more robust form – is considered legitimate or at least acceptable by all concerned, as illustrated by the fact that no leadership has refused to participate. This represents a significant development because the 'Retreat' has served to undermine comprehensively the notion that unwelcome issues traditionally regarded as domestic developments are, de facto, taboo in exchanges among foreign ministers. It would appear that it is now increasingly possible for ASEAN foreign ministers to broach any topic if their interests or standing, or those of other member governments or the Association as a whole, are affected. As Secretary-General Rodolfo Severino argued after the Singapore 'Retreat': 'While it was not heated, some grievances and even complaints about lack of action on this or that came out. So the willingness to say negative things has risen. Once that happens, you can't go back anymore' (quoted in Reyes 2000c).

Be that as it may, many of the characteristics of the 'Retreat' do not yet signal a full withdrawal from ASEAN's diplomatic and security culture. For one thing, the 'Retreat' has remained consistent with the norm of quiet diplomacy. When hosting the first 'Retreat', Professor Jayakumar refused to divulge to journalists the concrete substance of the discussions that had taken place. In other words, he declined to disentangle his summary account by providing insights on the different points of view articulated by himself and his colleagues during the four-hour session. Surin Pitsuwan did not even take questions after giving a short press briefing following the second 'Retreat' in Bangkok the year after. A press conference was called following the first informal retreat of ASEAN foreign ministers in Yangon, but again no details of the exchanges were released.

Second, while the 'Retreat' offers foreign ministers the opportunity to raise any topic, it would appear that the meetings have so far not been used to address in any detail, for example, bilateral disputes between member states. This is testified by the apparent reluctance of Manila and Kuala Lumpur to discuss further a dispute that arose in the first half of 1999 over two reefs in the South China Sea. Similarly, the border confrontation between the Royal Thai Army and Myanmar's armed forces in February 2001 apparently did not feature as a issue in Yangon the following April. In other words, while ASEAN leaders may have shed inhibitions about deliberating on sensitive issues of common concern in an ASEAN setting, this does not mean that the 'Retreat' has undermined the norms associated with ASEAN's diplomatic and security culture. Clearly, though, the advantage of holding the 'Retreat', especially in view of the alleged candid nature of ministerial discussions in this multilateral setting, is that it allows ASEAN foreign ministers to dismiss accusations that they are hostage to outdated conceptions of the norm of non-interference.

To see whether, beyond the surveillance mechanism and the 'Retreat', there are clearer manifestations of shifting collective understandings in relation to the core norms of ASEAN's diplomatic and security culture, the next two sections focus on ASEAN's response to the recent tragedy in East Timor and the ASEAN troika, respectively.

ASEAN and East Timor

In the eyes of many analysts and human rights activists ASEAN's record on East Timor before 1999 was shameful, to the point of complicity in the unfolding tragedy befalling the East Timorese (Inbaraj 1997). At no point following Jakarta's intervention in East Timor in 1975 had the issue formally featured in any ASEAN meeting.[7] Indeed, with the annexation of the former Portuguese colony President Suharto had rejected anything that smacked of interference in Indonesia's internal affairs. In the 1990s Jakarta exerted significant diplomatic pressure on other ASEAN countries to prevent NGOs from holding conferences on East Timor on their territory. ASEAN states complied with Indonesia's express wishes in all cases.

Notably, ASEAN's silence on East Timor continued under the reform-minded government of President B.J. Habibie, not least because he too regarded East Timor as an internal issue. And perhaps not surprisingly, therefore, East Timor still remained outside the remit of discussions within ASEAN when President Habibie first contemplated granting enhanced autonomy to the territory in autumn 1998. The same appears to have been the case when he offered the possibility of full independence should the autonomy option be rejected.[8] In the run-up to the popular consultation organised to establish clarity on East Timor's future status, President Habibie enlisted the services of the UN, not ASEAN, and restricted himself to announcing Jakarta's policy reversal on East Timor to his ASEAN colleagues (Chongkittavorn 1999a).

Notably, if the Indonesian leadership was initially reluctant to involve ASEAN in dealing with the East Timor issue, other regional governments were also reluctant to become involved. When the United Nations

Assistance Mission in East Timor (UNAMET) was formed to organise a 'popular consultation' on the political future of the territory, the Habibie government indicated that it would prefer the presence of ASEAN civil and police units to those from other countries. However, several ASEAN member states failed to respond (*The Nation*, 14 September 1999), suggesting that the respective governments were less than keen to adopt a role either individually or as a regional grouping. In the event, the Philippines, Thailand and Malaysia participated.

In view of ASEAN members' deference to Indonesia on East Timor, it is not necessarily surprising that the Joint Communiqué of the Thirty-second Ministerial Meeting makes no reference to the territory, although by this time a series of atrocities had been committed against East Timorese civilians. Also, the referendum on the territory's political future had been postponed to 30 August. While it was couched in shock and dismay, ASEAN states also found it difficult to respond to Jakarta, let alone criticise it publicly, after the clear victory of the pro-independence forces in East Timor led to widespread violence and destruction after 4 September. In the words of the late Gerald Segal, ASEAN governments – together with other Asian countries – initially restricted themselves to 'solidarity in silence about a military response to Indonesian atrocities' (Segal 1999). Indeed, from the perspective of an outside observer, ASEAN's discourse on sovereignty and the 'ASEAN way' seemed curiously out of touch with the increasing significance accorded to 'human security' in Western policy-making circles.

Only as calls multiplied for an immediate intervention to stop militia attacks on East Timorese civilians and refugees – apparently perpetrated with the intention of sparking off a civil war involving FALINTIL (*Forças Armadas de Libertaçao Nacional de Timor Leste*; Armed Forces of National Liberation of East Timor) – did ASEAN members cautiously respond to the unfolding events. For instance, ASEAN members reacted positively, but with some hesitation, to attempts by Western countries to have the issue discussed on the sidelines of the 1999 APEC 'Summit' Meeting in Auckland, especially given Indonesia's intended absence at the special meeting proposed for this purpose. When the meeting took place, two of Indonesia's neighbouring Malay states, Brunei and Malaysia, were absent and the remainder of ASEAN foreign ministers participated merely in their 'private and individual capacities' (Chongkittavorn 1999c).

However, in the face of the general public outcry at the scale and nature of the revenge attacks on East Timorese by the pro-integrationist militias and the obvious complicity of local Indonesian forces, several ASEAN governments found it increasingly difficult not to respond diplomatically to the developing tragedy. Thailand and Malaysia, for instance, indicated that if the United Nations approved a peacekeeping force they would participate. Many ASEAN policy-makers were deeply concerned about the implications of the East Timor tragedy for their individual and collective standing.

The Habibie government, meanwhile, drawing on the principle of non-interference to justify its position, pointed out that despite the violence the introduction of an armed international force into East Timor could only take place after the ratification of East Timor's vote on independence. At the time this was planned for November 1999.[9] In the event this position proved untenable, as Indonesia faced strong Western pressure to restore peace and security in the territory immediately or invite an international force in. This pressure continued to mount in view of the apparent implementation of a plan code-named *Operasi Wiradharma*, seemingly contrived in July, the aim of which was to deport East Timorese to West Timor before their further dispersal around the Indonesian archipelago.[10] However, within days of the aforementioned APEC meeting, Indonesia acquiesced to international pressure to accept international peace-keeping forces through the UN from what President Habibie described as 'friendly countries'. This decision followed threats by the IMF to review loans to Jakarta, and Washington's suspension of economic development assistance and arms supplies. It came at the end of a UN Security Council mission to Jakarta and East Timor.[11]

As arrangements for the establishment of a multinational force under Australian command proceeded, Indonesia's foreign minister, Ali Alatas, laid the ground for an agreement between his Thai counterpart and the then chief of Indonesia's armed forces to have troops from ASEAN countries join the international force (Dupont 2000: 166). Having been formally invited to join INTERFET, nevertheless only four ASEAN countries initially expressed a willingness to make a serious contribution: Thailand, Malaysia, Singapore, and the Philippines. In the event, Australia and Thailand ended up offering the biggest peace-keeping contingents, with a Thai general assuming deputy command. In contrast to Thailand, the Philippines and the Singapore, Malaysia sent only a token force to East Timor, because of her apparent disaffection at the decision to entrust Australia to lead the peace enforcement operation. The new entrants to the Association did not commit any civilian or military units to any East Timor operation. Significantly, ASEAN countries participated in INTERFET as individual countries only.

Reasons for ASEAN states' participation in INTERFET

At least five reasons may be identified why several ASEAN countries joined the international force for East Timor. The first was arguably to demonstrate solidarity with Indonesia. In the wake of the broad outcry at the destruction wrought in East Timor, President Habibie was forced to abandon his adamant opposition to an international force entering East Timor to restore order. President Habibie resented in particular that Australia was to lead this international force. This arose from a sense of betrayal. Australia had previously explicitly recognised the territory's annexation by Jakarta, but then suddenly undertook a major foreign policy shift by advising the administration of Dr Habibie that all options should be considered regarding a new status for East Timor in order to prevent a hardening of attitudes in the territory (Cotton 1999). Of particular significance in this respect was the receipt by Dr Habibie of a letter by the Australian, prime minister, Howard.[12]

To influence the command and composition of the international force, while not formally setting preconditions on the nationality of troops, at the last minute the Habibie government thus specifically asked the then ASC chair that ASEAN countries take a major, if not a leading, role in the force to be assembled. To the extent that a direct role by Australia could not be avoided, the participation of several ASEAN countries was seen as making the intervention more palatable for Jakarta. This was well appreciated by other ASEAN governments, who would not have joined INTERFET had it not been for Jakarta's explicit consent.

The second reason is linked to attempts to avert a further slide in Indonesia's international standing. As a proud member of international society and the leader of the non-aligned world in the early 1990s, Indonesia saw its prestige severely undercut by the events in East Timor. The most important factors in this regard were the proven complicity of the Indonesian National Army (TNI) in the atrocities committed and the leadership's apparent nonchalance to limit damage to the country's international image. The extent of this damage was exemplified by remarks made by UN Secretary-General Kofi Annan to the effect that Jakarta could not eschew responsibility for possible 'crimes against humanity'. Notably, the concern with Indonesia's international standing was not completely selfless. Some ASEAN states were clearly also worried about how the combustion of Indonesia's reputation would affect its own broader image as an Association.

Also, by participating in INTERFET, the respective ASEAN members hoped to expunge the memory of their alleged inaction in previous regional crisis situations and improve the Association's international image. As Kavi Chongkittavorn put it, '[a]n Indonesia being treated as a pariah state would greatly damage a wounded Asean which has been trying to recoup its losses since the admission of Burma two years ago' (Chongkittavorn 1999d). Above all, it was feared that if ASEAN members failed to respond to American and European demands to participate in a joint intervention force in East Timor its relations with ASEAN dialogue partners might be impaired.

Third, while unavoidable, ASEAN states found it politically damaging to allow Australia to lead an international force into Southeast Asia. This demonstrated ASEAN's incapacity to address regional problems on its own terms and indicated the limits of its ability to maintain regional stability. As the Thai deputy foreign minister, M.R. Sukhumbhand Paribatra, put it,

> We in Asean have been saying since 1971 that we want the region to be free from outside interference. Now a problem has arisen that can lead

to outside interference in regional affairs. So we must do something about it – we cannot logically stand still and do nothing – we must put our words into action.

(quoted in *The Nation*, 15 September 1999)

Clearly the reasoning expressed here alludes to the ZOPFAN Declaration, which the Suharto regime had fully endorsed over many years.

ASEAN members further believed that if they did not participate in INTERFET to curb the violence, the destruction and atrocities in East Timor might potentially have very negative implications for stability in Indonesia. At issue was the prospect of an intensification of the domestic power struggle in Indonesia, with unforeseeable consequences. Singapore thus considered it important to shore up the more moderate elements in the Indonesian armed forces. While denouncing the atrocities of rogue elements in the army, the Singapore government equally made clear, however, that little would be gained if in the effort to restore order in the territory and implement the result of the ballot the international community threatened Indonesia's stability by discrediting, without discrimination, its civil or military leaders. Another factor was the fear of the possible further break-up of the Indonesian archipelago. The events in East Timor were viewed as potentially having an impact on events in Aceh and Irian Jaya (Papua), and an accentuation of the secessionist struggles there was seen to lead to more regional instability. Some ASEAN leaders also worried about the possibility of the re-emergence of secessionist activities within their own borders. In this sense, the violence in East Timor not only threatened the future of Indonesian politics, but also undermined regional stability.

Finally, it is also possible to understand the participation of some ASEAN member governments in the context of intra-ASEAN politics. The Chuan government in Bangkok, for example, was clearly involved in the East Timor crisis with the aim of lifting Thailand to a higher ground of international morality, responsibility and credibility, which would allow Bangkok to become the new standard bearer in Southeast Asia (Phasuk 1999). Not surprisingly, therefore, Thailand pledged the largest number of troops besides Australia.[13] Also, a Thai officer, Major-General Songkitti Chakrabhat, director of the Supreme Command's information department and a former military attaché to Indonesia, assumed the role of deputy commander of INTERFET.

The significance of ASEAN states' participation in INTERFET and UNTAET

The participation of ASEAN members in an intervention force clearly marked a significant moment in the evolution of the 'ASEAN way', although it is important to recognise that only some ASEAN members participated as individual states. Indeed, for the first time several ASEAN governments had dispatched a considerable number of troops to restore order in a territory that for years had been acknowledged as having been incorporated into Indonesia. Moreover, INTERFET was not a traditional peacekeeping mission, but legitimated by a Chapter VII mandate of the UN Charter. The same applies to the UNTAET mission, established in October 1999 and implemented in February 2000,[14] to which core ASEAN members (Thailand, the Philippines, Singapore and Malaysia) again contributed both civilian and military personnel.[15] That said, it seems premature to consider the participation of these ASEAN members' troops as evidence of the demise of ASEAN's diplomatic and security culture. There are several points here.

First, personnel committed by ASEAN member states to participate in the international force did so at the explicit invitation of Indonesia, extended to Surin Pitsuwan in exchanges with Ali Alatas and General Wiranto on 14 September 1999. Second, ASEAN members' armed forces were not meant to engage in peace enforcement. Indeed, the Thai army chief, General Surayud Chulanont, made clear that Thai soldiers serving in INTERFET would only participate in peacekeeping operations to which Jakarta had given its assent. Significantly, the presence of individual ASEAN states in East Timor was therefore confined to the eastern rather than the western part of the territory, which borders on West Timor and where the danger of running into militia members was significantly higher. This pattern of deployment began to change only in 2001, when Singapore sent peacekeepers close to the border with West Timor (*Asian Defence Journal*, May–June 2001).

Third, ASEAN member governments clearly sought to respect as many of Indonesia's sensitivities as possible. For example, details of the aforementioned exchanges between Surin Pitsuwan and Ali Alatas and General Wiranto were treated as confidential. ASEAN foreign ministers decided not to discuss East Timor at their meeting on the sidelines of the 1999 UN General Assembly. Respect for Jakarta's sensitivities even went so far as Prime Minister Chuan informing UN Secretary-General Kofi Annan that Thailand would like to see Indonesian troops participate in the operations conducted by INTERFET.

Fourth, one participating ASEAN member appears to have joined in a multinational humanitarian mission to East *and* West Timor (i.e. inside Indonesia), but it did so only in response to another 'invitation' by Ali Alatas in late September 1999. This 'invitation' had been issued in reaction to concerns in the US and elsewhere about the apparent lack of safety for refugees from East Timor and the civilian character of the camps in which they were housed. Generally though, ASEAN countries strongly resisted suggestions by Australia and the United States to extend military operations into West Timor (i.e. Indonesian territory) when in hot pursuit of pro-Jakarta militias. ASEAN governments argued that such an action would constitute a flagrant breach of Indonesia's sovereignty. The Thai prime minister, Chuan Leekpai, reminded the US defence secretary that the mandate of the international force in East Timor was restricted to East Timor itself (Srivornart and Chimprahba 1999).

Fifth, ASEAN countries publicly voiced concern about allegedly 'aggressive' behaviour on the part of Australian soldiers after pictures of Western soldiers pointing their rifles at the heads of suspected pro-Jakarta militiamen appeared in the international media, pictures that greatly irked many Indonesians and irritated Jakarta's neighbouring governments. Sixth, when Australia claimed a proprietary role for itself (and the United States) to become more routinely involved in managing regional order ASEAN governments described the claims as inappropriate and protested against the so-called 'Howard Doctrine'. Notably, this included the Thai Ministry of Foreign Affairs, even though Thailand continued to work closely with Australia in leading INTERFET. The Malaysian deputy prime minister, Abdullah Ahmad Badawi, was more unequivocal, however, when he said, 'We don't wish to see any country appointing itself the protector or leader for this region. Asian countries are capable of looking after the region themselves and cherish peace for the region more than others' (quoted in Richardson 1999).

Finally, none of the governments that had decided to participate in INTERFET believed that it possessed an exemplary character for the future, let alone was the beginning of an ASEAN force geared to conduct humanitarian intervention. The Chuan government favoured a more proactive stance in bringing about intervention, while questioning whether ASEAN had the capability to pursue this without the assistance of friendly major powers. However, Malaysia's foreign minister, Datuk Seri Syed Hamid Albar, argued that Kuala Lumpur was 'wary of new concepts which might compromise sovereignty in the name of humanitarianism' (quoted in Wong 1999). The Philippine government stated two conditions for humanitarian intervention: a UN Security Council resolution and an invitation from the country to be intervened in (Baguioro 1999). Retired Indonesian foreign minister Ali Alatas, meanwhile, warned that, first, any new norm on humanitarian intervention must be based on the principles of legitimacy and universal applicability. He also warned (Alatas 2000) that external forces might initiate or exploit internal situations for their own political ends. In conjunction, these statements illustrate the lack of enthusiasm among ASEAN members even for UN-mandated peacekeeping activities in Southeast Asia. In this context, it is also significant that ASEAN countries did not support the call for a UN commission of inquiry to be sent to East Timor to investigate atrocities there.[16] In particular, they were reluctant to endorse the appointment of a UN rights expert for the territory as the first stage towards setting up a tribunal to try alleged war criminals. In the meantime Dr Mahathir went so far as to accuse anti-Indonesia 'parties' of exploiting Indonesia's economic problems to press for the August ballot in East Timor.

In short, while there can be no doubt that new ground has been broken with ASEAN participation in INTERFET, and that this has perhaps even illustrated the art of the possible as regards some of its members, this participation has neither amounted to nor automatically heralds a major change in the 'ASEAN way'. The fact that the participation of ASEAN countries in a peacekeeping operation in what was then still officially part of Indonesia would have been unimaginable only a few years earlier does not alter this assessment. Nor does the subsequent support given by some ASEAN countries to UNTAET, which was also based on Indonesia's consent and UN authorisation.[17] In other words, ASEAN members are still some way off *collectively* embracing new understandings of the salience of norms like non-intervention.

The next section examines whether the ASEAN troika represents the next stage of a meeting on the contours of an emerging further collective reconsideration of core ASEAN norms.

The institutionalisation of the ASEAN troika

ASEAN's response to the East Timor crisis in the run-up to the establishment of INTERFET compounded its already considerable credibility and image problem. Indicative of this assessment is the comment by Sebastian and Smith, who noted that 'East Timor became ASEAN's millstone when the Association failed to speak up and stop the rampage' (Sebastian and Smith 2000: 79). The consequences of key ASEAN member states' initial failure to respond early and collectively to the bloodshed in East Timor, not only cost the Association more of what remained of its international standing, but also virtually ensured that Australia was asked to manage this problem of regional order in Southeast Asia. This raised serious questions about the capacity of both ASEAN and the ARF to conduct preventive diplomacy. Notably, the ARF did not directly mention East Timor in the 1999 Statement by the ARF chair, Singapore. In was against this background that Thailand's premier, Chuan Leekpai, proposed the formal institutionalisation of an ASEAN troika at the Third Informal Summit of ASEAN leaders in Manila in November 1999.

The proposal built to some extent on the rather ambivalent experience of the troika that had been convened two years earlier to address the domestic and international crisis which followed Hun Sen's coup against Prince Norodom Ranariddh in July 1997. It was no doubt also motivated by the applause the Chuan administration had received from both the international media and foreign governments for contributing in a very positive way to the international force in East Timor. Significantly, Bangkok's participation in INTERFET and UNTAET had strongly underlined the Chuan government's claim to a new identity as a caring democracy that was prepared to defend proactively the rights and interests of humanity. Not surprisingly, therefore, Premier Chuan and his foreign policy team were keen to strengthen Thailand's credentials in this area even further, as it was Bangkok's unstated objective to renew ASEAN in a way that would help it inculcate a position of moral leadership of the Association. Even if they were wary of Thailand's motives, other ASEAN members were expected to find this idea agreeable because of a professed widespread belief among members that regional solutions should be found for regional problems. Thus, Thailand's foreign-policy-makers advocated the establishment of an ASEAN body to deal quickly with urgent and important regional political and security issues that were causing concern among ASEAN leaderships. To the extent that the principle of subsidiarity would apply, ASEAN could be responsible for preventive diplomacy in lieu of the ARF. Such preventive diplomacy would, if successful, then make the intervention of outside powers unlikely. In that sense, the ASEAN troika concept was a direct rejoinder to the agenda putatively sketched for the Association by ASEAN Secretary-General Rodolfo Severino, when he argued thus:

> Another step that ASEAN might take on the road to greater region-alism is to open itself to the possibility of taking regional action to help a member-country deal with internal difficulties that have regional or international dimensions; assist member-countries in resolving disputes between them; and keep actions and policies of one member-country from seriously harming others. This, of course, presupposes that ASEAN members would be willing to accept such involvement by their neighbors.
>
> (Severino 1999)

It was not before the Thirty-third ASEAN Ministerial Meeting in Bangkok, however, that the ASEAN troika concept was formally approved. As the time-lapse between the initial broad-based low-key support by ASEAN leaders and the eventual agreement on the troika's principles and purposes indicates, its inception proved contentious among ASEAN leaderships. This contention replicated in some ways the controversy surrounding the ongoing process of elaborating the concept and principles of preventive diplomacy in the ARF (see Chapters 5 and 6).

The ASEAN debate on the troika concept

While the Chuan government initially conceived of the troika as a permanent body institutionalised at ministerial level, most foreign policy leaders of other member states regarded this as uncalled for. For most of them, the troika proposal marked a clever effort to revitalise Surin Pitsuwan's proposal of flexible engagement in a different garb. In some ways, of course, the troika proposal went far beyond the (spurned) advocacy for flexible engagement, because it suggested not merely the possibility and legitimacy of flexibility in the application of the norm of non-interference among members, but a more sustained effort at preventive diplomacy in the name of ASEAN. Like flexible engagement, the troika concept raised a host of questions. Would the troika remain compatible with the norms of sovereign equality and non-interference? Would it apply to interstate disputes as well as to intra-state conflict? The complexity of the issue was framed by ASEAN's Secretary-General Rodolfo Severino:

> [W]hat if conflict does occur within a country in a form and to a degree that threatens other countries in Southeast Asia? Each such case would be different from others, perhaps even radically so. In this light, what norms are there to invoke? Would there be any? Could there be any?
>
> (Severino 2001)

Notably, while Surin's proposal for flexible engagement was shunned by all member states except the Philippines, the proposal for an ASEAN troika was not. As the following section shows, however, it was considerably modified in the period between November 1999 and July 2000. Burma came out most vocally against the troika's proposed power to address regional crises without a consensus, and pushed hardest to water down the new body's mandate (Crispin 2000).

The ASEAN troika compromise

The compromise achieved over the troika concept (ASEAN 2000a) may be summarised in five points. First, the 'ASEAN troika', originally intended to be a permanent institution at ministerial level, was reconceptualised as an 'ad-hoc body'. In other words, the troika is to be disbanded once it has addressed 'in a timely manner the urgent and important regional political and security issues and situations of common concern likely to disturb regional peace and harmony'. This compromise position had already evolved by the time of the Senior Officials Meeting in May 2000, as it became clear that very few ASEAN states were interested in a permanent body to handle a temporary crisis. Second, it was agreed that the troika would not be a decision-making body and was not intended to represent ASEAN beyond its assigned brief. Instead, it was meant to report and submit recommendations to ASEAN foreign ministers. Third, the troika is meant to work in accordance with norms enshrined in the ASEAN treaties and agreements, in particular the norms of consensus and non-interference. Fourth, the troika can be established on a consensual basis upon the request of the ASC chair or any other ASEAN foreign minister. Finally, it was agreed that the troika would normally be composed of the foreign ministers of the present, past and future chair countries of the ASEAN Standing Committee, although other compositions might also be considered. This constituted a change to the reasoning underlying the composition of the

1997 ASEAN troika, with the Philippines as chairman and Indonesia and Thailand as interested parties.

As was the case with flexible engagement, the compromise reached with respect to the troika as a vehicle for intramural preventive diplomacy would appear to constitute a further development of ASEAN's diplomatic and security culture, at least in conceptual terms. On the other hand, the compromise clearly re-emphasises the continued validity of the norms of sovereign equality, consensus as well as non-interference. The reiteration of these norms as possessing lasting validity reflected the unabated deep-seated apprehensions of some policy-makers about the uncertain outcomes of external involvement in domestic political processes. In a sense, to these leaders the troika concept resembled a sword of Damocles endangering regime preservation. That said, the troika proposal still further reinforces the increasingly dominant collective understanding whereby it is legitimate for members to raise internal or interstate issues of concern not only on a bilateral basis, but also in the context of ASEAN diplomacy.

This latter understanding is still emerging; it is not yet fully developed. The point becomes clear if we look, for instance, at the norm of non-interference. Although the Chuan government has seemingly accepted that the troika should refrain from addressing issues that are the internal affairs of ASEAN member countries, the agreement to this text has not necessarily implied that Thailand would accept, say, Yangon's understanding of what should be subsumed under this notion. Indeed, the point of Bangkok's previous proposal for greater flexibility in the practice of the principle of non-interference was that Thai foreign policy shapers favoured the view that some matters considered internal were not justifiably so labelled because they had cross-border implications. Drawing on the evolution of the concept of sovereignty in international law, Thailand has accordingly explicitly rejected the notion that the production and trafficking of drugs constitute only domestic issues. From Bangkok's perspective, the same is true for government policies that drive members of ethnic minorities across national state boundaries. Meanwhile, however, the SPDC in Myanmar is able to advocate a different and much narrower interpretation of the norm, as some earlier members themselves did during the Cold War.

Not surprisingly, while displaying to the international press an ebullient mood about the outcome of the Bangkok 'Retreat', the Chuan government was uncomfortable with the compromise decision on how the troika would be activated. Bangkok's foreign policy elite favoured the chair having as much latitude as possible to establish the troika. It was intimated that this was necessary from the outset to prevent the international media from claiming all too easily that the troika would be ineffective in practice. Last-minute ministerial discussions in Bangkok thus subsequently saw the Thais argue that the troika chair could in fact activate the troika on the basis of an initial exploration. As Surin Pitsuwan argued, the Troika chair 'could take exploratory steps on certain issues, he would consult, he would communicate, he could activate the troika, he could ask for the convening on an emergency basis' (quoted in Agence France Press [hereafter AFP], 25 July 2000). As Thai Foreign Ministry spokesman Don Pramudwinai further clarified, '[I]f from this exploration the troika is convinced that it should be functional in severe situations the troika can activate itself' (quoted in AFP, 25 July 2000). If other troika members disagreed, however, or other vigorous objections were raised, the troika would call for an emergency meeting of all members to discuss whether the troika should come into force.

Putting the troika into practice: a forlorn hope?

Regional analysts have not reacted very enthusiastically to the ASEAN troika compromise. For instance, Shawn Crispin argued that '[w]ith no clear mandate as to how, where and when the troika may be employed, Asean seems to have missed a golden opportunity to reinvigorate the grouping's sagging credibility as a pillar of peace and stability in the region' (Crispin 2000: 22). Certainly, it remains to be seen whether the Thai foreign minister, Surin Pitsuwan, was correct in confidently asserting that the 'Troika would serve to elevate ASEAN cooperation to a higher plane and further enhance ASEAN's unity and solidarity' (ASEAN 2000a). Short of activating it, the challenge for ASEAN will thus be to clarify what practices the troika will be able to engage in that allow it to fulfil its stated purpose while respecting the norms of consensus and non-interference in the internal affairs of member states. Significantly, several member states have already invoked the latter norms to limit the potential practical application of the troika – despite the emerging consensus among regional leaderships that increasingly fewer issues qualify as proper domestic affairs that should remain outside the remit of what can legitimately be discussed within ASEAN circles.

Indonesia's leadership, for example, has argued that Jakarta should be left to deal with the violence in Maluku, which since 1998 has left about 5,000 people dead and has displaced up to half a million. However, Jakarta has been unable or unwilling to stem the violence that has engulfed the religiously divided communities since early 1999, leaving the Muslim militia Laskar Jihad to wage a holy war against those of Christian faith (Murphy 2001; Dhume 2001). Notably, the Joint Statement passed at the Thirty-third ASEAN Ministerial Meeting made no reference to Maluku. It did, however, reaffirm – in a separate statement – Indonesia's territorial integrity, and called on Indonesia to reach a peaceful solution to its problems in Aceh and Irian Jaya (Papua) through dialogue and reconciliation consistent with its efforts to maintain the momentum of political and economic reforms (ASEAN 2000b).[18] Equally, the Philippine leadership under President Estrada quickly rejected the ASEAN troika as an appropriate vehicle to address internal crises linked to the Abu Sayyaf hostage-taking or Moro separatism. As the foreign minister, Siazon, declared, 'the MILF [Moro Islamic Liberation Front] issue is pure and simple a case of rebellion ... All my [ASEAN] colleagues understand that no self-respecting government would ever allow a secessionist group to occupy territory or agree to a breakup of its own country' (quoted in Reyes 2000b). The Malaysian foreign minister, Syed Hamid, has suggested that the troika would be unsuitable to deal with an array of issues that had brought about ASEAN bad press.

Within the first year following the finalisation of the troika concept, the question of whether to establish the troika was addressed only once by the incumbent chair of the ASC. This happened when the confrontation between the SPDC and opposition leader Aung San Suu Kyi deteriorated in September 2000 in the wake of the forcible removal of the Nobel Prize laureate from Rangoon's main railway station to prevent her from travelling outside the city.[19] When Suu Kyi was subsequently placed under house arrest again, UN Secretary-General Kofi Annan advised that the ASEAN troika should become involved. However, Vietnam – the chair of the ASEAN Standing Committee after the Thirty-third ASEAN Ministerial Meeting in Bangkok in July 2000 – refused to initiate the troika, even though the Thai government, as the past chair, reportedly supported such a move. Apparently, following a brief survey of ASEAN governments' opinions on the matter, Hanoi foreign-policy-makers had concluded that the invocation of the troika was not called for. As a spokeswoman for the Vietnamese Ministry of Foreign Affairs said, '[O]n the basis of consensus and non-interference in each other's internal affairs ... we recognise that the latest changes in Myanmar are Myanmar's internal affairs and external parties should not interfere' (Vietnamese Ministry of Foreign Affairs 2000). The Thai Ministry of Foreign Affairs meanwhile issued a statement which denied that it had called for the convening of the troika, but pointed out that it would not 'oppose any initiative that would activate' it (Thai Ministry of Foreign Affairs 2000). In the event, at least three things militated against the involvement of the troika in mediating between the Yangon government and the political opposition. First, Myanmar reacted very negatively to the idea. Second, support within the grouping for the invocation of the troika was very limited. Third, an initiative to influence the internal situation in Myanmar was already underway, headed by UN Special Envoy Razali Ismail, who secretly visited Myanmar in late June/early July and again in October to bring about a dialogue between the SPDC and the NLD including Aung San Suu Kyi. Significantly, not only was the troika not convened to address the domestic political quagmire in Myanmar, but it was not called on in the face of the mounting confrontation between Thailand and Myanmar in the first few months of 2001.

The Thailand–Myanmar spat

Thai–Myanmar relations have for several years experienced increasing strife. Among the many issues straining bilateral relations are the failure to demarcate the joint border, the fighting between the Burmese army and various ethnic insurgent groups, the flow of drugs from Myanmar into Thailand, and the suspension of fishery rights in Myanmar waters. Although several of these problems existed prior to the accession to power of the second Chuan government, it is under the latter that bilateral ties have encountered their most serious downturn. One reason for this is that the Chuan administration sought to replace the controversial policy of 'constructive engagement' by a more ideological and less business-oriented approach *vis-à-vis* Yangon, in the form of 'flexible engagement'. Difficult relations were then further exacerbated in the aftermath of the 1999 occupation of the Myanmar embassy in Bangkok.[20] Notably, Prime Minister Chuan did not once visit Myanmar during his term of office.

In February 2001 the longstanding diplomatic feud escalated into an armed confrontation. This confrontation led to the death of approximately 50–100 Burmese soldiers in heavy shelling as the Royal Thai Army pounded and then retook a military outpost which had been occupied by the Burmese two days earlier and which lay inside Thailand. Prior to the occupation Burmese forces had requested access to the outpost to launch a military strike against the Shan State Army. However, the Thai rangers stationed there refused.[21] Significantly, the ensuing military clash at Ban Pang Noon appeared to be linked to a subsequent artillery exchange across the Myanmar–Thai border. This exchange first saw what appeared to be an indiscriminate shelling of the Thai border town of Mae Sai and, in response, the Thai shelling of suspected *tatmadaw* positions around Tachilek. While the military encounters were in a sense only limited, the multiple resort to force marked the first major violations of the most significant norm of ASEAN's diplomatic and security culture – the non-use of force. While in earlier years minor military incidents had occurred between some members, particularly in the South China Sea, the spats along the Thai–Myanmar border were the first to result in a significant number of fatalities in a direct combat situation among two ASEAN member states. As such, those responsible for ordering the use of force violated the sanctity of ASEAN's core norm.

Both sides subsequently took steps to calm military tempers and limit the political fallout of the border clashes. In early April a regional border meeting was convened in Kengtung (Myanmar), at which Thailand's representative, the commander of the Third Army, Lieutenant-General Wattanachai, agreed with his Myanmar counterpart, Major-General Thein Sein, to pursue plans for a troop withdrawal and the demilitarisation of some of the disputed territory. Significantly, Wattanachai Chaimuenwong also elicited a commitment of sorts from Thein Sein to eradicate drug-production bases if the Thai side provided Yangon with the requisite intelligence data. It is too early to tell whether Myanmar will honour this commitment. Within weeks Myanmar officials and army leaders again refused to acknowledge the involvement of the United Wa State Army (UWSA) in the production and trade of drugs, let alone attribute blame to them for this.

Indeed, for some time SPDC representatives have argued that it is the Shan State Army that is producing and peddling drugs and that Bangkok is assisting its cause, not least by allowing it to use sanctuaries beyond the reach of Burmese troops. Yangon has, in turn, claimed that the Thai army has fabricated evidence to support its claims against UWSA, and accused Bangkok of making Myanmar a scapegoat for Thailand's drug woes. Yangon has similarly suggested that Thailand is complicit in or supportive of raids by ethnic Karen rebels based on the common border. The Thai government has strenuously denied these claims. However, it is generally accepted that historically Thailand's foreign and security policy has at times involved passive, if not active, support for insurgents. In early May 2001 the ruling regime in Yangon claimed that Thailand had launched air strikes inside Myanmar, whereas the Thais explained that one of its F-16 pilots had released a sonic boom (Associated Press 2001).

Given the direct military clash between government forces, the question is why the ASEAN troika was not convened to deal with this conflict. There would appear to be several points. First, several factors impede a rapid settlement of the border conflict. These include the ceasefire agreements between Yangon and ethnic insurgents, the involvement of minority groups in the production and trafficking of drugs, the apparent reliance of the SPDC on drug money to promote the development of at least certain parts of Myanmar, the country's political stasis, and internal power struggles. Second, as regards the Thai side, the assertive stance adopted by the Third Army under Lieutenant-General Wattanachai towards incursions into Thailand and the cross-border trafficking of drugs has proved popular with both large parts of the armed forces and the media.[22] However, it has put him at odds with former Prime Minister Chavalit Yongchaiyuth who became Defence Minister in the Thaksin administration in February 2001. The latter has been associated with a brand of business and personal diplomacy that in the past helped to satisfy particular Thai and Burmese interests, but during the premiership of Chuan Leekpai it was viewed as having been discredited and not necessarily being in Thailand's national interests given Bangkok's embrace of a democratic identity. Third, as the Singaporean analyst Lee Kim Chew (2001) has noted, '[t]heirs is a longstanding spat which ASEAN can do little to help. Nor do they welcome third-party intervention.' Fourth, the border conflict in its various dimensions is not a major news item and even the longstanding plight of refugees encamped along the Myanmar-Thai border has equally attracted only limited attention in most international media. There has thus been less of a need for ASEAN to be seen to act. Finally, following the ouster of the Chuan administration in the January 2001 elections, Thailand's new government has repeatedly signalled its preparedness to search for a diplomatic solution to the most divisive issues.

In the event, in June 2001 Premier Thaksin Shinawatra removed some of the heat underlying bilateral relations by conducting a domestically controversial official visit to Myanmar. The two sides signed a joint communiqué, in which they affirmed, among other things, that they would strengthen economic, technical and commercial co-operation, and agreed to normalise the border-crossing regime. They also signed a memorandum of understanding on co-operation in narcotic drugs, psychotropic substances and precursor chemicals control, and resolved to engage in quadrilateral co-operation involving Laos and China. Whether or not the visit and the pledges given will suffice to bring about a constructive bilateral relationship remains to be seen. Thaksin's visit was controversial, not least because previous ministerial intervention had proved unsuccessful. Indeed, in May 2001 Thai nationalism had been fanned by the shelling of a royal agricultural project and the publication of articles in the *New Light of Myanmar* (the mouthpiece of the SPDC) on relations between Thailand's rulers and colonial powers, which were widely deemed to be offensive to the monarchy. As Lieutenant-General Wattanachai had reportedly put it, 'If they want to fight, then let's fight at the border. Don't bring our monarchy into the conflict' (quoted in Kasitipradit and Nanuam 2001).

Conclusion

This chapter has examined ASEAN's attempts to enhance its international image and regain its role as a serious regional actor in the international politics of East Asia in the wake of the Hanoi Summit. It was argued that on the face of things the initiation of the ASEAN surveillance process and the ASEAN 'Retreat' suggested an emerging consensus among member states that international recognition depends on leaving behind certain aspects of the 'ASEAN way'. This was further illustrated by the relatively robust role played by some member states in East Timor and members' agreement on the troika concept. Thailand foreign policy leaders, in particular, have been keen to impress by exerting considerable diplomatic efforts to help change ASEAN leaders' interpretations and practices so that these become more consistent with those held by leaderships of the major Western powers and members of international civil society. However, as this chapter has demonstrated, any argument that ASEAN's initiatives amount to the demise of the 'ASEAN way' in the short term must be treated with caution. It is clear that, despite the participation of some ASEAN members in INTERFET and UNTAET, collective understandings with respect to ASEAN's diplomatic and security culture have not yet significantly shifted (also see Cotton 2001). Great significance continues to be attributed to the norms of non-interference, consensus and sovereign equality. This has complicated discussions on the finalisation of the troika concept and continues to stymie the possibilities of its application. Thus, though there may be leeway for advocates of the further development of ASEAN's diplomatic and security culture, those seeking to deny greater flexibility in its practice have equal leeway, if not more. Indeed, ASEAN leaders have continued to disagree about when it would be legitimate to allow the chair to initiate the troika to pursue preventive diplomacy, even in circumstances that clearly threaten regional peace and stability. This testifies to the strength of suspicion of some members and the concomitant need to have in place a normative framework that can mediate insecurity and estrangement.

The potential for ASEAN's diplomatic and security culture to unravel altogether is, no doubt, worrying both for those ASEAN leaders who have defended traditional or more conservative positions on the 'ASEAN way' and those who have advocated its further development. The potential for the demise of ASEAN's diplomatic and security culture has been illustrated by the recent military skirmishes on the Thai–Myanmar border and the parallel war of words.

The concluding chapter will seek to establish the short- to medium-term prospects for ASEAN's diplomatic and security culture.

Conclusion
On the prospects for ASEAN's diplomatic and security culture

This book has argued that ASEAN's diplomatic and security culture has been meant to mediate estrangement and insecurity in Southeast Asia. It has identified six norms as making up the core of the 'ASEAN way': sovereign equality; non-recourse to the use of force; non-interference and non-intervention; non-invocation of ASEAN to address unresolved bilateral conflict between members; quiet diplomacy; and mutual respect and tolerance. The book has found that, although a number of challenges have been levelled at the 'ASEAN way' by different members of the Association, centrepieces of this normative terrain, which took form only in the early 1970s, have throughout remained meaningful to the majority of leaderships in member states. This is not to say that even those leaderships that have found the edifice of ASEAN's diplomatic and security culture useful in part or in full to ward off challenges to their identity, legitimacy or security have not at times violated collective understandings of the constituent norms. Indeed, not a single core norm associated with the 'ASEAN way' has not been tested, challenged or violated. Notably, in view of developments in Thai–Myanmar relations in the first half of 2001, this assessment extends to the norm of the non-use of force in settling bilateral conflict.

The question to be explored in this concluding chapter focuses on the short- to medium-term prospects for ASEAN's diplomatic and security culture against the foil of possible scenarios for the medium to longer term. Arguably, there are three broad scenarios for the first decade of the twenty-first century. The first scenario posits the continued significance of the 'ASEAN way' but allows for the development of increasingly flexible interpretations of the basic norms of international society guiding ASEAN interactions, and the emergence over time of new norms that enjoy legitimacy among all Southeast Asian incumbent regimes. This scenario sees Southeast Asian leaderships remaining to some extent estranged from one another or suspicious of one another, but expects them nevertheless to continue engaging each other in processes of norm-elaboration and norm-rationalisation. The latter, so the scenario posits, is likely to occur through intramural discussion about the validity of the constituent elements of ASEAN's diplomatic and security culture, driven not least by civil society and extra-regional pressures and criticisms of existing interpretations and understandings of the 'ASEAN way'. Over time one would thus expect, for instance, that ASEAN members would attach less and less significance to the norm of non-interference, or to see the ASEAN troika or the ASEAN High Council in operation. This scenario plays on the notion of the development of the 'ASEAN way'.

The second scenario holds that ASEAN's diplomatic and security culture does not noticeably evolve because ASEAN leaders are reluctant to endorse shifts in collective understandings that to them might amount to a Pandora's box being opened and might ultimately result in the political demise of the more authoritarian regimes. In this scenario member states continue to insist that the norms of sovereignty, non-interference and consensus, in particular, are inserted into the various documents still being drafted on preventive diplomacy or dispute settlement. Moreover, this scenario posits that even if it is possible to spell out the meaning and principles of concepts like preventive diplomacy, its application in practice will run into difficulties as members stress due regard for the norms of consensus, consent and non-interference. Equally, this scenario assumes that, while on paper members agree to the establishment of the ASEAN troika or the ASEAN High Council, these instruments will not and cannot be invoked in practice.

The third scenario posits the demise of the 'ASEAN way'. This scenario assumes that there is likely to be a longer absence of consensus about the legitimacy of new collective understandings, not least in relation to the norms of sovereignty and non-interference. In this scenario ASEAN leaders may still point to the significance of respecting the validity of the legal-political norms underlying the 'ASEAN way' for regional security, but they are less and less constrained by these norms in intramural relations. Having been breached consistently, bilateral and multilateral ties within ASEAN would be expected to be damaged, leading to a further loss of standing of the Association, if not causing it to totter on the brink of collapse.

Although it is radical, this last scenario cannot be dismissed. While only a scenario, it is not completely divorced from contemporary events. ASEAN has for some years experienced a crisis of identity. This crisis of identity, reinforced by enlargement, was considerably compounded by the onset of economic adversity in 1997. This affected member states in different ways and led them to seek divergent paths to recovery. The different trajectories taken by Singapore, Malaysia and Indonesia are very instructive in this regard. Indeed, in 2001, three years after the height of the Asian crisis, ASEAN countries stood divided on the level of development achieved, the ideas and concepts underpinning the organisation and management of their political economy and political system, and their commitment to democracy, human rights and political change. Not surprisingly, therefore, challenges to all elements of ASEAN's diplomatic and security culture from within the Association have multiplied between 1997 and 2001. Efforts to push for constructive intervention or flexible engagement were noteworthy in this regard, as was the singular challenge to the norm of respect, associated, for instance, with the timing of Hun Sen's 1997 coup. As regards the norm of the non-use of force, ASEAN foreign ministers did follow in decrying ASEAN's de facto acceptance of the resort to force to evict an existing government in Cambodia, principally on the grounds of the non-interference principle. But they looked away in 2001 as the border dispute between Yangon and Bangkok unfolded.

Having outlined the possible future trajectories of ASEAN's diplomatic and security culture, this chapter now turns to assessing its probable short- to medium-term prospects. This assessment builds in significant measure on an understanding of the past, including the more recent past. Importantly, though, it does not seek simply to extrapolate the prospects for the future from the findings of the past. Rather, an attempt is made to understand the material and ideational structure within which regional leaders currently strive to overturn or defend certain interpretations of norms linked to the 'ASEAN way'.

Thus, in its first section, the Conclusion is concerned with briefly restating the reasons why some ASEAN leaders have attempted to promote new interpretations of core aspects of ASEAN's diplomatic and security culture. That section will also briefly reiterate the key reasons why public challenges to the 'ASEAN way', whether direct or indirect, have largely been repudiated by other member states. The second section examines the reasons why ASEAN decision-makers continue to ascribe meaning to the norms of the 'ASEAN way'. The third explores the domestic context in which ASEAN decision-makers operate and assesses to what extent the considerations about regime security and survival reinforce the view that the norms of the 'ASEAN way' should still be adhered to. The fourth section provides a brief overview of key parts of the normative and ideational structures currently pervasive in international society, as well as of specific actors from the emerging regional civil society that might have an impact on the future development of ASEAN's diplomatic and security culture. Bearing in mind both the structural constraints in which ASEAN decision-makers operate and their likely reasoning processes, the final section attempts to sketch very tentatively the possible development of ASEAN's diplomatic and security culture in the short and medium term.

The development of ASEAN's diplomatic and security culture

The 'ASEAN way' evolved against the backdrop of a struggle for independence, sovereign equality and regional autonomy in international society, as well as a struggle for state and regime security. Its emergence required, above all, acts of reconciliation between Jakarta and Kuala Lumpur, between Singapore and Jakarta, and between Kuala Lumpur and Singapore. Also, it depended on the willingness of the Philippines and Malaysia to agree to a *modus vivendi* in relation to Sabah. Only once these elementary steps in mutual recognition had been taken did the ASEAN-5 leaders begin to respect more or less scrupulously the political-legal norms and socio-psychological norms that I summarised as the 'ASEAN way' in the Introduction. Narrow interpretations of its norms were endorsed by ASEAN decision-makers because of common problems with local insurgency movements and the conviction of leaderships that, if bilateral relations and the wider region were to advance economically and politically, practices challenging the process of reconciliation were undesirable. All ASEAN member states have been prickly about challenges to their sovereignty, but Singapore – in view of its historical emergence and innate vulnerability – has been particularly sensitive in this regard.

The extent of the development of the 'ASEAN way'

The development of ASEAN's diplomatic and security culture has been the result of norm-rationalisation processes through diplomatic interaction and intra-leadership debates. In significant measure, however, the development of the 'ASEAN way' has also been the consequence of direct or indirect challenges to the validity of the dominant interpretations of supposedly shared norms or to the legitimacy of the way in which they were practised. That said, until the early 1990s only a few intramural challenges emerged and very few of these were successful. One example of this was Indonesia's pursuit of cocktail diplomacy. Chapter 4 also argued that ASEAN's endorsement of the composition of the Supreme National Council represented the necessary sacrifice of a pristine interpretation of the norms of non-intervention and the non-use of force in favour of the political advantages accruing from a settlement of the conflict. However, when the Cambodian conflict ended and UNTAC assumed its functions, ASEAN leaderships continued to endorse rather narrow interpretations of core elements of the 'ASEAN way', even while allowing for some ambiguity in their practice. This ambiguity was reinforced not least by the Association resorting to constructive engagement *vis-à-vis* Myanmar, even though by most measures this was a feeble attempt to influence domestic political events in a country that only signed up to the TAC in 1995 and which joined the Association two years later.

Although several member states have rejected challenges to the 'ASEAN way', this has not prevented the emergence of new collective understandings of some of its core norms. This is illustrated by the fact that the proposal for flexible engagement was initially spurned, before being implemented in the form of the 'Retreat' and subsequently in part rehashed in the elaboration of the ASEAN troika concept. More ambitious undertakings, such as those planned on the basis of this concept and the passing of rules for the operationalisation of the ASEAN High Council, have thus far defied practical implementation, since the formal requirements of consultation and consensus have complicated involvement in the internal affairs of member states by other member states in the name of the Association.

Reasons for intramural challenges to the 'ASEAN way'

The book has highlighted five key motivations for challenges to ASEAN's diplomatic and security culture. First, challenges emerged because during the Cold War Indonesia's foreign and security policy elite found unpalatable the political and potential security implications of stringently insisting on applying basic international norms, recognised as norms of the 'ASEAN way', to the wider international politics of Southeast Asia. Challenges have arisen, second, in reactions to extramural pressure on ASEAN to move beyond narrow understandings of the 'ASEAN way', especially in view of the anticipated consequences of failing to do so. Challenges have emanated, third, from the identity-formation processes of governments and the wider society they represent. The growth of civil society in their countries and the concomitant espousal of a democratic identity, for instance, have led some governments to reject norms of interstate and interpersonal conduct at leadership level that they increasingly see as protecting authoritarian regimes from legitimate criticism. Fourth, in some cases challenges to the 'ASEAN way' have also emerged because some leaders have sought to enhance their personal popularity and political legitimacy or felt it necessary to respond to perceived provocations by their ASEAN counterparts. It was said of Philippine President Estrada, for example, that he 'introduced a new courage to regional affairs' (Rajaretnam 2000: 41). Finally, challenges have also arisen in situations where leaderships have felt that their economic or political interests would be compromised or even seriously prejudiced by unswervingly abiding by the norms of ASEAN's diplomatic and security culture.

Having outlined the key reasons that led to the 'ASEAN way' being challenged from with the Association, it is equally useful to restate briefly why ASEAN members have continued to reject the suggestion that collectively moving beyond the more narrow understandings of ASEAN's core norms is necessary or inevitable.

Reasons for continued endorsement of the 'ASEAN way'

At least four arguments can be distinguished as to why the majority of ASEAN governments have rejected proposals whose implementation would ascribe legitimacy to more flexible and wide-ranging modes of intramural conduct, including preventive diplomacy and dispute settlement. These will now be discussed in turn.

The 'ASEAN way': a qualified success

The most basic argument in this regard is that many foreign policy decision-makers within ASEAN view the more or less scrupulous adherence to the 'ASEAN way' as a success story. There are three separate points here. First, the 'ASEAN way' has been a success because, from the perspective of ASEAN leaders, this shared diplomatic and security culture has helped them and their colleagues to maintain regional, interstate and regime security. As Acharya argued, 'ASEAN's norms have had important regulatory impact' (Acharya 2001: 202). Second, the 'ASEAN way' has provided parameters within which member states have been able to pursue their own identity-formation processes, including the elaboration of different socio-economic and political systems. Finally, ASEAN's diplomatic and security culture has generally served to avoid or mediate intramural alienation that might spring from violations of identity claims.

Significantly, for ASEAN leaders and officials the fact that ASEAN did not specify the criteria for an institutionalised role in preventive diplomacy as conflict mediation between member states until 2000 does not detract from the argument that the 'ASEAN way' has been a success. The same applies to members' longstanding reluctance to identify relevant criteria for the possible invocation of the ASEAN High Council, which has meant that most intramural bilateral conflicts have been shelved. As has been noted in this book, ASEAN states have in some instances relied on ad-hoc third-party mediation by other member countries to deal with disputes involving two other ASEAN member states. In some cases it has clearly been the view of decision-makers that sub-regional order would be none the worse if they delegated to external bodies the settlement of sensitive conflicts and emotive issues which might otherwise rekindle interstate or intramural tension.[1] In other instances third-party mediation has also occurred in relation to domestic disputes within ASEAN countries. As illustrated with respect to the situation in Mindanao, this mediation has tended to be informal, but nonetheless effective.

At the same time, it must be acknowledged that more or less strict compliance with traditional notions of the 'ASEAN way' has also had the potential to exacerbate challenges or threats to regional security. For instance, quiet diplomacy to address the smog-haze crisis appears to have delayed President Suharto's adoption of appropriate countermeasures, leading to a major regional environmental catastrophe. Equally, regional security was clearly impaired when secessionism forcefully reared its head in Aceh, in north Sumatra, in 1999, provoking counterinsurgency measures that in turn generated around 140,000 internally displaced people. Yet the problem was not addressed at the ASEAN level at the time. Indeed, while they were very concerned, not least because Aceh is geographically situated at the entry into the Malacca Strait, Singapore and Malaysia did not publicly criticise Jakarta for adopting a heavy-handed strategy *vis-à-vis* Aceh that was likely to make a political solution more difficult. Nor did ASEAN or individual member states publicly speak out when, following President Habibie's decision to have the status of the territory addressed through the ballot box, Jakarta began a campaign of violence to deter the East Timorese from siding against the pro-integrationist forces. As was discussed in Chapter 8, Australia was eventually tasked with leading a UN-mandated international force into East Timor. That said, these examples may demonstrate, not so much the irrelevance or ineffectiveness of the 'ASEAN way' in the eyes of ASEAN foreign policy elites, as the difficulty of applying its norms more flexibly to the Association's largest member, as has been done in relation to other ASEAN states. In sum, then, one should treat with caution both unabashedly positive assessments of ASEAN's diplomatic and security culture and conclusions about its alleged ineffectiveness or irrelevance. Despite the negative experiences, most ASEAN leaderships still appear to judge the 'ASEAN way' as an overall success.

The 'ASEAN way' and the major powers in East Asia

A second reason why ASEAN countries by and large still endorse the validity of ASEAN's diplomatic and security culture is linked to the long-standing attempt by the Association's members to engage the major powers in norm building. In particular, ASEAN has tried to win a formal commitment by the regional major powers to the norms of the non-use of force, sovereign equality and non-intervention/non-interference. In the 1970s ASEAN sought to do this by unilaterally issuing the ZOPFAN Declaration. In the 1990s ASEAN continuously promoted recognition and acceptance of the purposes and principles of the TAC for the peaceful settlement of disputes, as outlined in the Concept Paper for the ARF. If ASEAN were no longer to insist on the salience of the norms of the 'ASEAN way', so the likely train of thought, its members would find it difficult to press the regional major powers explicitly to recognise their validity in relation to the Association. Indeed, how important an objective a formal endorsement of the norms of the TAC is to ASEAN is evidenced by the efforts undertaken to make dialogue partners accede to the Second Protocol to the TAC. ASEAN has argued that accession to the TAC by the major powers would be an expression of their commitment to the Treaty's purposes and principles in the promotion of peace and stability in East Asia. The importance attributed by ASEAN member states to the legal-political norms of the 'ASEAN way' is further illustrated by attempts of the ASEAN Institutes of Strategic and International Studies (ISIS) – particularly ISIS Malaysia – and Russia to formulate a Pacific Concord at the ARF Track II level. The Pacific Concord is meant to be an all-encompassing normative framework designed to inform interstate conduct among countries in the Pacific in as obliging a manner as possible.[2] Significantly, as the book has argued throughout, ASEAN governments have not seen any contradiction between their promotion of the acceptance of basic norms of international society, particularly non-interference, and the individual ASEAN members' defence and security ties with external powers.

The 'ASEAN way' and the ARF

In part, ASEAN's continued commitment to its diplomatic and security culture must also be understood in the context of the further development of security co-operation in the ARF and the Association's role as its driving force. As previous chapters showed, by arrogating to itself the leading role in the ARF, ASEAN has sought to extend norms and related practices of the 'ASEAN way' to the ARF process because '[I]n the ASEAN context, there is some merit to the ASEAN approach' (ARF 1995). These efforts have been fairly successful, at both the declaratory and the practical level of ARF activity. First, ARF members noted that 'the first ARF meeting in Bangkok agreed to "endorse the purposes and principles of ASEAN Treaty of Amity and Cooperation in Southeast Asia as a code of conduct governing relations between states and a unique diplomatic instrument for regional confidence-building, preventive diplomacy, and political and security cooperation" (ARF 1995)'. Second, ARF members accepted the principle of sovereign equality as expressed in the practice of consensual decision-making. Third, the ARF membership agreed on an evolutionary approach to security co-operation that, first of all, emphasised ASEAN's interpersonal and non-confrontational method of confidence building. Fourth, the principle of quiet diplomacy has been made a feature of the ARF process, and this has naturally also applied to the bilateral meetings organised around the ministerial talks. Fifth, the norm of respect and tolerance has been largely observed, as illustrated by advance consultation among ARF senior officials and exchanges among participants that are usually described as candid but which in general appear not to have been unacceptably strident in tone. And, at least for the moment, the ARF is not meant to engage in conflict resolution.

However, Western non-ASEAN members of the ARF, in particular, have sought to proceed with the initiation of practical preventive diplomacy measures that potentially accord great importance to an expanded ARF chair and challenge norms of the 'ASEAN way'. China has rejected such a development and welcomed the continued relevance of ASEAN's diplomatic and security culture to the ARF. If they are to remain the ARF's driving force, core ASEAN's states know they need to be less shy in promoting more ambitious methods of preventive diplomacy in the ARF, (Chongkittavorn 1999b; Tay and Obood Talib 1997). However, in view of Beijing's concerns this does not mean an abandonment of the 'ASEAN way'. Indeed, to uphold ASEAN's own position in the ARF and to ensure that the Forum remains central to security co-operation in the wider East Asia ASEAN decision-makers accept that it is necessary to steer a middle path between defending 'the ASEAN' way and embracing new understandings of some of its norms.

The continued role of the 'ASEAN way' in mediating estrangement

The fourth reason for ASEAN's adherence to the 'ASEAN way' is linked to its function of mediating and preventing estrangement among state leaders and officials. The policy-makers of the founding states in particular have developed an understanding about the possible depth of resentment and ensuing suspicion that might arise as a consequence of unwarranted interference, not least in the form of condescending remarks expressed in public. As the political history of ASEAN suggests, critical comments, ill-considered remarks or pejorative references to other leaders, especially if made in public, have the potential to be perceived as personal slights, sometimes with quite negative long-term effects for bilateral ties. The underlying reason for this is often a sense of vulnerability, which may arise either from the geographical or economic strictures within which the leadership has to operate or even from self-perceived policy inadequacies relating to the economy, social and political stability, or value and governance systems. Significantly, to the extent that some leaders display public insensitivity or patronising behaviour, ASEAN's political history has also demonstrated the potential for various political forces to seize upon this in nationalist outrage. As such, ill-considered remarks can quickly take on the form of challenges to the political legitimacy of those at whom the remark was directly or indirectly addressed, making it all the more necessary to repulse it as unwarranted 'interference'.

By adhering to the norms of non-interference, restraint, respect and quiet diplomacy, ASEAN leaders have sought to give full justice to the possibilities that grievances or the political abuse of grievances can impair bilateral relations. ASEAN leaders realise that because bilateral relations are often delicate, trading rhetorical blows and allowing themselves to be seen to interfere in other member states' domestic politics is probably one of the best recipes to ruin the prospects for greater regional co-operation. As such, the motivation to abide by ASEAN's diplomatic and security culture builds on considerations more or less identical to those shared by the first generation of ASEAN leaders. For ASEAN governments, the 'ASEAN way' is not significant only in terms of its potential to *prevent* disputes, however. It is equally significant as a rallying point once its norms have been breached, to contain the conflict and to allow for a relatively speedy normalisation of ties. Just how relevant the norms of the 'ASEAN way' remain even to core sets of bilateral relations within the Association has been made evident by recent developments in Singapore–Malaysia and Singapore–Indonesia relations. In these two cases, the perceived disrespect for a country as a fully sovereign actor, and remarks deemed condescending and perceived as personal slights brought about or reinforced major diplomatic downturns (Leifer 2000; da Cunha 1999).

Having discussed four general reasons why ASEAN's diplomatic and security culture still matters to ASEAN decision's makers, in the next section we will examine to what extent individual ASEAN decision-makers still have other reasons to find ASEAN's diplomatic and security culture meaningful.

Decision-makers, regime security and the salience of the 'ASEAN way'

The new members

Reluctance to embrace partial new interpretations of existing norms or new norms has remained particularly pronounced among the State Peace and Development Council (SPDC, formerly SLORC) in Myanmar, the Vietnamese Communist Party (VCP), the Lao People's Revolutionary Party (LPRP) and Hun Sen's Cambodian People's Party.

Myanmar

Since the early 1990s the SPDC has been a target for global criticism and sanctions by Western countries because of its refusal to surrender political power to the opposition National League for Democracy (NLD). The ruling military regime in Yangon has also had to live with reional criticism, mostly conveyed by ASEAN members on the country's political developments, under the label of 'constructive engagement'. It is therefore not surprising that the SPDC has adamantly stood up for a more conservative or traditional view of what constraints the norms of sovereignty, non-interference and consensus should impose within ASEAN. Given the ongoing political struggle between the SPDC and the NLD,[3] the armed confrontation with several ethnic groups and the seemingly ambiguous role played by the military regime in the battle against drugs, it is unwarranted to expect Yangon not to insist that its counterparts adhere to the 'ASEAN way'. By invoking these norms Yangon has certainly played its part in stymieing the formation of rules on the functioning of the troika.

Vietnam

Strong opposition to moving beyond narrow collective understandings of ASEAN's diplomatic and security culture has also been voiced in Hanoi. As Vietnam's foreign minister, Nguyen Dy Nien, put it at the Thirty-third ASEAN Ministerial Meeting, '[t]he Association's time-tested fundamental principles and practices, first and foremost the principle of consensus and that of non-interference into each other's internal affairs, have bound us together and been a source of strength' (Nguyen Dy Nien 2000). As for the future, he added that '[w]e have every reason to firmly believe that outstanding or newly-emerging issues need to and will be effectively resolved in the "ASEAN way"' (Nguyen Dy Nien 2000). To understand Hanoi's stance, the following points should be noted. First, VCP leaders are concerned about the party's legitimacy at home, despite some success with economic reforms. Consequently, they are unwilling to become the target of unsolicited advice on how best to remould the country's political economy or to exercise its continued monopoly of political power. Second, VCP leaders are concerned that those unhappy with the regime can attract political and financial support from neighbouring countries and beyond. Such apprehension did not arise when resentful peasants vented their anger at the corruption and nepotism of local cadres in Thai Binh in 1997. However, it has arisen in the context of unrest in the provincial capitals of Pleiku and Buon Me Thuot, in the provinces of Gia Lai and Dac Lac, respectively, which has been linked to the struggle of the resurgent *Forces Unifiées pour la Libération des Races Opprimées* (FULRO) (Weggel 2001). Third, to the extent that Hanoi demands that other ASEAN members observe the 'ASEAN way' in intramural relations, this is seen as indirectly strengthening Vietnam's diplomatic hand in rejecting perceived interference by the United States to bring about peaceful evolution.

Lao PDR

The Lao leadership, too, is firm about the need to continue with the norms of ASEAN's diplomatic and security culture as a framework for bilateral and multilateral co-operation within ASEAN. This is not connected to major challenges to regime legitimacy in Laos itself. First, the question of regime legitimacy does not arise for a large part of the essentially apolitical population, and those for whom it might arise often tend to benefit from the methods of the ruling regime. Second, existing challenges to regime continuity have so far proved manageable for the LPRP. Indeed, continued military resistance against Vientiane has erupted repeatedly mostly in outlying parts of Laos, so that the wider impact has been limited. Yet for the LPRP there are at least five reasons for supporting in particular the norm of non-interference as conventionally interpreted. First, the regime is interested in further developing its own reform agenda so that it can reap the maximum benefit from the transformation of Laos' political economy. Second, the LPRP has no plans to relinquish its political monopoly position. Third, the leadership lacks the confidence that Lao citizens will have full confidence in the party as the process of economic reforms unfolds; it is mindful that domestic grievances might be exploited by overseas Lao groups interested in destabilising the regime. Fourth, the close co-ordination of foreign policy with Vietnam implies that as long as Vietnam promotes non-interference and consensual decision-making Laos will support Hanoi. Fifth, Lao leaders, cognisant of their country's geographical location, size and limited population and its shared history with Thailand, are particularly suspicious of Bangkok's ambitions to enhance its economic, cultural and political influence in Indochina. In sum, there is little prospect of Vientiane supporting proposals for revamping the 'ASEAN way' for some time to come.

Cambodia

There can be little doubt that, at least in the medium term, Phnom Penh will also continue to insist on the validity of the established understandings of the core norms of ASEAN's diplomatic and security culture. Many of the reasons why Cambodia also remains wedded to the 'ASEAN way' are similar to those of leaders in other Indochinese states. First, there can be little doubt that Hun Sen remains a deeply suspicious ruler with a fine understanding of his vulnerabilities and those of Cambodia at large, which might be exploited to his detriment. Second, Cambodian leaders, their good working relations with Hanoi and Bangkok notwithstanding, do not fully trust either. As regards Thailand, for example, there have been suspicions that elements of the Royal Thai Army have given refuge to anti-government Cambodian freedom fighters, some of which have US citizenship. And finally, as one Cambodian minister put it, 'No nation can accept any measure that curtails its sovereignty, even the most democratic and liberal country in the world. The right to fashion one's own destiny is sacrosanct and will always be guarded jealously' (Chhon 2000: 23).

The earlier members

It is a misconception to suggest that the 'ASEAN way' is first and foremost hostage to the concerns of the leaderships of the new members. The truth of the matter is that even among the old members several have been reluctant to endorse major conceptual or practical revisions of the 'ASEAN way'. For instance, the stance adopted by Malaysia or Brunei Darussalam in 1998 was conspicuous in its limited enthusiasm to defend, let alone promote, the agenda of those urging a rethink of the 'ASEAN way' in the form of 'flexible engagement' or 'enhanced interaction'. As the end of the millennium approached, their respective level of enthusiasm had not in most cases markedly increased.

Singapore

Singapore's leaders have long associated a major potential security risk with the consequences of a breakdown of the normative framework governing sub-regional order in Southeast Asia. Consequently it has – sometimes stridently – asserted its sovereignty, especially vis-à-vis Malaysia and Indonesia. Still, Singapore leaders have never thought they could rely only on the binding force of norms for its national security, which is why the city-state has sought to engage extra-regional powers in the Southeast Asian region and is prepared to spend a relatively high proportion of its budget on defence.[4] Significantly, while Singaporean officials continue to regard international norms as the first line of defence against possible external threats that might rekindle or exacerbate local ethnic and class antagonisms (Ganesan 1998: 583–4), they have recognised that ASEAN's diplomatic and security culture may need to adapt to changing realities. That Singapore was able to propose and establish the foreign ministers' 'Retreat' to mediate skilfully between the contending positions of fellow members on the 'ASEAN way' testifies to the astuteness of its diplomatic corps. Singapore also believes that ASEAN will have to embrace preventive diplomacy. In this regard, the city-state has clearly accepted that the principle of non-intervention does not *per se* override humanitarian considerations, but equally clearly its leaders do not subscribe to a doctrine of interventionism (Jayakumar 1999c).

Malaysia

Like policy-makers in Singapore, UMNO party leaders have also been reluctant to abandon ASEAN 'basics'. To the extent that concepts such as sovereignty and non-interference have enjoyed meaning in this context, the advocacy of their continued validity serves to sustain Malaysia's security and to secure respect for Kuala Lumpur in international affairs. As K.S. Nathan has argued, 'Malaysia's conception of security is a corporate aggregate of its own historical experience, its multiethnicity, its ethnonational vision, and its desire to seek recognition for its changed status from "object" to "subject" of international relations' (Nathan 1998: 548).[5] As had already been made manifestly clear by their denunciation of the 1998 pre-APEC dinner speech by then US Vice-President Al Gore, UMNO is prone to react strongly if outsiders are seen to provide support to their domestic political opponents. In addition, Kuala Lumpur has not been keen on discussions about the continued pursuit of core objectives of the National Economic Policy (NEP), which discriminates in favour of indigenous Malays in terms of achieving power and wealth and is regarded a key pillar of the regime security of UMNO. That said, the government's willingness to attract international investment on a scale not seen since the NEP reversed the trend of foreign ownership established under colonial rule (Gomez and Jomo 1997; ch. 2) indicates that Malaysia accepts in practice the erosion of economic autonomy. Moreover, Malaysia's political elites are not averse to enhancing intra-ASEAN co-operation to deal with challenges to the 'ASEAN way', even in ways that might legitimise new collective interpretations of ASEAN's core norms. However, for that to happen Kuala Lumpur would like the discourse of those challenging the 'ASEAN way' to be toned down. As Mohamad Jawhar explained, 'if you keep talking about interference and intervention, it will be very difficult. We should not use words which can be divisive. Let's just talk about cooperation' (quoted in *Asiaweek*, 1 September 2000).

Indonesia

After the political demise of President Suharto in May 1998 it was widely expected that Indonesia would embrace the democratic moment within ASEAN as well as the charge against the Association's longstanding collective interpretations of the 'ASEAN way'. Such expectations were reinforced by Jakarta's dependence on international financial institutions and Western capital in the wake of the outbreak of the Asian crisis. In the event, Dr Habibie and his government stayed the course on ASEAN's diplomatic and security culture. His successor to the presidency, Abdurrahman Wahid, also reaffirmed on various occasions the validity of these norms and of other core elements of the 'ASEAN way' for the Association's intramural relations. Significantly, one such instance was at the first ever session of the ASEAN People's Assembly (APA; see below, p. 231) in November 2000, when he vowed not to interfere in the Anwar Ibrahim affair even though he emphasised that he was personally close to him. One can identify at least four reasons for Jakarta's continued commitment to the longstanding interpretation of the 'ASEAN way'. First, following the loss of East Timor and in view of Jakarta's problems with secessionism in Aceh and Irian Jaya, the Wahid government was concerned about the possibility of Indonesia's territorial fragmentation. Second, Wahid represented secular nationalist and moderate Muslim interests that value an independent foreign policy as well as autonomous decision-making processes. As is perhaps indicated by his authoritarian leadership style, Wahid's interest in democratising regional politics in Southeast Asia also proved rather limited. As one analyst put it, 'Abdurrahman seems to show little to no interest in ASEAN internal politics, even in the matter of democratization' (Tesoro 2000: 45). Arguably, President Wahid increasingly also had personal reasons for opposing new collective understandings of the 'ASEAN way'. Put simply, Wahid wanted to benefit from the norm of non-interference seen against the backdrop of the many months of uncertainty about his political survival before he was impeached in a special session of the People's Consultative Assembly (MPR) for alleged corruption and incompetence.

However, even under Megawati Sukarnoputri, the country's new leader following President Wahid's forced political retirement, Indonesia's stance on the continued validity of the 'ASEAN way' has not changed. There are several reasons for this. First, apart from seeking to restore the Indonesian economy to better health, the new government has been bound to focus on domestic reform. On the agenda is an array of issues such as the relationship between parliament and the presidency, the role of the military, the place of religion and minorities in the polity, separatist tendencies in some provinces, and the relationship of the provinces to the centre. All these will take time to deal with. Second, Megawati has herself built up strong nationalist credentials that are likely to make her government resist external interference in the internal affairs of the Republic.

The Philippines

Various Philippine governments have supported moving beyond established understandings of ASEAN's diplomatic and security culture. As early as the 1970s, the Marcos regime proposed that conflicts among ASEAN members be dealt with by the Association. In the 1990s, under President Corazon Aquino, Manila more or less consistently endorsed strong involvement in Myanmar's political affairs. And, towards the end of the decade, President Estrada sought to substitute personal for official diplomacy to legitimise his frank comments on political developments in Malaysia. Recently the secretary of foreign affairs, Domingo Siazon, argued that there remained a 'need to concretize the principles and values that keep ASEAN member countries together' (Siazon 2000), which to Siazon entailed finalising the draft Rules of Procedure of the ASEAN High Council and endowing substance to the ASEAN troika.[6] Manila has also supported the idea of an ASEAN Human Rights Mechanism (see below, p. 230). As previously noted, Manila has been well disposed to resorting to preventive diplomacy involving ASEAN and non-ASEAN third parties to resolve the conflict in Mindanao.[7] Recent moves towards a ceasefire agreement between the government of the new resident, Gloria Macapagal-Arroyo, and the Moro Islamic Liberation Front (MILF) again testify to this.

Thailand

The administration of Chuan Leekpai may well go down in history as having vigorously challenged ASEAN's diplomatic and security culture in the aftermath of the Asian crisis, first with proposals for flexible engagement and an ASEAN troika and, finally, just before leaving office, by temporarily giving free rein to its Third Army in the country's border strife with Myanmar. However, Thai voters did not re-elect the Chuan administration in January 2001 and the incoming administration of Thaksin Shinawatra has not upheld Bangkok's challenge to the 'ASEAN way'. Indeed, on assuming office the foreign minister, Surakiart, immediately opened up a new foreign policy discourse stressing 'forward engagement' as opposed to 'flexible engagement'. While the latter was presented as an approach that had jeopardised relations with Thailand's neighbours, the former sought influence through deepening economic co-operation and greater economic integration (Crispin and Vatikiotis 2001). Significantly, during a visit by Prime Minister Thaksin and several members of his cabinet to Yangon in June 2001 Thailand and Myanmar reaffirmed basic norms of international society while agreeing to accelerate bilateral co-operation, particularly in combating the drug flow to Thailand. This was expressed in the signing of a joint communiqué and a memorandum of understanding on the prevention, repression, rehabilitation, crop substitution and information exchange on the drug trade. There is a possibility that if Myanmar moves towards meeting some of the longstanding Thai demands on issues relating, for instance, to the border and drug trafficking, the Thaksin administration may stick to its initial more conservative line on ASEAN's diplomatic and security culture. This could be the case in particular if the Burmese leadership invited Bangkok to inspect areas within Myanmar in which the Thai government believes drugs to be produced. In view of the uncertainty of these developments it remains to be seen whether Thai foreign-policy-makers will not resume its challenge to the established interpretations of what constitute legitimate practices of the 'ASEAN way'.

This section has examined the national positions on the 'ASEAN way' – bar one – held by individual member governments. Based on the above discussion, it is possible to divide ASEAN leaderships into three broad categories according to how they stand on the issue of the further development of the 'ASEAN way': 'obstructionists', 'cautious reformers' and 'practitioners of change'. Notably, at the beginning of the millennium it is the new entrants' leaderships that are most supportive of ASEAN's diplomatic and security culture as it was practised among the earlier members in the first two decades of the Association. The earlier members, on the whole, seem prepared to accept new understandings on how to practice key norms, yet only within limits. Following the recent accession to power of Thaksin as premier in Thailand, there is a possibility that only one country will, in the short to medium term, openly call for further refinement of the 'ASEAN way' – the Philippines. In other words, the majority of ASEAN member governments either desire the status quo ante or are by and large content with the status quo as regards the understandings and the practices of ASEAN's political and security culture. The next section briefly reviews to what extent ASEAN leaders are nevertheless likely to be subjected to pressure to allow for further processes of norm-rationalisation in the years ahead.

Extramural and civil society pressures on the 'ASEAN way'

ASEAN leaderships operate in regional as well as global material and ideational-discursive contexts. As regards the former, ASEAN countries continue to be dependent on access to external markets, particularly those of the United States and Japan. ASEAN states also require foreign direct investment to promote their economic development and industrialisation. Several ASEAN members – not least Indonesia and the Indochinese states –

are also dependent on international financial institutions to finance public debt and cover budget deficits. This reliance on external players no doubt makes at least some individual ASEAN countries susceptible to political pressure, not least on the 'ASEAN way'. As regards the ideational-discursive context, ASEAN decision-makers stand exposed to emerging shifts in the normative structure of international society, and attendant debates, say, on the legitimacy of humanitarian intervention. As was made clear in Chapter 8, several leaderships, particularly those in Bangkok and Singapore, have responded to global debates by proposing changes to ASEAN's traditional modes of interaction. Given that the relevant debates are set to proceed,[8] they can, for instance, be expected to have a bearing on ASEAN discussions on preventive diplomacy, as well as on other aspects related to its continuing process of self-evaluation and self-renewal. Beyond the general global normative context ASEAN leaderships are also exposed to pressure to rethink the validity of the 'ASEAN way' by Track II institutions, non-governmental organisations and regional civil society.

As a Track II institution, ASEAN–ISIS, a group of ASEAN-based think tanks or institutes of strategic studies, many of whose representatives have good or even excellent ties with senior officials in their respective countries, has, since the early 1990s, proved a relatively good vehicle for influencing ASEAN policy. Researchers of individual members of ASEAN–ISIS have engaged in constructive criticism of official ASEAN policy and floated ideas on how to help move the Association forward (Hernandez 1998; Wanandi 1999). As such, ASEAN–ISIS is a useful complement to relevant debates at the official level. Importantly, Professor Carolina Hernandez, president of the Institute for Strategic and Development Studies (ISDS) in Manila (the Philippine arm of ASEAN–ISIS) has not only played a major role in promoting new understandings of norms governing interaction between ASEAN members. In her capacities as president of ISDS and chairperson of ASEAN–ISIS, positions held concurrently in the late 1990s, she also supported civil society groups in advocating the establishment of an ASEAN Human Rights Mechanism.

ASEAN decision-makers will no doubt also continue to take note of recommendations emanating from the Council for Security Cooperation in Asia-Pacific (CSCAP). The CSCAP process has in the past been instrumental in exploring ideas not yet deemed fit for discussion at Track I level. Still, much of its work has prepared the ground for subsequent official decisions, as illustrated by the CSCAP input into the draft on the definition and principles of preventive diplomacy. For the future, a closer informal relationship between the ARF and CSCAP is in the wings.

There will also continue to be exchanges between the Working Group for an ASEAN Human Rights Mechanism and ASEAN senior officials (held since 1996), which may have a bearing on the future development of the 'ASEAN way'. The rationale for the possible establishment of an ASEAN Human Rights Mechanism with governmental support was originally to redress the situation whereby only a few opportunities arose for the region to take stock of human rights developments from the standpoint of ASEAN. This concerned, in particular, the right to development and the balance between the rights of the individual and those of the community. Over the years, however, the Working Group has pursued a number of objectives challenging the 'ASEAN way' on the road towards establishing a regional human rights mechanism, conceived as an intergovernmental body promoting human rights in co-operation with civil society. Among other things, the Working Group has sought acknowledgement as an 'important catalyst for the promotion of human rights in ASEAN'. Efforts have, second, been directed towards the establishment of a national human rights institution in every ASEAN country. A third objective has been an ASEAN declaration on human rights as a basis for the establishment of a regional mechanism. The fourth objective has been the creation of a unit within the ASEAN Secretariat to focus on human rights-related concerns within the region (Working Group for an ASEAN Human Rights Mechanism, undated). So far, most governments in Southeast Asia have not been enthusiastic about seeing an ASEAN Human Rights Mechanism set up. Several have rejected the idea that there should even be a national human rights commission.[9] The objections are manifold. [10]

Beyond the challenge posed by the Working Group, it will become increasingly difficult for governments of ASEAN countries to prevent 'intrusion' into 'domestic affairs' by NGOs (Sukma 2000: 4). Just prior to the Thirty-third ASEAN Ministerial Meeting regional civil-society groups met to warn the representatives of ASEAN member states that the conduct of foreign affairs was no longer the prerogative of a certain elite. What member states needed to do, it was argued, was to transcend the die-hard mutual suspicion they cloaked with the principle of non-interference and open their minds to friendly recommendations from neighbours.

A good recent indication of how developments in Track III[11] diplomacy are posing challenges for the 'ASEAN way' was the convening of the inaugural APA, hosted by the Indonesian Centre for Strategic and International Studies in Batam, Riau, in November 2000. APA brings together several hundred participants from across Southeast Asia for discussions on issues such as globalisation, poverty, women's empowerment, human rights, good governance and the environment. The Assembly sees itself as a counterpoint to the 'fraternity of government officials' that is ASEAN. As this phrase indicates, the starting-point for APA was the argument that ASEAN states have failed to create a moral commitment and a personal sense of unity amongst their peoples. At the same time, the idea of an APA builds on the realisation that for NGOs to be successful in influencing intergovernmental dialogues, it is necessary for regional civil society to have some institutionalised expression and the capacity to act regionally. In the event, the establishment of the APA was made possible as part of the Southeast Asia Co-operation Project (SEACP), which is funded mainly by institutions and foundations in Canada, Japan, Europe and the United States. Its key purpose is to broaden support for the principles and practices of human security as well as to enable civil society actors to have better access to national and ASEAN-level policy discussions. While APA represents a Track III activity, ASEAN–ISIS sees itself as playing a major role as an intermediary between ASEAN governments and civil-society groups. Despite the fact that the first session of the Assembly ended without a firm conclusion or a final declaration, it is to be expected that regional civil-society representatives will continue to exert pressure on ASEAN leaders to accommodate the concept and practice of human security. This may lead to the further development of the 'ASEAN way'.

Prospects

This chapter began by identifying three long-term scenarios for ASEAN's diplomatic and security culture: evolution, stasis and demise. It is, of course, not possible to predict the extent to which the future of the 'ASEAN way' will resemble one of these scenarios by, say, 2010. The short- to medium-term prospects of ASEAN's diplomatic and security culture are likely to depend on whether member-state governments believe that this normative framework, which has served to mediate both insecurity on the part of individual leaders and estrangement between them, should evolve. There are significant domestic reasons for ASEAN decision-makers to opt for the status quo on the 'ASEAN way', but equally there are old and new voices seeking an overhaul of its underlying understandings. Surely the thinking of state leaders on the further development of ASEAN's diplomatic and security culture will depend on the policy-making context, i.e. economic circumstances, social and political stability, relations with the major powers and the extent of moral pressure from inside the ASEAN countries. As all leaders of ASEAN countries accept that the 'ASEAN way' is of some utility in maintaining peace and stability in Southeast Asia and remain concerned about the implications of loosening constraints associated with the constituent norms, some features of the 'ASEAN way' will probably endure for some time.

Immediate prospects

In the short term the norms of sovereign equality, with its corollary of consensual decision-making, non-interference and the non-use of force are likely to be reaffirmed by ASEAN, even while the Association is busy defining the concept of preventive diplomacy and formulating the principles underpinning its application. Similarly, the rules for the operation of the ASEAN High Council are, at least implicitly, also likely to emphasise the salience of these norms. Since ASEAN members all reject coercive measures, ASEAN is likely to focus on the requirement of consent both for preventive diplomacy and for the operation of the High Council. At the same time, the 'Retreat' is likely to remain the most useful encounter during which to exchange views about the future relevance and significance of the Association. However, to the extent that more or less all issues become legitimate subjects for discussion among ASEAN member states, the norm of quiet diplomacy will remain meaningful to ASEAN policy-makers in the conduct of their intramural relations. In view of the prevailing mutual suspicions among members, the activation of the ASEAN troika cannot be taken for granted.

Medium-term prospects

It is reasonable to expect that the 'ASEAN way' will evolve further in the medium term as the process of norm-rationalisation within the Association and the ARF continues. Should a relevant situation arise, ASEAN governments might, for example, shift from the mere limited conceptual endorsement of new intramural instruments, say in the field of preventive diplomacy, to their practical adoption. It is likely that the concept of human security will feature more prominently in discussions among regional analysts and ASEAN leaderships, since they may have to make greater allowance for it in the context of relevant debates on preventive diplomacy in the ARF and ASEAN. One of the effects of this may be that they further specify the criteria for certain agreed procedures to be implemented. However, it would be a mistake to assume that this implies that ASEAN is copying extra-regional ideas and practices of regionalism (Higgott 2000). In conclusion, it makes sense to expect the 'ASEAN way' to be resilient but not impervious to change. This implies that ASEAN leaders will continue to find themselves in a predicament. As the former Thai prime minister Anand Panyarachun formulated it: '[W]e often do not know when it is more appropriate to apply the old rules or the new, and all the while the shadow of history and institutional inertia confound our ability to keep up with the times' (Panyarachun 2000). There can be no doubt that how ASEAN members address this predicament will determine any future assessment of the Association.

Notes

Introduction

1 Diplomacy may be understood as the process of dialogue and negotiation by which states conduct their relations and pursue their purposes by means short of war (Watson 1991: 11). Der Derian has thought about diplomacy as a process of 'mediation between estranged individuals, groups or entities' (1987: 6). Culture may be understood as a set of evaluative and cognitive standards (such as norms, rules, values, or models) that define what entities and actors exist in a system, how they operate in a given context and how they relate to one another (Jepperson, Wendt and Katzenstein 1996: 56).

2 R.J. Vincent, who like Hedley Bull was associated with the so-called English School, argues that 'Diplomatic Culture is the culture derived from the aristocratic cosmopolitanism of dynastic Europe which provides custom, precedent and manners for the rather precious society of diplomatists' (cited in Der Derian 1996: 90). On the English School, see Dunne (1998) and Robertson (1998).

3 See, for example, Buzan (1991), Buzan, Waever and de Wilde (1998) or Terriff, Croft, James and Morgan (1999). For a very useful contribution with a focus on East Asia, see Alagappa (1998).

4 On 'trust', also see Rengger (1997).

5 By lifeworld is meant that stockpile of interpretation patterns which, linguistically organised, is culturally transmitted, and linked to the processes of socialisation of each individual, thereby forming contexts of relevance or common situation definitions (Habermas 1987: 119–52).

6 See Ero (1999) in relation to Africa.

7 Busse (1999) and Nischalke (2000) make a similar distinction, but distinguish between what they term 'behavioural' and 'procedural' norms. Nischalke subsumes the following norms under the category of the 'ASEAN way': *musyawarah* and *mufakat*, informality and non-confrontational behaviour in the process of foreign policy co-ordination.

8 See Chalmers (1996: ch. 2) for a similar account.

9 The present account of the 'ASEAN way' as a framework for mediating estrangement and insecurity thus does not include as key elements the norms of 'regional autonomy', 'collective self-reliance' or 'no ASEAN military pact' that were identified by Acharya (2001).

10 Hadi Soesastro listed twelve principles as making up the 'ASEAN way':

> the principle of co-operative peace; the principle of seeking agreement and harmony; the principle of respect for territorial integrity; the principle on non-interference in the domestic affairs of member states; the principle of egalitarianism; the principle of decision-making by consensus; the principle

of sensitivity, politeness, non-confrontation and agreeability; the principle of mutual caring; the principle of quiet, private and elitist diplomacy versus public washing of dirty linen and diplomacy through the media; the principle of solidarity; the principle of being non-Cartesian, non-legalistic and concentrating on process and content; the principle of pragmatism.

(Soesastro 1995: iii–iv)

Also see Sopiee (1998: 28, footnote 1) for a slightly different list of principles.

11 For Michael Leifer, ASEAN constituted a *security community* only in terms of intramural conflict avoidance and management (Leifer 1986: 123–5). He otherwise used the term *diplomatic community* (1989) in recognition of ASEAN's collective diplomatic efforts and cohesion in facing off Vietnam over Cambodia and laying some of the groundwork for the Paris Peace Accords.

12 Adler and Barnett (1998) argue that even if a dyad within the community goes to war, this does not necessarily amount to the demise of a security community.

13 In Acharya (2001: 63) the first usage of the term 'ASEAN way' is dated to around 1974.

14 Martha Finnemore and Kathryn Sikkink (1998) have argued that a norm violator might bring about a 'norm cascade'. This would be the case if other social actors support the norm violation and press for a new norm.

15 For influential works in this area, see Wendt (1999), Finnemore (1996), Adler (1997), Katzenstein (1996), Bull (1977) and Ruggie (1998).

16 Alagappa has associated a range of values with political survival, such as:

[The] consolidation of the ideational basis that underpins the construction of nation and state and constitutes the basis for political domination; preservation of internal order and political stability; promotion of economic growth, development, and distributive justice; preservation of the sociocultural essence of the nation; and the preservation and enhancement of an international context, both normative and material, that is conducive to the attainment of these and other values, interests, and goals.

Alagappa (1998: 682)

17 This builds on Jürgen Habermas's (1996) persuasive argument put forward in relation to deliberative democracy, whereby every subject of the law must also be its author for a norm to be both legally valid and legitimate.

18 Struggles for recognition by social forces in ASEAN states have not always paralleled those of the elites. Indeed, in many cases leaderships have arguably denied respect to at least some of their citizens in ways that have prompted the latter to engage in struggles for recognition against their leaders or state.

19 Emphasis in the original.

1 Early origins of the 'ASEAN way' – the struggle for respect and sovereignty

1 See Sandhu *et al.* (1992), Broinowski (1982, 1990), Sukrasep (1989) and Antolik (1990). Exceptions of sorts are Jorgensen-Dahl (1982) and Acharya (2001).

2 On the example of Kelantan, see Suwannathat-Pian (1988: 184–92). Also see Hooker (1988a: 386–8).

3 On the political economy of 'colonial Southeast Asia', see Reid (1993) and Gunder Frank (1998).

4 The collapse of the traditional interstate system in what would later be conceived as Southeast Asia occurred more or less at the same time as the demise of the

Chinese tribute system. On the latter, see Fairbank (1968), Zhao Suisheng (1997: ch. 2) and Hunt (1996: ch. 2).

5 The United States relinquished its extra-territorial rights in 1920, Japan did so only in 1924, Britain and France in 1925. Evocation rights continued for some time even after the promulgation of Siam's legal codes; extra-territoriality finally came to an end in 1939 (Gong 1984a: 234–7).

7 As Kratoska and Batson (1992: 253) put it, 'The unprecedented scale and carnage of the hostilities served to undermine any pretensions that Western civilization possessed inherent moral superiority' (Kratoska and Batson 1992: 253).

8 Comprehensive bibliographical entries for the political leaders of the founding ASEAN states can be found in Leifer (1996a).

9 This section can only give the most cursory of overviews in line with the limited intention to illustrate the significance of a struggle for recognition in the pursuit of sovereign equality.

10 In the Siamese–French Treaty of 1867 Siam surrendered her claims over Cambodia in return for France's recognition of Siam's rights over the old Cambodian provinces of Battambang and Siemrap. For details of the French–Siamese territorial conflict, see Hall (1981: ch. 41). In 1893 France claimed all Siamese territories east of the Mekong River and temporarily occupied parts of south-eastern Siam in the lead-up to the Salisbury–Courcel settlement of 1896.

11 This loss of jurisdiction over foreign nationals extended not only to British citizens, but also to an array of nationals from other European powers and the United States. Treaties similar to the Treaty of Friendship and Commerce with Britain were concluded with, for example, France (1856), the United States (1856), Denmark (1858), Portugal (1859), Holland (1860) and Prussia (1862).

12 The Federated Malay States consisted of Perak, Selangor, Negri Sembilan and Pahang.

13 The Tunku expressed his resentment in the following way: 'But for the new Federal Ministers we had no homes, no cars, no welcome, and were treated like unwanted outcasts and intruders' (Rahman 1986: 56). The Tunku was also less than enthusiastic about the quality of his housing:

> The roof leaked when it rained heavily, wetting us in bed, so my wife and I had to get up and move the bed to another corner. Unfortunately, however, the bedding got wet, and we had to remove it and sleep on the wooden plank floor. Naturally, I couldn't sleep all night, and I swore that the British must go quickly.
>
> (Rahman 1986: 56)

14 Dato' Abdullah Ahmad described the Tunku as having 'had the Malay aristocratic arrogance of birth, style, and privileges and generosity' (Abdullah Ahmad 1985: 12). The Tunku was the son of the Sultan of Kedah, Sultan Abdul Hamid Halim Shah. His mother was Thai-Burmese.

15 It has been said of Singapore's Foreign Minister Sinnathamby Rajaratnam that there 'was within him the swallowed bile of the colonised Asian' (Bloodworth 1986: 19). Also see Lee Kuan Yew (1998) for an autobiographical account by Singapore's Senior Minister.

16 The rise of millennial movements indicated the extent of alienation by the wider peasant population at the perceived intrusiveness of colonial administrative procedures. Significantly, their occurrence developed, in particular, against a combination of local grievances and unbearable colonial insults. These would leave Muslims in Aceh 'to be prepared to die a martyr's death rather than to submit to the rule of kāfir' (Ileto 1992: 229).

17 As Robert van Niel put it: 'In their world-view, they expected to pay taxes, tribute, and services in return for a protection of their life-style which involved an adequate return of material goods, chiefly food, and the maintenance of cosmological harmony and hierarchy' (van Niel 1980: 110).

18 See Pascual (1962) for the socio-economic context and the development of Rizal's thought.

19 As Ileto put it, *kalayaan* denoted a situation 'when society would be turned on its head, when all men would be brothers, leaders would be Christ-like, all forms of oppression would end and property would be shared; in other words, when their image of kalayaan would turn into lived experience' (Ileto 1979: 207). Indeed, according to Ileto,

> [Kalayaan] points out precisely the possibility that folk religious traditions and such cultural values as *utang na loob* (meaning a lifelong debt to another for some favour bestowed) and *hiya* (meaning shame), which usually promote passivity and reconciliation rather than conflict have latent meanings that can be revolutionary.
>
> (Ileto 1979: 10)

2 Post-war origins of the 'ASEAN way' – from estrangement and conflict to regional reconciliation and accommodation

1 The Philippines peacefully achieved independence in 1946. The Indonesian struggle for independence ended in 1949. Malaya gained independence in 1957. Singapore only became a separate independent country in 1965, following its exit from the Malaysian Federation, of which it had become a part in 1963. Prior to that it had become a separate British colony in 1945 and a self-governing State (under British sovereignty) in 1959, with foreign and defence affairs falling into the purview of Britain and internal security becoming joint responsibility. Thailand had retained its independence, but, as we have noted, had succeeded in removing vestiges of extraterritoriality only in 1939.

2 Upon US representations, Thailand and the Philippines at first threatened to boycott the Conference if the PRC was going to participate, but later agreed to attend in order to 'balance' communist participation (Soerjono 1964: 42–3). Malaya was not represented as the Tunku failed to obtain observer status.

3 Manila had started to assert itself against Washington during the Quirino presidency. However, it took the American refusal, in Spring 1962, to settle the war damage claims to embarrass political elites in Manila in such a way as to lead them to portray Americans as ungrateful and to intensify efforts to seek greater nationalist credentials.

5 Article VIII of the Anglo-Malayan Defence Treaty of 1957, which extended only to the Federation of Malaya, was revised in this Agreement so

> that the Government of the Federation of Malaysia will afford to the Government of the United Kingdom the right to continue to maintain the bases and other facilities at present occupied by their service authorities within the State of Singapore and will permit the United Kingdom to make such use of these bases and facilities as the United Kingdom may consider necessary for the purpose of assisting in the defence of Malaysia, and for Commonwealth defence and *for the preservation of peace in Southeast Asia.*
>
> (my emphasis)

See Article VI of the Agreement of July 1963 between the United Kingdom Government and Governments of Territories of the Future Malaysia, reprinted in Gullick (1967: 103).

6 For a balanced assessment of the circumstances leading to Singapore's independence, see Leifer (2000: 27–32).

7 The final agreement consisted of three points:
1 the cessation of hostile acts;
2 the immediate establishment of diplomatic relations;
3 'in order to resolve the problems between the two countries arising out of the formation of Malaysia' the Malaysian government was to afford an opportunity to the people of Sarawak and Sabah 'to reaffirm in a free and democratic manner through general elections, their previous decision about their status in Malaysia' (Weinstein 1969: 93–4).

8 Viewing Malaysia as a possible buffer against communism, under Suharto the Army Strategic Command apparently sought to establish contacts within Kuala Lumpur as early as 1964, with a view to terminating confrontation (Anwar 1994: 29).

9 The key passage reads as follows:

> Being in Agreement that foreign bases are temporary in nature and should not be allowed to be used directly or indirectly to subvert the national independence of their countries, and that the arrangements of collective defence should not be used to serve the particular interest of any of the big powers.
>
> (reprinted in Jorgensen-Dahl 1982: 38)

The full texts of the Manila Agreements are reprinted in Mackie (1974: 336–40).

10 ASA was dissolved on 30 August 1967.

11 This principle declared all waters surrounding, between and connecting the islands constituting the Indonesian state, regardless of their extension or breadth, to be integral parts of the territory of the Indonesian state and therefore to be part of the internal waters under the exclusive sovereignty of Indonesia.

12 See extract of Statement by Mr R. Ramani, Malaysian Permanent Representative to United Nations General Assembly, 9 December 1964. Official Records, Doc. A/PV, 19th Session, p.68, reprinted in Boyce (1968: 126–7).

13 For details of the scope of communist insurgencies facing ASEAN countries and their counter-insurgency operations, see the contributions in Jeshurun (1985).

3 ZOPFAN and the ASEAN Regional Forum – the extramural dimension of ASEAN's struggle for security and recognition

1 See Paragraph 5 of the Preamble, in which ASEAN countries articulated their determination to 'ensure their stability and security from external interference in any form or manifestation in order to preserve their national identities in accordance with the ideals and aspirations of their peoples' (ASEAN 1967).

2 See Chin Kin Wah (1987) on the Anglo-Malayan/Malaysian alliance.

3 Thanat Khoman remarked, for instance, that 'Thailand refuses to recognize the jurisdiction and competence of the United States Foreign Relations Committee over the foreign policy of Thailand' (Khoman 1970b: 12).

4 According to Dewi Fortuna Anwar (1996: 34), the concept of national resilience, developed by the Institute for National Defence, was discussed from 1968 and adopted as state policy in 1973. Suharto defined national resilience thus:

internally: the ability to ensure the necessary social changes while keeping one's own identity, with all its vulnerability, and externally, it is the ability to face all external threats, regardless of their manifestations. 'National resilience' therefore, covers the strengthening of all the component elements in the development of a nation in its entirety, thus consisting of resilience in the ideological, political, economic, social, cultural and military fields.

(Quoted in Hänggi 1992: 121, fn 11)

5 On the strategic triangle that developed out of these changes, see the contributions in Ross (1993). See Burr (1998) for recently published material on Henry Kissinger's diplomacy at the time.
6 The Singaporean and Indonesia delegations had produced a joint paper on the future of ASEAN–PRC relations, the Philippines had formulated a proposal to convene a pan-Asian summit, and Malaysia submitted a working paper on the ZOPFAN proposal (Hänggi 1992: 131–4).
7 Hans Indorf (1975: 23) has convincingly argued that the distinction initially made by the Association between the political and regular activities always remained 'rather artificial'. In Singapore in April 1972 ASEAN leaders formally decided to meet informally once a year to discuss international developments affecting the region (ASEAN 1972).
8 For the notion of 'possession' and 'milieu' goals, see Wolfers (1962: ch. 5).
9 Thailand and the Philippines assisted the US war effort by dispatching a limited number of troops and by offering air bases for US operations. Malaysia provided arms and training facilities.
10 The other Indochinese countries had participated as observers at various times. Laos had done so in 1969, 1973 and 1974; the Khmer Republic under Marshal Lon Nol in 1971, 1973 and 1974; and South Vietnam (Republic of Vietnam; RVN) in 1969 and 1971.
11 See Stuart-Fox (1997: 156–67) for the events leading up to the establishment of the Lao People's Democratic Republic.
12 See J. Taylor (1991) and B. Singh (1996) on the conflict in East Timor.
13 The key move towards improving bilateral relations had been the closure of American bases in Thailand at Bangkok's request (Thayer 1990: 143).
14 The Cambodian conflict will be covered in more detail in Chapter 4.
15 On the evolution of the Archipelagic Doctrine, see Djalal (1996: 124–30) and Leifer (1978: 17–25).
16 Vietnam gained membership in APEC in November 1998, but at the time of writing is not yet a member of the World Trade Organisation (WTO).
17 Vietnam and the United States reached an agreement in principle on a bilateral trade agreement on 25 July 1999.
18 Such details can be found in Frost (1993: esp. 58–66) and Zagoria (1997: 164–8).
19 Membership in ASEAN was conferred on Laos only on 23 July 1997, as was Myanmar, and Cambodia was admitted on 30 April 1999.
20 For examinations and assessments of the various security issues involved, see the contributions in Lau Teik Soon and Suryadinata (1988), Simon (1988) and Scalapino *et al.* (1990).
21 China's challenge to the 'ASEAN way' will be explored in greater detail in Chapter 5.
22 See the Agreement Concerning the Sovereignty, Independence, Territorial Integrity and Inviolability, Neutrality and National Unity of Cambodia (1991). The guarantor powers are China, France, the United Kingdom, Russia, the United States, the ASEAN countries, Myanmar, Laos, Vietnam, Australia, India, Japan, Canada and the former Yugoslavia (as the then representative of the Non-Aligned Movement). The guarantor powers are to engage in consultations

in the event of a violation of Cambodia's neutrality. This Agreement was linked to the Agreement on a Comprehensive Political Settlement of the Cambodian conflict that aimed at the neutralisation of domestic conflict.

23 See Leifer (1996b) for a more detailed account of the establishment of the ARF.

24 In 1993 Singapore brokered a compromise whereby the EAEG would become the East Asian Economic Caucus within APEC.

25 The extent to which ASEAN has succeeded in winning the respect of the major powers for the norms associated with the 'ASEAN way' will be explored in some detail in Chapters 5 and 6.

26 Suharto's successor, President B.J. Habibie, abrogated the security agreement in the wake of Australia's role in the UN-sponsored intervention force in East Timor in 1999.

4 The Cambodian conflict and the 'ASEAN way' – the struggle for a pristine interpretation of principles

1 For detailed such works see Morris (1999), Draguhn and Schier (1987) and Heder (1981). See Chandler (1998) for a general introduction to Cambodia and Leifer (1967) for Cambodia's search for security.

2 The invasion, for instance, also violated the Declaration on Principles of International Law Concerning Friendly Relations and Co-operation among States in accordance with the Charter of the United Nations, UNGA Res. 2625 (XXV), 25 UN GAOR, supp. (no. 28) 121, UN doc. A/8028 (1971).

3 It should be noted that ASEAN countries were far less instrumental in reaching the accord than was Sino–Soviet normalisation, the end of the Cold War and P5 collective co-operation on the Cambodian crisis. These wider geostrategic changes led the four Cambodian factions to negotiate more ardently, not least because it became apparent that external assistance would ebb away (Peou 1997: chs 4, 5).

4 For a chronology, see Raszelenberg and Schier (1995). See Berry (1997) on the significance of Australia's diplomatic role in the three years before the Paris Peace Agreements. On the 1989 Paris Peace talks, see Acharya, Lizée, and Peou (1991).

5 On the record of the United Nations in Cambodia see Berdal and Leifer (1996), Heder and Ledgerwood (1996) and Peou (1997: pt III).

6 This focus on the legal-political principles of ASEAN's diplomatic and security culture constitutes a major difference to the accounts by Acharya (2001: ch. 3) or Nischalke (2000). Both have primarily been interested in the extent to which the norms of consultation and consensus were challenged in the course of formulating ASEAN's Cambodia policy.

7 The number of Cambodian refugees increased from 14,782 at the end of 1978 to 154,766 at the end of December 1981 (Theeravit 1982: 570; also see Robinson 1998: chs 4 and 5).

8 Thailand's vulnerability was very real, although the events in Cambodia were also used by the military to justify the acquisition of arms. On this point, see Regaud (1992: 168).

9 It should be noted, however, that Vietnam had sought to reach an agreement whereby the Indochinese states would ensure that no aid reached the Thai communist insurgents through the three Indochina countries in return for Bangkok's recognition of the Heng Samrin regime.

10 Normalisation was taken off Indonesia's immediate foreign policy agenda after anti-Chinese riots erupted in Indonesia in April 1980. Jakarta also rejected what would have amounted to a symbolic visit to Indonesia of China's Party Chairman Hua Guofeng in 1980 (van der Kroef 1981b).

11 See see Marks (1996: ch. 2) on the demise of the Communist Party of the Philippines.
12 To avoid misunderstandings Singapore also supported the adoption of the military dimension. Early on in the conflict Singapore proposed ASEAN military co-operation at the multilateral level. Only Manila supported this proposal. It has since been revealed that Singapore, Thailand, Malaysia, the United States and China spent US$1.3 billion to provide military support to the Khmer Rouge and the non-communist resistance.
13 For some of the annual votes on the situation in Kampuchea, see UNGA Resolutions 34/22 (14.11.79), 35/6 (22.10.80), 36/5 (21.10.81), 37/6 (28.10.82), 38/3 (27.10.83), 39/5 (30.10.84), 40/7 (5.11.85), 41/6 (21.10.86) and 42/3 (14.10.87).
14 Singapore's efforts proved resoundingly successful. Only thirty-four countries recognised the PRK during the early to mid-1980s. Of these, only ten had an embassy in Phnom Penh: Bulgaria, Cuba, Czechoslovakia, the GDR, Hungary, India, Laos, Poland, the Soviet Union and Vietnam.
15 The Vietnamese had not called for a humanitarian intervention before they invaded Kampuchea, but their subsequent justifications emphasised concerns about the humanitarian situation under the rule of Pol Pot. On intervention and humanitarian intervention, see the contributions in Bull (1984). See Wheeler (2000) for a recent contribution arguing strongly in favour of humanitarian interventions.
16 A previous instance of humanitarian intervention was that of India in East Pakistan in 1971. See Leifer (2000) for the most comprehensive account of Singapore's sense of vulnerability.
17 It has been argued that, all in all, Vietnam's invasion of Democratic Kampuchea in fact was 'a reasonable act of self-defence', especially in view of the destruction of Vietnamese villages and the massacres of Vietnamese civilians by the Khmer Rouge (Klintworth 1989: 28).
18 For an analytical and an autobiographical account of the horrors under Pol Pot, see Kiernan (1996) and Ngor (1988).
19 The coalition consisted of the Khmer Rouge, the KPNLF and the royalist FUNCINPEC. Prince Sihanouk was installed as president, Son Sann as prime minister. The Khmer Rouge remained the predominant military force within the coalition. Maintaining the foreign affairs portfolio, they also represented the CGDK at the UN and would have been permitted to take the label of Democratic Kampuchea with them in the event of any coalition split (van der Kroef 1981a).
20 The amended clause is reprinted in Raszelenberg and Schier (1995: 43).
21 The main points of this appeal aimed at the complete withdrawal of foreign troops from Kampuchea, the right to self-determination of the Khmer people and compliance by all states to refrain from interference in Kampuchea's internal affairs.
22 The first seminar had taken place before Benny Murdani's visit to Vietnam. Participants had included Pham Van Dong and Nguyen Co Thach.
23 Michael Leifer (1982: 15–17) has noted that the 1977 treaty forming a special relationship between Vietnam and Laos did not evoke serious security concerns in neighbouring capitals.
24 After further reflection, Vietnamese leaders did accept the Kuantan formula in a UN speech in October 1980.
25 The following draws on Peou (1997: 34–7).
26 Interestingly, no comment was made on the state of bilateral affairs with Singapore's neighbours in the official *Singapore 1988*.

27 See Chee (1989: 24) on Singapore's viewpoints on the shift in position undertaken by Thailand.
28 The *de jure* position was associated with the Ministry of Foreign Affairs, whereas the de facto position was linked to the Thai military. Thailand's Foreign Ministry was relegated to playing second fiddle as the incoming prime minister, Chatichai Choonhavan, himself assumed responsibility over foreign affairs and later shared responsibility with the deputy premier and defence minister, Chavalit Yongchaiyuth.
29 Singapore and Indonesia had in the meantime sought to overcome bilateral frictions through accelerated processes of confidence building. Indonesia, for instance, offered military training facilities to Singapore. Both sides financed the construction of an air weapons range in Siabu, Sumatra, in 1988. Also, several meetings between President Suharto and Prime Minister Lee Kuan Yew took place to improve the relationship. For example, the minister of defence, General Murdani, and the Commander-in-Chief of Indonesian Armed Forces, General Try Sutrisno, visited Singapore, while B.G. Lee Hsien Loong and Chief of General Staff Lieutenant-General Winston Choo visited Indonesia.

5 China's relations with ASEAN – challenging or reinforcing the 'ASEAN way'?

1 The Five Principles of Peaceful Co-existence (mutual respect for territorial integrity and sovereignty, mutual non-aggression, non-interference in each other's internal affairs, equality and mutual benefit, and peaceful co-existence) were put forward in 1953 in the context of Sino-Indian relations and incorporated in the 1982 PRC constitution.
2 See Reid (1996) for an account of the discontinuities of private trade and political intervention in relations between China and polities in Southeast Asia.
3 The Second Protocol amending the TAC and allowing states outside Southeast Asia to accede with the consent of all Southeast Asian countries was only agreed in 1998.
4 See Friedman (1996) on the pitfalls of direct translations of political discourses in relation to China.
5 Other contentious issues concerned the extension of most-favoured nation (MFN) status and the resolution passed by the US Congress to deny Beijing's bid to host the 2000 Olympics (Chen Peiyao 1995).
6 The US claimed that Beijing had made available to rogue states material that would allow for the production of weapons of mass destruction. Also, it was alleged that China had supplied suitable delivery systems to countries to which such exports were prohibited by US law, primarily Pakistan, Iran, and Libya. The US further argued that the sale of Chinese M-11 and M-9 missiles to countries like Pakistan was incompatible with the Chinese pledge to 'observe' the Missile Technology Control Regime.
7 The other two stages were preventive diplomacy and the 'elaboration of approaches to conflict'. The terminology originally envisaged for the third stage, conflict resolution, was rejected by the Chinese delegation.
8 The PRC published a second White Paper (*China's National Defense* 1998) on the occasion of ARF 5 that is more comprehensive and informative. A further White Paper was released in 2000.
9 The Agreement was signed by China, Russia, Kazakhstan, Tajikistan and the Kyrgyz Republic. In June 2001 the group included Uzbekistan, to form the Shanghai Co-operation Organisation.
10 China agreed with the Philippines on an eight-point code of conduct with regard to disputed maritime territory. This includes a pledge to resolve the Spratly

Islands dispute peacefully and in accordance with international law, including UNCLOS. However, the Philippine president, Fidel Ramos, acknowledged at the time of the signing that it remained unclear precisely how the agreement could be implemented, as the question of sovereignty had not been dealt with.

11 Track I diplomacy involves emissaries of sovereign states in official interaction. Track II diplomacy also involves government officials, among others, but the latter engage each other only in their personal capacities. Any conclusions or recommendations emerging from meetings are in no way binding upon governments, nor are the proceedings of such meetings declamatory of the position of any state. Governments are thus able to dismiss any conclusions or recommendations as they choose, but free to adopt anything useful that may transpire.

12 Estimates of China's defence expenditure have varied. See Bernstein and Munro (1998: 70–2) for one of the more extreme conclusions. A careful discussion of the matter is in Gurtov and Byong Moo Hwang (1998: ch. 9).

13 Interestingly, it has been pointed out that China's interpretation of the Law of the Sea has reflected that of Vietnam, whose officials have also drawn straight baselines along its coast, subsuming huge areas of sea as internal waters (Tonesson 2000: 209–10).

14 Michael Leifer has also characterised these events as 'a defining diplomatic moment for China in ordering its priorities with the states of Southeast Asia' (Leifer 1997b: 168).

15 Earlier in 1998 Vietnam had apparently built structures on Orleana and Kingston Shoals, which are also claimed by the PRC.

16 While differences over the geographic extension of the code remained, other contentious points appear to have been settled. The Philippines and China agreed on a compromise wording to ensure no new occupation or structures would be built in the disputed areas. Malaysia's concerns on the interpretation of disputes as questions of territorial integrity or sovereignty were settled by an agreement that these be decided on a case-by-case basis.

17 For the Vietnamese position, see Luu Van Loi (1996).

18 On dialectical thinking in Chinese foreign policy, also see G. Chan (1999: ch. 2).

19 This chapter does not seek to establish whether China's 'partnerships' with other major powers are blessed with much substance.

20 Interestingly, in the interviews conducted by the author in early July 1998 most of the Chinese interlocutors opined that, irrespective of what happened in Jakarta, China would follow a policy of 'stability' by not interfering in the Indonesian domestic political context.

21 These are: (1) China–Thailand Joint Statement on a Plan of Action for the 21st Century, signed in Bangkok, 5 February 1999; (2) China–Vietnam Joint Statement, signed in Beijing, 27 February 1999. During President Tran's visit to Beijing in December 2000 the two sides subsequently also signed a Joint Statement on All-round Co-operation in the New Century, Beijing, 25 December 2000; (3) Joint Statement by the Government of Malaysia and the People's Republic of China on the Framework for Future Bilateral Relations, signed in Beijing, 31 May 1999; (4) China and Brunei Joint Communiqué on the Orientation of Future Bilateral Relations, issued in Beijing, 24 August 1999; (5) China–Singapore Joint Statement on Bilateral Cooperation, issued in Beijing, 11 April 2000; (6) Joint Statement by the People's Republic of China and the Republic of Indonesia on the Future Directions of Bilateral Co-operation, signed in Beijing, 8 May 2000; (7) Joint Statement between the Government of the People's Republic of China and the Government of the Republic of the Philippines on the Framework of Bilateral Co-operation in the Twenty-First Century, signed in Beijing, 16 May 2000; (8) Joint Statement of the People's Republic of China and the Union of Myanmar on the Framework of Future

Bilateral Relations and Co-operation, signed in Beijing, 6 June 2000; (9) Joint Statement by the People's Republic of China and the Lao People's Democratic Republic on the Framework of Their Bilateral Co-operation, Vientiane, 12 November 2000; (10) Joint Statement by the People's Republic of China and the Kingdom of Cambodia on the Framework of Their Bilateral Co-operation, Phnom Penh, 13 November 2000.

22 The China–Malaysia statement notes, for example, the possibility of bilateral co-operation in the defence industry sector. Another example is the envisaged security co-operation between Bangkok and Beijing by way of confidence-building measures as well as military diplomacy. The Indonesia–China statement also contains a reference to co-operation in defence and political and regional security. Statements signed with Cambodia, Laos and Myanmar stress security co-operation against cross-border crime, particularly smuggling, drug and aliens trafficking, as well as military exchanges.

23 My emphasis.

24 In an attempt to break out of its diplomatic isolation and to win greater international recognition, Taiwan's vice-president, Lien Chan, for instance, went to Singapore for a 'family holiday' during New Year 1998. Premier Vincent Siew visited the Philippines in January and Kuala Lumpur in April. The Malaysian deputy prime minister, Anwar Ibrahim, stopped over in Taipei in February following high-profile visits by Taiwanese delegations to Thailand, Malaysia and Indonesia in January (*SÜDOSTASIEN aktuell*, March 1998: 71). Taiwan also proposed contributing US$4 billion to an Asian Monetary/Fund but failed to contribute to the financial assistance given under the auspices of the International Monetary Fund (IMF).

25 Unfortunately for ASEAN, the truth of the matter is that the ARF was next to irrelevant to the improvement in US–China relations in the period 1996–8. Singapore's foreign minister Jayakumar admitted as much at the Thirty-First ASEAN Ministerial Meeting in July 1998.

26 See Yahuda (1999) and Shambaugh (1999) for more detailed discussions of China's security perceptions of the West after the bombing of the Chinese Embassy in Belgrade.

27 A similar response emerged when in April 2001 an American EP3 spy-plane was forced to make an emergency landing on the island of Hainan.

6 The US challenge to the 'ASEAN way'

1 For an account of these events, see Lintner (1990).

2 The question what purpose these elections were to serve has been a matter of scholarly debate. See Siemers (1996) for an argument running contrary to the perceived wisdom.

3 See Siemers (1999) for a thoughtful argument on whether the confrontational stance adopted by Washington has served to improve the prospects for democracy and human rights in Myanmar.

4 As Madeleine Albright put it, 'When we urge a government to engage in dialogue with a legitimate political movement, as we are doing in the case of Burma, that is not interference. That is standing up for the expressed will of that country's people' (Albright 1998).

5 For insightful discussions of the 'Asian values' debate, see Dupont (1996) and Robison (1996). While the 'Asian values' discourse generally challenged the US belief in the merits of liberal democracy, there was another reason why Washington sought to repulse it. Ultimately the question was whose societal and political ideas and values might serve as a possible model for the further political development of the PRC. For many Americans the demise of communism and

authoritarianism in China would be Washington's 'final victory' in international society. Accordingly, advocates of the US model of political, economic and social development felt challenged by the small but quite vocal group of leaders, especially in Singapore (Mahbubani 1995), who proclaimed the virtues of an alternative ideas of governance supposedly geared toward economic success as well as social and political stability. As Diane Mauzy argued, the United States saw Singapore in particular as 'interfering with its democratizing goals by offering and/or recognizing a rival approach that emphasizes order, stability, and economic development while discouraging rapid political liberalization' (Mauzy 1997: 225).

6 See Carey (1997: 1, 24) on the problematic use of 'Myanmar'.

7 See *SÜDOSTASIEN aktuell*, January 1997: 29–30 for details.

8 As Chapter 7 will demonstrate, it took the financial and economic crisis of 1997/8 for Thailand's then Democrat-led government under Chuan Leekpai to respond to Western pressure on Myanmar, irrespective of the other reasoning processes involved.

9 ASEAN member governments did not give any public support to the formation of the Committee Representing the People's Parliament in August 1998, nor to the subsequent establishment of a virtual parallel government in December that year (*SÜDOSTASIEN aktuell*, November 1998: 460–3).

10 See Carter and Perry (1999: 92–9) for an insider's account of some aspects of the crisis. On the origins and significance of the crisis, see Garver (1997). It should be noted that ASEAN as a grouping did not adopt a position on the conflict, although Singapore publicly voiced its concerns, and other officials did so privately.

11 The US subsequently succeeded in engaging China in bilateral security dialogues and confidence-building measures at all levels considered appropriate and possible, including that of the Joint Chiefs of Staff. During the visits to the US by China's President Jiang Zemin in October 1997, the visit by US Secretary of Defense to Beijing in January 1998, and that of President Clinton to China in June 1998, a number of confidence-building measures were agreed. These included the exchange of visits by senior officials, reciprocal visits of warships, discussion of mutual approaches to humanitarian relief, agreements to observe one another's exercises, and agreements to de-target strategic missiles as well as on procedures to avoid incidents at sea.

12 For more encompassing discussions, see the contributions in Ball and Acharya (1999).

13 To the extent that ASEAN leaders followed debates in the United States about the interrelationship between preventive diplomacy and preventive defence, the perceived challenge to their understanding of preventive diplomacy as initially pre-crisis and non-coercive activities has been accentuated. Preventive defence, a concept introduced by former Secretary of Defense William Perry in 1996, is about preventing the emergence of existential threats to US interests, deterring those threats that the US cannot prevent, and defeating those threats that the US cannot deter, using force where necessary.

14 Other ASEAN governments have of course also played an important role in steering the development of preventive diplomacy forward, for instance as ARF chairs or as co-chairs of the ISG–CBM.

15 See, in particular, the contributions by Tay (1997) and CSCAP Singapore (1999).

16 An overview of the extent of security co-operation at the time can be found in J. Young (1992).

17 On the revitalisation of the US–Japan alliance, see Asher (1997), Mochizuki (1997), Green and Cronin (1999) and Armacost 1996). As regards the security dilemmas arising from the revitalisation, see Garrett and Glaser (1997) and Christiansen (1999).

18 For details, see transcripts of interviews with US Secretary of Defense William Cohen (US Department of Defense 1999a, 1999b).
19 See Blair (2000) for a recent statement on the establishment of such 'security communities'.
20 On the 'unconscious resentment' of the US at the ZOPFAN proposal see Wilson (1975: 106).
21 Singapore is the largest US trading partner among the ten ASEAN countries and the top destination among the ASEAN countries for US foreign investment.
22 Russia, China and Vietnam preferred not to participate, despite having been invited (*Far Eastern Economic Review*, 12 April 2001: 8).
23 The ratification in 1999 of the Agreement Regarding the Treatment of United States Armed Forces Visiting the Philippines allows for the resumption of normal military-to-military contacts, including regular ship visits and periodic joint exercises. In February 2000 the Philippines hosted the 'Balikatan' exercise, which involved over 4,000 US and Philippine troops. The Philippines provided 750 troops to the International Force in East Timor (INTERFET) and supplied the first military commander to the multinational peacekeeping force of the United Nations Transitional Administration in East Timor (UNTAET). Cobra Gold 2001 involved some 13,000 troops in the Third Army region of northern Thailand. Its focus was on peacekeeping and disaster relief.
24 Other concerns relate to the precise nature of the legally binding negative security assurances from protocol parties, the ambiguity of language concerning the permissibility of port calls by ships which may carry nuclear weapons, and the procedural rights of protocol parties to be represented before the various executive bodies set up by the treaty to ensure its implementation.
25 China had initially objected to the inclusion of continental shelves and EEZs in the SEANWFZ Treaty, but then withdrew its reservation in view of the agreed inclusion of a 'policy statement' that would clarify that claims to the exclusive economic zones would not be prejudiced by the Treaty (interview with Indonesian official, 7 July 1998).

7 The concept of flexible engagement and the practice of enhanced interaction – intramural challenges to the 'ASEAN way'

1 Non-interference is not only a key principle in the Bangkok Declaration and the TAC. It has also, albeit indirectly, been incorporated into the ASEAN Vision 2020, where the TAC in Southeast Asia is envisioned as a binding code of conduct for the governments and peoples of the region (ASEAN 1997).
2 The EU–ASEAN Joint Co-operation Committee finally met in Bangkok in May 1999. Myanmar was allowed to attend but not to speak.
3 For details, see Siemers (1996) and Than (1997, 1998).
4 The ASEAN troika pursued two key issues: halting the armed hostilities between forces loyal to Prince Ranariddh and those loyal to Hun Sen; and organising free and fair elections in which all parties and political personalities would be able to participate freely. ASEAN had initially also conveyed concerns about the constitutionality of the appointment of Ung Huot as first prime minister. ASEAN countries were also later consulted on Japan's 'four pillars initiative'.
5 The respective accounts of this issue by both the Singaporean and Malaysian governments are contained in *Straits Times* (1 August 1998: 37–40). Also see Leifer (2000:149–51).

6 President Estrada also called Anwar a friend of the Philippine people, drawing parallels between him and José Rizal, the national hero of the Philippines, who was executed by the Spanish in 1896. The Philippine media drew parallels between the fate of Benino Aquino and Datuk Seri Anwar Ibrahim. (*Philippine Daily Inquirer*, 4 October 1998).

7 Among the new irritants complementing existing ones in Singapore–Malaysia relations in September 1998 were the prohibition of so-called Central Limit Order Book trades and the Senior Minister's account (Lee Kuan Yew 1998) of his country's exit from Malaysia. In September Malaysia served the required one-day notice to inform the city-state that it would cancel all special approvals and waivers enabling the aircraft of the Rebpulic of Singapore Air Force to enter Malaysian airspace. Similar restrictions were subsequently imposed on Singapore ships. However, Malaysia did not unambiguously spell out whether the restrictions on ships applied only to military vessels. In early October Malaysia's defence minister complained that Singapore had repeatedly violated the country's territorial integrity '[s]even times, water five times' (*Straits Times*, 2 October 1998). This followed Malaysia's earlier unprecedented notice that its forces would not participate in military exercises under the umbrella of the FPDA planned for October 1998 (Jayasankaran 1998). Malaysia's then defence minister, Datuk Seri Syed Hamid Albar, also called into question whether the FPDA was still meeting Malaysia's defence needs (*Straits Times*, 27 October 1998).

8 Kuala Lumpur decided later that most of the 220,000 workers to be allowed into Malaysia would be Indonesians, with Thais in second place (*Straits Times*, 21 November 1998).

9 In September 1992 the then foreign minister, Roberto Rómulo, and President Ramos had declared that the Philippines would no longer pursue the claim to Sabah.

8 ASEAN's diplomatic and security culture after the Hanoi Summit – has 'old' thinking been dominating 'new' practices?

1 For generally positive accounts of ASEAN's response to the Asian Crisis, see Funston (1999) and Chalermpalanupap (1999).

2 Several ASEAN countries of course participated in the UNTAC mission in Cambodia, but Phnom Penh had not yet become a member at the time.

3 The ASEAN troika must not be confused with the ASEAN High Council set up under the TAC. Rules of procedure of the latter were released at the ASEAN Ministerial Meeting in July 2001 (ASEAN 2001). These rules challenge the norm that member states do not call on the Association to help resolve disputes among signatories of the TAC. However, a closer reading suggests that it is not a foregone conclusion that the ASEAN High Council will become operational to deal with intramural disputes any time soon.

4 Notably, the ASP is only one of several similar surveillance processes operated by the Association in the area of economic co-operation. The AFTA Council has, for instance, supervised the acceleration of AFTA agreed at Hanoi, whereby the ASEAN-6 states were meant to reduce the rate of their tariffs to 0–5 per cent in at least 90 per cent of tariff lines by the year 2000. In the area of investments, the ASEAN Investment Area Council supervises the implementation of the Framework Agreement on the ASEAN Investment Area. This shows that in economic co-operation a consensus has obtained whereby policy implementation by member states in distinct areas is open to scrutiny.

5 The forum of ASEAN Finance and Central Bank Deputies and its working group, the ASEAN Select Committee for the ASP, have institutionally supported

the ASP. It has been further assisted by the ASEAN Surveillance Co-ordinating Unit based at the ASEAN Secretariat, and the ASEAN Surveillance Technical Support Unit based at the Asian Development Bank in Manila.

6 The membership of the ASEAN Select Committee comprises senior officials from the ASEAN Finance Ministries and Central Banks.

7 In the immediate aftermath of Indonesia's intervention in East Timor Singapore was the only country to, first, abstain and then absent itself when the United Nations General Assembly voted on resolutions on East Timor in 1975 and 1976, respectively (B. Singh 1996). In effect, ASEAN's stance played a significant role in helping Suharto offset Indonesia's loss of international standing in the non-aligned world in the aftermath of the intervention in East Timor.

8 For a useful overview of the developments in East Timor leading up to UNTAET, see A. Smith (2000). On East Timor, also see J. Taylor (1999).

9 The results of the 'popular consultation' were recognised by Jakarta on 19 October 1999.

10 This plan was as vile as the violence planned around March under *Operasi Sapu Jagad* (Operation Clean Sweep), the goal of which was to exterminate leaders, cadres and supporters of the anti-integration movement. See Dunn (2001) for details of the atrocities committed in East Timor. On violence against East Timorese women, also see Mythans (2001).

11 For details, see United Nations Security Council (1999).

12 As Leaver has argued, the letter left Dr. Habibie 'inventing an indigenous version of the botched decolonization process that had prompted Indonesia's original invasion' (Leaver 2001:28).

13 Bangkok's offer of a total of 1,778 troops was the second largest after Australia's.

14 For details of its mission, see UNTAET (undated). For an early critical assessment of UNTAET, see Chopra (2000).

15 East Timorese independence activist José-Ramos Horta vetoed a leading peacekeeping role by Malaysia in the UNTAET phase on the grounds that Kuala Lumpur was 'on the side of Indonesia' and that Malaysia 'doesn't care about human rights' (*The Nation*, 19 October 1999).

16 The Wahid administration passed a decree in April 2001 whereby a national inquiry to be set up will only have the authority to investigate violations of human rights committed after 30 August 1999.

17 ASEAN countries have actively supported UNTAET. A Filipino officer and, subsequently, a Thai general have commanded UNTAET's military force, a Malaysian has served as the chief of staff of the UNTAET Administration Office, and a sizeable number of Filipinos and Thais have been among the UN peacekeepers deployed in East Timor (UNTAET, undated).

18 According to ASEAN (2000c: para. 22), the foreign ministers reiterated their continuing support for the sovereignty, territorial integrity and. national unity of Indonesia, which includes the Provinces of Aceh and Irian Jaya (Papua). The foreign ministers also commended the efforts and measures taken by the Indonesian government to restore peace and order.

19 See *SÜDOSTASIEN aktuell* (March 2001: 140–5) for an account of the background to these events.

20 Myanmar leaders decided to close the joint border with Thailand after the seizure of Myanmar's embassy in Bangkok in 1999. Thailand refused to expel the perpetrators, as Myanmar leaders demanded, on human rights grounds.

21 The Thai government reportedly engaged Myanmar in military-to-military diplomacy after the seizure of the outpost at Ban Pang Noon in Mae Fah Luang district by 200–500 Burmese troops. Although an agreement on a withdrawal

appears to have been reached at the diplomatic and township border level, this agreement was not implemented, so that the Royal Thai Army proceeded to recapture the base (Ashayagachat 2001).

22 Thailand's National Security Council has declared the drug menace sweeping the country to be the number one security threat. In justifying his tough line, Lieutenant-General Wattanachai can also build on the comments of the Supreme Army commander, General Surayud Chulanont. In 1999 the commander reportedly said that he was determined 'to win the war against drugs even if it meant fighting a border war against drug armies or the army of Myanmar' (cited in Brooke 2000: 11).

Conclusion – on the prospects for ASEAN's diplomatic and security culture

1 Malaysia and Indonesia have agreed to involve the International Court of Justice (ICJ) on the question of Sipadan and Ligitan. Overlapping territorial claims by Singapore and Malaysia to the rocky shoal of Pedra Branca, where Horsburgh Lighthouse is located, have also been referred to the ICJ for arbitration.

2 For the rationale for a Pacific Concord and a critical appraisal, see Mohamed Jawhar Hassan (1996) and Evans (1996), respectively.

3 The domestic situation in Myanmar has improved somewhat since the initiation of a dialogue between the military-run government and Daw Aung San Suu Kyi in October 2000. The SPDC has since released more than 150 people held for political reasons. Nonetheless, it seems certain that the military regime has no ambition to quit politics in the short to medium term.

4 In 2001 the proportion of defence spending amounted to 36 per cent of the city-state's budget.

5 See Kamarulzinam Abdullah (1999) for a recent assessment of the threat to Malay security posed by the manipulation of religion.

6 The rules of procedure were agreed in 2001. Details to be found at http://www.aseansec.org/view.asp?file=/amm/amm/hanoi03htm.

7 As regards the peace talks between Manila and the MNLF, Indonesia became involved through the participation in the Organisation of Islamic Countries (OIC), which gave Jakarta a mandate in 1993 to deal with the Moro issue. In the event, Indonesian diplomats relied on an approach that built on the Cocktail party approach used in bringing together the parties of the Cambodian conflict and as applied in the informal South China Sea workshops, i.e. informal talks without preconditions (Djalal 1999: 203).

8 As Kofi Annan argued, it remains 'essential that the international community reach consensus – not only on the principle that massive and systematic violations of human rights must be checked, wherever they take place, but also on ways of deciding what action is necessary, and when, and by whom' (Annan 1999; see also Annan 2000).

9 Human rights have thus not featured explicitly in ASEAN's key documents. Even the ASEAN Vision 2020, adopted by all member states in 1998, does not expressly refer to human rights, but merely stresses the importance of 'total human development regardless of gender, race, religion, or social and cultural background'.

10 Some ASEAN governments have argued that the creation of a regional human rights mechanism could not precede the establishment of national human rights commissions. Another concern raised focuses on the possibility that human rights organisations could be pursuing a political agenda beyond the concern

for human rights and that they might unwittingly or knowingly become the pawns of foreign NGOs. Some ASEAN leaders also remain very uncomfortable with the proposed initiative on the basis that complete freedom of expression or association poses a threat to peaceful ethnic and religious co-existence. Indeed, these decision-makers regard the ASEAN Human Rights Mechanism as a vehicle designed both to endanger national stability and to bring about their respective political demise.

11 Track III diplomacy involves civil society representatives, i.e. NGO experts, academics, business people and other grassroots representatives.

Bibliography

Abdullah Ahmad (1985) *Tengku Abdul Rahman and Malaysia's Foreign Policy, 1963–1970* (Kuala Lumpur: Berita Publishing).

Abdullah Ahmad Badawi (1998) 'Opening Statement at Thirty-First ASEAN Ministerial Meeting', Manila, 24 July 1998, at http://www.aseansec.org/view.asp?file=/amm/amm31osm.htm.

Abin, Rais (1991) 'Developments in Indonesia–Singapore Bilateral Relations: Politics', in Lau Teik Soon and Bilveer Singh (eds) *Singapore–Indonesia Relations: Problems and Prospects* (Singapore: Singapore Institute of International Affairs), pp. 95–100.

Acharya, Amitav (1991) 'Association of Southeast Asian Nations: "Security Community" or "Defence Community"?', *Pacific Affairs* 64(2): 159–78.

—— (1992) 'Regionalism and Regime Security in the Third World: Comparing the Origins of the ASEAN and the GCC', in Brian L. Job (ed.) *The Insecurity Dilemma: National Security of Third World States* (Boulder, CO: Lynne Rienner), pp. 143–64.

—— (1993) *A New Regional Order in South-East Asia: ASEAN in the Post-Cold War Era*, Adelphi Paper 279 (London: Brassey's/International Institute for Strategic Studies).

—— (1994) *An Arms Race in Post-Cold War Southeast Asia? Prospects for Arms Control* (Singapore: Institute of Southeast Asian Studies).

—— (1995) 'ASEAN & Human Rights Management in Southeast Asia', in James T.H. Tang (ed.) *Human Rights and International Relations in the Asia Pacific* (London and New York: Pinter), pp. 167–82.

—— (1996a) 'ASEAN and Conditional Engagement', in James Shinn (ed.) *Weaving the Net: Conditional Engagement of China* (New York: Council of Foreign Relations), pp. 220–48.

—— (1996b) 'A Regional Security Community in Southeast Asia?', in Desmond Ball (ed.) *The Transformation of Security in the Asia/Pacific Region* (London: Frank Cass), pp. 175–200.

—— (1997) 'Ideas, Identity and Institution-building: from the "ASEAN way" to the "Asia-Pacific way"', *The Pacific Review* 10(3): 319–46.

—— (1998a) 'Better Try Constructive Intervention', *The Nation*, 17 June 1998: A4.

—— (1998b) 'Collective Identity and Conflict Management in Southeast Asia', in Emanuel Adler and Michael Barnett (eds) *Security Communities* (Cambridge: Cambridge University Press), pp. 198–227.

—— (1999a) 'Containment, Engagement, or Counter-Dominance? Malaysia's response to the rise of China', in Alastair Iain Johnston and Robert S. Ross (eds) *Engaging China: The Management of an Emerging Power* (London and New York: Routledge), pp. 129–51.

—— (2001) *Constructing a Security Community in Southeast Asia: ASEAN and the Problem of Regional Order* (London and New York: Routledge).

Acharya, Amitav and J. D. Kenneth Boutin (1998) 'The Southeast Asia Nuclear Weapon-Free Zone Treaty', *Security Dialogue* 29(2): 219–30.

Acharya, Amitav, Pierre Lizée and Sorpong Peou (eds) (1991) *Cambodia – The 1989 Paris Peace Conference: Background Analysis and Documents* (New York: Kraus International Publications).

Adler, Emanuel (1997) 'Seizing the Middle Ground: Constructivism in World Politics', *European Journal of International Relations* 3(3): 319–63.

Adler, Emanuel and Michael Barnett (1998) 'A Framework for the Study of Security Communities', in Emanuel Adler and Michael Barnett (eds) *Security Communities* (Cambridge: Cambridge University Press), pp. 29–65.

Agence France Press (2000) 'ASEAN expected to Formally Adopt Crisis Mediation "Troika"', 25 July 2000.

Agreement Concerning the Sovereignty, Independence, Territorial Integrity and Inviolability, Neutrality and National Unity of Cambodia (1991), reprinted in James Mayall (ed.) (1996) *The New Interventionism 1991–94* (Cambridge: Cambridge University Press), pp. 157–60.

Agreement Regarding the Treatment of United States Armed Forces Visiting the Philippines (1998), Manila, 10 February 1998.

Aguinaldo, Emilio with Vicente Albano Pacis (1957) *A Second Look at America* (New York: Robert Speller & Sons).

Ahmad Rithaudeen (1979) 'Kampuchean Problem and Nonalignment', *Contemporary Southeast Asia* 1(3): 205–10.

Alagappa, Muthiah (1987a) *The National Security of Developing States: Lessons from Thailand* (Dover, MA: Auburn House).

—— (1987b) *Towards A Nuclear-Weapons-Free Zone in Southeast Asia* (Kuala Lumpur: ISIS Malaysia).

—— (1991) 'Regional Arrangements and International Security in Southeast Asia: Going Beyond ZOPFAN', *Contemporary Southeast Asia* 12(4): 269–305.

—— (ed.) (1995) *Political Legitimacy in Southeast Asia: The Quest for Moral Authority* (Stanford, CA: Stanford University Press).

—— (1998) 'Conceptualizing Security: Hierarchy and Conceptual Traveling', in Muthiah Alagappa (ed.) *Asian Security Practice: Material and Ideational Influences* (Stanford, CA: Stanford University Press), pp. 677–97.

Alatas, Ali (2000) 'Jakarta's Diplomacy Challenges', *Straits Times*, 2 April 2000.

Albright, Madeleine K. (1997) 'Statement to Fourth ASEAN Regional Forum Plenary', 27 July, at http://www.state.gov/www/statements/970727.html.

——(1998) 'Intervention at the Fifth ASEAN Regional Forum Plenary', Manila, 27 July.

——(1999) Transcript of Press Conference, Singapore, 25 July.

Anderson, Benedict R.O'G. (1990) *Language and Power: Exploring Political Cultures in Indonesia* (Ithaca and London: Cornell University Press).

——(1991) *Imagined Communities: Reflections on the Origin and Spread of Nationalism* (London:Verso).

Anderson, Jennifer (1997) *The Limits of Sino–Russian Strategic Partnership*, Adelphi Paper 315 (Oxford: Oxford University Press/International Institute for Strategic Studies).

Ang Cheng Guan (2000) 'The South China Sea Dispute Revisited', *Australian Journal of International Affairs* 54(2): 201–15.

Annan, Kofi A. (1999) 'Two Concepts of Sovereignty', originally published in the *Economist*, 18 September 1999, available at http://www.un.org/Overview /SG/Kaecon.htm.

—— (2000) 'We the Peoples: The Role of the United Nations in the 21st Century', http://www.un.org/millennium/sg/report/full.htm.

Antara News Agency, 2 April 1998, in *Summary of World Broadcasts* FE/3194 B/5, 6 April 1998.

Antolik, Michael (1990) *ASEAN and the Diplomacy of Accommodation* (New York: M.E. Sharpe).

Anwar, Dewi Fortuna (1994) *Indonesia in ASEAN: Foreign Policy and Regionalism* (Singapore: Institute of Southeast Asian Studies).

—— (1996) *Indonesia's Strategic Culture: Ketahanan Nasional, Wawasan Nusantara and Hankamrata*, Australia–Asia Papers no. 75 (Centre for the Study of Australian–Asian Relations, Nathan, Griffith University, May 1996).

Anwar Ibrahim (1997) 'Crisis Prevention', *Newsweek*, 21 July: 29.

ARF (ASEAN Regional Forum) (1994) 'Chairman's Statement', First Meeting of the ASEAN Regional Forum, Bangkok, 25 July 1994.

—— (1995) *The ASEAN Regional Forum: A Concept Paper*, annexed to the Chairman's Statement of the Second Meeting of the ASEAN Regional Forum, 1 August 1995, at http://www.aseansec.org/view.asp?file=/politics/arf—ch2c.htm.

—— (1998a) 'Chairman's Statement', The Fifth Meeting of the ASEAN Regional Forum, Manila, 27 July 1998.

—— (1998b) Annex E to the 'Chairman's Statement', Fifth ASEAN Regional Forum, 27 July 1998.

—— (1998c) Annex F to the 'Chairman's Statement', Fifth ASEAN Regional Forum, 27 July 1998.

—— (1998d) *Co-Chairs' Consolidated List of Possible New ARF CBMs*, annexed to the 'Chairman's Statement', Fifth Meeting of the ASEAN Regional Forum, Manila, 27 July 1998.

—— (1999) 'Chairman's Statement', Sixth Meeting of the ASEAN Regional Forum, Singapore, 26 July 1999.

—— (2000a) 'Chairman's Statement', Seventh Meeting of the ASEAN Regional Forum, Bangkok, 27 July 2000.

—— (2000b) *Concept and Principles of Preventive Diplomacy*, Bangkok, 27 July 2000.

—— (2001a) 'Document on the Concept and Principles of Preventive Diplomacy', at http://www.aseansec.org/view.asp?file=/amm/arf8doc5.htm.

—— (2001b) 'Co-Chair's Paper on the Terms of Reference For the ARF Experts / Eminent Persons (EEPs)', at http://www.aseansec.org/view.asp?file=/amm/ arf8doc7.htm.

—— (2001c) 'Enhanced Role of the ARF Chair (Shared Perspectives Among ARF Members)', at http://www.aseansec.org/view.asp?file=/amm/arf8doc6.htm.

Armacost, Michael H. (1996) *Friends or Rivals? The Insider's Account of U.S.–Japan Relations* (New York: Columbia University Press).

ASEAN (1967) 'Bangkok Declaration', Bangkok, 8 August 1967.

—— (1971a) 'Zone of Peace, Freedom and Neutrality Declaration (Kuala Lumpur Declaration)', Kuala Lumpur, 27 November 1971.

—— (1972) 'Joint Press Statement', The ASEAN Foreign Ministers Meeting to Discuss International Developments Affecting the Region, Manila, 13–14 July 1972.

—— (1973) 'Joint Press Statement', The ASEAN Foreign Ministers' Meeting to Assess the Agreement on Ending the War and Restoring Peace in Vietnam and to Consider its Implications for Southeast Asia, Kuala Lumpur, 15 February 1973.

—— (1976a) 'Treaty of Amity and Co-operation in Southeast Asia', Bali, 24 February 1976.

—— (1976b) 'Declaration of ASEAN Concord', Bali, 24 February 1976.

—— (1979a) 'Statement' by Indonesian Foreign Minister Mochtar Kusumaatmadja as Chairman of the ASEAN Standing Committee on the Escalation of the Armed Conflict Between Vietnam and Kampuchea, Jakarta, 9 January 1979.

—— (1979b) 'Joint Statement', Special Meeting of ASEAN Foreign Ministers on the Current Political Development in the South-East Asian Region, Bangkok, 12 January 1979.

—— (1979c) 'Joint Statement on Refugees', Bangkok, 12 January 1979.

—— (1979d) 'Joint Communiqué', Twelfth ASEAN Ministerial Meeting, Bali, 30 June 1979.

—— (1985) 'Joint Statement by the ASEAN Foreign Ministers on the Kampuchean Problem', Kuala Lumpur, 8 July 1985.

—— (1986a) 'Joint Statement on the Situation in the Philippines', Jakarta, 23 February 1986.

—— (1986b) 'Joint Communiqué', The Nineteenth ASEAN Annual Ministerial Meeting, Manila, 28 June 1986.

—— (1987a) 'Joint Communiqué', The Twentieth ASEAN Annual Ministerial Meeting, Singapore, 16 June 1987.

—— (1987b) 'Joint Press Release of the Informal ASEAN Foreign Ministers' Meeting', Bangkok, 16 August 1987.

—— (1992) 'Singapore Declaration', issued at the Fourth ASEAN Summit, 28 January 1992.

—— (1993) 'Chairman's Statement', ASEAN's Post-Ministerial Conferences Senior Officials Meeting, Singapore, 20–21 May 1993.

—— (1995) 'Statement by the ASEAN Foreign Ministers on the Recent Developments in the South China Sea', 18 March 1995.

—— (1997) 'ASEAN Vision 2020', Kuala Lumpur, 15 December 1997, at http://www.aseansec.org/summit/vision97.htm.

—— (1998a) 'Terms of Understanding on the Establishment of the ASEAN Surveillance Process', Washington, DC, 4 October 1998.

—— (1998b) 'Hanoi Plan of Action', Hanoi, 16 December 1998.

—— (1999) 'Joint Communiqué', The Thirty-Second Ministerial Meeting, Singapore, 23–24 July 1999, at http://www.aseansec.org/view.asp?file=/politics/pramm32.htm.

—— (2000a) 'The ASEAN Troika', Bangkok, 24–25 July 2000, at http://www.aseansec.org/view.asp?file=/amm/as—troika.htm.

—— (2000b) 'Joint Statement of ASEAN + 3 in Support of the Sovereignty, Territorial Integrity and National Unity of Indonesia', Bangkok, 24–28 July, at http://www.aseansec.org//view.asp?=/amm/js—acir.htm.

—— (2000c) 'Joint Communiqué', The Thirty-Third Ministerial Meeting, Bangkok, 24–25 July 2000.

—— (2001) 'Rules of Procedure of the High Council of the Treaty of Amity and Cooperation in Southeast Asia', Hanoi, 23–27 July 2001.

ASEAN–ISIS (1991) *Time for Initiative: Proposals for the Consideration of the Fourth ASEAN Summit* (Jakarta: ASEAN Institutes of Strategic and International Studies), 4 June 1991.

Ashayagachat, Acharya (2001) 'Rangoon Envoy Given Protest Note', *Bangkok Post*, 13 February 2001.

Asher, David L. (1997) 'Fresh Perspectives on East Asia's Future: A U.S.–Japan Alliance for the Next Century', *Orbis* 41(3): 343–75.

Asian Defence Journal (2001) May–June 2001, p.49.

Asiaweek (2000) 'Interview: We Must Stick Together', 1 September 2000.

Aspinall, Edward, Gerry van Klinken and Herb Feith, (eds) (1999) *The Last Days of President Suharto* (Clayton, VIC: Monash Asia Institute, Monash University).

Associated Press (2001) 'Myanmar: Thailand Made Airstrikes', 11 May 2001.

Baguioro, Luz (1999) 'Intervene Only if You Are Invited to Do So', *Straits Times*, 21 November 1999.

Ball, Desmond and Amitav Acharya (eds) (1999) *The Next Stage: Preventive Diplomacy and Security Cooperation in the Asia-Pacific Region* (Canberra: Strategic and Defence Studies Centre, Australian National University/Institute of Defence and Strategic Studies, Nanyang Technological University, Singapore).

Battersby, Paul (1998) 'Border Politics and the Broader Politics of Thailand's International Relations in the 1990s: From Communism to Capitalism', *Pacific Affairs* 71(4): 473–88.

Berdal, Mats and Michael Leifer (1996) 'Cambodia', in James Mayall (ed.) *The New Interventionism 1991–1994: United Nations Experience in Cambodia, Former Yugoslavia and Somalia* (Cambridge: Cambridge University Press), pp. 25–58.

Berita Harian, 30 March 1998, in *Summary of World Broadcasts* FE/3190 B/4, 1 April 1998.

Bernstein, Richard and Ross H. Munro (1998) *The Coming Conflict with China* (New York: Vintage Books).

Berry, Ken (1997) *Cambodia: From Red to Blue: Australia's Initiative for Peace* (St Leonards, NSW: Allen & Unwin/Department of International Relations RSPAS, ANU).

Blair, Dennis (2000) 'On US Security Concerns in Asia', Statement before the House International Relations Committee, Subcommittee on Asia and the Pacific, 8 March 2000, at http:// www.house.gov/international—relations/ap/ussecur/ blair.htm.

Bloodworth, Dennis (1986) *The Tiger and the Trojan Horse* (Singapore: Times Book International).

Boutros-Ghali, Boutros (1992) 'Agenda of Peace: Preventive Diplomacy, Peace-making and Peace-keeping', reprinted as Appendix A in Adam Roberts and Benedict Kingsbury (1993) *United Nations, Divided World: The UN's Roles in International Relations*, second edition (Oxford: Oxford University Press), pp. 470–98.

Boyce, Peter (1968) *Malaysia and Singapore in International Diplomacy: Documents and Commentaries* (Sydney: Sydney University Press).

Broinowski, Alison (ed.) (1982) *Understanding ASEAN* (London and Basingstoke: Macmillan).

—— (ed.) (1990) *ASEAN into the 1990s* (London and Basingstoke: Macmillan).

Brooke, Micool (2000) ' "Drug Invasion" Fuels Thai Force Modernisation Programme', *Asian Defence Journal* 5/2000, pp. 10–13.

Brown, T. Louise (1991) *War and Aftermath in Vietnam* (London and New York: Routledge).

Bull, Hedley (1977) *The Anarchical Society: A Study of Order in World Politics* (Basingstoke and London: Macmillan).

—— (ed.) (1984) *Intervention in World Politics* (Oxford: Clarendon Press).

Bull, Hedley and Adam Watson (1984) 'Conclusions', in Hedley Bull and Adam Watson (eds) *The Expansion of International Society* (Oxford: Clarendon Press), pp. 425–35.

Burr, Wilhelm (ed.) (1998) *The Kissinger Transcripts: The Top-Secret Talks with Beijing and Moscow* (New York: New Press).

Burton, John (ed.) (1990) *Conflict: Human Needs Theory* (Basingstoke: Macmillan).

Busse, Nikolas (1999) 'Constructivism and Southeast Asian Security', *Pacific Review* 12(1): 39–60.

Buszynski, Leszek (1988) 'The Philippines, ASEAN and the Future of the American Bases', *The World Today* 44(5): 82–5.

—— (1992a) 'Southeast Asia in the Post-Cold War Era: Regionalism and Security', *Asian Survey* XXXII(9): 830–47.

—— (1992b) 'ASEAN's Security Dilemmas', *Survival* 34(2): 90–107.

—— (1992c) *Gorbachev and Southeast Asia* (London and New York: Routledge).

—— (1994) 'Thailand's Foreign Policy: Management of a Regional Vision', *Asian Survey* XXXIV(8): 721–38.

—— (1995) 'China and the ASEAN Region', in Stuart Harris and Gary Klintworth (eds) *China as a Great Power: Myths, Realities and Challenges in the Asia-Pacific Region* (New York: St. Martin's Press), pp. 161–84.

—— (1998) 'Thailand and Myanmar: The Perils of "Constructive Engagement" ', *Pacific Review* 11(2): 290–305.

Buzan, Barry (1991) *Peoples, States and Fear: An Agenda for International Security Studies in the Post-Cold War Era*, second edition (Hemel Hempstead: Harvester Wheatsheaf).

Buzan, Barry, Ole Waever and Jaap de Wilde (1998) *Security: A New Framework for Analysis* (Boulder, CO: Lynne Rienner).

Caballero-Anthony, Mely (1998) 'Mechanisms of Dispute Settlement: The ASEAN Experience', *Contemporary Southeast Asia* 20(1): 38–66.

Carey, Peter (1997) *From Burma to Myanmar: Military Rule and the Struggle for Democracy*, Conflict Studies Paper 304 (London: Research Institute for the Study of Conflict and Terrorism).

Carr, E.H. (1946) *The Twenty Years' Crisis: An Introduction to the Study of International Relations* (London and Basingstoke: Macmillan).

Carter, Ashton B. and William J. Perry (1999) *Preventive Defense: A New Security Strategy for America* (Washington, DC: Brookings Institution Press).

Chaipitat, Kulachada (2001) 'ASEAN Members Are "Now More Stable" ', *The Nation*, 15 April 2001.

Chalermpalanupap, Termsak (1999) 'ASEAN-10: Meeting the Challenges' at http://www.aseansec.org/secgen/articles/asean—10.htm.

Chalmers, Malcolm (1996) *Confidence-Building in South-East Asia* (Bradford: Westview Press).

Chan, Gerald (1999) *Chinese Perspectives on International Relations: A Framework for Analysis* (Basingstoke and London: Macmillan).

Chan, Joseph (1995) 'The Asian Challenge to Universal Human Rights: A Philosophical Appraisal', in James T. H. Tang (ed.) *Human Rights and International Relations in the Asia Pacific* (London and New York: Pinter), pp. 25–38.

Chan Heng Chee (1969) 'Singapore's Foreign Policy, 1965–1968', *Journal of Southeast Asian History* 10(1): 177–91.

—— (1971) *Singapore: The Politics of Survival, 1965–1967* (Singapore and Kuala Lumpur: Oxford University Press).

Chanda, Nayan (1986) *Brother Enemy: The War after the War* (New York: Collier Books).

—— (2001) 'So Much Oil, So Hard To Get', *Far Eastern Economic Review*, 21 June 2001: 28–9.

Chanda, Nayan, Rigobarto Tiglao and John McBeth (1995) 'Territorial Imperative', *Far Eastern Economic Review*, 23 February: 14–16.

Chandler, David (1998) *A History of Cambodia*, second edition (Chiang Mai: Silkworm Books).

Chang, C.Y. (1983) 'The Sino-Vietnam Rift: Political Impact on China's Relations with Southeast Asia', *Contemporary Southeast Asia* 4(4): 538–64.

Chang Pao-min (1985) *Kampuchea Between China and Vietnam* (Singapore: Singapore University Press).

Che Man, W.K. (1990) *Muslim Separatism: The Moros of Southern Philippines and the Malays of Southern Thailand* (Singapore: Oxford University Press).

Chee, Stephen (1989) 'Southeast Asia in 1988', in Ng Chee Yuen (ed.) *Southeast Asian Affairs 1989* (Singapore: ISEAS), pp. 3–36.

Chen Jie (1993) 'Human Rights: ASEAN's new importance to China', *The Pacific Review* 6(2): 227–37.

Chen Peiyao (1995) 'Big-Power Relations in the Asia-Pacific Region', *IISS Journal* (Shanghai) 1(3): 1–11.

—— (1998) 'Grand Adjustment of Sino-U.S. Relations: On a Constructive Strategic Partnership', *IISS Journal* (Shanghai) 5(2): 1–8.

Chhon, Keat (2000) 'Flexible Engagement vs Non-Interference: Cambodia's Official Position', in Kao Kim Hourn (ed.) *ASEAN's Non-Interference Policy: Principles Under Pressure?* (London: ASEAN Academic Press), pp. 21–4.

Chin Kin Wah (1987) *The Defence of Malaysia and Singapore: The Transformation of a Security System 1957–1971* (Cambridge: Cambridge University Press).

—— (1991) 'The Five Power Defence Arrangements: Twenty Years After', *Pacific Review* 4(3): 193–203.

—— (1995) 'ASEAN: Consolidation and Institutional Change', *Pacific Review* 8(3): 424–39.

China's National Defense (1998) (Beijing: Information Office of the State Council of the People's Republic of China).

Ching, Frank (1997) 'ASEAN Faces New Challenges', *Far Eastern Economic Review*, 14 August: 30.

Choi, Kang and Panitan Wattanayagon (1997) 'Development of Defence White Papers in the Asia-Pacific Region', in Bates Gill and J.N. Mak (eds) *Arms, Transparency and Security in South-East Asia*, SIPRI Research Report no. 13 (Oxford: Oxford University Press), pp. 79–92.

Chongkittavorn, Kavi (1998) 'Thai Proposal Needs ASEAN Support', *The Nation*, 13 July: A4.

—— (1999a) 'Indonesia to Help East Timor into ASEAN', *The Nation*, 17 February, at http://202.44.251.4/nationnews/1999/199902/19990217/39186.html.

—— (1999b) 'Asean Clout Lacking in Regional Forum', *The Nation*, 31 May.

—— (1999c) 'ASEAN Lacking Unanimity for Talks', *The Nation*, 9 September 1999.

—— (1999d) 'ASEAN Peace-keepers Must Go to Timor', *The Nation*, 13 September 1999, at http://202.44.251.4/nationnews/1999/199909/19990913/49535html.

Chopra, Jarat (2000) 'The UN's Kingdom of East Timor', *Survival* 42(3): 27–39.

Christiansen, Thomas J. (1999) 'China, the U.S.–Japan Alliance, and the Security Dilemma in East Asia', *International Security* 23(4): 49–80.

Clad, James (1998) 'The "Passing Gendarme": Military Power and Economic Access', in Selig S. Harrison and Clyde V. Prestowitz, Jr (eds) *Asia After the 'Miracle': Redefining U.S. Economic and Security Priorities* (Washington, DC: Economic Strategy Institute), pp. 245–56.

Cook, Paul and Martin Minogue (1997) 'Economic Reform and Political Conditionality', in Peter Carey (ed.) *Burma: The Challenge of Change in a Divided Society* (Basingstoke and London: Macmillan), pp. 183–208.

Cossa, Ralph A. (1996) 'Bilateralism Versus Multilateralism: An American Perspective', *Korean Journal of Defence Analysis* VIII(2): 7–27.

—— (1998) 'Mischief Reef: A Double Betrayal', *PacNet Newsletter* no. 49, 22 December, at http://www.csis.org/html/pac4998.html.

Cotton, James (1999) 'Peacekeeping in East Timor: An Australian Policy Departure', *Australian Journal of International Affairs*, 53(3): 237–46.

—— (2001) 'Against the Grain: The East Timor Intervention', *Survival* 43(1): 127–42.

Crispin, Shawn W. (2000) 'Ties That Bind', *Far Eastern Economic Review*, 10 August 2000, at http://www.feer.com/articles/2000/0008—10/p22region.html.

Crispin, Shawn W. and Michael Vatikiotis (2001) 'Back to Business', *Far Eastern Economic Review*, 22 February 2001: 26–7.

Cronin, Patrick M. (1992) 'Pacific Rim Security: Beyond Multilateralism?', *Pacific Review* 5(3): 209–20.

Cronin, Richard P. (1997) 'Congress and U.S. Policy Towards ASEAN and Southeast Asia', *Borneo Review* VIII(2), December 1997: 103–17.

CSCAP draft on preventive diplomacy principles, see *Preventive Diplomacy: Definition and Principles*, http://www.cmc.sandia/gov/CSCAP/statemtpd.htm.

CSCAP Singapore (1999) 'Review of Preventive Diplomacy Activities in the Asia-Pacific Region', in Desmond Ball and Amitav Acharya (eds) *The Next Stage: Preventive Diplomacy and Security Cooperation in the Asia-Pacific Region* (Canberra: Strategic and Defence Studies Centre, Australian National University/Institute of Defence and Strategic Studies, Nanyang Technological University, Singapore), pp. 293–323.

Cumings, Bruce (1999) *Parallax Visions: Making Sense of American–East Asian Relations at the End of the Century* (Durham: Duke University).

da Cunha, Derek (1993) 'Whittling Away Asia's Security Bedrock', *Wall Street Journal Europe*, 27 July: 6.

—— (1998) 'Concerns Loom Over Security', *Straits Times*, 19 July, at http://www.asia1.com.sg/straitstimes/pages/cpe1—0719.html.

—— (1999) 'Singapore in 1998: Managing Expectations, Shoring-up National Morale', *Southeast Asian Affairs 1999* (Singapore: Institute of Southeast Asian Studies), pp. 271–90.

'Declaration on Principles of International Law Concerning Friendly Relations and Co-operation among States in accordance with the Charter of the United Nations' (1971) UNGA Res. 2625 (XXV) 25 UN GAOR, supp. (no.28) 121, UN Doc. A/8028.

Der Derian, James (1987) *On Diplomacy: A Genealogy of Western Estrangement* (Oxford: Basil Blackwell).

—— (1996) 'Hedley Bull and the Idea of Diplomatic Culture', in Rick Fawn and Jeremy Larkins (eds) *International Society after the Cold War: Anarchy and Order Reconsidered* (London: Macmillan), pp. 84–100.

Desker, Barry (1991) 'Developments in Indonesia–Singapore Bilateral Relations: Politics', in Lau Teik Soon and Bilveer Singh (eds) *Singapore–Indonesia Relations: Problems and Prospects* (Singapore: Singapore Institute of International Affairs), pp. 101–10.

Deutsch, Karl W., Sidney A. Burrell, Robert A. Kann, Maurice Lee Jr, Martin Lichterman, Raymond E. Lindgren, Francis L. Loewenheim and Richard W. van Wagenen (1957) *Political Community and the North Atlantic Area: International Organization in the Light of Historical Experience* (Princeton, NJ: Princeton University Press).

Devan, Janadas (1998) 'Will the US Never Learn', *Straits Times*, 27 November 1998.

Dhume, Sadanand (2001) 'Islam's Holy Warriors', *Far Eastern Economic Review*, 26 April 2001: 54–7.

Dittmer, Lowell (1997) 'Unstable Outlook: China's Quest for a Coherent Foreign Policy', *Harvard Asia Pacific Review* 2(1): 14–17.

Djalal, Dino Patti (1996) 'The Geopolitics of Indonesia's Maritime Territorial Policy (Jakarta: Centre for Strategic and International Studies).

—— (1999) 'The Indonesian Experience in Facilitating a Peace Settlement Between the Government of the Republic of the Philippines and the Moro National Liberation Front', in Desmond Ball and Amitav Acharya (eds) *The Next Stage: Preventive Diplomacy and Security Cooperation in the Asia-Pacific Region* (Canberra: ANU/Institute of Defence and Strategic Studies in Singapore), pp. 199–207.

Doronila, Amando (1998) 'Estrada's Brawling Style of Diplomacy', *Philippine Daily Inquirer*, 9 November 1998.

Dosch, Jörn (1995) 'Die Relevanz des integrationstheoretischen Ansatzes von Karl W. Deutsch für die Assoziation südostasiatischer Nationen (ASEAN)', *Welt-Trends* Nr. 7: 66–85.

Draguhn, Werner and Peter Schier (eds) (1987) *Indochina: der permanente Konflikt* [Indochina: The Permanent Conflict], third extended edition (Hamburg: Institute für Asienkunde).

Dunn, James (2001) 'Crimes Against Humanity in East Timor, January to October 1999: Their Nature and Causes', http://www.etan.org/etanpdf/pdf1/dunn.pdf.

Dunne, Tim (1998) *Inventing International Society. A History of the English School* (Basingstoke: Macmillan).

Dupont, Alan (1996) 'Is There An "Asian Way"?', *Survival* 38(2): 13–33.

—— (2000) 'ASEAN's Response to the East Timor Crisis', *Australian Journal of International Affairs* 54(2): 163–70.

EIU (1998) *EIU Country Report*, 2nd quarter 1998, Vietnam (London: Economist Intelligence Unit).

—— (1999) *EIU Country Report*, 1st quarter 1999, Malaysia, Brunei (London: Economist Intelligence Unit).

Embassy of the People's Republic of China, Washington DC (1998) 'The Question of the South China Sea: Its Origins and Current Status', at http://www.china-embassy.org/Cgi-Bin/Press.pl?SouthChinaSea.

Emmerson, Donald K. (1996a) 'Indonesia, Malaysia, Singapore: A Regional Security Core?', in Richard J. Ellings and Sheldon W. Simon (eds) *Southeast Asian Security in the New Millennium* (Armonk, NY: M.E. Sharpe), pp. 34–88.

—— (1996b) 'US Policy Themes in Southeast Asia in the 1990s', in David Wurfel and Bruce Burton (eds) *Southeast Asia in the New World Order: The Political Economy of a Dynamic Region* (Basingstoke and London: Macmillan), pp. 103–27.

Ero, Comfort Ekhuase (1999) 'The Evolution of Norms in International Relations: Intervention and the Principle of Non-Intervention in Intra-African Affairs' unpublished PhD thesis, University of London, LSE.

Estrada, Joseph Ejercito (1998) 'East Asia at the Crossroads', Keynote Address at the World Economic Forum's East Asia Economic Summit, Singapore, 13 October, at http://www.erap.com/web/speeches/speech11.htm.

Evans, Grant and Kelvin Rowley (1990) *Red Brotherhood at War: Vietnam, Cambodia and Laos since 1975* (London and New York: Verso).

Evans, Paul M. (1996) 'Towards a Pacific Concord', in Mohamed Jawhar Hassan and Sheikh Ahmad Raffie (eds) *Bringing Peace to the Pacific* (Kuala Lumpur: ISIS Malaysia), pp. 5–25.

Fairbank, John King (ed.) (1968) *The Chinese World Order: Traditional China's Foreign Relations* (Cambridge, MA: Harvard University Press).

Fifield, Russell H. (1968) *The Diplomacy of Southeast Asia: 1945–1958* (Hamden, CT: Archon Books).

—— (1980) 'ASEAN: The Perils of Viability', *Contemporary Southeast Asia* 2(3): 199–212.

Finkelstein, David and Michael McDevitt (1999) 'Competition and Consensus: China "New Concept of Security" and the United States Security Strategy for the East Asia-Pacific Region', *PacNet Newsletter*, no. 1, 8 January 1999.

Finnemore, Martha (1996) *National Interests in International Society* (Ithaca, NY: Cornell University Press).

Finnemore, Martha and Kathryn Sikkink (1998) 'International Norm Dynamics and Political Change', *International Organization* 52(4): 887–917.

Freeman, Nick J. (1998) 'Laos: No Safe Haven from the Regional Tumult', in Derek da Cunha and John Funston (eds) *Southeast Asian Affairs 1998* (Singapore: Institute of Southeast Asian Studies), pp. 141–57.

Friedman, Edward (1996) 'Goodwill Lost in Translation', *Far Eastern Economic Review*, 1 August: 27.

Frost, Frank (1993) *Vietnam's Foreign Relations: Dynamics of Change*, Pacific Strategic Papers (Singapore: Institute of Southeast Asian Studies).

Funston, John (1979) 'The Third Indochina Conflict', *Contemporary Southeast Asia* 1(3): 268–89.

—— (1998a) 'ASEAN: Out of Its Depth?', *Contemporary Southeast Asia* 20(1): 22–37.

—— (1998b) 'Thai Foreign Policy: Seeking Influence', in Derek da Cunha and John Funston (eds) *Southeast Asian Affairs 1998* (Singapore: Institute of Southeast Asian Studies), pp. 292–306.

—— (1999) 'Challenges Facing ASEAN in a More Complex Age', *Contemporary Southeast Asia* 21(2): 205–19.

Ganesan, Narayanan (1998) 'Singapore: Realist cum Trading State', in Muthiah Alagappa (ed.) *Asian Security Practice: Material and Ideational Influences* (Stanford, CA: Stanford University Press), pp. 579–607.

Gao Jiquan (1996) 'China Holds High the Banner of Peace' (in *Jiefangjun Bao* [Liberation Army Daily], 27 June 1996), in *Summary of World Broadcasts* FE/2651 G/5–G/6, 29 June 1996.

Garrett, Banning and Bonnie Glaser (1994) 'Multilateral Security in the Asia-Pacific Region and its Impact on Chinese Interests: Views from Beijing', *Contemporary Southeast Asia* 16(1): 14–34.

—— (1997) 'Chinese Apprehensions about Revitalization of the U.S.–Japan Alliance', *Asian Survey* 37(4): 383–402.

Garver, John W. (1992) 'China's Push Through the South China Sea: The Interaction of Bureaucratic and National Interests', *China Quarterly*, no. 132, December 1992: 999–1,028.

—— (1997) *Face Off: China, the United States, and Taiwan's Democratization* (Seattle and London: University of Washington Press).

—— (1998) 'Sino-Russian Relations', in Samuel S. Kim (ed.) *China and the World: Chinese Foreign Policy Faces the New Millennium* fourth edition (Boulder, CO: Westview Press), pp. 114–32.

Gates, Robert M. (1996) 'Preventive Diplomacy: Concept and Reality', *PacNet Newsletter*, no. 39, 27 September, at http://www.csis.org.html/pac3996.html.

Giddens, Anthony (1984) *The Constitution of Society: Outline of a Theory of Structuration* (Cambridge: Polity Press).

Gilks, Anne (1992) *The Breakdown of the Sino-Vietnamese Alliance, 1970–1979* (Berkely, CA: Institute of East Asian Studies, University of California).

Godwin, Paul H.B. (1996) 'From Continent to Periphery: PLA Doctrine, Strategy and Capabilities Toward 2000', *China Quarterly*, no. 146, June 1996: 443–87.

Goh Chok Tong (2001) 'Managing Strategic Change in East Asia', Keynote Address to the US–ASEAN Business Council at the US Ambassadors Tour 2001 Annual Dinner, Washington, DC, 12 June 2001.

Gomez, Edmund Terence and K. S. Jomo (1997) *Malaysia's Political Economy: Politics, Patronage and Profits* (Kuala Lumpur: Cambridge University Press).

Gong, Gerrit W. (1984a) *The Standard of 'Civilisation' in International Society* (Oxford: Clarendon Press).

—— (1984b) 'China's Entry Into International Society', in Hedley Bull and Adam Watson (eds) *The Expansion of International Society* (Oxford: Clarendon), pp. 171–84.

Gordon, Bernard K. (1966) *The Dimensions of Conflicts in Southeast Asia* (Englewood Cliffs, NJ: Prentice-Hall).

Grader, Sheila (1988) 'The English School of International Relations: Evidence and Evaluation', *Review of International Studies* 14(1): 29–44.

Green, Michael J. and Patrick M. Cronin (eds) (1999) *The US–Japan Alliance: Past, Present, and Future* (New York: Council on Foreign Relations Press).

Gullick, J.M. (1967) *Malaysia and its Neighbours* (London: Routledge & Kegan Paul).

Gunder Frank, Andre (1998) *ReOrient: Global Economy in the Asian Age* (Berkeley, CA: University of California Press).

Gurtov, Melvin (1970) *Southeast Asia Tomorrow: Problems and Prospects for U.S. Policy* (Baltimore and London: John Hopkins Press).

—— (1971) *China and Southeast Asia – The Politics of Survival: A Study of Foreign Policy Interaction* (Lexington, MA: D.C. Heath & Co.).

Gurtov, Melvin and Byong Moo Hwang (1998) *China's Security: The New Roles of the Military* (Boulder, CO: Lynne Rienner).

Gyaw, Ohn (1998) *Statement at the Thirty-First ASEAN Ministerial Meeting*, Manila, 24 July 1998, at http://www.aseansec.org/view.asp?file=/amm/amm31osu.htm.

Habermas, Jürgen (1984) *The Theory of Communicative Action, Volume I: Reason and the Rationalization of Society*, trans. T. McCarthy (Boston, MA: Beacon Press).

—— (1987) *The Theory of Communicative Action, Volume II: Lifeworld and System: A Critique of Functionalist Reason*, trans. T. McCarthy (Boston, MA: Beacon Press).

—— (1992) *Nachmetaphysisches Denken, philosophische Aufsätze* [Post-Metaphysical Thinking: Philosophical Essays] (Frankfurt/M: Suhrkamp).

—— (1996) *Between Facts and Norms: Contributions to a Discourse Theory of Law and Democracy*, trans. W. Rehg (Cambridge, MA: MIT Press).

Hall, D.G.E. (1981) *A History of South-East Asia*, fourth edition (Basingstoke and London: Macmillan).

Hamzah, B.A. (1992) 'Introduction: ZOPFAN – Its Strategic Intent', in B.A. Hamzah (ed.) *Southeast Asia and Regional Peace: A Study of the Southeast Asian Concept of Zone of Peace, Freedom and Neutrality (ZOPFAN)* (Kuala Lumpur: ISIS), pp. 1–9.

Hänggi, Heiner (1992) *Neutralität in Südostasien: das Projekt einer Zone des Friedens, der Freiheit und der Neutralität* [Neutrality in Southeast Asia: The Project for a Zone of Peace, Freedom and Neutrality] (Bern: P. Haupt).

Haron, Mohamed (1998) 'Understanding Malaysia's Strategic National Perspective', *Asian Affairs* 1(3): 19–34.

Heder, Stephen (1981) 'The Kampuchean–Vietnamese Conflict', in David W.P. Elliott (ed.) *The Third Indochina Conflict* (Boulder, CO: Westview Press), pp. 21–67.

Heder, Steve and Judy Ledgerwood (eds) (1996) *Propaganda, Politics, and Violence in Cambodia: Democratic Transition under United Nations Peace-keeping* (New York: M.E. Sharpe).

Heine-Geldern, Robert (1973) 'Conceptions of State and Kingship in Southeast Asia', in John T. McAlister, Jr (ed.) *Southeast Asia: The Politics of National Integration* (New York: Random House), pp. 74–89.

Henderson, Jeannie (1999) *Reassessing ASEAN*, Adelphi Paper 328 (Oxford: Oxford University Press/ISIS).

Hernandez, Carolina G. (1998) 'Towards Re-examining the Non-Intervention Principle in ASEAN Political Co-operation', *Indonesian Quarterly* 26(3): 164–70.

Hiebert, Murray (1997) 'All For One', *Far Eastern Economic Review*, 7 August: 26.

Hiebert, Murray and Michael Vatikiotis (1997) 'Conflict of Interests', *Far Eastern Economic Review*, 24 July: 18–19.

Higgott, Richard (2000) 'The International Relations of the Asian Economic Crisis: A Study in the Politics of Resentment', in Richard Robison, Mark Beeson, Kanishka Jayasuriya and Hyuk-Rae Kim (eds) *Politics and Markets in the Wake of the Asian Crisis* (London and New York: Routledge), pp. 261–82.

Hill, Michael and Lian Kwen Fee (1995) *The Politics of Nation Building and Citizenship in Singapore* (London and New York: Routledge).

Hirschfield, Claire (1968) 'The Struggle for the Mekong Banks, 1892–1896', *Journal of Southeast Asian History* 9(1): 25–52.

Hitchcock, David I. (1997) *Factors Affecting East Asian Views of the United States*, CSIS Report (Washington, DC: Center for Strategic & International Studies).

Hoang Anh Tuan (1993) 'Why Hasn't Vietnam Gained ASEAN Membership', *Contemporary Southeast Asia* 15(3): 280–91.

—— (1996) 'ASEAN Dispute Management: Implications for Vietnam and an Expanded ASEAN', *Contemporary Southeast Asia* 18(1): 61–80.

Honneth, Axel (1995a) *The Struggle for Recognition: The Moral Grammar of Social Conflicts* (Cambridge: Polity Press).

—— (1995b) 'Author's Introduction', in Axel Honneth (1995) *The Fragmented World of the Social: Essays in Social and Political Philosophy*, edited by Charles Wright (New York, AL: State University of New York Press), pp. xi–xxv.

Hooker, M.B. (1988a) 'English Law in Sumatra, Java, The Straits Settlements, Malay States, Sarawak, North Borneo and Brunei', in M.B. Hooker (ed.) *Laws of South-East Asia, Volume II: European Laws in South-East Asia* (Singapore: Butterworth & Co.), pp. 299–446.

—— (1988b) 'The "Europeanization" of Siam's Law 1855–1908', in M.B. Hooker (ed.) *Laws of South-East Asia, Volume II: European Laws in South-East Asia* (Singapore: Butterworth & Co.), pp. 531–607.

Hughes, Christopher R. (1995) 'China and Liberalism Globalised', *Millennium* 24(3): 425–45.

Hunt, Michael H. (1996) *The Genesis of Chinese Communist Foreign Policy* (New York: Columbia University Press).

Huxley, Tim (1984) *The ASEAN States Defence Policies, 1975–1981: Military Responses to Indochina*, Working Paper 88 (Canberra: Strategic and Defence Studies Centre, Australian National University).

—— (1993) *Insecurity in the ASEAN Region*, Whitehall Paper 23 (London: Royal United Services Institute for Defence Studies).

—— (1998) 'A Threat in the South China Sea? A Rejoinder', *Security Dialogue* 29(1): 113–18.

Ileto, Reynaldo Clemena (1979) *Pasyon and Revolution. Popular Movements in the Philippines, 1840–1910* (Quezon City, Metro Manila: Ateneo de Manila University Press).

—— (1992) 'Religion and Anti-Colonial Movements', in Nicholas Tarling (ed.) *The Cambridge History of Southeast Asia, Volume II: The Nineteenth and Twentieth Centuries* (Cambridge: Cambridge University Press), pp. 197–248.

Inbaraj, Sonny (1997) *East Timor: Blood and Tears in ASEAN*, revised edition (Chiang Mai: Silkworm Books).

Indonesia–Malaysia Joint Communiqué (1970) reprinted in *Asia-Pacific Recorder* 1(2), May 1970: 26–8.

Indorf, Hans H. (1975) *ASEAN: Problems and Prospects*, Occasional Paper no. 38 (Singapore: Institute of Southeast Asian Studies).

—— (1984) *Impedimemts to Regionalism in Southeast Asia: Bilateral Constraints Among ASEAN Member States* (Singapore: Institute of Southeast Asian Studies).

Innes-Brown, Marc and Mark J. Valencia (1993) 'Thailand's Resource Diplomacy in Indochina and Myanmar', *Contemporary Southeast Asia* 14(4): 332–51.

Irvine, Roger (1982) 'The Formative Years of ASEAN: 1967–1975', in Alison Broinowski (ed.) *Understanding ASEAN* (London: Macmillan), pp. 8–36.

Ishak bin Tadin (1960) 'Dato Onn and Malay Nationalism, 1946–1951', *Journal of Southeast Asian History* 1 (1960), pp. 56–88.

Jackson, Karl D. (1982) 'U.S. Policy, ASEAN, and the Kampuchean Crisis', in Robert Scalapino and Jusuf Wanandi (eds) *Economic, Political and Security Issues in Southeast Asia in the 1980s* (Berkeley, CA: Institute of East Asian Studies, University of California), pp. 124–39.

Jackson, Keith (1971) ' "Because It's There ..." A Consideration of the Decision to Commit New Zealand Troops to Malaysia Beyond 1971', *Journal of Southeast Asian Affairs* 2(1): 22–31.

Jayakumar, S. (1996) 'The Southeast Asian Drama: Evolution and Future Challenges', Georgetown University Inaugural Distinguished Lecture on Southeast Asia, Washington, DC, 22 April.

—— (1997a) 'Opening Statement', Thirtieth ASEAN Ministerial Meeting, Kuala Lumpur, 24 July, at http://www.aseansec.org/view.asp?file=/amm/amm31osu.htm.

—— (1997b) 'ASEAN at Thirty: Accomplishment and Challenges', Speech to the Los Angeles World Affairs Council and the Asia Society, Southern California Center, Los Angeles, 18 November, at http://www.lawac.org/speech/jayakum.html.

—— (1998) 'Opening Statement', Thirty-first ASEAN Ministerial Meeting, Manila, 24 July, at http://www.gov.sg/mfa/speeches/index.htm.

—— (1999a) 'Closing Statement' as Chairman of the Thirty-Second ASEAN Standing Committee, 21 July 1999, at http://www.mfa.gov.sg.

—— (1999b) 'Remarks by Singapore Foreign Minister Jayakumar on Return from AMM Retreat on 23 July 1999', at http://www.gov.sg/mfa/amm/speeches/1999072302.html.

—— (1999c) 'Will the UN Survive in the 21st', Address given at the Fifty-fourth United Nations General Assembly, New York, 24 September, at http://www.gov.sg/mfa/speeches/index.htm.

—— (2000) 'Opening Statement', Thirty-third ASEAN Ministerial Meeting, Bangkok, 24 July 2000, at http://www.aseansec.org/view.asp?file=/amm/amm33osg.htm.

Jayasankaran, S. (1998) 'Under the Gun', *Far Eastern Economic Review*, 3 September: 20.

Jepperson, Ronald L., Alexander Wendt and Peter J. Katzenstein (1996) 'Norms, Identity, and Culture in National Security', in Peter J. Katzenstein (ed.) *The Culture of National Security: Norms and Identity* (New York: Columbia University Press), pp. 33–75.

Jeshurun, Chandran (ed.) (1985) *Governments and Rebellions in Southeast Asia* (Singapore: Institute of Southeast Asian Studies).

Ji Guoxing (1998) 'China Versus South China Sea Security', *Security Dialogue* 29(1) 1998: 101–12.

Johnston, Alastair Iain (1996) 'Learning Versus Adaptation: Explaining Change in Chinese Arms Control Policy in the 1980s and 1990s', *China Journal* no.35, January 1996: 27–61.

Joint Press Release on Indonesian Foreign Minister's Visit to Vietnam (1987) in *Summary of World Broadcasts* FE/8633/A3/1, 30 July 1987.

Joint Statement of the Meeting of Heads of State/Government of the Member States of ASEAN and the President of the People's Republic of China (1997) Kuala Lumpur, 16 December 1997.

Jorgensen-Dahl, Arnfinn (1982) *Regional Organization and Order in South-East Asia* (Basingstoke and London: Macmillan).

Kamarulzaman Askandar (1996) *ASEAN as a Process of Conflict Management: ASEAN and Regional Security in Southeast Asia: 1967–1994*, unpublished PhD thesis, University of Bradford, Department of Peace Studies.

Kamarulzinam Abdullah (1999) 'National Security and Malay Unity: The Issue of Radical Religious Elements in Malaysia', *Contemporary Southeast Asia* 21(2): 261–82.

Kasitipradit, Sermsuk and Wassana Nanuam (2001) 'Thaksin to Speed Up Visit to Rangoon', *Bangkok Post*, 30 May 2001, at http://www.asiamedia.ucla.edu/Weekly2001/06.05.2001/Thailand.htm.

Katzenstein, Peter J. (ed.) (1996) *The Culture of National Security: Norms and Identity in World Politics* (New York: Columbia University Press).

Kelly, James A. (2001) 'U.S. Policy in East Asia and the Pacific: Challenges and Priorities', Testimony before the Subcommittee on East Asia and the Pacific, House Committee on International Relations, Washington, DC, June 12, 2001, at http://www.state.gove/p/eap/rls/2001/3677.htm.

Kerkvliet, Benedict J. (1977) *The Huk Rebellion: A Study of Peasant Revolt in the Philippines* (Berkeley, CA: University of California Press).

Kerr, Pauline, Andrew Mack and Paul Evans (1994) 'The Evolving Security Discourse in the Asia-Pacific', in Andrew Mack and John Ravenhill (eds) *Pacific Cooperation: Building Economic and Security Regimes in the Asia-Pacific Region* (St Leonards, NSW: Allen & Unwin Australia), pp. 233–55.

Khasnor, Johan (1984) *The Emergence of the Modern Malay Administrative Elite* (Singapore: Oxford University Press).

Khoman, Thanat (1970a) 'Thailand and Cambodia', Speech at Asian and Pacific Nations Conference on Cambodia in Djakarta, 16–17 May 1970, reprinted in *Asia Pacific Record: Basic Documents and Vital Speeches* 1(4), July 1970: 3–6.

—— (1970b) 'Speech to American Chamber of Commerce', reprinted in *Asia-Pacific Record: Basic Documents and Vital Speeches* 1(6), September 1970: 9–12.

Khoo Boo Teik (1995) *Paradoxes of Mahathirism: An Intellectual Biography of Mahathir Mohamed* (Kuala Lumpur: Oxford University Press).

Kiernan, Ben (1996) *The Pol Pot Regime: Race, Power, and Genocide in Cambodia Under the Khmer Rouge, 1975–79* (New Haven, CT, and London: Yale University Press).

Kim, Samuel S. (1994) 'China's International Organizational Behaviour', in Thomas W. Robinson and David Shambaugh (eds) *Chinese Foreign Policy: Theory and Practice* (Oxford: Clarendon Press), pp. 401–34.

Kirby, William C. (1994) 'Traditions of Centrality, Authority and Management in Modern China's Relations', in Thomas W. Robinson and David Shambaugh (eds)

Chinese Foreign Policy: Theory and Practice (Oxford: Clarendon Press), pp. 13–29.

Klintworth, Gary (1989) *Vietnam's Intervention in Cambodia International Law* (Canberra: Australian Government Publishing Service).

Koh, Tommy B. (1998) *The Quest for World Order: Perspectives of a Pragmatic Idealist* (Singapore: Times Academic Press).

Kolko, Gabriel (1985) *Vietnam: Anatomy of War 1940–1975* (London and Sydney: Unwin).

—— (1997) *Vietnam: Anatomy of a Peace* (London and New York: Routledge).

Kratochwil, Friedrich V. (1989) *Rules, Norms, and Decisions: On the Conditions of Practical and Legal Reasoning in International Relations and Domestic Affairs* (Cambridge: Cambridge University Press).

Kratoska, Paul and Ben Batson (1992) 'Nationalism and Modernist Reform', in Nicholas Tarling (ed.) *The Cambridge History of Southeast Asia: The Nineteenth and Twentieth Centuries, Vol. 2* (Cambridge: Cambridge University Press), pp. 249–324.

Krepon, Michael (ed.) (1997) *Chinese Perspectives on Confidence-building Measures*, Report No. 23, May (http://www.stimson.org/cbm/china/cbmrpt.htm).

Kusuma-Atmadja, Mochtar (1990) 'Some Thoughts on ASEAN Security Co-operation: An Indonesian Perspective', *Contemporary Southeast Asia* 12(3): 161–71.

—— (1993) 'The Prospects of Establishing a NWFZ in South-East Asia', in Bunn Nagara and K.S. Balakrishnan (eds) *The Making of a Security Community in the Asia-Pacific* (Kuala Lumpur: ISIS Malaysia, Proceedings of the Seventh Asia-Pacific Roundtable, 6–9 June 1993), pp. 295–301.

Lachica, Eduardo (1971) *The Huks; Philippine Agrarian Society in Revolt* (New York: Praeger).

Lam, Willy Wo-Lap (1999) *The Era of Jiang Zemin* (Singapore: Prentice-Hall).

Lau Teik Soon (1969) 'Malaysia–Singapore Relations: Crisis of Adjustment, 1965–1968', *Journal of Southeast Asian History*, 10(1): 155–76.

Lau Teik Soon and Leo Suryadinata (eds) (1988) *Moving Into the Pacific Century: The Changing Regional Order in the Asia-Pacific* (Singapore: Heinemann Asia).

Leaver, Richard (2001) 'The Meanings, Origins and Implications of "the Howard Doctrine"', *Pacific Review* 14(1): 15–34.

Lee Kim Chew (1998a) 'ASEAN Unity Showing Signs of Fraying', *Straits Times*, 23 July: 30.

—— (1998b) 'Jaya Opposes Change to ASEAN Policy', *Straits Times*, 24 July: 3.

—— (2001) 'Distrust Bedevils Thai–Myanmar Relations', *Straits Times*, 11 April.

Lee Kuan Yew (1970) 'Modern Non-Alignment', *Asia Pacific Record* 1(7), October 1970: 10–12.

—— (1998) *The Singapore Story: Memoirs of Lee Kuan Yew* (Singapore: Prentice-Hall).

Lee Lai To (1981) 'Deng Xiaoping's ASEAN Tour: A Perspective on Sino-Southeast Asian Relations, *Contemporary Southeast Asia* 3(1): 58–75.

—— (1999) *China and the South China Sea Dialogues* (Westport, CT: Praeger).

Lee Poh Ping (1982) 'The Indochinese Situation and the Big Powers in Southeast Asia: The Malaysian View', *Asian Survey* XXII(6): 516–23.

Legge, J.D. (1972) *Sukarno: A Political Biography*, second edition (Sydney, London and Boston: Allen & Unwin).

Leifer, Michael (1967) *Cambodia: The Search for Security* (London: Pall Mall Press).

—— (1968) *The Philippine Claim to Sabah* (Zug: Inter Documentation).

—— (1972) *Dilemmas of Statehood* (Singapore: Asia Pacific Press).

—— (1978) *International Straits of the World: Malacca, Singapore, and Indonesia* (Alphen aan den Rijn: Sijthoff and Noordhoff)

—— (1982) 'Kampuchea and Laos – Critical Issues for ASEAN', in Robert Scalapino and Jusuf Wanandi (eds) *Economic, Political and Security Issues in Southeast Asia in the 1980s* (Berkeley, CA: Institute of East Asian Studies, University of California), pp. 13–22.

—— (1983) *Indonesia's Foreign Policy* (London: Allen & Unwin/Royal Institute of International Affairs).

—— (1986) 'The Role and Paradox of ASEAN', in Michael Leifer (ed.) *The Balance of Power in East Asia* (London: Macmillan), pp. 119–31

—— (1988) 'Israel's President in Singapore: Political Catalysis and Transnational Politics', *Pacific Review* 1(4): 341–51.

—— (1989) *ASEAN and the Security of South-East Asia* (London and New York: Routledge).

—— (1993) 'Indochina and ASEAN: Seeking a New Balance', *Contemporary Southeast Asia* 15(3): 269–79.

—— (1995a) 'Vietnam's Foreign Policy in the Post-Soviet Era: Coping with Vulnerability', in Robert S. Ross (ed.) *East Asia in Transition: Toward a New Regional Order* (New York: M.E. Sharpe), pp. 267–92.

—— (1995b) 'Chinese Economic Reform and Security Policy: The South China Sea Connection' *Survival* 37(2): 44–59.

—— (1996a) *Dictionary of the Modern Politics of South-East Asia* (London and New York: Routledge)

—— (1996b) *The ASEAN Regional Forum: Extending ASEAN's Model of Regional Security*. Adelphi Paper 302 (Oxford: Oxford University Press/International Institute for Strategic Studies).

—— (1997a) 'China and the U.S.: Common Standards of Engagement', *TRENDS* (Annex to *Business Times*, Singapore, weekend edition), 25–26 January: iv.

—— (1997b) 'China in Southeast Asia: Interdependence and Accomodation', in David S.G. Goodman and Gerald Segal (eds) *China Rising: Nationalism and Interdependence* (London and New York: Routledge), pp. 156–71.

—— (1997c) 'ASEAN and the Question of Cambodia: Regional Limitations of Enlargement', *IISS Strategic Comments* 3(7): 1–2.

—— (1999a) 'The ASEAN Peace Process: A Category Mistake', *Pacific Review* 12(1): 25–38.

—— (1999b) 'Indonesia's Encounters with China and the Dilemmas of Engagement', in Alastair Iain Johnston and Robert S. Ross (eds) *Engaging China: The Management of an Emerging Power* (London and New York: Routledge), pp. 87–108.

—— (2000) *Singapore's Foreign Policy: Coping with Vulnerability* (London and New York: Routledge)

Leong, Stephen (1987) 'Malaysia and the People's Republic of China in the 1980s', *Asian Survey* XXVII(10): 1,109–26.

Lewis, John W. and Xue Litai (1994) *China's Strategic Seapower: The Politics of Force Modernisation in the Nuclear Age* (Stanford, CA: Stanford University Press).

Liang, Chi-shad (1997) 'Burma's Relations with the People's Republic of China: From Delicate Friendship to Genuine Co-operation', in Peter Carey (ed.) *Burma: The Challenge of Change in a Divided Society* (Basingstoke and London: Macmillan), pp. 71–93.

Lim, Robyn (1998) 'The ASEAN Regional Forum: Building on Sand', *Contemporary Southeast Asia* 20(2), August 1998: 115–36.

Lintner, Bertil (1990) *Outrage: Burma's Struggle for Democracy* (London: White Lotus).

—— (1994) *Burma in Revolt: Opium and Insurgency Since 1948* (Boulder, CO: Westview Press).

—— (1998) 'Home Grown Crisis', *Far Eastern Economic Review*, 30 July 1998: 52–3.

Liu Huaqiu (1995) 'Step-by-Step Confidence Building for the Asian Region: A Chinese Perspective', in Ralph A. Cossa (ed.) *Asia-Pacific Confidence and Security Building Measures* (Washington, DC: Center for Strategic and International Studies), pp. 119–36.

Luu Van Loi (1996) *Le différend vietnamo-chinois sur les archipels: Hoang Sa et Truong Sa* (Hanoi: The Gioi).

Lyon, Peter (1963) *Neutralism* (Leicester: Leicester University Press).

—— (1969) *War and Peace in South-East Asia* (London: Oxford University Press/Royal Institute of International Affairs).

McBeth, John (1997) 'No Meddling', *Far Eastern Economic Review*, 19 June: 16–17.

McCloud, Donald (1986) *System and Process in Southeast Asia: The Evolution of a Region* (Boulder, CO: Westview Press).

Macintyre, Andrew J. (1987) 'Interpreting Indonesian Foreign Policy: The Case of Kampuchea, 1979–1986', *Asian Survey* XXVII(5): 515–34.

McKenna, Thomas M. (1998) *Muslim Rulers and Rebels: Everyday Politics and Armed Separatism in the Southern Philippines* (Berkeley, CA: University of California Press).

Mackie, J.A.C. (1974) *Konfrontasi: The Indonesia–Malaysia Dispute 1963–1966* (Kuala Lumpur: Oxford University Press).

McMichael, Heath (1987) *Indonesian Foreign Policy: Towards a More Assertive Style*, Australia–Asia Papers no. 40 (Centre for the Study of Australian–Asian Relations, Nathan, Griffith University).

McNamara, Robert S. with Brian Van De Mark (1995) *In Retrospect: The Tragedy and Lessons of Vietnam* (New York: Vintage Books).

McSweeney, Bill (1999) *Security, Identity and Interests: A Sociology of International Relations* (Cambridge: Cambridge University Press).

McTurnan Kahin, Audrey R and George McTurnan Kahin (1995) *Subversion as Foreign Policy: The Secret Eisenhower and Dulles Debacle in Indonesia* (New York: New Press).

McTurnan Kahin, George (1956) *The Asian–African Conference: Bandung, Indonesia, April 1955* (Ithaca, NY: Cornell University Press).

—— (1970) *Nationalism and Revolution in Indonesia*, second edition (Ithaca, NY: Cornell University Press).

Magdalena, Federico V. (1997) 'The Peace Process in Mindanao: Problems and Prospects', in Daljit Singh (ed.) *Southeast Asian Affairs 1997* (Singapore: Institute of Southeast Asian Studies), pp. 245–59.

Mahbubani, Kishore (1992) 'New Areas of ASEAN Reaction: Environment, Human Rights and Democracy', *ASEAN–ISIS Monitor*, no.5, October–December 1992: 13–17.

—— (1995) 'The Pacific Impulse', *Survival* 37(1): 105–20.

Malik, J. Mohan (1997) 'Myanmar's Role in Regional Security: Pawn or Pivot?', *Contemporary Southeast Asia* 19(2): 52–73.

Manning, C.A.W. (1962) *The Nature of International Society* (London: LSE).

Marks, Thomas A. (1996) *Maoist Insurgency Since Vietnam* (London: Frank Cass & Co.).

Mauzy, Diane K. (1997) 'The Human Rights and "Asian values" Debate in South-east Asia: Trying to Clarify the Key Issues', *Pacific Review* 10(2): 210–36.

Milne, R.S. (1963) 'The Uniqueness of Philippine Nationalism', *Journal of Southeast Asian History* 4: 82–96.

Mochizuki, Mike M. (ed.) (1997) *Toward a True Alliance: Restructuring U.S.–Japan Security Relations* (Washington, DC: Brookings Institution Press).

—— (2000) 'The US–Japan Alliance: Beyond the Guidelines', *PACNET Newsletter* 35, 1 September, at http://www.csis.org/pacfor/pac0035.html.

Mochizuki, Mike and Michael O'Hanlon (1998) 'A Liberal Vision for the US–Japanese Alliance', *Survival* 40(2): 127–34.

Mohamed Jawhar Hassan (1996) 'Towards a Pacific Concord', in Mohamed Jawhar Hassan and Sheikh Ahmad Raffie (eds) *Bringing Peace to the Pacific* (Kuala Lumpur: ISIS Malaysia), pp. 37–45.

Mohamed Najib Tun Razak, Datuk (1995) *Asia-Pacific's Strategic Outlook: The Shifting of Paradigms* (Petaling Jaya: Pelanduk Publications).

Möller, Kay (1998a) *Sicherheitspartner Peking? Die Beteiligung der Volksrepublik China an vertrauens- und sicherheitsbildenden Maßnahmen seit Ende des kalten Krieges* [Beijing as a Security Partner? The Participation of the People's Republic of China in Confidence- and Security-Building Measures since the End of the Cold War] (Baden-Baden: Nomos Verlagsgesellschaft).

—— (1998b) 'Cambodia and Burma: The ASEAN Way Ends Here', *Asian Survey* XXXVIII(12): 1,087–104.

Moore, Barrington, Jr (1967) *Social Origins of Dictatorship and Democracy: Lord and Peasant in the Making of the Modern World* (London: Allen Lane/Penguin Press).

—— (1978) *Injustice: The Social Bases of Obedience and Revolt* (Basingstoke and London: Macmillan).

Morris, Stephen J. (1999) *Why Vietnam Invaded Cambodia: Political Culture and the Causes of War* (Stanford, CA: Stanford University Press).

Muhammad Ghazali Shafie (1968/1987) 'Statement by the Leader of the Malaysian Delegation to the Malaysia/Philippines Official Talks on the Philippines Claim to Sabah, 15th July 1968', reprinted as 'The Philippine's Claim to Sabah', in S. Rajaratnam (1987) *The Prophetic & the Political. Selected Speeches and Writings of S. Rajaratnam*, edited by Chan Heng Chee and Obaid ul Haq (Singapore: Graham Brash), pp. 118–29.

—— (1980/1982) 'Problems in Southeast Asia: Hopes and Fears. Speech to the Malaysian Armed Forces Staff College, Kuala Lumpur, 9 June', reprinted in Muhammad Ghazali Shafie (1982) *Malaysia: International Relations, Selected Speeches* (Kuala Lumpur: Creative Enterprise Sendirian Berhad), pp. 311–21.

—— (1992) 'Prospects for a Zone of Peace, Freedom and Neutrality (ZOPFAN) in Southeast Asia', in B.A. Hamzah (ed.) *Southeast Asia and Regional Peace: A Study of the Southeast Asian Concept of Zone of Peace, Freedom and Neutrality (ZOPFAN)* (Kuala Lumpur: ISIS), pp. 39–45.

Murphy, Dan (2001) 'Indonesian Crime in the Moluccas', *International Herald Tribune*, 12 January 2001.

Mythans, Seth (2001) 'Women of East Timor Live with Legacy of Rape', *International Herald Tribune*, 2 March 2001.

Nair, Shanti (1998) *Islam in Malaysian Foreign Policy* (London and New York: Routledge).

Narine, Shaun (1997) 'ASEAN and the ARF: The Limits of the "ASEAN way"', *Asian Survey* XXXVII(10): 961–78.

Nathan, K.S. (1998) 'Malaysia: Reinventing the Nation', in Muthiah Alagappa (ed.) *Asian Security: Material and Ideational Influences* (Stanford, CA: Stanford University Press), pp. 513–48.

Ngor, Haing S. (1988) *Surviving the Killing Fields: the Cambodian Odyssey of Haing S. Ngor* (London: Chatto & Windus).

Nguyen Dy Nien (2000) 'Opening Statement', Thirty-Third ASEAN Ministerial Meeting, Bangkok, 24 July 2000, at http://www.aseansec.org/view.asp?file=/amm/amm33ovn.htm.

Nguyen Hong Thao (1998) 'China's Maritime Moves Raise Neighbours' Hackles', *Viet Nam News*, 26 July: 7.

Nguyen Manh Hung (1973) 'The Two Vietnams and the Proposal for a Neutralized Southeast Asia', in Lau Teik Soon (ed.) *New Directions in the International Relations of Southeast Asia* (Singapore: Singapore University Press/Institute of Southeast Asian Studies), pp. 137–45.

Nischalke, Tobias Ingo (2000) 'Insights from ASEAN's Foreign Policy Co-operation: The "ASEAN way": A Real Spirit or a Phantom', *Contemporary Southeast Asia* 22(1): 89–112.

Noble, Lela Garner (1975) 'Ethnicity and Philippine–Malaysian Relations', *Asian Survey* XV(5): 453–72.

Nuechterlein, Donald E. (1965) *Thailand and the Struggle for Southeast Asia* (Ithaca, NY: Cornell University Press).

Ott, Marvin C. (1998) 'From Isolation to Relevance: Policy Considerations', in Robert I. Rotberg (ed.) *Burma: Prospects for a Democratic Future* (Washington, DC: Brookings Institution Press), pp. 69–83.

Panyarachun, Anand (2000) 'A Secure Asean Will Take Re-invention', Address at the First Meeting of ASEAN Army Commanders, Cha-am, 21 November 2000, reprinted in *Bangkok Post*, 22 November 2000, at http://www.scoop.bangkokpost.co.th/bkkpost/2000/bp2000—nov/bp20001122/221100 —news27.html.

Paribatra, Sukhumbhandh (1987) 'ASEAN: Meeting and Failing the Vietnamese Challenge', *Indochina Issues* 95, November 1987.

—— (1998) 'Preparing ASEAN for the Twenty-First Century', Singapore, 31 July, at http://www.mfa.go.th/Policy/fm03.htm.

Paribatra, Sukhumbandh and Chai-Anan Samudavanjia (1986) 'Internal Dimensions of Regional Security in Southeast Asia', in M. Ayoob, (ed.) *Regional Security in the Third World: Case Studies from Southeast Asia and the Middle East* (London and Sydney: Croom Helm), pp. 57–91.

Pascual, Ricardo R. (1962) *The Philosophy of Rizal* (Manila: Pedro B. Ayuda).

Peou, Sorpong (1997) *Conflict Neutralization in the Cambodian War: From Battlefield to Ballot-Box* (Kuala Lumpur: Oxford University Press).

Peterson, M.J. (1997) *Recognition of Governments: Legal Doctrine and State Practice, 1815–1995* (Basingstoke and London: Macmillan).

Phasuk, Sunai (1999) 'Thailand Gives Asean New Meaning', *The Nation*, 24 September 1999.

Pibulsonggran, Nitya (1989) 'Statement on the Situation on Kampuchea, UNGA, 15 November 1989', in *Thailand Foreign Affairs Newsletter* no. 11/1989: 6–8.

Pitsuwan, Surin (1998a) 'Currency Turmoil in Asia: The Strategic Impact', Remarks at the Twelfth Asia-Pacific Roundtable in Kuala Lumpur, 1 June 1998, at http://www.mfa.go.th/Policy/fm01.htm.

—— (1998b) 'Keynote Address' by the Minister of Foreign Affairs of Thailand at the Seminar in Commemoration of the Forty-ninth Anniversary of the Faculty of Political Science, Thammasat University, 12 June 1998, at http://www.mfa.go.th/Policy/fm02.htm.

—— (1998c) 'Opening Statement', Thirty-first ASEAN Ministerial Meeting, Manila, 24 July 1998.

Porter, Gareth (1980) 'Kampuchea's Seat: Cutting the Pol Pot Connection', *Indochina Issues* 8, July 1980.

—— (1981) 'ASEAN and Kampuchea: Shadow and Substance', *Indochina Issues* 14, February 1981.

—— (1982) 'Vietnam Plays a Negotiating Card', *Indochina Issues* 29, October 1982.

Poulgrain, Greg (1998) *The Genesis of Konfrontasi: Malaysia, Brunei, Indonesia, 1945–1965* (Bathurst: Crawford House).

Pretzell, Klaus-Albrecht (1997) 'The Consequences of "ASEAN 10"', *SÜDOSTASIEN aktuell*, July 1997: 324–27.

Puthucheary, Mavis (1987) 'The Administrative Elite', in Zakaria Haji Ahmad (ed.) *Government and Politics of Malaysia* (Singapore: Oxford University Press), pp. 94–110.

Quinn-Judge, Paul (1980) 'ASEAN's Vietnam Problem: Confrontation or Dialog?', *Indochina Issues* no. 9, August 1980.

Rahman, Tunku Abdul (1986) *Political Awakening* (Petaling Jaya, Selangor: Pelanduk Publications).

Rajaratnam, S. (1979) 'Statement' at the Twelfth ASEAN Ministerial Meeting in Bali, 28 June 1979.

—— (1987) *The Prophetic & the Political: Selected Speeches and Writings of S. Rajaratnam*, edited by Chan Heng Chee and Obaid ul Haq (Singapore: Graham Brash).

—— (1989) 'Riding the Vietnamese Tiger', *Contemporary Southeast Asia* 10(4): 343–61.

Rajaretnam, M. (2000) 'Principles in Crisis: The Need for New Directions', in Kao Kim Hourn (ed.) *ASEAN's Non-Interference Policy: Principles Under Pressure?* (London: ASEAN Academic Press), pp. 37–49.

Ramage, Douglas E. (1995) *Politics in Indonesia: Democracy, Islam and the Ideology of Tolerance* (London and New York: Routledge).

Raszelenberg, Patrick and Peter Schier (1995) *The Cambodia Conflict: Search for a Settlement, 1979–1991: An Analytical Chronology* (Hamburg: Institut für Asienkunde).

Razak, Tun Abdul bin Datuk Hussein, 'World Political Situation and Trends', reprinted in *Asia Pacific Record* 1(11), February 1971: 6–9.

Regaud, Nicolas (1992) *Le Cambodge dans la tourmente: le troisième conflit indochinois 1978–1991* (Paris: Fondation pour les Études de Défense Nationale /L'Harmattan).

Reid, Anthony (1993) *Southeast Asia in the Age of Commerce 1450–1680: Expansion and Crisis*, vol. 2 (New Haven, CT, and London: Yale University Press).

—— (1996) 'Flows and Seepages in the Long-term Chinese Interaction with Southeast Asia', in Anthony Reid (ed.) *Sojourners and Settlers: Histories of Southeast Asia and the Chinese* (St Leonards, NSW: Asian Studies Association of Australia/Allen & Unwin), pp. 15–50.

Rengger, Nicholas (1997) 'The Ethics of Trust in World Politics', *International Affairs* 73(3): 469–87.

Reyes, Alejandro (2000a) ' "Splendid" Is the Word', *Asiaweek*, 25 July 2000, at http://www.asiaweek.com/asiaweek/intelligence/2000/07/25/.

—— (2000b) 'A Frank and Not-so-frank Talk with the Philippine Foreign Secretary', *Asiaweek*, 25 July 2000.

—— (2000c) 'Adrift: But the Powerhouse Economies of the Region's Northeast May Provide a Lifeline', *Asiaweek*, 1 September 2000.

Reynolds, Craig J. (1991) 'Introduction', in Craig J. Reynolds (ed.) *National Identity and Its Defenders, 1939–1989* (Chiang Mai: Silkworm Books), pp. 1–40.

Richardson, Michael (1982) 'ASEAN and Indo-Chinese Refugees', in Alison Broinowski (ed.) *Understanding ASEAN*, pp. 92–114.

—— (1998a) 'Japan's Lack of Leadership Pushes ASEAN Toward Cooperation With China, *International Herald Tribune*, 17 April, at http://www.iht.com /IHT/MR/98/mr041798.html.

—— (1998b) 'Habibie Cancels Visit to Kuala Lumpur', *International Herald Tribune*, 7 October, at http://www.iht.com/IHT/MR/98/index.html.

—— (1998c) 'Timing of China's Move on Spratlys Raises Asian Suspicions', *International Herald Tribune*, 2 December: 4.

—— (1999) 'Asians Criticize Australia for Playing Role of "U.S. Deputy" ', *International Herald Tribune*, 27 September, at http://www.iht.com/IHT/MR/99/ mr092799.html.

Robertson, B.A. (ed.) (1998) *The Structure of International Society* (London: Pinter).

Robinson, W. Courtland (1998) *Terms of Refuge: The Indochinese Exodus and the International Response* (London: Zed Books).

Robison, Richard (1996) 'The Politics of "Asian values" ', *Pacific Review* 9(3): 309–27.

Roff, William R. (1994) *The Origins of Malay Nationalism*, second edition (Kuala Lumpur: Oxford University Press).

Ross, Robert S. (ed.) (1993) *China, the United States and the Soviet Union: Tripolarity and Policy Making in the Cold War* (Armonk, NY: M.E. Sharpe).

Rotberg, Robert I. (1998) 'Prospects for a Democratic Burma', in Robert I. Rotberg (ed.) *Burma: Prospects for a Democratic Future* (Washington, DC: Brookings Institution Press), pp. 1–7.

Roth, Stanley O. (1998) 'Multilateral Approaches to Regional Security', Presentation at Henry L. Stimson Center, 21 July, at http://www.stimson.org/cbm/asls /roth.htm.

Ruggie, John Gerard (1998) *Constructing the World Polity: Essays on International Institutionalization* (London: Routledge).

San Pablo-Baviera, Aileen (1998) 'Security Challenges of the Philippine Archipelago', in Derek da Cunha and John Funston (eds) *Southeast Asia 1998* (Singapore: Institute of Southeast Asian Studies), pp. 213–26.

Sandhu, K. S., Sharon Siddique, Chandran Jeshurun, Ananda Rajah, Joseph L. H. Tan and Pushpa Thambipillai (1992) *The ASEAN Reader* (Singapore: Institute of Southeast Asian Studies).

Scalapino, Robert, Seizaburo Sato, Jusuf Wanandi and Sung-Joo Han (eds) (1990) *Regional Dynamics: Security, Political and Economic Issues in the Asia-Pacific Region* (Jakarta: Centre for Strategic and International Studies).

Schier, Peter (1982) 'The Indochina Conflict from the Perspective of Singapore', *Contemporary Southeast Asia* 4(2): 226–35.

Schier, Peter and Manola Schier-Oum (1985) *Prince Sihanouk on Cambodia: Interviews and Talks with Prince Norodom Sihanouk*, second edition (Hamburg: Institut für Asienkunde).

Schwab, Orrin (1998) *Defending the Free World: John F. Kennedy, Lyndon Johnson, and the Vietnam War, 1961–65* (Westport, CT: Praeger).

Scott, James M. (1996) *Deciding to Intervene: The Reagan Doctrine and American Foreign Policy* (Durham and London: Duke University Press).

Sebastian, Leonard C. and Anthony L. Smith (2000) 'The East Timor Crisis: A Test Case for Humanitarian Intervention', in Daljit Singh (ed.) *Southeast Asian Affairs 2000* (Singapore: Institute of Southeast Asian Studies), pp. 64–83.

Segal, Gerald (1999) 'Concern for East Asians Ought to Begin at Home', *International Herald Tribune*, 14 September 1999, at http://ds.dial.pipex.com/gsegal/ih14se99.htm.

Severino, Rodolfo C., Jr (1998) 'ASEAN Vision 2020: Challenges and Prospects in the New Millennium', Remarks by the Secretary-General of ASEAN at the Eighth Southeast Asia Forum, Kuala Lumpur, 15 March, at http://www.aseansec.org/secgen/visi2020.htm.

—— (1999) 'Regionalism: The Stakes for Southeast Asia', Address by the Secretary-General of the Association of Southeast Asian Nations at the Institute of Defence and Strategic Studies, Singapore, 24 May, at http://www.asean.or.id/secgen/sg—idss.htm.

—— (2001) *ASEAN: Building the Peace in Southeast Asia*, Paper presented at the Fourth High Level Meeting between the United Nations and Regional Organizations on Cooperation for Peace-Building, New York, 6–7 February 2001, at http://www.aseansec.org/secgen/sg—peace.htm.

Seymour, James D. (1998) 'Human Rights in Chinese Foreign Relations', in Samuel S. Kim (ed.) *China and the World: Chinese Foreign Policy Faces the New Millennium* (Boulder, CO: Westview Press), pp. 217–38.

Shambaugh, David (1996) 'Containment or Engagement of China? Calculating Beijing's Responses', *International Security* 21(2): 180–209.

—— (1999) 'China's Military Views the World: Ambivalent Security', *International Security* 24(3) (winter 1999/2000): 52–79.

Shamira Bhanu Abdul Azeez (1998) *The Singapore–Malaysia 'Re-Merger' Debate of 1996* (Hull: University of Hull).

Sheng Lijun (1995a) *China's Policy Towards the Spratly Islands in the 1990s*, Working Paper No. 287 (Canberra: Australian National University, Strategic and Defence Studies Centre).
—— (1995b) 'China's Foreign Policy Under Status Discrepancy, Status Enhancement', *Contemporary Southeast Asia* 17(2): 101–25.
Shi Chunlai (1999) 'Preventive Diplomacy and the Asia-Pacific Region', in Desmond Ball and Amitav Acharya (eds) (1999) *The Next Stage: Preventive Diplomacy and Security Cooperation in the Asia-Pacific Region* (Canberra: Strategic and Defence Studies Centre, Australian National University/Institute of Defence and Strategic Studies, Nanyang Technological University, Singapore), pp. 173–86.
Siazon, Domingo L., Jr (1997) 'Opening Statement' at the Thirtieth ASEAN Ministerial Meeting, Kuala Lumpur, 24 July.
—— (2000) 'Opening Statement' at the Thirty-Third ASEAN Ministerial Meeting, Bangkok, 24 July 2000, at http://www.aseansec.org/view.asp?file=/amm/amm33osp.htm.
Siemers, Günter (1996) 'Zum geplanten politischen System in Myanmar' [On the Planned Political System in Myanmar], *SÜDOSTASIEN aktuell*, May 1996: 250–6;
—— (1998) 'Suu Kyi in Myanmar: von Konfrontation zu Kollision?' [Suu Kyi in Myanmar: From Confrontation toward Collision?], *SÜDOSTASIEN aktuell*, January 1998: 384–402.
—— (1999) 'Warum keine erfolgreichere Myanmar Politik?' [Why is There Not a More Successful Myanmar Policy?], *SÜDOSTASIEN aktuell*, January 1999: 57–63.
Simon, Sheldon W. (1988) *The Future of Asian-Pacific Security Collaboration* (Lexington, MA: Lexington Books).
—— (1989) 'ASEAN Security in the 1990s', *Asian Survey* XXIX(6): 580–600.
—— (1990) 'The United States and Conflict Reduction in Southeast Asia', *Contemporary Southeast Asia* 12(2): 83–100.
—— (1998a) 'Security Prospects in Southeast Asia: Collaborative Efforts and the ASEAN Regional Forum', Paper presented at the Thirty-ninth ISA Annual Convention, Minneapolis, 17–21 March.
—— (1998b) *The Economic Crisis and ASEAN States' Security* (Carlisle, PA: Strategic Studies Institute).
Singapore 1988 (Singapore: Information Division of the Ministry of Communications and Information).
Singh, Ajit *Dato* (1996) 'Opening Address' at the International Seminar to Commemorate the Silver Anniversary of CSIS on One Southeast Asia in a New Regional and International Setting, Jakarta, 18 September, at http://www/aseansec.org/dato/csis25.htm.
Singh, Bilveer (1990) *The Soviet Union in Singapore's Foreign Policy: An Analysis* (Kuala Lumpur: ISIS Malaysia).
—— (1992) *ZOPFAN and the New Security Order in the Asia-Pacific Region* (Petaling Jaya: Pelanduk Publications).
—— (1996) *East Timor, Indonesia and the World: Myths and Realities*, second edition (Kuala Lumpur: ADPR Consult (M) Sdn. Bhd).
—— (2000) *Succession Politics in Indonesia: The 1998 Presidential Elections and the Fall of Suharto* (Basingstoke and London: Macmillan).

Singh, D.S. Ranjit (1984) *Brunei 1839–1983: The Problems of Political Survival* (Singapore and Oxford: Oxford University Press).

Sirikrai, Surachai (1990) 'Thai Perceptions of China and Japan', *Contemporary Southeast Asia* 12(3): 247–65.

Smith, Anthony (2000) 'East Timor: Status Quo Ante Bellum', *Panorama* 2(2): 7–32.

Smith, Martin (1991) *Burma, Insurgency and the Politics of Ethnicity* (London and New Jersey, CT: Zed Books).

Snitwongse, Kusuma (1998) 'Thailand's Year of Stability: Illusion or Reality', in Mohammed Ayoob and Ng Chee Yuen (eds) *Southeast Asian Affairs 1988* (Singapore: Institute of Southeast Asian Studies), pp. 269–86.

Soenarno, Radin (1960) 'Malay Nationalism, 1900–1945', *Journal of Southeast Asian History* no. 1 (March 1960): 1–28.

Soerjono, Wirjodiatmodjo Raden (1964) *Der Gedanke der Blockfreiheit in Südostasien. Geschichte und Deutung der Solidaritätskonferenzen der Colombo-Staaten 1954–1961* [The Idea of Non-Alignment in Southeast Asia: History and Meaning of the Solidarity Conferences of the Colombo States 1954–1961] (Stuttgart: Kohlhammer Verlag).

Soesastro, Hadi (1995) 'Foreword', in Hadi Soesastro (ed.) *ASEAN in a Changed Regional and International Political Economy* (Jakarta: Centre for Strategic and International Studies), pp. iii–iv.

—— (ed.) (1997) *One Southeast Asia in a New Regional and International Setting* (Jakarta: Centre for Strategic and International Studies).

Solidum, Estrella D. (1988) 'The United States Military Presence as an Issue in Philippine Politics: A View from the Philippines', *Pacific Review* 1(4): 385–99.

Sopiee, Mohamed Noordin (1975) 'Towards a "Neutral" Southeast Asia', in Hedley Bull (ed.) *Asia and the Western Pacific: Towards a New International Order* (Sydney: Nelson), pp. 132–58.

—— (1998) 'ASEAN Towards 2020: Strategic Goals and Critical Pathways', in Stephen Leong (ed.) *ASEAN Towards 2020: Strategic and Future Directions* (Kuala Lumpur: ISIS Malaysia/ASEAN Academic Press), pp. 21–8.

Srivoranart, Vorapun and Marisa Chimprahba (1999) 'US to Aid Deployment of Thai Troops in Timor', *The Nation*, 2 October 1999.

State Council of the PRC (1995) *China: Arms Control and Disarmament* (Beijing: Information Office of the State Council of the People's Republic of China).

Storey, Ian James (1999) 'Creeping Assertiveness: China, the Philippines and the South China Sea Dispute', *Contemporary Southeast Asia* 16(1): 95–118.

Stuart, Douglas T. and William Tow (1995) *A U.S. Strategy for the Asia-Pacific*, Adelphi Paper 299 (Oxford: Oxford University Press/International Institute for Strategic Studies).

Stuart-Fox, Martin (1982) 'Resolving the Kampuchean Problem: The Case for an Alternative Regional Initiative', *Contemporary Southeast Asia* 4(2): 210–25.

—— (1997) *A History of Laos* (Cambridge: Cambridge University Press).

Sudo, Sueo (1992) *The Fukuda Doctrine and ASEAN: New Dimensions in Japanese Foreign Policy* (Singapore: ISEAS).

Suharto, (1970) Speech at the Conference of Non-Aligned Nations in Lusaka on 9 October 1970, reprinted in *Asia Pacific Record* 1(4), July 1970: 10–16.

Sukma, Rizal (1994) 'Recent Developments in Sino-Indonesian Relations: An Indonesian View', *Contemporary Southeast Asia* 16(1): 35–45.

—— (1999) *Indonesia and China: The Politics of a Troubled Relationship* (London and New York: Routledge).

—— (2000) 'US–Southeast Asia Relations After the Crisis: The Security Dimension', at http://www.asiafoundation.org/publications/rpt-amer.html.

Sukrasep, Vinita (1989) *ASEAN in International Relations* (Bangkok: Aksornsiam Press).

Suryadinata, Leo (1985) *China and the ASEAN Sates: the Ethnic Chinese Dimension* (Singapore: Singapore University Press).

—— (1991) 'Indonesia–Vietnam Relations Under Suharto', *Contemporary Southeast Asia* 12(4): 331–46.

—— (1996) *Indonesia's Foreign Policy Under Suharto: Aspiring to International Leadership* (Singapore: Times Academic Press).

—— (1998) 'China's Hands-Off on Indonesia', *Far Eastern Economic Review*, 16 April: 31.

Suwannathat-Pian, Kobkua (1988) *Thai–Malay Relations: Traditional Intra-Regional Relations from the Seventeenth to the Early Twentieth Century* (Singapore, Oxford and New York: Oxford University Press).

—— (1995) *Thailand's Durable Premier: Phibun through Three Decades 1932–1957* (Kuala Lumpur: Oxford University Press).

Talbott, Strobe (1994) 'Opening Statement' at the Post-Ministerial Conference, Bangkok, 27 July, at http://www.asean.or.id/amm/pmc27osu.htm.

Tambiah, Stanley Jeyaraja (1987) *The Buddhist Conception of Universal King and its Manifestations in Southeast Asia* (Kuala Lumpur: University of Malaya).

Tan Lian Choo (1991) 'Personality Politics in Thailand', in Sharon Siddique and Ng Chee Yuen (eds) *Southeast Asian Affairs 1991* (Singapore: Institute of Southeast Asian Studies), pp. 279–97.

Tang Jiaxuan (1998) Statement of the People's Republic of China at the Post-Ministerial Conference, Manila, 28 July, at http://www.aseansec.org/amm/pmc31osh.htm.

—— (1999) 'Address' at China–ASEAN Dialogue, Singapore, 27 July 1999.

Tassell, Tony (1998) 'ASEAN Plans to Monitor Risks in Region', *Financial Times*, 8 October: 7.

Tate, D.J.M. (1971) *The Making of Modern South-East Asia: The European Conquest*, vol. I (Kuala Lumpur: Oxford University Press).

Tay, Simon S.C. (1997) 'Preventive Diplomacy and the ASEAN Regional Forum: Principles and Possibilities', reprinted in Desmond Ball and Amitav Acharya (eds) (1999) *The Next Stage: Preventive Diplomacy and Security Cooperation in the Asia-Pacific Region* (Canberra: Strategic and Defence Studies Centre, Australian National University/Institute of Defence and Strategic Studies, Nanyang Technological University, Singapore), pp. 117–155.

Tay, Simon S.C. and Obood Talib (1997) 'The ASEAN Regional Forum: Preparing for Preventive Diplomacy', *Contemporary Southeast Asia* 19(3): 252–68.

Taylor, George E. (1964) *The Philippines and the United States: Problems of Partnership* (New York and London: Praeger).

Taylor, John G. (1991) *Indonesia's Forgotten War: The Hidden History of East Timor* (London: Zed Books).

—— (1999) *East Timor: The Price of Freedom* (London: Zed Books)

Terriff, Terry, Stuart Croft, Lucy James and Patrick Morgan (1999) *Security Studies Today* (Cambridge: Polity Press).

Tesoro, Jose Manuel (2000) 'Abdurrahman's Indonesia', *Panorama* 2(2): 33–50.

Thai Ministry of Foreign Affairs (1998) *Thailand's Non-Paper on Flexible Engagement*, at http://www.thaiembdc.org.pressctr/pr/pr743.htm.

—— (2000) *Clarification on News Reports Concerning ASEAN Troika*, 28 September 2000.

Thambipillai, Pushpa (1985) 'ASEAN Negotiating Styles: Asset or Hindrance?', in Pushpa Thambipillai and J. Saravanamuttu, *ASEAN Negotiations: Two Insights* (Singapore: Institute of Southeast Asian Studies), pp. 3–28.

Than, Tin Maung Maung (1997) 'Myanmar Democratisation: Punctuated Equilibrium or Retrograde Motion', in Anek Laothamatas (ed.) *Democratization in Southeast and East Asia* (Singapore: Institute of Southeast Asian Studies), pp. 167–214.

—— (1998) 'Myanmar: Preoccupation with Regime Survival, National Unity, and Stability', in Muthiah Alagappa (ed.) *Asian Security Practice: Material and Ideational Influences* (Stanford, CA: Stanford University Press), pp. 390–416.

Than, Tin Maung Maung and Mya Than (1997) 'Myanmar: Economic Growth in the Shadow of Political Constraints', in Daljit Singh (ed.) *Southeast Asian Affairs 1997* (Singapore: Institute of Southeast Asian Studies), pp. 205–230.

Thayer, Carlyle A. (1990) 'ASEAN and Indochina: The Dialogue', in Alison Broinowski (ed.) *ASEAN into the 1990s* (Basingstoke and London: Macmillan), pp. 138–61.

—— (1999) 'Vietnamese Foreign Policy: Multilateralism and the Threat of Peaceful Evolution', in Carlyle A. Thayer and Ramses Amer (eds) *Vietnamese Foreign Policy in Transition* (Singapore: ISEAS), pp. 1–24.

Theeravit, Khien (1982) 'Thai–Kampuchean Relations: Problems and Prospects', *Asian Survey* XXII(6): 561–76.

Tian Zhongqing (1995) 'An Analysis of the Asia-Pacific Multilateral Security Dialogue', *SIIS Journal* (Shanghai) 1(3): 40–52.

Tilman, Robert O. (1976) 'Mustapha's Sabah, 1968–1975: The Tun Steps Down', *Asian Survey* XVI(6): 495–509.

Time Asia (1998) Interview with Dr Surin Pitsuwin by Tim Larimer, 2 November, at http://www.cgi.pathfinder.com/time/asia/magazine/1998/981102/surin1.html.

Tonesson, Stein (2000) 'Vietnam's Objective in the South China Sea: National or Regional Security', *Contemporary Southeast Asia* 22(1): 199–220.

Tongdhamachart, Kramol (1982) 'Thai Perspectives on the Conflict in Kampuchea', in Robert Scalapino and Jusuf Wanandi (eds) *Economic, Political and Security Issues in Southeast Asia in the 1980s* (Berkeley, CA: Institute of East Asian Studies, University of California), pp. 75–81.

Towards a Southeast Asian Community: A Human Agenda: A Statement on the Future Southeast Asian Community to the Leaders and Peoples of Southeast Asia, Manila, 23 August 1996.

Townsend-Gault, Ian (1996) 'Confidence and Cooperation in the South China Sea: The Indonesia–Canada Initiative', in Jusuf Wanandi (ed.) *Regional Security Arrangements: Indonesian and Canadian Views* (Jakarta: Centre for Strategic and International Studies in Co-operation with CSCAP Indonesia), pp. 69–80.

—— (1998) Preventive Diplomacy and Pro-Activity in the South China Sea', *Contemporary Southeast Asia* 20(2): 171–90.

Turnbull, C.M. (1977) *A History of Singapore, 1819–1975*, first edition (Oxford: Oxford University Press).

Um, Khatarya (1991) 'Thailand and the Dynamics of Economic and Security Complex in Mainland Southeast Asia', *Contemporary Southeast Asia* 13(3): 245–70.

United Nations Security Council (1999) *Report of the Security Council Mission to Jakarta and Dili*, S/1999/976, 14 September 1999, at http://www.un.org/peace /etimor/docs9926220E.htm.

UNTAET (undated) http://www.un.org/peace/etimor/etimor.htm.

US Department of Defense (1998) *The United States Security Strategy for the East Asia-Pacific Region*, at ht tp://www.defenselink.mil/pubs/easr98.

—— (1999a) Secretary Cohen's Press Conference in Darwin, 29 September 1999, at ht tp://www.defenselink.mil:80/news/Sep1999/t09291999t0929coh.html.

—— (1999b) Secretary Cohen's Press Conference in Bangkok, 1 October 1999, at ht tp://www.defenselink.mil:80/news/Oct1999/t10011999—t001bang.html.

US Department of State (1997) *Conditions in Burma and U.S. Policy toward Burma* (Washington, DC: US Department of State).

——(1998) *Thailand Country Report on Human Rights Practices for 1997* (Washington, DC: US Department of State).

—— (1999) *Conditions in Burma and U.S. Policy Toward Burma* (for period 28 March 1999–28 Sept 1999).

Valencia, Mark J. (1996) 'The Spratly Imbroglio in the Post-Cold War Era', in David Wurfel and Bruce Burton (eds) *Southeast Asia in the New World Order: The Political Economy of a Dynamic Region* (Basingstoke and London: Macmillan), pp. 244–69.

van der Kroef, Justuf M. (1979) 'Hanoi and ASEAN: Is Coexistence Possible', *Contemporary Southeast Asia* 1(2): 164–78.

—— (1981a) 'ASEAN, Hanoi, and the Kampuchean Conflict: Between "Kuantan" and a "Third Alternative"', *Asian Survey* XXI(5): 515–35.

—— (1981b) '"Normalizing" Relations with the People's Republic of China: Indonesia's rituals of Ambiguity', *Contemporary Southeast Asia* 3(1): 187–218.

—— (1988) 'Cambodia: The Vagaries of "Cocktail" Diplomacy, *Contemporary Southeast Asia* 9(4): 300–20.

van Ness, Peter (1970) *Revolution and Chinese Foreign Policy: Peking's Support for Wars of National Liberation* (Berkeley: University of California Press).

van Niel, Robert (1979) 'From Netherlands East Indies to Republic of Indonesia, 1900–1945', in Harry Aveling (ed.)*The Development of Indonesian Society. From the Coming of Islam to the Present Day* (New York: St Martin's Press), pp. 106–65.

Vasavakul, Thaveeporn (1997) 'Vietnam: The Third Wave of State Building', in Daljit Singh (ed.) *Southeast Asian Affairs 1997* (Singapore: Institute of Southeast Asian Studies), pp. 337–63.

Vietnamese Ministry of Foreign Affairs (2000) 'On the Current Situation in Myanmar', Answers by MOFA's Spokeswoman Phan Thuy Thanh to foreign correspondents, 17 October 2000, at http://www.mofa.gov.vn/English/Press/press-release.htm.

Wanandi, Jusuf (1979) *Security Dimensions of the Asia-Pacific Region in the 1980s* (Jakarta: Centre for Strategic and International Studies).

—— (1988) 'An Introduction to China's Role in Regional Problems', in Joyce K. Kallgren, Noordin Sopiee and Soedjati Djiwandono (eds) *ASEAN and China: An Evolving Relationship* (Berkeley, CA: University of California Press), pp. 177–88.

—— (1996) *Asia Pacific After the Cold War* (Jakarta: Centre for Strategic and International Studies).

—— (1997a) 'ASEAN Wise in Deferring Cambodia's Entry', *PacNet Newsletter* no. 29, 18 July, at http://www.csis.org/html/pac2997.html.

—— (1997b) 'A Lesson for ASEAN', *Far Eastern Economic Review*, 24 July: 34.

—— (1998) 'The Strategic Implications of the Economic Crisis in East Asia', *The Indonesian Quarterly* 26(1): 2–6.

—— (1999) 'ASEAN's Challenges for Its Future', *PacNet Newsletter* no. 3, January, at http://www.csis.org/pacfor/pac0399.html.

Wang Gungwu (1968) 'Early Ming Relations with Southeast Asia: A Background Essay', in John King Fairbank (ed.) *The Chinese World Order: Traditional China's Foreign Relations* (Cambridge, MA: Harvard University Press), pp. 34–62.

—— (1962/1992) 'Malayan Nationalism', in *Community and Nation: China, Southeast Asia and Australia* (St Leonards, NSW: ASAA/Allen & Unwin), pp. 187–96.

Wannamethee, Phan (1992) 'ZOPFAN: A Blueprint for Regional Co-existence', in B.A. Hamzah (ed.) *Southeast Asia and Regional Peace: A Study of the Southeast Asian Concept of Zone of Peace, Freedom and Neutrality (ZOPFAN)* (Kuala Lumpur: ISIS), pp. 89–103.

Watson, Adam (1991) *Diplomacy: The Dialogue Between States* (London: Routledge).

Weatherbee, Donald E. (1984) 'ASEAN Regionalism: The Salient Dimension', in Karl D. Jackson and M. Hadi Soesastro (eds) *ASEAN Security and Economic Development* (Berkeley, CA: California University Press), pp. 259–68.

—— (ed.) (1985) 'Diplomacy of Stalemate', *Southeast Asia Divided: The ASEAN–Indochina Crisis* (Boulder, CO, and London: Westview Press), pp. 1–30.

Weggel, Oskar (1998) 'Chinas Außenpolitik am Ende des 20. Jahrhunderts, Teil 3: Strategien', *CHINA aktuell*, August 1998: 817–25.

—— (2001) 'Ethnische und soziale Klopfzeichen in Vietnam', *SÜDOSTASIEN aktuell*, May 2001: 319–26.

Weinstein, Franklin B. (1969) *Indonesia Abandons Confrontation: An Inquiry into the Functions of Indonesian Foreign Policy* (Ithaca, NY: Cornell University).

—— (1976) *Indonesian Foreign Policy and the Dilemma of Dependence: From Sukarno to Suharto* (Ithaca, NY: Cornell University Press).

Wendt, Alexander (1999) *Social Theory of International Politics* (Cambridge: Cambridge University Press).

Wheeler, Nicholas J. (2000) *Saving Strangers: Humanitarian Intervention in International Society* (Oxford: Oxford University Press).

White House (1997) *A National Security Strategy for A New Century* (Washington, DC).

Whiting, Allen S. (1995) 'Chinese Nationalism and Foreign Policy After Deng', *The China Quarterly* 142: 295–316.

—— (1997) 'ASEAN Eyes China: The Security Dimension', *Asian Survey* XXXVII(4): 299–322.

Williams, Michael C. (1992) *Vietnam at the Crossroads* (London: Pinter/Royal Institute of International Affairs).

Wilson, Dick (1975) *The Neutralization of Southeast Asia* (New York: Praeger).

Wilson, W. (1918) 'President Woodrow Wilson's Fourteen Points', Address delivered in Joint Session before the Senate and the House of Representatives, 8 January 1918 (http://www.lib.byu.edu/rdh/wwi/1918/14points.html).

Winters, Jeffrey (1998) 'The Risks and Limits of Corporate Foreign Policy', in Selig
    S. Harrison and Clyde V. Prestowitz, Jr (eds) *Asia After the Miracle: Redefining
    U.S. Economic and Security Priorities* (Washington, DC: Economic Strategy Insti-
    tute), pp. 223–44.
Wolfers, Arnold (1962) *Discord and Collaboration: Essays on International Politics*
    (Baltimore and London: Johns Hopkins University Press).
Wong, Douglas (1999) 'KL wary of new concept', *Straits Times*, 21 November 1999.
Working Group for an ASEAN Human Rights Mechanism (undated) website
    http://www.rwgmechanism.com.
Wu Xinbo (1998) 'China: Security Practice of a Modernizing and Ascending Power',
    in Muthiah Alagappa (ed.) *Asian Security Practice: Material and Ideational Influ-
    ences* (Stanford, CA: Stanford University Press), pp. 115–56.
Yahuda, Michael (1986) *The China Threat*, ISIS Seminar Paper (Kuala Lumpur:
    ISIS).
—— (1996) *The International Politics of the Asia-Pacific, 1945–1995* (London and
    New York: Routledge).
—— (1997) 'How Much has China Learned About Interdependence', in David S.G.
    Goodman and Gerald Segal (eds) *China Rising: Nationalism and Interdepen-
    dence*(London and New York: Routledge), pp. 6–23.
—— (1999) 'After the Embassy Bombing', *China Review* no. 14, at
    http://www.gbc.org.uk/yahuda14.htm.
Yoon, Suthichai (1998) 'Declare Victory and Retreat', *The Nation*, 23 July: A4.
Young, Jeffrey D. (1992) *U.S. Military Interaction with Southeast Asian Countries*,
    CRS Report for Congress 92–241 F, 27 February.
Young, Peter Lewis (1997) 'The Five Power Defence Arrangement – A Review',
    Asian Defence Journal 5/97: 5–9.
Zagoria, Donald S. (1997) 'Joining ASEAN', in James W. Morley and Masashi
    Nishihara (eds) *Vietnam Joins the World* (Armonk, NY: M.E. Sharpe), pp.
    154–72.
Zakaria Haji Ahmad (1979) 'Vietnamese Refugees and ASEAN', *Contemporary
    Southeast Asia* 1(1): 66–74.
Zha Daojiong (2000) 'China and the May 1998 riots of Indonesia: Exploring the
    Issues', *Pacific Review* 13(4): 557–75.
Zhang Jialin (1994) ' "China Threat" – A New Breed of the Old Myth', *SIIS Journal*
    1(1) (1994): 63–87.
Zhao Suisheng (1997) *Power Competition in East Asia: From the Old Chinese World
    Order to Post-Cold War Regional Multipolarity* (Basingstoke and London:
    Macmillan).

Index

ABRI (Armed Forces of Indonesia) 85,
92, 94, 104, 105
Abdul Razak Baginda 175
Abdullah Ahmad Badawi 155, 177, 186,
188, 203,
Abdurrahman Wahid 227
Abu Sayyaf 208
Aceh 201, 208, 219, 227, 236n16, 248n
Adat 23
Aguinaldo, Emilio (President) 29
Ahmad Rithaudeen 92, 94
Alatas, Ali 75, 77, 108, 148, 174, 178,
202, 203
Albright, Madeleine 145, 154, 244n4
All Burma Students Democratic Front
177
AMPERA (Amanat Penderitaan
Rakyat) 44
Anand Panyarachun 79, 233
Anglo-Japanese Alliance 20
Anglo-Malayan/Malaysian Defence
Agreement (AMDA) 54, 237n5,
238n2
Annan, Kofi 200, 202, 209, 249n8
anti-colonialism: in Indonesia 27–29; in
Malaya 23–26; in Philippines 29–31;
in Singapore 26–27; (also see extra-
territoriality)
Anwar Ibrahim, Datuk Seri 147, 166,
167, 180, 183, 184, 185, 186, 187, 227,
244n24, 247n6
Aquino, Benino 247n6
Aquino, Corazon 73, 168, 228
Association of Southeast Asia (ASA):
16, 35–36, 42–3, 46, 238n10
Association of Southeast Asian Nations
(ASEAN): ASEAN Appeal 93, 99
(also see Cambodia conflict);
Bangkok Declaration 43–44, 44, 53,

63, 80, 146, 238n1; Concept Paper for
the ARF 77, 78, 115, 118, 151, 152,
155, 157; Declaration of ASEAN
Concord 63, 64, 65; Declaration on
the South China Sea 115, 123, 126,
152; dialogue partners 189, 200;
diplomatic and security culture (see
'ASEAN way'); and East Timor
197–204, 248n7; enlargement 10, 69,
70, 165, 166, 191; 'five-plus-two'
proposal 93, 94 (also see Cambodia
conflict); Free Trade Area 71, 79,
146, 189, 247n4; Hanoi Plan of
Action 189, 190, 192; Hanoi Summit
15, 188, 189–190, 191; High Council
50–51, 78, 190, 192, 215, 217, 219,
228, 232, 247n3, 249n6; Human
Rights Mechanism 228, 230,
249–50n10; Institutes of
International and Strategic Studies
76, 167, 220, 230, 232; and
INTERFET 199–204, 246n23;
People's Assembly 227, 231, 232;
Post-Ministerial Conferences (PMC)
76, 77; and preventive diplomacy 10,
205, 213, 221, 230, 232, 233; reasons
for constructive engagement of
Myanmar 143–4; relations with
Myanmar 145–46; relations with
Japan 72; relations with PRC 71, 76,
122, 123–9, 130–32, 134–37,
243n13–16; relations with US 71, 79,
139–40, 147–49, 161–64; relations
with Vietnam 62–63, 66–67, 69–71,
74, 81–2, 83; 'Retreat' 15, 192,
194–196, 197, 207, 212, 217, 225, 233;
Secretariat 64, 146, 167; Surveillance
Process 15, 192, 193–94, 247n4; and
Taiwan Strait Crisis 245n10; Treaty

of Amity and Co-operation in Southeast Asia (TAC) 14, 50, 53, 63, 64, 65, 77, 78, 115, 135, 141, 146, 152, 157, 189, 217, 221, 220, 246n1, 247n3; troika 15, 192, 195, 204–209, 211, 212, 215, 217, 228, 233, 246n4, 247n3; troika mission in Cambodia 174, 175; Vision 2020 171, 189, 249n9; and ZOPFAN (see under ZOPFAN)

ASEAN-China Senior Officials Meeting 125–6, 129

ASEAN Plus Three 112, 134;

ASEAN Regional Forum: Annual Security Outlook (ASO) 156, 157; and China 116–122, 151, 152, 157–158; confidence building 118–120, 151–152, 155–157; and East Timor 204; 'good offices'152, 153, 156, 157; Inter-sessional Support Group on Confidence-Building Measures (ISG-CBM) 119, 152, 155, 156, 157, 245n14; origins of 76–77; preventive diplomacy 78, 120–122, 152–154, 155–157, 205, 221, 226, 233; Register of Experts/Eminent Persons (EEPs) 156, 157; Track II 120, 220; Troika 154, 157; and United States 150–154, 158; and ZOPFAN 78–79;

'ASEAN way': and Al Gore 187–88; ambiguous practice 46–7, 168–169, 214, 217; Cambodia on 225; conceptualisations of 3–4, 6, 234–35n10; criticism of 7, 8; and 'constructive engagement' 143, 145–147, 217; core norms of 1, 7, 214; demise of 8, 10, 190, 213; development of 10, 14, 49–50, 64, 189, 193–4, 196, 197, 203–204, 205–7, 212, 217–18, 221, 229; as diplomatic and security culture 3, 6–7; and enhanced interaction 183–7; and enlargement 148, 165–166, 215; and flexible engagement 165–83; intramural challenges to 10, 50, 82, 94, 100, 101–103, 106, 107–108, 111, 166, 169–170, 183–7, 204–6, 211, 214, 215–16, 217, 218; Indonesia's on 227–28; Lao PDR on 224–25; Malaysia on 226–27; Myanmar on 223; origins 9, 14, 16–17, 31; Philippines on 228; and PRC 14, 113–115, 122–29, 129–37, 221;

prospects for 15, 216, 232–33; purpose 50, 69–70, 214, 218–223; pressures on 229–31; as qualified success 64, 219–220; reaffirmation of 188, 218–223; and 'Retreat' 196–97; scenarios for 214–16, 232; Singapore on 225–26; Thailand on 228–29; and United States 14, 140–41, 143, 145–6, 149, 150–1, 153–4, 160–61, 187–88; Vietnam on 70, 223–24; and ZOPFAN 52 (also see ASEAN; constructive engagement; enhanced interaction; flexible engagement; ZOPFAN)

Asia-Europe Meeting (ASEM) 112, 126, 129, 134, 178,

Asia Pacific Economic Co-operation (APEC) 69, 79, 129, 134; 239n16; 240n24; summit in Kuala Lumpur 184, 185, 186, 187; summit in Auckland 198

Asian Development Bank 193

Asian financial crisis 7, 8, 10, 14, 112, 124, 139, 146, 162, 165, 166, 170, 180, 215, 227

Asian values 144, 174, 244n5

Aung San Suu Kyi 142, 144, 145, 149, 182, 196, 209, 249n3

Australia 54, 58, 150, 156, 220,

balance of power 13, 62, 74, 75,

Ban Pang Noon (Thailand) 210

Bandung Conference 9, 34–35, 41, 237n2

Bandung Declaration 35

Bangkok Accord 42

Bangkok Declaration (see ASEAN); origins 43–44

Barican, Fernando 187

Barisan Socialis 49

Battambang 22

bebas-aktif principle (see Indonesia)

Blair, Dennis, Admiral 159, 162

Bolkiah, Prince Mohamed 181

Boutros-Ghali, Boutros 120, 121, 153,

Brandt, Willy 48

Brunei Darussalam 38, 88, 114, 156, 180, 181

Bowring Treaty 19, 20

bunga mas 18

Buon Me Thuot (Vietnam) 224

Burma (see Myanmar)

Bush, George 110, 140, 141

Cambodia 33, 43, 50, 55, 148: July 1997
   coup 166, 174, 204, relations with
   Thailand 225; accession to ASEAN
   174–5,
Cambodia conflict: ASEAN reaction to
   Vietnam's intervention 83–88, 241;
   and China 99, 102, 103, 109, 110;
   Coalition Government of
   Democratic Kampuchea) 89, 90, 92,
   93, 94, 95, 100, 102, 103, 106, 109,
   110; 'cocktail party/diplomacy' 94,
   95, 101–104, 107, 108, 111; Eight-
   Point proposal 95, 102; Framework
   Document 109, 110; and Indonesia
   92, 93–94, 95, 98–101, 111;
   International Conference on
   Kampuchea (ICK) 90, 91, 93, 95, 99,
   140; International Conferences in
   Paris 1989/1991 109, 110; Jakarta
   Informal Meetings (JIM I/II) 103,
   104, 108; Kuantan principle 93, 98,
   241n24; and Malaysia 92, 93, 94, 98;
   Paris Peace Agreements 74, 109, 110,
   167, 175, 235n11, 239–40n22, 240n4;
   Supreme National Council 108, 109,
   110, 111, 217; Thai reversal on
   106–109, 242n28; and United States
   91, 110; Vietnam intransigence
   97–100; Vietnam's military
   withdrawal 73, 109 (also see ASEAN
   Appeal; Democratic Kampuchea;
   Hun Sen; Khmer Rouge; Khmer
   People's National Liberation Front;
   Kuantan Doctrine, FUNCINPEC;
   Norodom Sihanouk, People's
   Republic of Kampuchea; State of
   Cambodia)
Cambodian People's Party (CPP) 165,
   223
Castro, Fidel 145
Ceauescu, Nicolae 95
Centre for Strategic and International
   Studies, Jakarta 94, 105, 231
chakravartin 17–18
Chart Thai Party 107
Chatichai Choonhavan 70, 106, 107,
   108, 111, 176, 242n28
Chavalit Yongchaiyuth 83, 106, 166, 176,
   211
Chettha Thanajaro 162
Chi Haotian 119
Chin Peng 26, 37, 114
Chin Siong 27

China (see People's Republic of China)
Chinese Communist Party (CCP) 70, 86,
   113, 133,
Choo, Winston 242n29
Chuan Leekpai 8, 162, 172, 176, 184,
   202, 203, 204, 205, 210, 211, 228,
   245n8
Chulalongkorn (King) (Rama V) 21
Clinton, Bill 145, 245n11;
   administration of 142, 148, 172, 173,
Coalition Government of Democratic
   Kampuchea (CGDK) (see Cambodia
   conflict)
Cobra Gold Military Exercises 159, 162
colonialism 19–20 (also see anti-
   colonialism)
Communist Party of the Philippines 87
CSCE 78
constructivism 11
constructive engagement 143, 145–146,
   164, 172, 173, 175, 176, 217, 223 (also
   see 'ASEAN way')
constructive intervention 167, 168, 216
   (also see Anwar Ibrahim; flexible
   engagement)
Co-operative security (see security)
Corregidor Affair 9, 16, 46
Council for Security Co-operation in the
   Asia-Pacific (CSCAP) 118, 121, 157,
   230; CSCAP Singapore 156

Democratic Kampuchea (DK) 67, 81, 89
   (also see Cambodia conflict)
Democratic Karen Buddhist Army 176
Democratic People's Republic of Korea
   (DPRK) 150
Democratic Republic of Vietnam (DRV)
   (see Vietnam)
Deng Xiaoping 87, 91, 114
DEPHANKAM (Department of
   Defence and Security, Indonesia) 105
DEPLU (Department of Foreign
   Affairs, Indonesia) 85, 86, 92
Dhanabalan, S. 93
Dien Bien Phu 33
Diplomacy: definition of 234; 'golf'
   diplomacy 43; official diplomacy 184,
   186; personal 184, 186; quiet
   diplomacy 3, 7, 138, 146, 153, 169,
   173, 178, 183, 184, 188, 189, 190, 196,
   217, 219, 221, 222; Track I 243n11;
   Track II 230, 243n11(also see
   ASEAN-ISIS, ASEAN Regional

Forum, CSCAP); Track III 231, 250n11 (also see ASEAN People's Assembly)
diplomatic community 82, 235n12
diplomatic culture 2, 10, 234n2
Diplomatic and security culture: and 'ASEAN way' 3–7; demise of 13; emergence of 12;
extension of 13; as particular normative terrain 3, 5; shared normative terrain 1-2
Dutch East Indies (see Indonesia)

East Asia Economic Grouping (EAEG) 79
East Timor 64, 86, 108, 148, 156, 161, 162, 197–201, 202, 203, 204, 220, 227, 248n8–17 (also see INTERFET)
'enhanced interaction' 14, 166, 168, 182, 183, 184, 186, 187, 189, 190, 196, 225; and Indonesia 185; and Malaysia 185–87; and Philippines 184–5; and Thailand 184 (also see 'ASEAN way')
Estrada, Joseph 184, 185, 186, 187, 218, 228, 247n6
European Union 6, 142, 144, 172, 173, 174, 182
Evans, Gareth 78,
Exclusive Economic Zone 124
Extra-territoriality 19, 20–21, 73:Thailand and relinquishment of 21–22, 236n5, n11, 237n1

FALINTIL (Armed Forces of National Liberation of East Timor) 198
'flexible engagement' 8, 10, 14, 166, 167, 168, 169, 170, 190, 205, 206, 210, 216, 225, 228: and ASEAN Troika 205, 206; and constructive intervention 167, 168; and enhanced interaction 182–83; Malaysia on 177–179, 180; meaning of 168; and non-interference 167, 168; Myanmar on 180, 182; official Thai rationale 170–172; reasons for proposing 172–177; reasons for rejecting 177–183; Singapore on 179, 180–181; Thailand on 166, 167, 170–177; Vietnam on 180, 181 (see enhanced interaction, ASEAN Troika; also see 'ASEAN way', Surin Pitsuwan)
Five Powers Defence Arrangements 58, 65, 73, 76,

Five Principles of Peaceful Co-existence 66, 113, 135, 136, 242n1
Forces Unifées pour la Libération des Races Opprimées (FULRO) 224
forward engagement 228
Fourteen Points 20
French-Siamese territorial conflict 236n10
FRETILIN (Revolutionary Front for an Independent East Timor) 86
Fukuda Doctrine 88
FUNCINPEC (United National Front for an Independent, Neutral, Peaceful and Co-operative Cambodia) 109, 175, 241n19

Gates, Robert M. 153
General Agreement on Tariffs and Trade 69
Geneva Conference 54
Ghafar Baba, Tun 186
Goh Keng Swee 26
Goh Chok Tong 79, 162
Gorbachev, Mikhail 72, 78, 106,
Gore, Albert 187, 188, 226
Greater East Asia Co-Prosperity Sphere 26, 31
Grenada 104
Guam Declaration 54 (see Nixon Doctrine)
Gyaw, Ohn 182

Ha Van Lau 97
Habibie, Bacharuddin Jusuf 178, 185, 186, 197, 199, 220, 227, 240n26, 248n12
Hall, D.G.E. 24, 31
Heng Samrin regime 83, 88, 89, 90, 95,
Hernandez, Carolina 167, 230
Herzog, Chaim 105, 169,
Howard, John 200
Howard Doctrine 203
Hua Guofeng 240n10
humanitarian intervention 203, 230, 241n15
Hun Sen 94, 101, 102, 103, 106, 108, 109, 110, 174, 175, 246n4
Hussein Onn 47, 87, 93, 98,

ilustrados 29
India 56, 241
Indonesia: Archipelago Declaration 37, 45, 238n11; Archipelagic Principle 68;

and ASA 35–36, 42–3; and Bandung Conference 34–35; *bebas-aktif* principle 34, 41, 44, 101; on Cold War 33–34; under colonial rule 27–29; Djakarta Conference on Cambodia 56; *konfrontasi*(confrontation) 9, 36–37, 39, 40–43, 238n7; and Malaysia 36–38, 41, 42, 43–45, 75–6, 186, 216, 238n8, 247n8, 249n1; nationalism 27–29; and PR China 34–35, 45, 48, 56, 64, 76, 86, 92, 101, 114, 124, 132–35, 240n10, 243n20; regional reconciliation 42–45; relations with Australia 79, 199–200, 240n26; and Singapore (see Singapore); and Thailand 107–108; and United States 105, 148–49; on Vietnam's intervention in Cambodia 85–86 (also see 'ASEAN way', enhanced interaction, neutralisation of Southeast Asia; ZOPFAN)
Indonesian Communist Party (PKI) 41, 49, 64, 86,
Indonesian Muslim Intellectuals' Association 105
Informal Meeting on Cambodia (IMC) 109
International Force in East Timor (INTERFET) 15, 192, 199, 201, 202, 204, 212, 246n23 (see East Timor; ASEAN)
International Court of Justice 249n1
International Military Education and Training (IMET) 148 (also see United States)
IMF 193, 244n24
Irian Jaya 201, 208, 227
Ismail, Tun Dr 54

Japan 26, 88, 112, 150, 160,
Jakarta Agreement 42
Jakarta Informal Meetings (JIM) (see Cambodia conflict)
Jayakumar, S 8, 161, 174, 178, 179, 192, 195, 196,
Jiang Zemin 245n11
Juanda Kartawijaya 37

kalayaan 30, 237n19
Kampuchean People's Revolutionary Armed Forces 81

Kampuchean People's Revolutionary Council 81
Karen National Union 175–176
Katipunan 29
Kaysone Phomvihan 63,
Kedah 18, 22
Kelantan 18, 22, 87
Ketahanan Nasional (National Resilience) 44, 57, 65, 238–39n4
Khmer People's National Liberation Front (KPNLF) 92, 93, 103, 109, 241n19
Khmer Rouge 81, 88, 91, 92, 93, 99, 103, 109, 110, 114, 241n12, n17, n19
KOGAM (Crush Malaysia Command) 43
Koh, Tommy, Professor 89, 90, 97
Konfrontasi (see Indonesia)
Kravichien, Thanin 67
Kubilai Khan 86
Kusuma-Atmadja, Mochtar 68, 94, 102, 108

Lao People's Revolutionary Party (LPRP) 63, 181, 223, 224
Laos 10, 33, 43, 50, 54, 55, 66, 77, 92, 106, 148, 180, 212, 239n10: relations with Thailand 225; relations with Vietnam 224, 225, 241n14
Laskar Jihad 208
Le Duan 62, 63
League of Nations 22
Lee Hsien Loong 106, 242n29
Lee Kuan Yew 26, 27, 38–40, 47, 48, 57, 72, 91, 162, 236n15, 242n29
Li Peng 72, 129
Lian Chan 244n24
lifeworld 3, 234n5
Lim Yew Hock 27
Liu Huaqiu 118, 120
London Agreement 38

Macapagal, Diasdado 36, 40
Macapagal-Arroyo, Gloria 228
MacArthur, Douglas (General) 30
McNamara, Robert S. 140
Mae Sai (Thailand) 210
Mahathir Mohamed 47, 75, 144, 148, 178, 180, 188, 190, 203
Mahbubani, Kishore 7
Majapahit 18
Malacca Straits 45, 48, 57
Malaya: under colonial rule 23; factors

underlying Malay nationalism 24;
moves toward independence 25;
merger with Singapore 38
Malayan/Malaysian Chinese Association
(MCA) 25, 39
Malayan/Malaysian Communist Party
(MCP) 26, 37, 87, 114, 169,
Malayan Indian Congress (MIC) 25
Malayan People's Anti-Japanese Army
26
Malayan Union 24–25
Malaysia: and Indonesia (see Indonesia);
Internal Security Act 183, 185;
'Malaysian Malaysia' 39; May 1969
riots 55; New Economic Policy 226;
and the Philippines 9, 45–46, 47,
186–87, 217; and People's Republic of
China 55, 64, 87, 119, 124, 244n22;
proposal for neutralisation of
Southeast Asia 54–56; reform
movement (reformasi) 183, 185, 188;
and Singapore (see Singapore); and
Thailand 184, 186; and United
Kingdom 38; and United States 73,
188; on Vietnam's intervention in
Cambodia 87, 96–97 (also see
enhanced interaction, flexible
engagement; neutralisation of
Southeast Asia)
Malik, Adam 42, 48, 100,
Maluku 208
mandala 17
Manglapus, Raul 73, 144,
Manila Agreements 238n9
Manila Declaration (see ASEAN
Declaration on the South China Sea)
Manila Pact (See Southeast Asia
Collective Defence Treaty)
Mao Zedong 26
Marcos, Ferdinand 40, 45, 73, 87, 88,
168, 182
Marhaenism 28
Megawati Sukarnoputri 227, 228
Milne, R.S. 30
Mindanao 219, 228
Mischief Reef (see South China Sea)
Mochtar Kusuma-Atmadja, Professor
65, 82, 94, 102, 108,
Mohamad Jawhar 227
Murdani, Benny Gen. 94, 99, 241n22,
242n29
Mongkut, King (Rama IV) 20, 21
Moro Islamic Liberation Front 208, 228

Moro National Liberation Front
(MNLF) 87, 168, 249n7
Muchtar Pakpahan 148
Muhammad Ghazali Shafie (Tan Sri) 46,
54, 55, 73, 87, 92, 94, 96, 97
musyawarah 4, 234n7
mufakat 4, 234n7
multipolarity 134
Myanmar: and ASEAN 143–144,
146–147; and PR China 72; Rohingya
Muslims 147; State Law and Order
Restoration Council (SLORC) 141,
142, 144, 147, 172; State Peace and
Development Council (SPDC) 141–2,
173, 182, 207, 209, 211, 223; and
Thailand (see Thailand); and United
States (see United States); (also see
flexible engagement)

Najib Tun Razak, Datuk Mohamad 73
Nakayama, Taro 77
National Liberation Front of South
Vietnam 62
National League for Democracy (NLD)
142, 182, 209, 223 (see Myanmar)
National Peasants Union 31
Ne Win, General 148
Neutralisation of Southeast Asia 53, 54,
60, 61, 74: Indonesia on proposal for
56–57, 58; Malaysian reasons for
proposing 55–56 (also see Malaysia);
Philippines on proposal for 57;
Singapore on proposal for 57;
Thailand on proposal for 56; North
Vietnam on proposal for 62; South
Vietnam on proposal for 61–62; (also
see ZOPFAN)
New Emerging Forces (NEFOS) 41
New International Economic Order 105
New World Order 141
New Zealand 54, 58,
NGOs 154, 231
Nguyen Co Thach 94, 98–99, 102, 104,
241n22
Nguyen Duy Trinh 67
Nguyen Dy Nien 223, 224
Nguyen Manh Cam 124
Nguyen Van Thieu 61, 63
Nixon Doctrine 52, 54
Non-aligned Movement 41, 89, 97
Non-aligned Conference: in Colombo
66; in Dar es Salaam 55; in Havana
89; in Lusaka 61;

Norm: behavioural 234n7; cascade 235; legal-rational norms 5; legal-political 6; function 1, 12; procedural 234n7; rationalisation 11, 214, 217, 229, 233; socio-cultural norms 4;
of consensus 206, 207, 208, 212, 223; of non-interference 1, 5, 6, 7, 10, 16, 45, 49, 50, 52, 58, 59, 60, 61, 62, 64, 66, 70, 74, 76, 78, 114, 129, 132, 134, 135, 146, 151, 152, 155, 160, 166, 168, 169, 175, 177, 192, 193, 198–99, 206, 207, 208, 212, 214, 220, 221, 222, 224, 226, 227, 231, 246n1 (also see ZOPFAN); of non-intervention 1, 3, 7, 49, 50, 52, 64, 66, 82, 92, 93, 104, 107, 111, 114, 165, 204, 214, 220; of non-involvement of ASEAN to address unresolved bilateral conflict 1,7, 46, 49, 50, 169, 177, 214; of non-use of force 1, 3, 8, 16, 41, 49, 50, 52, 61, 62, 64, 74, 76, 82, 92, 93, 104, 111, 114, 122–23, 129, 152, 153, 165, 210, 214, 216, 220; of mutual respect and tolerance 1, 6, 7, 49, 59, 129, 165, 214, 216, 221,222; of quiet diplomacy 1, 7, 146, 153, 169, 173, 178, 183, 184, 188, 189, 190, 196, 214, 233; of restraint 123–25, 129, 152, 222; of sovereign equality 1, 7, 16, 17–18, 31, 32, 52, 58, 61, 62, 70, 74, 78, 96, 129, 135, 212, 214, 216, 220, 221; of sovereignty 17, 18, 24, 47, 59, 82, 107, 114, 116, 128, 151, 152, 155, 160, 165, 182, 198, 202, 203
NAFTA 72
NATO 137
New Order regime 42, 44, 48, 49, 57 (also see Indonesia)
Nguyen Van Thieu regime 61, 63
North Korea 56
North Vietnam (Democratic Republic of Vietnam) 56, 61
Nurul Izzah Anwar 184

Old Established Forces (OLDEFOS) 41
Onn bin Jaafar, Dato 25
Organisation of Islamic Countries (OIC) 249n7

Pacific Concord 220, 249n2
Panyarachun, Anand 79, 233
Paribatra, M.R. Sukhumbhand 11, 96, 171, 173, 200,

Paris Peace Conference 22
Paris Peace Agreements of 1973, 62
Paris Peace Agreements/Accords of 1991 (see Cambodian conflict)
Pattani United Liberation Organisation (PULO) 169
Pedra Branca 249n1
People's Action Party 27, 39
People's Army of Vietnam (PAV) 81, 100, 106
People's Consultative Assembly (MPR) 227
People's Liberation Army 123
People's Liberation Army (Navy) (PLAN) 101, 123
People's Republic of China (PRC) 14, 45, 48, 55, 56, 57, 152, 212: and ASEAN (see ASEAN); and ASEAN Regional Forum 135–37; and ASEAN way (see ASEAN way) 114, 122–4, 132, 137, 138; Belgrade embassy bombing 137; confidence building 118–20; Joint Statements 134; and Cambodia 110; and Japan 116, 117; Middle Kingdom complex 130; new concept of security 136; on 'partnerships' 130–1; preventive diplomacy 120–2, 155, 157; and Russia 131; and South China Sea 74, 115, 122–29, 138; and Soviet Union 52, 106, 110; and United States 52, 58, 91, 131, 137, 151, 242n6, 244n25, 245n11
People's Republic of Kampuchea 82, 83, 87, 88, 89, 90, 91, 94, 95, 97, 99, 101, 102, 103, 104, 106, 109, 110, 111, 176 (also see Cambodia conflict)
Perlis 18, 22
Perry, William 150
Pham Van Dong 81, 241n22
Philippines: Base Line Act 46; *cacique* class 30; and Indonesia 46; nationalism 29–31; and PR China 119, 124, 126–7, 242–43n10; relations with US 30–31, 32–33, 36, 44, 57, 73, 162–163, 237n3; on Vietnam's intervention in Cambodia 87–88; Visiting Forces Agreement 163, 246n23;
Phibul Songkram, Field Marshal 22, 23, 33, 176
Pitsuwan, Surin 10, 166, 167, 168, 170, 182, 184, 196, 205, 207, 208,

PKI (see Indonesian Communist Party)
Pleiku (Vietnam) 224
Pol Pot 86, 90, 95, 102, 103, 241n15, n18,
Prem Tinsulanond 98, 106,
preventive defence 158–60, 245n13 (also
    see United States)
Pridi Phanomyong 22
priyayi 27

Qian Qichen 133
Qing dynasty 20

Rahman, Tunku Abdul 25, 35, 37–40,
    46, 47, 54, 236n13, n14
Rajaratnam, Sinnathamby 26, 49, 84, 85,
    104, 107, 236n15
Ramos, Fidel 168, 247n9
Ranariddh, Prince Norodom 166, 174,
    246n4
ratu adil (just ruler) 28
Razak, Tun Abdul bin Datuk Hussein
    42, 47, 54, 55, 61
Razali Ismail 209
Republic of Vietnam (RVN) (see
    Vietnam)
Rizal, José 29, 237n18, 247n6
Rómulo, Carlos 36, 50,
Rómulo, Roberto 123, 247n9
Roth, Stanley O. 154
Royal Thai Army 8, 176, 197, 210, 211,
    225, 248–9n21
Rusk, Dean 33
Russia 77

Sabah and Sarawak 38, 42, 238n7
Sabah dispute 9, 36, 42, 46, 47, 50, 57,
    187, 217
Saddam Hussein 145
Samad Ismail 27
Samudavanjia 11
San Francisco Treaty System 150, 160
Santer, Jacques 131
Sarekat Dagang Islam (Islam Trading
    Society) 28
security: co-operative security 78, 117;
    human 198, 232; ontological security
    2, 11; regime 149, 180–2, 190, 216,
    219, 226
security community 9, 159, 160, 235n11,
    246n19
security culture 2
security regime 9

Severino, Rodolfo C., Jr 167, 196, 205,
    206,
Shan State Army 210, 211
Shanghai Academy of Social Sciences
    124
Shanghai Agreement 118
Shanghai Co-operation Organisation
    242n9
Shi Chunlai 120
Siam: and colonial powers 19, 21;
    struggle for membership in
    international society 21–22; (also see
    extra-territoriality)
Siazon, Domingo L., Jr 167, 182, 187,
    208, 228
Siddhi Savetsila 98, 106,
Siemrap 22
Sihanouk, Norodom 89, 94, 102, 103,
    108, 109,
Singapore: Armed Defence Forces 106;
    on ASEAN defence co-operation 76;
    on basic norms of international
    society 64, 74, 85, 89–90, 96; and
    Cambodia power sharing
    arrangement 110; on 'cocktail
    diplomacy' 102, 103–104 (also see
    Cambodia conflict); under
    colonialism 26; defence spending
    249n4; diplomacy to reverse
    Vietnam's intervention in Cambodia
    89–90; and East Timor 202, 248n7;
    and Indonesia 48–49, 85, 104–105,
    201, 217, 222; and Malaysia 38–40,
    47–48, 76, 105–106, 217, 222, 246n5,
    247n7; and People's Action Party
    (PAP) 27; on preventive diplomacy
    154–155 (also see ASEAN Regional
    Forum); and PR China 76, 134, 155;
    and Thailand 107, 242n27; and
    United States 44, 57, 72, 74, 89, 105,
    155, 161–162, 244–5n5, 246n21; on
    Vietnam's intervention in Cambodia
    84–85, 90–91, 96
Singh, Ajit (Dato) 6
Sipadan and Ligitan 249n1
Socialist Republic of Vietnam (SRV)
    (see Vietnam)
sociological turn in IR 11
Soenarso 43
Songkitti Chakrabat 201
Son Sann 92, 241n19
South China Sea 14, 71, 72, 73, 122–29,
    179, 197: code of conduct 126–7;

Investigator Shoal 127; workshop on Managing potential conflicts in the 125, 249n7; Mischief Reef 115, 123, 124, 125, 126, 161; Paracel Islands 124; Scarborough Shoal 124, 127; Spratlys 124, 126; Tennent Reef 127
South Korea 112
South Vietnam (Republic of Vietnam) 61
Southeast Asia Collective Defence Treaty (Manila Pact) 33
Southeast Asia Co-operation Project 231
Southeast Asian Association for Regional Co-operation (SEAARC) 43
Southeast Asian Friendship and Economic Treaty 35
Southeast Asia Nuclear Weapons Free Zone (SEANWFEZ) 68, 163–164, 246n25: and great powers 68, 164, 246; Treaty on 68, 140
Southeast Asia Treaty Organisation (SEATO) 33, 57, 62,
Soviet Union 69, 84, 88, 89, 91, 92, 102,
standard of civilisation 20–22
State of Cambodia (SOC) 109, 110, 111 (also see Cambodia; Cambodia conflict)
State Law and Order Restoration Council (SLORC) (see Myanmar)
State Peace and Development Council (SPDC) (see Myanmar)
struggle for recognition: as anti-colonialism and nationalism in Southeast Asia 17, 19–20, 20–31; and conflict 12; as enduring process 12; underpinning ZOPFAN 60–61 (also see ZOPFAN)
Suharto 40, 43, 44–5, 48, 56, 61, 75, 93, 98, 99, 100, 101, 132, 133, 148, 166, 174, 176, 219, 227, 238n8, 242n29
Sukarno 28, 31, 35, 37–38, 40, 41, 44, 45
Surayud Chulanont 177, 202, 249n22
Surin Pitsuwan (see Pitsuwan, Surin)
suwannaphum 107, 176
suzerainty 18, 21
Suzuki Zenko 88
Syed Hamid Albar, Datuk Seri 203, 209, 247n7

Tachilek (Myanmar) 210
Taiwan Strait 150
Talbott, Strobe 149

Tan Siew Sin 39
Tang Jiaxuan 120, 121, 132, 133, 137
tatmadaw 8, 143, 210
Thaksin Shinawatra 211, 228
Thai Binh 224
Thailand 8, 55: and anti-communism 23, 33; and ASEAN Troika 204–5, 209 (see ASEAN Troika); democratic identity and foreign policy 173, 211; and Laos 84; and Myanmar 8, 143, 172, 175–6, 209–212, 216, 228–29, 248n20, n21; Myanmar as an issue in Thai foreign policy 172–73; and PR China 56, 72, 83, 84, 88, 99, 134; repeal of extraterritoriality 21–22; and Soviet Union 106; and United States 23, 33, 83, 162, 238; and Vietnam 56, 83–84, 98; on Vietnam's intervention in Cambodia 83–84, 96; (also see enhanced interaction; flexible engagement)
Than Shwe 144
Thanat Khoman 33, 36, 42, 43, 56, 58, 61, 238n3
Thanom Kittikachorn 56
Thein Sein, Major-Gen 210
Third-party mediation 40, 43, 168, 219, 228, 249n7
Treaty of Amity and Co-operation (see ASEAN)
Trengganu 18, 22, 87
Try Sutrisno 242n29
Tun Mustapha bin Datuk Harun 46, 168

UMNO (United Malays National Organisation) 25, 39, 180, 226
Ung Huot 246n4
United Kingdom: withdrawal from East of Suez 27, 52, 54
United Nations 88, 91,116, 129, 197:
United Nations Assistance Mission in East Timor 198
United Nations Charter 82, 97, 135, 152, 202
United Nations Conventional Arms Register 118, 152
United Nations General Assembly 55, 82, 89, 97, 102, 104, 142, 157, 248n7
United Nations Human Rights Commission 142, 148
United Nations Security Council: 78, 89, 137, 199, 203; 248n11; permanent members (P5) 82, 109, 110

United Nations Law of the Sea
(UNCLOS) 68, 105, 243
United Nations Transitional
Administration in East Timor
(UNTAET) 192, 201–2, 212, 246n23,
248n8, n14–15, n17 (see East Timor)
United Nations Transitional Authority
in Cambodia (UNTAC) 72, 82, 110,
217, 240n5, 247n2
United States: Asia-Pacific Regional
Iniative 159; as a benign power 71,
139; confidence building 151, 156;
democracy promotion 71; East Asia
Strategy 158–160; International
Military Education and Training
(IMET) 148; and Japan 139, 159; and
Northeast Asia 150; Pacific
Command 159; perceived
disengagement from Southeast Asia
71; preventive defence 158–60,
245n13; preventive diplomacy
153–54, 158, 160, 164, 245n13;
relations with Myanmar 141–143,
144–145, 244n4; and Vietnam War 52
(also see ASEAN, 'ASEAN way',
ASEAN Regional Forum)
United Wa State Army 210–11

Vietcong 56
Viet Minh 33, 34
Vietnam: relations with ASEAN (see
ASEAN); and 'ASEAN way'
('ASEAN way'); and ASEAN troika
209; and Laos 66, 224; and PR China
67, 114, 70, 82, 86, 110, 119, 124;
post-1975 relations with United
States 67; and Second Indochina War
52, 54, 56, 62, 63; and South China
Sea 127, 128 (also see South China
Sea); (also see flexible engagement)
Vietnamese Communist Party 62, 69, 81,
86, 181, 223
Vo Dong Giang 67

Wahid, Abdurrahman 133, 227
Wanandi, Jusuf 105
Wattanachai Chaimuenwong, Lt-Gen
210, 211, 212
West Irian 37 (see Irian Jaya)
Wilson, Woodrow 20
Wiranto, General 202
World Bank 193
World Trade Organisation (WTO) 69

ZOPFAN (Zone of Peace, Freedom and
Neutrality) 14, 50–51, 52, 62, 65, 72,
95, 140, 141: actualisation of 73;
component concepts 59–60;
compromise 53–54, 57–8; debate
about reviving ZOPFAN 73–74;
definition 59; and foreign bases 73;
Kuala Lumpur Declaration 52, 53,
58, 59, 60, 61, 63, 65, 74, 201, 220;
and major powers 61, 68, 74, 114;
operational goals of 58, 65–66,
67–68, 79; origins of 53–54; as
proposed normative framework for
intra-regional relations 59–65; Post-
Cold war debate on 73; 1975
proposals to realise 63; and
SEANWFEZ 68; and Treaty of
Amity and Co-operation 53; and
Vietnam 53, 62–63, 66; Working
Group on (WGZOPFAN) 68; (also
see neutralisation of Southeast Asia)

Made in the USA
Middletown, DE
25 January 2018